THE INSIDER

THE INSIDER

A Life of Virginia C. Gildersleeve

NANCY WOLOCH

Columbia University Press

New York

Columbia University Press
Publishers Since 1893
New York Chichester, West Sussex
cup.columbia.edu

Library of Congress Cataloging-in-Publication Data
Names: Woloch, Nancy, 1940- author.
Title: The insider : a life of Virginia C. Gildersleeve / Nancy Woloch.
Description: New York : Columbia University Press, [2022] | Includes index.
Identifiers: LCCN 2021030688 (print) | LCCN 2021030689 (ebook) |
    ISBN 9780231204248 (hardback) | ISBN 9780231204255 (trade paperback) |
    ISBN 9780231555449 (ebook)
Subjects: LCSH: Gildersleeve, Virginia Crocheron, 1877–1965. | Deans (Education)—
    New York (State)—Biography. | Barnard College—Alumni and alumnae—Biography. |
    Women's colleges—New York (State)—History—20th century. | Women in
    higher education—New York (State)—History—20th century. | Antisemitism in
    higher education—United States—History—20th century.
Classification: LCC LB875.G542 W65 2022 (print) | LCC LB875.G542 (ebook) |
    DDC 378.0092 [B]—dc23/eng/20211006
LC record available at https://lccn.loc.gov/2021030688
LC ebook record available at https://lccn.loc.gov/2021030689

Columbia University Press books are printed on permanent
    and durable acid-free paper.
Printed in the United States of America

Cover image: Detail of Virginia C. Gildersleeve. Class photo, 1899. © Barnard Archives.
Cover design: Lisa Hamm

Contents

THE INSIDER

Introduction

The newly appointed dean of Barnard College faced the crowd that had gathered for her inauguration in February 1911 with assurance. Although the college had recently been beset with problems, she recalled, and she was "conscious of skating on very thin ice," the new appointee, only thirty-three, took office with impressive advantages. Not only a native New Yorker with family connections, not only a Barnard graduate (class of '99), she had also been a graduate student at Columbia and, most recently, as an instructor, she had swiftly ascended the academic ranks. Welcomed by students, faculty, alumnae, and trustees, the new dean— the "inside" candidate—knew the terrain she was about to take over. Or, as a New York newspaper had just declared, "Miss Gildersleeve Has Grown Up With the Institution She Now Heads."[1]

Swept into prominence, Virginia C. Gildersleeve (1877–1965) enjoyed a long career in higher education and world affairs. Dean of Barnard College (in effect president) for over three decades, from 1911 to 1947, president Virginia left her stamp on higher education for women: She led an admired institution, promoted women's capacity for intellectual work, organized the Seven College Conference (the "Seven Sisters"), and avidly defended the liberal arts tradition. Virginia also had an impact in foreign relations. Founder of the International Federation of University Women (IFUW), started in 1919, she carved out a global role for educated women, pursued the elusive goal of peace, developed expertise on the Middle East, and assembled a strong set of foreign policy credentials. In 1945, at the pinnacle of her foreign policy role, she served as the sole woman member of the United States delegation to the Charter meeting of the United Nations in San Francisco. Virginia's dual career of high achievement reflects both her advantaged background and exceptional leadership skill. "She is a person who instinctively commands deference from others," as an IFUW colleague declared.[2]

But barriers to a laudatory study abound. A series of disruptive episodes undercut Virginia's record of accomplishment. She acquired a reputation for bias in Barnard admissions: Like other elite colleges of the early twentieth century, Barnard discriminated against Jewish applicants, and its dean drew criticism (deserved) for endorsing bigotry. Beyond that, in the early 1930s, both on campus and in the press, Virginia voiced an indulgent view of Nazi policies; she did her best thereafter to ignore her (brief) apology for fascism and egregious error in judgment. After World War II and after she left Barnard, Virginia entered another zone of conflict; she became active in U.S. anti-Zionism, a national movement opposed to the founding of Israel; her leadership in the postwar anti-Zionist campaign further enraged critics of her anti-Semitism while at Barnard. These three developments reinforced one another: each was a distinct area of contention, however, embedded in its own set of circumstances. The book explores Virginia's penchant for controversy in historical context; it considers her drive to adopt a defiant, contrarian stance—or what she called her "mulish" tendency—as well as to compete and excel.

Virginia left another set of challenges to scrutiny, too. To deflect critics and deter biographers, she published a well-received and widely read autobiography (1954), not necessarily a reservoir of truth but full of engaging material—on family roots, Columbia history, managerial style, colleagues in academia and foreign affairs, and on the UN's formative moments, during which she argued against mention of equal rights for women in the UN Charter (yet another source of controversy). Praising her friends and trashing her enemies, Virginia seeks in her memoir to shape her own role in the historical record. She also brings up her sequential relationships with two "intimate" companions, first, Caroline Spurgeon, British scholar and literary critic, best known for her work on Shakespeare's imagery, and then Elizabeth Reynard, Barnard English professor, Navy officer in World War II, and expert on American folklore and literature. At the same time that she compiled material for her autobiography, in the early 1950s, Virginia destroyed her personal papers, which, presumably, would have conveyed something more about her private life. Yet it is possible to reconstruct a great deal about the two sets of couples and about the pattern of single-sex relationships that recur among women faculty and other women professionals in the early twentieth century.

One recent analyst of Virginia's significance, philosopher Stephen Turner, posits that a "failure of empathy" prevents us (the modern audience) from fully engaging with a Progressive-Era figure like Virginia or appreciating her achievements.[3] He has an excellent point. Historians of the past few decades have given the Progressives a drubbing; we now approach them with caution, including those like Virginia who, shaped by facets of the Progressive Era, endured for decades. I suggest, conversely, that in Virginia's case, "failure of empathy" has a second and equally salient meaning: Virginia's inability to empathize with others impeded her from reaching many of her contemporaries and prevents her from reaching most of us (in the modern audience) as well. Virginia was at once highly sensitive to aspects of her social environment—on meeting a new acquaintance, for instance, a critic noted, she liked to "place" the newcomer in class and status—and at the same time tone-deaf to the messages and undercurrents of the social environment, as well as to the way that it changed over time.

This book, then, reels with tensions and contradictions, and often with feuds and resentments. It addresses the privileged identity that Virginia enjoyed: the circumstances into which she was born, the advantages that flowed her way, and the educational capital that she accumulated. It explores her role as an "insider," in-the-know and well-connected, and on occasion, as an "outsider." It deals with her resourcefulness in higher education, her strategy for gaining influence in academic life ("working from within"), the ways that she acquired and deployed expertise, and her drive to take part in the almost inaccessible world of foreign affairs. It examines the institutions with which Virginia was involved, from women's colleges to foreign policy networks to anti-Zionist lobbies. It explains her stance in the early-twentieth-century women's movement, that is, as a public figure concerned with women's status but opposed to demands for equal rights for women, as at the United Nations in 1945. It assesses her effort to create, revise, and protect her own role in history, primarily through personal narrative. Finally, the book discusses ambition, competition, and rivalry, a triumvirate of powerful themes that resonate throughout Virginia's life and that drew me to examine it.

Virginia C. Gildersleeve saw herself as on the cutting edge of modern women's roles, and she sometimes was. Part of a generation of women that attended college in the 1890s and that relied on higher education to gain entry to careers and public life, Virginia—and her counterparts—hoped for educational parity. They wanted to achieve for women the same type of higher education that elite colleges and universities had long provided for men. Virginia filled a special niche in this cohort. She sought to open new space for women in academic life, to increase women's access to the professions, and to shape a role for women in world affairs. To do so required talent, tactics, and invention. Virginia fared best when enmeshed with institutions that she founded or controlled where she could capitalize on her personal status and leadership skill. The book considers the achievements she made, the setbacks she faced, and her moments of confrontation and conflict.

CHAPTER ONE

Roots: 1877–1911

Born in her family's New York City brownstone in 1877, Virginia Crocheron Gildersleeve absorbed a sense of entitlement that shaped her
long career in higher education and public affairs. In part, her entitled
identity reflected her own dominant persona, which she revealed in her
autobiography of 1954, *Many a Good Crusade*, and which was evident in
her early years to family members. Virginia was always a center of family
life, doted upon by her mother and her father, a New York judge, and
by her older brothers, Alger, born in 1869, who became a civil engineer,
and Harry, whose tragic death at age twenty in 1891 threw the household into crisis; the turmoil only increased Virginia's central role in the
family. Her sense of identity also rested on social class. To grow up on
Forty-Eighth Street off Fifth Avenue, within range of neighbors that
included Vanderbilts, Astors, and Rockefellers, connoted position and
advantage. Though Virginia qualified the family's privilege with a memorable disclaimer—"My mother used to remark that we were not 'in
society,' exactly," she wrote, "We were professional people"—she enjoyed
the benefit that a degree of social status could provide.[1]

Not least, Virginia's sense of entitlement rested on her pride in
ancestry, the knowledge that each of her parents descended from a long
line of American-born forebears going back to the early seventeenth
century (the Gildersleeves) and, in the case of the Crocherons, the late

seventeenth century. However hardscrabble the lives of these remote relatives may have been and often were, at least the family roots reached far enough back in time to claim a place in early American history and above all to ensure membership in a ruling caste—white, Protestant, proud, and secure. For such status, Virginia was indebted to her mother, Virginia Crocheron, whose ancestors had run small farms in Staten Island since the 1670s and later established an outpost in 1820s Alabama, and to her self-made father, Henry Alger Gildersleeve—Civil War officer, marksman, athlete, lawyer, and jurist—originally of Dutchess County, New York.

THE CROCHERONS OF STATEN ISLAND

In 1904 the *New York Times* sent a reporter to New Springville, Staten Island to interview reclusive Mary Elizabeth Crocheron, 73, who lived alone in an old mansion on a seventy-acre estate that had been mortgaged to nearby St. Andrews Protestant Episcopal Church. Wandering around the house amid the fine furniture that her family had collected and that she refused to sell, such as the Chippendale-style sideboard, Mary Elizabeth Crocheron wore the clothes of her youth—the 1850s—because, now living on charity and in debt to St. Andrews, she had no others. Miss Crocheron, said the *Times*, was the last of the Crocherons in Staten Island, where they had farmed since the seventeenth century. Other Crocheron descendants, unmentioned in the *Times*, lived in the greater metropolitan area, including the two Virginia Crocheron Gildersleeves, mother and daughter, of West Forty-Eighth Street, who represented, respectively, the seventh and eighth generations of the Crocheron family. Virginia the younger, Barnard '99, was then teaching freshman composition at the college.[2]

Like their impoverished relative, Virginia Gildersleeve and her mother were proud descendants of a single progenitor, Jean Crocheron, originally from Flanders, Belgium, and said to have arrived in the late seventeenth century as a stowaway in a barrel. Jean, who settled in Staten Island around 1670, was a Huguenot escapee from anti-Protestant prejudice in Europe even before the Revocation of the Edict of Nantes (1685), a policy that intensified persecution of Protestants in France. According to Virginia's brother, Alger Gildersleeve, who began in the 1920s to explore their family history, Jean Crocheron was a member of a sect of twelfth-century French dissenters called Waldense that became Protestant in the 1600s. Jean Crocheron traveled to New York from Holland, a common route for Huguenots, who, after leaving France or other places in Europe, often went to England or Holland on their way to the new world. When Alger tried to track the Huguenot roots of the progenitor, he found that the New Jersey Huguenot Society, rather than its New York counterpart, listed Jean as a member, which makes sense, as Staten Island lies closer to New Jersey than to New York. The Staten Island population in the 1670s contained a small Huguenot community, including some other Waldensians, as well as some English and Dutch settlers. In Algonquian, the name "Staten Island" means "the bad place."[3]

By 1677, Jean Crocheron owned a farm of 188 acres on western Staten Island. The land Jean cultivated was near Fresh Kills, an area of tidal creeks and coastal marshland that seventeenth-century settlers called "the big swamp." Landfill at Fresh Kills in the mid-twentieth century became a huge dump for New York City garbage. Jean's estate in 1696, at his death, according to one inventory, contained a lot of money: at least 200£ of currency in a box, plus gold, pieces of eight, livestock, wheat, rye, and fifteen books, including a Bible. The estate also listed a "negro family, man, woman, and boy," or, as in a second inventory, "a negro man, an Indian woman, and her child"—in either case a reminder of slavery's importance to the Staten Island economy. "Every farmer whose necessities required it, was the owner of one or more slaves," according to a nineteenth-century history of Staten Island. Slavery played a significant role in both the colony of New York and well into the nineteenth century in New York State, where it ended only gradually, between 1799 and 1827.[4] (After 1799, children born to slave mothers were free but required to work for the mother's master as indentured servants until the late 1820s. All New York slaves were finally freed on July 4, 1827.)

Until slavery ended, the Crocheron farming families of Staten Island owned one to four slaves; so did many neighbors. Crocherons also owned grain mills, gristmills, and sawmills. Some Crocherons became local judges or town supervisors. Two served in Congress, Henry (Democratic-Republican), 1815–1817, and his brother Jacob (Jacksonian Democrat), 1829–1831. Crocherons married other Huguenots and also among the English and Dutch; they spread out and multiplied. Families with up to ten sons or even more ensured the proliferation of the family name. Virginia's great-great-grandfather, farmer Henry Crocheron (1744–1796), for instance, had nine sons (and four slaves). Crocheron daughters, under their married names, lived in places such as Brooklyn, Long Island, and upstate New York, as well as locally. Some sons vanished into New Jersey; most stayed in Staten Island. Staten Islanders, including Crocherons, were loyal to England in the Revolution, or uncommitted; thirty thousand British troops were stationed at one point on Staten Island.[5]

In 1818, John Jay Crocheron (no connection to the first Chief Justice, John Jay), bachelor great-uncle of Virginia, led a group of family members from Richmond Village, Staten Island, to Dallas County, Alabama. The date was crucial. Slavery was soon to fade away in New York State, but the Southwest was just opening up to settlement and slave-owning. Alabama became a territory in 1817 and a state in 1820. Land was available and profit beckoned (the same circumstances that had once attracted settlers to Staten Island). Some newcomers to Alabama brought with them hundreds of slaves; if Staten Island was a "bad place," Alabama was a worse place, one that fused the most retrograde facets of the West and the South. Why go there? To acquire land, to grow cotton, to buy slaves, to buy more land, to grow more cotton, and so on. To provide yet further opportunity for white settlers, the federal government around 1830 sent most of the Indian population, the Creeks and Choctaws, out to Indian Territory, now Oklahoma. Again, the Crocherons prospered. Their main goal: to produce cotton to transport by steamship back to Staten Island, and to ship consumer goods from there to Alabama.[6]

John Jay Crocheron and his relatives settled in an area around Selma, Alabama, on the Alabama River. John Jay had a 200-slave plantation at Elm Bluff and many enterprises, including steamships. He also became director of a state bank. In the Civil War, too old to fight, he would finance a company of cavalry called the Crocheron Light Dragoons. John Jay's younger brother Henry, co-founder of Crocheron and Perine, a mercantile firm, built a mansion about twenty miles away from Elm Bluff in Cahaba, a town populated by well-off slave-owning families. Yet another brother and Virginia's grandfather, Richard Connor Crocheron, moved to the Cahaba house in 1840 and remained there for a decade.

Richard held an interest in one of the Crocheron businesses, the New York and New Orleans Steamship Company, which ran four ships between New York, New Orleans, and Havana—the *Black Warrior*, the *Catawba*, the *DeSoto*, and the *Bienville* (all names from Alabama history). Richard's daughter, Virginia Crocheron, was born in Alabama in 1844. Widowed around 1850, and devastated, Richard freed his slaves and moved with his three children back to New York, to a house at 28 West Forty-Seventh Street. Many family members, however, remained in Alabama, and some migrated elsewhere in the South or Southwest, such as Richard's brother Henry, who moved in 1837 to Texas, which had just won independence from Mexico and offered new prospects for landowning and profit.[7]

Virginia Crocheron Gildersleeve (the younger) loved the history of Cahaba, the distinctive town in which Crocherons spent the winters; in the summers they traveled to the cooler climate of Staten Island. Located on the banks of the Alabama River, Cahaba enjoyed easy transport and thriving enterprise; by 1820, the town had two newspapers, a land office, a state bank, stores, hotels, boardinghouses, schools, and many businesses. John Jay and a Crocheron relative, for instance, ran a store that sold groceries, hardware, glass, and brandy. Most important, the grand homes of Cahaba, like the Crocheron mansion, provided a busy social center, miles removed from the cotton fields and slave labor that economically sustained Cahaba's homeowners. A town history of 1908 suggests the appeal of the antebellum Cahaba lifestyle: "The people, being generally wealthy, with many slaves and large plantations located nearby or in the surrounding country, had an abundance of leisure to extend a generous hospitality, which they did in a royal manner," wrote the admiring town historian, "and there was no limit to the round of visiting and entertainment, which was continuous and practically endless."[8]

The state capital until 1826, Cahaba had occasional trouble with the river that its mansions overlooked; after a flood of 1825, the statehouse collapsed, and the capital moved first to Tuscaloosa and then to Montgomery. Cahaba flooded again in 1833, but Cahabans always rebuilt. Two of the many local Crocherons, Daniel and Michael, uncles of John Jay, ran a brickyard, which profited from the ongoing building and rebuilding. Social events continued with vigor, even after floods; Cahaba remained well known for its "mode of life" and "educated and cultured people," the town historian wrote, at least until 1865, "until the ruin that overswept the South after the Civil War."[9]

At the war's end, the Crocheron mansion, with its Federal-style portico and brick columns, was the site of a meeting between the Union general James H. Wilson and the notorious Confederate general Nathan Bedford Forrest, for surrender and exchange of prisoners after the nearby battle of Selma. A Confederate prison at Cahaba released some 5,000 Union soldiers as Wilson cleared the area. Soon after the war's end, the town burned down, including the Crocheron mansion; only its brick columns still stood, amid weeds. Cahaba became a ghost town. Virginia the younger visited Alabama in 1917, a few years into her Barnard deanship, when she traveled to Montgomery and Selma to find relatives, explore Cahaba history, and speak at a local girls' school, the Margaret Booth School. "This morning I visited the State Capitol [in Montgomery], where Jeff Davis was inaugurated," Virginia wrote to her mother. "The director of the department of the archives seemed to know all about Cahaba." Much taken with the Alabama connection, Virginia considered herself a Southerner and a Cahaban. Her mother never returned.[10]

Back in New York City after 1850, the Crocheron youngsters went to school. Virginia Crocheron attended the Moravian Academy for Girls, a school founded in 1742 in Bethlehem, Pennsylvania, and then, as a teenager, with her brother John and sister Henrietta, a well-regarded secondary school in Poughkeepsie, New York, the Cottage Hill Academy; this was run by noted educator Milo P. Jewett, who had previously run a girls' school in Alabama. Jewett became the first president of Vassar College, started in 1861, a pioneer venture in higher education for women. Virginia Crocheron hoped to attend the new college but instead went home to keep house for her father on Forty-Seventh Street. In her daughter's account, her brother John introduced her to a young man, Henry Alger Gildersleeve, in New York. They wed in 1868. A nominal Quaker, Henry, at his prospective wife's insistence, joined the Episcopal Church; the family in decades to come, nominally Episcopalian, was notably secular. Still, Henry's change of faith would reward his daughter: Columbia, rooted in the Church of England, as were other prominent New York institutions, still chose its leaders only among Episcopalians. After marriage, the life of Virginia Crocheron the elder merged into that of the Gildersleeve family.

THE RISE OF HENRY A. GILDERSLEEVE

Virginia Gildersleeve's father, Henry Alger Gildersleeve, was almost always the right man in the right place in the right time. He was also among the ninth generation of Gildersleeves, a huge family whose progenitor, Richard Gildersleeve, had been born in 1601 in Suffolk, East Anglia, a major source of Puritan migrants to the new world. Richard arrived in the Massachusetts Bay Colony in 1635. Stopping first at Watertown, Massachusetts, he joined a small band of settlers who pushed farther, to Connecticut, where he alit in Wethersfield in 1636. Ever disputatious, Richard challenged authority wherever he went, moved on, and kept moving. The founding member of seven towns in succession, he ended up in Hempstead, Long Island, in 1643. There he served as a magistrate under Dutch rule, 1644–1664, and a commissioner under British rule. Richard died in 1681. For half a century, he had argued with everyone. He had battled Pequots, hounded Quakers, and defied royal governors; he had also negotiated treaties, sought individual rights (his own), and repeatedly founded self-governing entities.[11]

Patriots in the American Revolution, Gildersleeves were mobile, enterprising, and prolific. They spread out all over the east and moved west to Ohio. Henry A. Gildersleeve came from a New York State branch. His father, Smith James Gildersleeve, a temperance advocate, had been a Quaker until disavowed for marrying Rachel Alger, a bride from outside the Society of Friends. Smith James ran a shoe store in Poughkeepsie with his youngest son, Elmer. The two older sons held other ambitions.[12]

Born on a farm in Clinton, New York, in 1840, Henry Alger Gildersleeve attended the district school, the Hudson River Institute, and the Cottage Hill School in Poughkeepsie. He then taught school back in Clinton and hoped to enter Union College in Schenectady. But the start of the Civil War changed his plans. Henry raised a company of 114 men for the Dutchess County regiment, the 150th New York infantry. Mustered in in 1862, the regiment fought in the Battle of Gettysburg in 1863 and then in campaigns in Maryland and Virginia. Henry then took a special post that involved New York recruitment. He returned to his regiment in June 1864 in time to join General Sherman for the Battle of Atlanta and the March through Georgia. Promoted continually, Henry became one of three majors in the 150th; he ended the war as a lieutenant colonel, with praise from Lincoln, many honors, and the loyalty of many veterans of the 150th who would vote for him in New York State judicial elections in years to come. His high-achieving younger brother, Frank Van Buren Gildersleeve (this family supported the Democratic Party), an army surgeon in the same regiment, won the same impressive military rank; Frank moved on to Amherst, medical school, and success in medicine.[13]

Now twenty-five years old, Henry A. Gildersleeve ("Alger" to his friends) began to pursue a career. His triumph of timing continued; he took part in the postwar growth of the legal profession. Henry began his training by working for a prominent New York City lawyer, Henry W. Johnson; at the same time, he took courses at Columbia's Department of Law, recently started in 1858. Then led by Professor Theodore W. Dwight, the Department of Law became, as of 1873, Columbia Law School. Dwight was known for inventing a system of legal education, the Dwight method, which focused on applied law—as opposed to the case method, which was inductive, more intellectual, and demanded more reading. The Dwight system, in contrast, taught practical skills; the student memorized a few works on legal principles and participated in moot court. Once again, Henry A. Gildersleeve enjoyed good luck. Professor Dwight, by coincidence or not, came from the very same hometown; he had formerly been a professor of law, history, and political economy at Hamilton College in Clinton, New York. Dwight welcomed the young veteran and indulged him thereafter with letters of recommendation. The young Gildersleeve, who moved fast, never graduated (the law school course was two years and many never finished it). Instead, after only one year, in 1866, he took the required exam and joined the New York bar in Poughkeepsie. One year after leaving the Union army, Henry A. Gildersleeve was ready to practice law.[14]

During his first decade of practice in New York City, Gildersleeve became known for marksmanship and leadership. He joined the National Guard and was elected lieutenant colonel of the 12th Regiment of New York State. In this capacity he defended a New York City arsenal at Thirty-Fifth Street and Seventh Avenue in the Orange riots of 1871, a clash between Irish Catholics and Protestants in which each group charged the other with subverting republican institutions. Gildersleeve also became a founder of the National Rifle Association, an organization formed in New York in 1871 to remedy the poor shooting skills shown by Union soldiers. The NRA goal: to encourage "rifle practice and to promote a system of aiming drill and target firing among the National Guard." Henry A. Gildersleeve served first as secretary and then as president in 1880–81. Democratic politics claimed his time, too. Finally, Gildersleeve won applause as an athlete. In 1874, he led a U.S. rifle ream to Ireland for a famous contest at Creedmoor, watched by thousands (rifle competition was then a spectator sport), which the United States won. A return match in England in 1875, before 20,000 spectators, brought another U.S. victory. In his first and only book, *Rifles and Marksmanship* (1876), Gildersleeve shared the skill sets that led to triumph in competition. According to the *American Rifleman*, these included "good eyesight, rare nerve, excellent judgment and application." Each prize in a rifle match gave the young lawyer a chance to hone his talent in public address; he would deliver his best-known speech in 1889 to commemorate the Battle of Gettysburg on the battlefield with the survivors of his regiment.[15]

In 1875, capitalizing on his fame in marksmanship, skill in oratory, influence as a Democrat, and the support of the former members of his regiment, Henry A. Gildersleeve won election as judge in the Court of General Sessions, New York City, a trial court, where he worked for fourteen years on criminal cases. In 1889, when he ran for reelection, he lost (this rarely happened to him), and returned to the practice of law, but only briefly. In May 1891, Governor David B. Hill appointed Gildersleeve to fill a vacancy on the state Superior Court, a trial court that no longer exists; six months later Gildersleeve won election to his post. In 1896 a new state constitution abolished the Superior Court; it became part of the state Supreme Court (in New York state, a trial court, as opposed to the state's highest court, the Court of Appeals). Thus, Gildersleeve became a state Supreme Court justice. He won reelection to the state Supreme Court in 1905 for another fourteen-year term and served for a period as Presiding Justice of the Appellate term in First Department, a branch of the state Supreme Court. By his retirement from the court in 1909, Virginia's father had won many marks of distinction in his field.[16]

Admired for his fair decisions, Judge Gildersleeve enjoyed high repute among colleagues. His good reputation on the bench held import for his daughter's career; for Virginia, the judge's status and success served as a stepping-stone to her own prominence. To impart a sense of impartiality in his opinions, the judge used several tactics. First, he showed great familiarity with the facts of the case at hand, which he reviewed in detail. He also gave intense attention to the claims of both sides, including the losing side, either to mention some valuable points made by the opposing lawyers or simply to consider in depth all arguments, no matter how futile or irrelevant, before stating a conclusion. Critics might on occasion find the judge unpredictable but never inattentive. Three decisions of the early 1890s, which his peers thought most important, convey Gildersleeve's judicial style. The decisions suggest the role of law in shaping the lively urban business world at the century's end. They also underscore the rise of the corporation as a powerful legal entity; in one way or another, in each major opinion, Henry A. Gildersleeve upheld corporate rights and set forth what they were.[17]

One decision involved horse racing. Horse breeder Edward Corrigan claimed that his colt, Huron, had won first place in a race called The Futurity, run in 1891 by the Coney Island Jockey Club. Huron, according to Corrigan, had outrun Dave Gideon's horse, His Highness. A fight broke out between the two horse owners; the jockey club, the corporation that ran the racetrack, disqualified Huron. Corrigan sued to claim the prize money he thought should have been his. The jockey club claimed that it had the right to determine who would enter races and the right to bar Corrigan and his horses from entry in further races. Corrigan then sued for an injunction to gain entry into future races. The Superior Court in 1891 granted the injunction to Corrigan, but a three-judge panel set aside the injunction in *Edward Corrigan v. The Coney Island Jockey Club* (1892). The rules of the corporation, the jockey club, prevailed, wrote Henry; with the injunction dismissed, the case would be tried. Henry's opinion won attention in part because Corrigan, big businessman and frequent litigant, was a friend of Mark Hanna, prominent Republican and soon best known as henchman of President McKinley. The case about Huron was tried in 1893; Corrigan lost.[18]

In his 1892 *Corrigan* opinion, Henry favored the Coney Island Jockey Club. The executive committee of the jockey club had been properly the "final arbiter" of the race of 1891 when it disqualified Huron. Committee members had "acted in good faith and had sufficient evidence before them to justify their conclusion." Executive committees of jockey clubs and social clubs were "supreme within themselves," Henry added. "[I]n the absence of fraud, courts should not interfere with their decisions." The horse breeder's demand to enter a subsequent race was as invalid as his challenge to the race results of 1891. Corrigan had waited over a year and then "came forward at the last moment, and demanded an entrance for his horse," Henry wrote. "His demands could not have been granted, without doing great injustice to the other competitors and to patrons of the turf generally." Again, members of the executive committee of the jockey club were "fully warranted in the course that they pursued." Henry's opinion validated corporate rights.[19]

A second case, *Homiston v. Long Island Railroad* (1893), dealt with public transit. The court considered whether a conductor might eject a passenger from a train if, as in one summary, "not given sufficient evidence that the traveler is entitled to ride." Conflict over a train ticket arose between conductor and passenger at the Jamaica station, a major junction, after the passenger changed trains; the conductor of the second train demanded a ticket. But the passenger claimed that he had not been given a "duplex" ticket to cover both train rides. A fight broke out between conductor and passenger, and the conductor, assisted by the brakeman, threw the passenger off the train; the passenger eventually paid the fare, returned to the train, and continued his trip, but sued the railroad. Henry reversed the judgment of an earlier court that the plaintiff had been wrongfully removed from the train. The previous judge, Henry wrote, should have let the case go to the jury instead of deciding it himself. The *Homiston* case demanded a new trial.[20]

An operatic performance, Henry's opinion reviewed the many questions on train travel that the jury had not had a chance to consider. Was the conductor on the first train, for instance, which ran from the village of Queens to Jamaica, remiss in not giving the plaintiff a duplex ticket? Did the plaintiff make clear to the conductor of the first train that his final destination was Flatbush Avenue, Brooklyn? Had the clanging of engine bells precluded a clear conversation? Once the plaintiff boarded the second train, to Brooklyn, without the required ticket, was the conductor justified in removing him from the train, an action that allegedly injured his person and his feelings? Did the railroad err in not making the duplex ticket available to the passenger at the very start of his journey? All questions of fact should have been put before the jury, Henry concluded. His opinion gave the Long Island Railroad another chance.

A third decision, *Jaeger v. Le Boutillier* (1893) involved improper and unfair competition in the garment trade, or more specifically, knockoffs. Jaeger's woolen underwear for women, produced according to a system invented by a German professor in Stuttgart, was sold at many prominent stores such as B. Altman's. Conflict arose between the Jaeger's Sanitary Woolen System Company and a firm on Fourteenth Street in New York City, Le Boutillier, that manufactured and sold underwear using the "Jaeger" name. Were the Fourteenth Street products illegal? Yes, though the decision was complex. The Jaeger manufacturer, it turned out, did not have the exclusive right to use the name "Jaeger" for its system of producing the garments; the manufacturer, the plaintiff, was not the first among makers of woolen underwear to sell items under that name in either Germany or the United States. But the defendant, the Fourteenth Street firm, had used cotton as well as wool in its product and thus deviated from the Jaeger concept or system; it was guilty of unfair competition. Henry's decision in this case delved into the importance of trademarks and helped set standards of manufacture in the garment industry.[21]

When he retired in 1909, Judge Gildersleeve became a referee for the state Supreme Court, a post granted to former justices. The Democratic Party (Tammany Hall) briefly considered Henry as a mayoral candidate. He served as guardian for a Murray Hill neighbor, Mrs. Caroline Astor (*the* Mrs. Astor, who had run New York society for decades), by then a wealthy widow with dementia; he continued his memberships in athletic clubs and other clubs, including the Century Club, where he was friendly with fellow member and Columbia president Nicholas Murray Butler; and he kept up with fishing, hunting, and golf, recreations in which his daughter became his partner. Virginia remembered learning to shoot as well as going to court with her father as a five-year-old. She also recalled the judge's outstanding reputation: "Often convicts, when they got out of Sing Sing, to which my father had sentenced them, came to call on him," and sought his help to get jobs.[22] Though Virginia declared her mother the preferred—and more influential—parent, Henry's career and achievement profoundly boosted her own.

As in earlier years, both parents, Virginia the elder and Henry, who had lost two previous daughters as infants, kept up a pattern of devotion to their favored, youngest child.

FAMILY LIFE IN THE UPPER ESTATE

The upper–class residential neighborhood of Murray Hill, where the Gildersleeves lived in Virginia's childhood, ran along Fifth and Madison Avenues from around Twenty-Third Street to Fiftieth Street. Buffered by elevated railways on Third and Sixth Avenues, the neighborhood was untainted by commerce and industry—free from tenements, breweries, factories, and slaughterhouses, like those on the far East Side. Murray Hill housed upscale residents such as merchants and bankers, some very wealthy, and a smattering of professionals; it had fashionable churches, handsome homes, and the best private clubs.[23]

Columbia University owned the northernmost piece of Murray Hill, the "Upper Estate," a twenty-acre, four-block stretch from Forty-Seventh Street to Fifty-First Street between Fifth and Sixth Avenues. A gift from New York State to Columbia College in 1814, the tract at first seemed a burden to the college. But by 1870 Columbia had found a use for the area: real estate development. Construction by the college included some rows of houses off Fifth Avenue. "Little Virginia was born at 28 West 48th Street in one of those four story brownstone front houses with a high 'stoop,' " her brother Alger recalled. "Soon after the Civil War, Columbia College had developed the area, by covering it with similar homes, all built closely together, and they were occupied by families of the upper middle class." Alger remembered an atmosphere of urban anomie; the neighborhood, as he recalled it, was not quite Edith Wharton territory. "These families were strangers, and there was no social life," he stated. "No one 'called on' anyone." Still, the Upper Estate and nearby streets housed most of the educational institutions with which the family was involved. Columbia was located at Madison Avenue and Forty-Ninth Street, until it moved to Morningside Heights in 1896; Barnard was in a brownstone at Madison and Forty-Fourth Street, and Virginia's secondary school, the Brearley School, was on East Forty-Fifth Street.[24]

Virginia remembered a four-story brownstone on a "quiet and respectable street," with similar homes inhabited by "solid American families"—the Griswolds, Prestons, McGees, Whitfields, Rhinelanders, and Frelinghuysens—"a few of them more wealthy and socially prominent than we were." Young or older, Virginia could skillfully weigh and assess social position. Nearby families, she recalled, had the same level of household help, "two maids—a cook and a chambermaid waitress—and they had someone come in by the day to do the washing. The servants were almost invariably Irish." The family spent summers outside the city, usually in Ellenville in Ulster County.[25]

Virginia's story of her childhood included an episode about which she had been told by family members: as a very small child, she had defied parental directions. She had started to get down from her high chair at breakfast without saying, "Please excuse me," and resisted demands that she do so ("I won't"), even though forced to remain in the chair for hours. Finally, the family gave in. The next day, when she was ready to do so, Virginia acceded to the original request. The incident, she felt, defined her character: "Any kind of pressure or threat stirs up some mulish trait in my disposition." This insight resonates. Virginia's visual memories began with educational experiences (nineteenth-century memoirists, similarly, sought hints of their future callings in early memories). The future dean recalled herself on her seventh birthday in 1884 at a desk in a fourth-floor room of the family brownstone that had been fitted out as a classroom; she also recalled being dropped off, in March 1888, when she was ten, at her first school at Fifth Avenue and Forty-Ninth Street by her brother Harry, on his way to nearby Columbia College. The incident provided a chance for diversion into a favorite memory: Harry. "Had this brother of mine lived on with his gay personality, his loyal affection for his little sister, his popularity, his brilliance, life, I think, would have been different for me in a number of ways," Virginia stated. Her recollections often circled back to Harry, and her memories of Harry were usually self-referential.[26]

A typescript describing the people who influenced Virginia's life, compiled by her friend and would-be biographer Dorothea Setzer, gave primacy to Virginia's mother: "A strong character who sent her to college when she did not want to go. Expressed an interest in all her activities, and encouraged her. In later life, allowing her complete freedom to follow her own inclinations. Her saws and maxims made a profound impression on her daughter." Virginia's father, wrote Setzer, influenced her to a lesser degree than her mother "and mainly by his example. He taught her to shoot, and saw to it that she had a gun suitable to her age as she grew up. He gave her an interest in sports and an outdoor life, which was not at all attractive to her mother." When Virginia compared her parents on the basis of social relations, she presented another equation. "Father had an inner friendliness and loved people, though outwardly he gave a rather grim and frightening impression which scared many people who did not know him well," Virginia recalled. "On the other hand, mother was outwardly vivacious and friendly, making visitors believe that she was most cordial and interested in them, when, as a matter of fact, she cared nothing for anyone outside of her immediate family." Virginia's mother seems the more frightening.[27]

It was Harry, Henry Alger Gildersleeve, Jr. (1871–1891), however, who was "the brilliant, radiant figure of my childhood." Harry "combined the characteristics of both parents in a happy fashion and was well liked and social." He was brilliant, in his sister's view. "But what I remember chiefly about Harry is his love of his little sister and his fondness for taking her about with him," she reported; he told her about evolution and took her with him to the Columbia College library at Madison Avenue and Forty-Ninth Street. Harry entered the college at age fifteen, graduated at age nineteen, and earned a master's degree at Columbia at age twenty. "Unlike Alger and myself, he was ambitious, and he was going into law," wrote Virginia. Then, in the summer of 1891, all three Gildersleeve offspring contracted typhoid, which they picked up in Sharon, Connecticut. "Harry had a light case but he got up too soon, had a relapse, developed peritonitis and died," wrote friend Dorothea Setzer. "His death was a blow from which her mother never recovered; she retired from the world and made home a gloomy place in which to be." To Virginia, Harry's death was a turning point: "At that moment a black curtain cut my life in two."[28]

Virginia remembered her surviving brother, Alger Crocheron Gildersleeve (1869–1952), as "a quiet boy but always doing interesting things." Alger had a scientific streak; he did chemical experiments at the back of the fourth floor, raised white mice on the front of the fourth floor, and kept a wild fox in the backyard. A cello and banjo player, he introduced his sister to music. Alger attended the Columbia College School of Mines (soon to become the engineering school), class of '89, before embarking on his career. "I was the elder brother of little Virginia, nearly nine years her senior," Alger remembered, "so when I was preparing for college she was still a little girl. Of course we never played together. As a matter of fact, our family never played indoor games. They just sat around and read." Alger recalled, too, the family's secularism. "The family in which the Dean was raised could not be called a 'religious' one. Prayers were personal affairs, and Grace was never said before meals." Much as he saw himself as distinct from other family members, those who "just sat around and read," Alger was always devoted to Virginia and in touch continually. He visited her in England, where she spent the summers in later life; contributed his research on family history for her memoir; and defended her from criticism.[29]

A loyal Columbia alumnus, Alger served the university in 1918 as engineer or contractor for the reconstruction of the Columbia Club at 4 West Forty-Third Street. For much of his adult life, after his marriage in 1910, he lived in Far Rockaway, a beach resort community in southeast Queens until the 1950s, when the subway reached it. Starting in the 1920s, Alger became an amateur genealogist. He wrote a study of his and Virginia's ancestor, a great-grandfather on their mother's side, John Gelb (b. 1744), an organ builder and immigrant from Germany to the United States in 1797. He also kept track of Crocheron relatives, North and South. With defiant impiety about the family legacy (Alger had a droll wit), he saved clippings about those who were arrested for vagrancy or deposited in asylums. Finally, he corresponded with Crocheron connections to compile a family history. Typically, Alger introduced himself and Virginia as members of the ninth generation and asked for family news. "Let me congratulate you on your flourishing branch with its many twigs," Alger responded in 1928 to a Southern correspondent, Edmund Parker Crocheron. "There are no children in our family, but my sister, the Dean, has a thousand girls up at Barnard."[30]

At Harry's death in 1891, when Virginia was 14, the family coped with the disaster by taking a trip to Europe. This and subsequent family voyages got Virginia started on a lifetime of travel. When the family returned in 1891, Virginia's parents enrolled her in the Brearley School, recommended to the Gildersleeves as New York's best educational opportunity. Samuel Brearley, Jr., had founded the school in 1884, with money borrowed from a Harvard classmate (class of '71). After college, Samuel Brearley had worked as a private tutor and attended Oxford. Planning to teach at a private boys' school, he became convinced of a need in New York City for the intellectual education of young women. The school's reputation soared; when Samuel Brearley died in 1886, "the Brearley," with twenty faculty and 120 students, turned away applicants. Virginia long remembered the school's brownstone building at Madison Avenue and Forty-Fourth Street and the devoted headmaster, James Greenleaf Croswell, whose lively correspondence with students, current and former, suggests a joyful and winning personality. Virginia studied French, German, Latin, Greek, and European history. Her best friends at Brearley, Alice Castree (Williams) and Elizabeth (Bessie) Coffin (Thomasson) remained friends later in life.[31]

In her last two years at Brearley, Virginia recalled, her mother began speaking of college: "She said I had brains but no nerves." ("No nerves" meant no propensity to nervous afflictions, such as were thought to afflict young women in college, according to a late nineteenth-century authority). Typically, Brearley graduates who attended college went to Bryn Mawr; this pattern became a tradition. But Virginia's mother, with whom educational decisions rested, wanted Virginia the younger to go to nearby Barnard. Still mourning the loss of her gifted son Harry, Virginia the elder made sure that her daughter remained close to home. There was a Brearley/Barnard connection, too: Caroline D. Choate, wife of prominent lawyer Joseph Choate and neighbor in Murray Hill's "Upper Estate"; the Choates lived a block away at 50 West Forty-Seventh Street. Caroline Choate, who had campaigned for women's acceptance at Columbia in 1882–1883, had persuaded Samuel Brearley to found his school in 1884, and had then recommended the school to her friends the Gildersleeves. When Barnard began five years later, Caroline Choate became a trustee and vice chairman of the board of trustees, on which she served until 1929. Thus, when Virginia entered Barnard in 1895, it was perhaps at the suggestion of this devoted trustee, seen by her fellow board members as "a very tower of strength to the young and struggling College."[32]

Founded in 1889, Barnard owed its existence to Columbia College's refusal to admit undergraduate women, a proposal that had rumbled around the Columbia administration for about a decade. In 1882–1883, eight committed women—among them Caroline D. Choate and Lillie Devereux Blake, petitioned president of Columbia Frederick Barnard to accept women at the college. President Barnard supported the idea; the Columbia trustees rejected it. Instead, Columbia created a special "Collegiate Course" in which women could take exams but not classes. But tenacious women and their supporters continued to press for a chance for liberal arts degrees at Columbia. Finally, advocate Annie Nathan Meyer, who, with "pathetic eagerness," in her words, had attended the half-baked "Collegiate Course," a "stony substitute" for the college experience, joined other advocates of women's higher education to start a separate institution for women. Barnard, distinctively, had a separate board of trustees and separate finances, and eventually—though not at first—a separate faculty.[33]

Barnard followed the model of the "affiliated" (or coordinate) college, which Annie Nathan Meyer described as a hybrid. "The affiliated college stands midway between the college for women on the one hand, and the coeducational college on the other," Meyer told the National Council of Women in 1891. "You will call it a compromise, possibly it is." Affiliated colleges had started at Cambridge and Oxford. Girton College at Cambridge in 1869 was the first, and others followed, mainly in the 1890s; the universities did not yet grant degrees to women. In 1879 Harvard established its "Annex," renamed Radcliffe in the 1890s. Radcliffe students took Harvard classes but received separate degrees. Proponents of affiliated colleges might also have noticed short-lived Evelyn College (1887–1897) at Princeton, then the College of New Jersey. With at most fifty students and usually far fewer, often faculty daughters, Evelyn depended totally on Princeton—for faculty, trustees, libraries, labs, curricula, exams, and academic standards; but its students, said the university, could not earn Princeton degrees until the new institution grew more secure, which never occurred. Instead, enrollment fell and Evelyn College closed, soon to be forgotten. The affiliated college of the 1890s was still a work in progress.[34]

Barnard, in contrast, survived and later prospered. In 1895, when Virginia entered, it was a tiny place, smaller than "the Brearley," and located in a house on Madison Avenue. When Columbia moved to Morningside Heights in 1897, Barnard followed; the young college took root in its uptown habitat, Milbank Hall, west of Broadway and overlooking the Hudson River. "We rattled around in the great space of our new Barnard buildings" Virginia remembered. In her student papers, Virginia reveled in the new location and in the appeal of Morningside Heights, "amid scenes of inspiring beauty." She appreciated the "rocky slopes of Morningside Park;" the "glittering darkness of winter, when the lights of the city flashed coldly below;" and the expansive views, from Grant's Tomb and the West Side rooftops to the lower Hudson Valley. "The charm of the heights fastened on me," she wrote.[35]

Virginia joined a class of twenty-two in 1895; her classmates came mainly from Manhattan, Brooklyn, and New Jersey, and one from upstate New York. "All were more or less on the same social level," Virginia recalled. In this instance, as in others linked to social relations and status, Virginia continually measured, weighed, assessed, and compared, both at the time and in retrospect. At the start, the classmates followed the same schedule. They studied English, Latin, Greek, math, and a modern language, French or German; Virginia took French. Downtown or uptown, Columbia professors walked a few blocks to teach Barnard classes. Virginia profited from four years of "Rhetoric," with its innumerable theme papers, and especially enjoyed Greek, where she found "joy in beauty, exhilaration of adventure, illumination of the mind." Greek was required for admission at the time, as well as for freshmen; "tho I never thought of specializing in the classics," Virginia recalled, "I chose to continue it [Greek], one course a year thru all the rest of my colleges days." Though she never chose a major, Virginia veered between English and history; even as an undergraduate she appreciated an interdisciplinary approach. Her straight A's for freshman year "should fill the entire family with pride," wrote Mrs. N.W. Liggett, the Barnard bursar, who, during the temporary absence of a dean, ran the tiny college herself (Mrs. Liggett never used a first name). "I think you have taken away something, in addition to scholarship, that will doubtless prove as valuable to you, and that is a closer and broader knowledge of human nature." In retrospect, Virginia agreed. The most important part of her college education, she believed, "was experience in human relations, the ability to know and understand people of various kinds, to appreciate them and to enjoy helping to organize them."[36]

Virginia described herself as "shy, snobbish, solemn" at the start of her college career, but soon became a class leader. Her first two friends were Edith Striker from East Orange, New Jersey and Alte Stilwell, from Harlem in upper Manhattan, then a well-off residential neighborhood. As at Brearley, Virginia made friends two at a time. Later, as dean, she would speak appreciatively of college friendships: "Not only do they make the rest of your life more joyful," she told Barnard students in 1914, "but they add lustre to college and make you love it." But she urged students to shun the hazards of friendship: "sentimental indulgence, which makes you mope in corners," "losing of your personality," or "over-demonstration of affection," all symptoms of the college "crush." Agnes Ernst (Meyer), class of '07, journalist and trustee (1935–1954), recalled a story related to her about Virginia as an object of crushes. "When she [Virginia] was a senior, many girls in the lower classes had remote crushes on her," Agnes Meyer stated in the 1950s. "She personified the role of the female scholar in college of the period and while they admired her extravagantly and tried to emulate her, none could get very close to her, or cultivate a human friendly relationship."[37]

Within her own class, however, Virginia nurtured relationships with favored friends—no doubt encouraged by her mother, who became an honorary class member and who gave parties for her daughter's classmates. Virginia's two very best friends at Barnard, who entered in junior year, each held Columbia connections. Alice Duer (1874–1942), a descendant of Rufus King of Massachusetts, signer of the Constitution and chairman of the Columbia Board of Trustees, was a great-granddaughter of William A. Duer, a president of Columbia College (1829–1842). Three years older than her classmates, Alice had postponed college until she could pay for it through her earnings in magazine fiction and journalism (her father had gone bankrupt), and later became a prolific author. Alice steadily praised Virginia and her achievements. "There was not, I believe, a single member of the class of Ninety-Nine who did not think, from our freshman year, that Virginia Gildersleeve would one day be Dean of Barnard," Alice claimed. Virginia, remembering Alice—and always measuring herself against others—was a rival as well as an admirer; she found Alice's talent daunting. She recalled sitting in philosophy class in Columbia's Low Memorial Library in December 1898, during senior year, staring at Alice and thinking how modest her own gifts were, in comparison. "I sum up my own capacities," Virginia wrote, "I have respectable marks, a respectable mind, and just no talent at all."[38]

Virginia's other best friend also had a connection to Columbia. Marjorie Putnam Jacobi (1878–1966) was the daughter of pioneer woman doctor Mary Putnam Jacobi (the daughter of publisher George Palmer Putnam) and Dr. Abraham Jacobi, a professor at the College of Physicians and Surgeons, which became part of Columbia in 1892. "Miss G. was the most prominent girl in her class, adored by its members, who voted her class president sophomore and senior years, and then permanent president," Marjorie recalled in the 1950s, looking back on their college experience—though sometimes shifting to the present. "She has a great gift for keeping things running smoothly, and a lawyer's dexterity in getting her own way. Hers is a judicial temperament, terrifically logical, objective, and without prejudice. She was always a good sport . . . having already acquired a reputation as a golfer, which sport she practiced and enjoyed with her adoring father. . . . Always perfectly tailored, her outstanding physical characteristics were her beautiful dark eyes." Marjorie became a Barnard Alumnae Trustee.[39]

In freshman year, Virginia joined the Barnard chapter of Kappa Kappa Gamma (KKG), a national fraternity (sororities were then called "fraternities"), founded around 1870; it was Barnard's first fraternity, as of 1891, and for Virginia's first two years the only one. Although "Kappa" had at first admitted the entire freshman class, it quickly dropped that policy. By 1895, the fraternity took pride in its exclusiveness—it valued social rank and family connections—and in the academic ability of its members; choosing among applicants, it accepted only the "very brightest & best of all who came." A major purpose of "Kappa" was to exclude Jews, who constituted about one fifth of the class of '99 and played no part in Virginia's circle or recollections. Virginia's first pair of close friends, Edith and Alte, joined the fraternity; when her new and more favored friends, Alice and Marjorie, joined the class in junior year, she secured "Kappa" membership for them as well. The fraternity steered Virginia into dramatic performances. "As an undergraduate, Miss G always played the part of a boy," Annie Nathan Meyer remembered.

While other girls in boys' parts borrowed clothes from a father or brother, Meyer recalled, Virginia's mother "always took Virginia to Rogers Peet and got clothes that fit her." Meyer's other memory of Virginia as a student was of college dances—all-women events, at which Barnard students filled one another's dance cards. "Her brother brought her to the college dances and walked around disconsolately until time to take her home," Annie Nathan Meyer declared. "She took herself very seriously and never did foolish things."[40]

Virginia got to know Columbia students, too, especially on the literary magazine, *The Morningside*, where she joined the board of editors. Here she met, among others, Frederick Keppel '99, future Dean of Columbia College and her colleague-to-be on all-important university committees. By senior year, most of Virginia's courses were at Columbia; there she shared classes with Columbia undergraduates and met some of her most distinguished professors. Franklin Giddings, who taught Principles of Sociology, was a founder of his field and Columbia's first sociology professor. Virginia impressed Nicholas Murray Butler, her philosophy professor and a friend of her father's; rising rapidly in his field and in university politics, Butler would become president of Columbia in 1902. James Harvey Robinson, who taught European history, was "by far the greatest teacher I ever studied under." Virginia's seventy-page, handwritten senior thesis, on the Committee of Public Safety in the French Revolution, written for Robinson, argued that "the theories of this group are, one and all, thoroughly imbued with the spirit of Rousseau." In Virginia's view, the essay lacked distinction; this is true. Still, her study of the committee members, however "impractical and fanatical," in her opinion, fostered what she saw as Barnard's goal: "to give us a liberal education, to broaden and develop evenly our minds."[41]

Intense self-consciousness characterized college women, as suggested in a paper that Virginia wrote as a senior on changes in the student population. During her four years at Barnard, she posited, a new type of student had arrived, one quite different from the old type of "sober-minded" student like herself—serious and diligent. The new type of student, in contrast, more superficial and less studious, attended college to socialize and enjoy "college life." How should Barnard view such a collegian? Virginia adopted a positive stance. The Barnard experience, she felt, would democratize the new arrivals, and there might be something to learn from the newcomers, too. Their fun-loving, frivolous approach to the college experience—their interest in rites and rituals, in theatricals and varsity teams—might offer benefit. One benefit: the newcomers probably aided Barnard, Virginia concluded, in its competition with other women's schools ("Vassar, Bryn Mawr, and most of our other sister colleges"). Thus, in the space of four pages, Virginia identified two types of female collegiate rivalry: between contingents of students, old and new, and among sister colleges. The essay suggests Virginia's ability to assess her social environment. It also reflects a transition that historians have subsequently noticed: as the numbers of college women rose, the studiousness of the early generation of college women waned. The new group of women collegians, well-off and less academically inclined, as Virginia suggested, held more social goals.[42]

Class loyalty also defined early college women. The class of '99 treasured its collective identity and distinctive qualities. "We have never been by nature frivolous and gay," Ninety-Niners declared in *Mortarboard*, the college yearbook, "but this year we have surprised even ourselves by the dignity and social mindedness we have displayed. Studiousness is widespread among us." The serious cast of Ninety-Niners gave way to frivolity on Friday afternoons: "We cheer ourselves for an hour with innocent games, ballad writing, and the perusal of light literature," declared *Mortarboard*. But diligence prevailed; the high standards of '99, its boosters claimed, might even intimidate incoming classes. With a final gust of self-regard, Ninety-Niners looked forward to the future of the class, to the endurance of its values, friendships, and memories. The legacy of '99, announced *Mortarboard*, included "a broader view of life, an armor against prejudice and bigotry, comrades we have grown to admire and love." In their limericks about class members, *Mortarboard* editors noted Virginia's success as a student, her ability to inspire envy, and the impact of her father's profession: "There once was a girl with a brief/ Of prodigies she was the chief/ She wrote argumentation/ That won commendation/ And awakened our envious grief."[43]

Self-involved and competitive, though lacking a clear direction, Virginia graduated first in her class and won the prestigious Fiske Prize for graduate study in 1899–1900. To shift to graduate work at Columbia, she later stated, was "the easiest thing for a Barnard graduate to do." Her best friends, she noted, were getting married. Alice Duer married

William Miller and went off with him to Costa Rica, where he was in business. Later known as suffragist and prolific novelist, Alice became an advisory editor of the *New Yorker* and Hollywood scriptwriter. Marjorie Jacobi in 1900 married George McAnemy, who would have an exceptional career as journalist, municipal reformer, and New York City official; he served as Manhattan borough president, on New York City's Board of Aldermen (now the City Council) and as comptroller. Virginia's Brearley friends married, too. Bessie Coffin had wed her British third cousin, Franklin Thomassen, on a trip to Europe in the summer after her junior year in secondary school; the couple saw Virginia in England in years to come. But Virginia moved gradually into academic life.[44]

To remain single after college was not unusual for Virginia's cohort. Only about half of women who graduated from college in the 1890s married, a decline from the marriage rate among women college graduates of the 1860s and 1870s, and greatest in the northeast, where women were more likely to attend women's colleges. Of the twenty-eight who had been at any time part of the Barnard class of '99, about half married. To contemporaries, the low marriage rates among college alumnae, compared to the general population, rested on a mix of choice and circumstance. Factors mentioned at the time included a greater desire for independence and rising expectations of marriage, or, as a Berkeley graduate student of 1895 suggested, "the bent toward congenial marriage may lessen the actual probability of marriage." The college woman was also "under less pressure to accept what falls below her standard than the average woman, because she can better support and occupy herself alone." Employment options for women graduates rose: they could find jobs not only in teaching, which grew dramatically, and in new women's professions, such as social work, but on college faculties—in women's colleges, big universities, and teacher training schools, which proliferated. In addition, the competitive marriage market took a toll. As the Berkeley graduate student dryly observed, "the remaining cause of the low marriage rate [among women college graduates] is that many men dislike intellectual women, whether because such women are really disagreeable or because men's taste is at fault."[45]

Still other factors may have shaped Virginia's path. These include some version of the "family claim," an expression used by settlement leader Jane Addams in her memoir of 1910 to describe her own post-college floundering in early 1880s; the family, Addams argued, required the service of the female college graduate (herself).[46] In Virginia's case, the "family claim" took the form of her own reluctance to leave her close-knit, firmly structured, upper-middle-class family of origin, whose members seemed superior—in their own view—to all others and whose emotional organization excluded outsiders. Few suitors, for instance, could have competed with the memory of Virginia's idealized brother Harry. More important, Virginia's frequent companion, model of behavior, and major influence, her mother, Virginia the elder, "cared nothing for anyone out-side of her immediate family." Virginia's brother, Alger, who saw himself as the family oddball, did not marry until he was over forty; the Gilder-sleeve version of the "family claim" may have shaped the paths of both surviving offspring. In any case, Virginia lived with her parents for the rest of their lives and established her own household only in her forties, after her parents died; thereafter her domestic life and affective relation-ships involved other women, her "intimate" companions.

The role in which Virginia saw herself in her undergraduate essay of 1899—as an intermediary or interlocutor between two types of students or cohorts—also suggests what her predicament might have been as a new college graduate. Virginia came of age between two generations of college women, historian Patrick Dilley points out, the pioneer activists and the next cohort. She fell "somewhere between the two," he observes, and "perhaps never fit very neatly into either."[47] To not fit in neatly was a challenge. Virginia had no clear-cut path forward, in short; she would have to invent one.

POST-GRADUATE DRIFT

After Virginia graduated from Barnard in 1899, she traveled to Europe with her parents and a friend, and entered graduate school at Columbia. The university had started to accept women for graduate work, gradu-ally and unevenly, in the early 1890s, following a proposal of the uni-versity president Seth Low (who succeeded President Barnard, served from 1890 to 1901, and then became mayor of New York City). Low's initiative enabled Columbia to keep pace with a few of its competitors (Yale and Penn), which had by then admitted women to graduate work. But some Columbia professors resisted, and some departments would not grant degrees to women. The Faculty of Political Science, which Virginia entered, as a Fiske Scholar in Political Science for 1899–1900, had only recently agreed, in 1898 and with reluctance, to admit women to its graduate program and as graduate degree candidates.[48]

At Columbia, Virginia studied with her admired undergraduate professors, James Harvey Robinson in French history and Franklin Giddings in sociology, along with Charles Osgood in American history. In 1900 she received an MA in medieval history. Her master's thesis, an exercise in bibliography for Professor Robinson, was "Some Materials for Judging the Actual Effects of Feudalism in France." The essay was a description of relevant documents plus a "critical bibliography . . . roughly classifying the important primary sources" and evaluating their potential usefulness—treaties, petitions, correspondence, marriage acts, and collections of archival material. Virginia then entered a period of meandering toward an academic career—a sequence of years, in her account, during which external factors—as opposed to professional goals—determined each successive next step.[49]

"In June, 1900 I received the degree of Master of Arts in medieval history," Virginia wrote. "I did not know what I wanted to do next." A passage in her autobiography, looking back from the 1950s, focuses on this moment as a juncture in which she wrestled with indirection and then swerved away from a conventional path toward an academic one:

> I decided to take a year off and just look around. Nearly all my intimate friends had married, or were about to do so, fortunately to men I greatly liked. Growing up in a predominantly masculine household, I had met plenty of men and all my life in Columbia University and elsewhere I worked closely with them. If my plan for a year off had been carried through and I had leisure to see a little more of a certain one of the polite eligible gentlemen who in those far-away days so formally courted decorous young ladies, I should, I think, have been married and lived my life in such glamorous lands as China, France, and Peru. Instead I was drawn into new and absorbing activities that diverted my mind until, at the age of thirty-three, I became Dean and acquired a very large "family" at Barnard College—a family capable of getting into so many scrapes and needing so much attention, and generally so lacking

in adequate housing and in orderly habits, that often I have felt sympathetic kinship with the domestic responsibilities of the Old Woman Who Lived in a Shoe.

What actually happened was that I received very early in the new school year, a letter from Professor William Tenney Brewster, of the Department of English, saying that the freshman class was unexpectedly large and that it was necessary to have an additional section of "English A." Would I be willing to conduct this?[50]

In the dense first passage, filled with imprecise language and jolts back and forth in time, Virginia conveys a situation of fluidity; her use of the word "certain," embedded in the third sentence, underscores uncertainty. Thus, she skirts the "marriage question." The vague reference to a onetime, youthful, heterosexual, romantic relationship may have been a custom in the memoirs of women who preferred single-sex relationships. At no point in these lines, significantly, does Virginia, the subject, seem to decide anything—either to ignore a suitor or to teach in college; rather, the situation around her determined her direction and pushed her one way or another.

But Virginia made some decisions, too. She seized the chance to return to Barnard in 1900 and teach freshman composition, a course known for its demands on instructors; in his own section, for instance, which he taught for some thirty years, Professor Brewster assigned—and graded—daily themes. The position offered to Virginia, he explained, was a half-job. "I am writing to you to know if you would consider an offer to do some teaching at Barnard College in the English Department," Brewster told Virginia. "The unusual size of the freshman class has so upset our calculations that we are shorthanded. . . . Specifically, we need someone to take charge of a section of about thirty freshmen for one hour of recitation, one hour of impromptu theme-writing, and between three and four hours of consultation." Virginia was to earn $250 a year (almost $7,300 today), half the pay of an "assistant" in English. She gained in return professional direction. "Thus, in a modest and experimental manner," she recalled, "I entered the teaching profession."[51]

The five-year experiment succeeded only in part: to teach freshman English held no promise of a professional future. Virginia could not expect to exceed the rank she held, assistant and tutor, or to teach classes in literature. Rather, her teaching stint led to an offer to teach even *more* freshman English. The English Department decided to confer all its sections of English A, the freshman course, to one sole instructor: Virginia would be that person. At this point, the young assistant made a firm decision. The horrible prospect of grading one hundred student papers a week, in her estimate, impelled her to request a leave from Barnard and to apply for further graduate work at Columbia. This time she turned to the Department of English, under the Faculty of Philosophy, which, in 1891, under its new dean, Nicholas Murray Butler, had admitted women to graduate courses and degrees, and was no doubt friendlier to women than was the History Department. Meanwhile, at Barnard, the class of 1906 was so impressed with Virginia's past teaching that it dedicated the 1906 *Mortarboard* to her.[52]

Virginia turned to English literature with a focus on Shakespeare. Her professors included William P. Trent on English literature of the seventeenth and eighteenth centuries; George P. Krapp on Anglo-Saxon poetry and the history of English; John W. Cunliffe on sixteenth century literature; and three specialists in Shakespeare, Ashley A. Thorndike, William W. Lawrence, and William Allan Neilson, who, as president of Smith College, would encounter Virginia often when she became dean. At her preliminary exams for the doctorate in October 1907, Virginia fielded questions from a group of her instructors. "When did the English language begin? What had been spoken in Great Britain before this?" asked Professor Krapp. "Where did the Angles and Saxons reside on the continent?" "When did English emerge after the Conquest?" asked Professor Lawrence. "What king was reigning at the beginning of the thirteenth century?" "Outline Spenser's life and work," demanded Professor Thorndike. "Name other important poets of the seventeenth century." Professor Brewster from Barnard, too, joined in the questioning: "What literary controversy was in progress about the end of the seventeenth century?" asked Brewster. "Compare [Swift's] attitude in *A Modest Proposal* with that in the last part of *Gulliver*."[53]

Virginia received praise for her interdisciplinary dissertation, "Government Regulation of Elizabethan Drama," in part a study of law. Exploration of Elizabethan theater and Shakespeare's audience members led Virginia to ask: What laws, local and national, affected drama? She looked at parliamentary statutes, royal proclamations, council orders, and laws and patents concerning the status and licensing of players, licensing of playhouses, and the reach of censorship. She found a centralization of power over drama in a member of the king's household, Master of the King's Revels, who developed a form of monopoly: only favored companies received royal patents to perform. The controversy over power to control drama that developed in Elizabethan London between the Royal Council and the municipal government, Virginia stated, illuminated the civil war that was soon to come. Puritans became infected with hatred of the Court, and in a final Puritan triumph, the Long Parliament in 1642, 1647, and 1648 prohibited all theatrical performances whatsoever.[54]

With expectation of a doctorate, Virginia met rejection at Barnard. The current dean, Laura D. Gill, told Virginia in the spring of 1907 that her two-year leave for graduate study was over, that the Barnard English faculty had recently expanded, and that there would be no room for her on the teaching staff. But—with the sort of good fortune that shaped her father's career in law—Virginia overcame this rebuff. First, she received an outside job offer. Professor Cunliffe, with whom she had studied sixteenth-century literature at Columbia, took a post at the University of Wisconsin as department chair and offered Virginia an associate professorship. Virginia declined, as she could not, she believed, leave her parents, then in their sixties. Still, the outside offer was a positive sign. Next, fortunately for Virginia, Dean Gill resigned at the end of 1907, and Professor Brewster became acting dean of Barnard; another of Virginia's Columbia professors, William Trent, chaired the Barnard section of the English Department. With her patrons in place, Virginia became a lecturer at Barnard, to teach sophomore English (for an annual salary of $800). "[T]hen came the most extraordinary stroke of good luck that ever befell a young teacher," she recalled: the Shakespeare course at Barnard, offered previously by Professors Neilson and Thorndike, needed an instructor. Professor Thorndike got tired of giving the class at Barnard and "nobody on the Columbia side wanted to do it either." So Columbia hired Virginia to teach the Shakespeare class at Barnard (another $500). In 1909 she reported to Professor Trent that the course enrolled forty, a number that she predicted would rise. The same year she gave an advanced course in medieval literature, including Chaucer. Within a year, Virginia had staked out a central role in English instruction at Barnard. Her rise from rejection to significance had been meteoric.[55]

Ever conscious of power relations, Virginia solidified her status in the English Department by reaching downward and upward. She proved her value to Barnard students by writing ballads with them at the student-run "Fireside Club," an extracurricular group, as she had so recently done on Friday afternoons with members of the class of '99. At the same time, she was appointed to the faculty committee that supervised the master's degree, "just as if I had been a young man of promise." Her teaching repertoire grew further: In the spring of 1910 the English Department gave Virginia permission to teach a graduate course on a subject of her choice; she chose the history of English verse and prepared exhaustively. In the fall, with a class of seven graduate students (five women and two men), Virginia analyzed the sources that fed "the great river of English poetry," going back to the Anglo-Saxon, Latin, Old French, and Italian, and tried, in her trademark interdisciplinary style, to draw links between visual art and poetry.[56]

Two years after receiving her doctorate, then, by her own account, Virginia had become a rising star of her department. She also assumed a college-wide office as Secretary of the Faculty and took a post in the Barnard alumnae association, too. Soaring high on a wave of professional triumph and, at the same time, carefully counting her steps of ascent, Virginia suddenly confronted a new opportunity.[57]

In December 1910, the young English instructor, now an assistant professor, received an invitation to become dean of Barnard College. That invitation was by no means a simple matter. It involved a prolonged, four-year search by college officials and trustees, and an intense conflict between two of the forces on whom Virginia would depend for decades in her time as dean, President Butler of Columbia and the Barnard College Board of Trustees, especially the Barnard Treasurer, George A. Plimpton. At issue were the powers that the dean would exert, the qualities to be sought in candidates, the merits of the individuals considered, and the relationship between the college and the university.

CHOOSING A DEAN

Since Barnard was founded in 1889, several educators had shaped the position of dean. Unlike some of its rival women's colleges—such as Bryn Mawr, Mount Holyoke, Vassar, and Wellesley—Barnard had no president; its status as an affiliate or coordinate college meant that the Columbia president, as of 1902 Nicholas Murray Butler, was the sole president on campus. Like Columbia College, Teachers College, or Columbia Law School, Barnard College was one of the president's fiefs, each with a dean. To the deans fell the tasks of running their institutions as well as negotiating for their constituencies in the larger arena of the university. How they managed this double mission determined their success.

Virginia's predecessors had a mixed record. Ella Weed (Vassar '73), the first dean or equivalent of a dean and a founding trustee, served from 1889 to 1894. A cautious leader, Weed employed, in historian Andrea Walton's words, "the principle of sameness and the strategy of subordination." Under her direction, Barnard adopted Columbia's entrance exam, curriculum, and academic standards; at the same time, Weed avoided potential sources of conflict linked to women, such as women's suffrage; she died in office. Emily James Smith (Putnam), Bryn Mawr '89, had studied Greek at Cambridge and served Barnard with distinction from 1894 to 1900. During her term, the student body grew, the curriculum expanded, and in a major contract with Columbia in 1900, Barnard won the power to hire its own faculty. Much admired (including by Virginia, one of her students), Emily married publisher George Putnam in 1899 and soon left the deanship but remained a devoted teacher of classics at the college. Her successor, Laura D. Gill (Smith, '81), had teaching experience but lacked graduate degrees; during her term, from 1901 to 1907, she sought to build the college a dormitory, which it much needed. But Gill floundered as obstacles arose. She clashed with the dean of Teachers College over whether TC could train undergraduates (no), fought with bursar N. W. Liggett, argued with several Jewish students over Saturday classes in a popular history course, and alienated trustee Annie Nathan Meyer by not having the college piano tuned. By 1907, Gill was enmeshed in a web of dispute.[58]

Most grievously, after a letter of complaint from a group of alumnae (a group that included Virginia's influential classmate Alice Duer Miller), Gill antagonized Columbia president Nicholas Murray Butler, who charged that Barnard, under Gill, was "not springing vigorously forward with full life and increased prestige." Among Butler's objections: Miss Gill had used the income of the Pure Science Fund, established by trustee Elizabeth Anderson, to "punish professors whom she did not like, and to give new facilities to those whom she did like," as the president wrote to Barnard treasurer Plimpton. "The whole episode was exceedingly discreditable." Butler's disapproval crushed Gill's authority, and she resigned under pressure. "Miss Gill had executive ability but lacked tact," recalled Virginia, whom Gill had refused to hire in 1907; the former dean, in Virginia's view, had always felt out of place at Barnard, as if "surrounded . . . by aliens." Laura D. Gill defended her stance in a surge of distressed letters to lawyer Silas Brownell, the head of Barnard's board of trustees, who had advised her to use more moderate language in her letter of resignation to Butler. "[M]y judgment has possibly been at fault," Gill told Brownell days after leaving office. "I should have respected myself more, to have had an open fight, been killed and left unburied on the field, than I do to [have] been what you call 'moderate.' " Still anguished by what she called "the Columbia situation," Gill summed up her Barnard experience as "a long nightmare."[59]

As Gill's plight suggests, to clash with Butler goaded fate. Ambitious, domineering, and egocentric, Nicholas Murray Butler ran Columbia like an empire. A Columbia College graduate of 1882, Butler excelled as a philosophy professor; became prominent in the National Education Association, a progressive reform group; founded a journal (*Educational Review*); rose quickly in academic affairs; and won his colleagues' votes in 1890 to become the first dean of the Faculty of Philosophy, where he presided for 12 years. He then served as university president for four decades, from 1902 to 1945. Under Butler, Columbia became an internationally recognized institution, "the greatest capital of the mind that the world has ever seen," as Butler claimed at seventy-five. A master at marketing and active in Republican politics, Butler ran for U.S. president in 1920 ("Butler Means Business"). Critics abounded. According to his biographer, Michael Rosenthal, Butler was "only comfortable with the well-to-do and well-connected." He was derided for social climbing, craving public homage, "toadying to the rich and powerful," surrounding himself with sycophants, and leaving a trail of corpses. In the words of one chair of the Columbia Board of Trustees, George Rives, "he values himself for his worst qualities." Butler's dominance pervaded all parts of campus life. "He rules the university as an absolute autocrat; he permits no slightest interference with his will," one critic charged. "He furiously attacks or cunningly intrigues against anyone who shows any trace of interference."[60] No wonder that a subordinate ran into trouble.

With Dean Gill's resignation, Butler appointed William T. Brewster, Virginia's former professor and chair of the English Department, to be acting dean of Barnard, a position he held through 1910. Butler's goals: to absorb Barnard more firmly into Columbia, to place it under supervision of Columbia trustees, and essentially to control it himself. He needed a dean indebted to him to fall in with this plan: Acting Dean Brewster was his person. But Barnard trustees were not ready to gratify Butler—to give up their quasi-independent college and in the process abolish their own positions. Nor did they want to see the acting dean installed permanently. Instead, they sought a woman dean responsible to themselves. The most active trustees, who led the campaign to find a dean, were Elizabeth Milbank Anderson, an heiress who had joined the board in 1894, funded construction of Barnard's first building in 1896, and supported Miss Gill; and college treasurer George A. Plimpton, the dynamic head of Ginn and Co., a leading educational publishing house, who served on the boards of several colleges, including his alma mater, Amherst (class of '76). Appointed to Barnard's board of trustees in 1893 by Emily James Smith to replace the previous treasurer, financier Jacob Schiff, the polymath Plimpton, buoyant, gregarious, energetic, and contentious enough to take on Columbia's president, showed boundless capacity to seek a woman dean and to foil Butler's plans.

Plimpton threw himself into the search, which sped up as 1909 began. He asked everyone he knew—a wide circle—for recommendations; suggestions poured in. One contact, Vassar trustee James M. Bruce, proposed Lida Shaw King, Vassar '90, a professor of classics at Brown and dean of its women's college (later Pembroke), "a woman of the highest character and rare personal endowment." Wellesley president Caroline Hazard told Plimpton about possible candidate Katherine M. Edwards, Cornell '88, a Wellesley Greek professor, "of attractive personal appearance and excellent manner . . . so much vitality and executive power." Hazard also proposed Susan Almira Bacon, a French literature professor at Mount Holyoke, "handsome, graceful in manner, a woman of the world, and a good scholar. . . . I do not know much about her executive ability." Still, said Hazard, "she comes of distinguished people—the right kind of people for the Dean of Barnard to come from." M. Carey Thomas, president of Bryn Mawr, claimed first that she could not think of anyone, but then suggested Mary Coes, Radcliffe '87, an official of that college and about to become its dean in 1910. "I do not believe she would in any way overstep her prerogative," Thomas noted, perhaps thinking of the turmoil linked to Laura Gill. In October 1909, Plimpton shared with his fellow trustee, Elizabeth Milbank Anderson, some of the suggestions he had collected. His list included two new candidates: Lois Kimball Mathews, Stanford '03, a history instructor at Vassar, who within a few years became dean of women at the University of Wisconsin, and Lucy Sprague, Radcliffe '00, one of the most talented candidates proposed in the search and the first dean of women at Berkeley, which sought mightily to retain her. "In regard to the Dean, I have four women on the string," Plimpton told Mrs. Anderson. "I think Butler has come to the conclusion that we are going to insist on a woman dean and he has got to make the best of it."[61]

Plimpton occasionally dismissed a suggestion, too, as in the case of the accomplished reformer Sophonisba Breckinridge, Wellesley '88, in 1909 an assistant professor of social economy at the University of Chicago, where she had earned a JD and PhD, and dean of the new Chicago School of Civics and Philanthropy, which trained social workers. "Miss Breckinridge I know all about," Plimpton told M. Carey Thomas, who had ventured her name. "I know her personally, but I do not think she would do for New York." It is possible that Sophonisba, an associate of Jane Addams and Hull House in Chicago, seemed to Plimpton too closely linked to labor reform. Or perhaps Sophonisba would not "do for New York" because the Chicago School of Civics and Philanthropy, which she led, was embroiled in a feud with the New York School of Philanthropy, with which Columbia had links; the feud concerned the nature of social work as a profession. Alternatively, Sophonisba's roots in the former Confederacy might have been Plimpton's main source of concern or perhaps a threat of scandal attached to the Breckinridge family might have stirred caution among Barnard trustees. Sophonisba's father, a former Kentucky congressman, had been sued for breach of promise in 1894 after a nine-year extramarital affair. Beyond that, Sophonisba was currently enmeshed in a romantic triangle with two women colleagues in Chicago.[62]

President Butler, meanwhile, unable to resist an academic search, had joined it; he, too, like Plimpton, proposed names and met with candidates. Butler voiced interest variously in Lucy Sprague, whom he had contacted in the fall of 1909; in Lida Shaw King, an admired administrator; and in other candidates, such as, briefly, Clara B. Spence, founder and head of the Spence School on the Upper East Side and a Barnard trustee, who had declined in 1908. At the same time Butler took steps to insure his own control. "My feeling is stronger than ever," he wrote to Plimpton in October 1909, "the interests of the college will be best promoted by electing Mr. Brewster dean, and by bringing in a strong woman—Miss Sprague or someone else—to a professorship, and with a special title that will give her authority over the domestic and personal life of the college women."[63]

Two months later, in December 1909, Butler still sought the right woman candidate. "The trouble is to find the woman," he wrote to trustee chair Silas Brownell. "My own acquaintance is pretty wide . . . but thus far (with a few exceptions) I have not seen or heard of any one in all respects suitable to the task." At that point, with no end to the search in sight, Butler mentioned Virginia for the first time:

> We have in our own ranks Miss Virginia Gildersleeve, a woman who, if she were in any other institution than our own, we should be anxiously seeking in connection with the Barnard Deanship. She is a talented and successful administrator in the fields in which she has experience and she has a personality which is very attractive to many younger women and which gives her large influence over them.

But Butler had reservations about Virginia, too: "She is very much the junior, in rank and service, of those whom she would be invited to lead." Were that not an obstacle, Butler concluded, "then Miss Gildersleeve's name ought also to be carefully considered."[64]

As 1910 began, pressure mounted; the search had stumbled and lurched for months. Butler now charged forward. On April 9, he appointed Acting Dean Brewster to a new position that he (the president) had just introduced, provost; Brewster thus held two posts, one permanent (provost) and one temporary, acting dean. A week later, on April 18, Butler built on his previous step. He proposed to the Barnard board of trustees that the deanship should be divided, that "the head of the College, the Dean, should be a woman, and that the office having to do with the details of the business and educational administration of the College should be filled by the present acting dean, W. T. Brewster, as 'Provost.' " In short, under this plan, all power would go to Brewster, the provost; the new woman dean would just be a figurehead, or as Virginia later put it, a "chaperone to the students." In June, Butler proposed a new name for the (newly modified) dean's position: Virginia's classmate, Alice Duer Miller, another former student and an activist among Barnard alumnae. Alice's social status was her winning card, in the president's view. "She is a born leader of the highest type, related to the Duers, the Kings, the Mackays, and all their circle," Butler told Plimpton. "She would be able, on the scholarly side, to teach mathematics, and on the personal side to give dignity and weight to the public representation of Barnard."[65]

But Alice lacked academic credentials, trustees noted; she was also the mother of a young child. By now, some opposition had arisen among trustees to Lucy Sprague, who, reluctant to leave Berkeley, withdrew in the summer of 1910; and Butler, it turned out, rejected Lois Kimball Mathews. "I know that the trustees do not want to urge anybody who is objectionable to you, and I am sure you feel the same," Plimpton told Butler on June 8, 1910. "I think if we find a Barnard graduate it would solve that problem. I would take Mrs. Miller without any hesitation whatsoever if she were not a married woman." And then he added, "I had rather have a first-rate married woman than a second or third-rate unmarried one."[66]

Turning to his confidante Mrs. Anderson, who shared his dislike of Acting Dean Brewster, Plimpton complained that his suggestions had been sidelined; he had "found" such leading candidates as Lida Shaw King, still under scrutiny, and Lois Kimball Mathews, whom Butler had recently rejected. "If I should find the angel Gabriel, Butler would probably turn him down," Plimpton told Mrs. Anderson. Butler's maneuver to disempower the prospective woman dean, however, upset Plimpton even more.

> Possibly he [Butler] may think he has Brewster, and he may be indifferent to what woman is there. But the understanding [of the trustees] is that the Dean of Barnard is the head of Barnard and Brewster is under her. She is superior to him in every way, educationally and socially, in fact she is the *head* of the college . . . Any other interpretation will be everlastingly opposed by me. Now Butler has had his way in regard to the Provost, and I say let us select a Dean after our own hearts. . . . your words have not fallen on hollow ground. . . . I do not propose to get out until things are made right there, if I have to stay and fight the whole battle alone.[67]

In October 1910, one of the last major candidates, Lida Shaw King, withdrew, because Butler's new rules had diminished the role of dean. "I should not care to take a position where I would not be the head of the educational work," King wrote to Plimpton on October 18, 1910.[68]

By now the once-crowded field of women under consideration had narrowed. Candidates had left the field of contest, trustees had voiced doubts about one or another, or Butler had disliked them. "My dear Plimpton," Butler wrote to the Barnard treasurer on November 14, 1910. "I understood you to say the other day that you thought a certain name would be acceptable to the Trustees." But Butler had one last ploy in reserve. On Nov 18, 1910, he wrote to Plimpton with a new offer. Barnard was running out of funds, Butler posited, and discontent prevailed. The president proposed to raise funds to pay Barnard's debts and to increase the college budget if Barnard would turn itself over to the Columbia University trustees. "I think the time has come to look this question fairly in the face," the president declared. Butler's last maneuver, to take over Barnard, had been the president's main goal all along, ever since the search for a dean had begun. The Butler proposal and events around it, according to historian Robert McCaughey, represent Barnard's "first merger crisis" with Columbia (though not its last).[69]

When the trustees rebelled at Butler's latest proposal, he backed off and returned to "a certain name." On Dec 9, 1910, at a meeting of the

Barnard trustees, Butler nominated Virginia to be dean. As the president commented, according to the account of a future trustee, there was "no one else in sight." Butler listed for the trustees all of Virginia's achievements at Barnard and Columbia. That she taught a course to Columbia graduate students—her current course on the history of verse—was an invaluable advantage, Butler emphasized; no other candidate could match such an academic feat. Significantly, Butler also reiterated the division of power that he had imposed. All academic power would go to the provost; the new dean would be the provost's aide.[70]

That arrangement for a diminished deanship did not suit Virginia, who delayed her response. Unwilling to accept the downgraded dean's position—or to be a mere "chaperone to the students," she bargained for a restoration of power to the dean. Butler seemed to acquiesce, though he ceded little; in his next set of revised rules, he provided that the dean had to consult the provost about every major decision. But Virginia sized up the situation astutely: Butler was going to stall before giving in to her demands. She accepted the deanship, even under imperfect conditions, on December 16, 1910. "I am glad to tell you that everybody seems enthusiastic over our new Dean," George Plimpton wrote to his ally, Mrs. Anderson. "We have been at it a long time, but I think we have made no mistake. I think Miss Gildersleeve is the best woman we could have possibly secured." Plimpton remained concerned, however, that Butler had not formally restored power to the dean. "The old man dies hard, doesn't he," Plimpton wrote to fellow trustee Arthur G. Milbank on December 21, 1910. "He probably thinks there is more than one way to skin a cat. But I guess we are equal to the emergency."[71]

It took months before Butler would finally revise the rules. In March 1911, weeks after she became dean, Virginia still sought a resolution to the issue. But shrewdly she ignored the president's delaying tactics, and eventually Butler complied. Looking back on her decision to accept the deanship, Virginia cited "my reluctance to have another stranger come in as Miss Gill had done and mess up my college again."[72]

Meanwhile, Chairman Silas Brownell, on behalf of the Board of Trustees, sent a triumphant message to the Barnard community. "In our twenty years Barnard College has educated a leader for our work," he proclaimed, "a Dean born and bred in New York, prepared in the Brearley, graduated from Barnard, earned in our Columbia University the highest degree open to women, promoted through all the Faculty grades to the head of the college as Dean. . . . What she hopes to accomplish in her new office will be told you by herself in her inaugural."[73]

Barnard had at last found the right candidate, an ideal insider, or in Plimpton's words, "a dean after our own hearts." Moreover, as President Butler had said (at least allegedly), there was "no one else in sight."

Through reminiscence and other writing, Virginia left a rich record narrative of the development of a complex personality, full of contradictions. As a reviewer of her autobiography later observed, Virginia did not seem to initiate events; rather, in her own account, events that occurred around her shaped the path that she followed. At first undirected, or, in her words, not "ambitious," she could still compete fiercely, excel in her studies, and rise fast in her profession. A rule abider who "never did foolish things," as Annie Nathan Meyer noted, she was nonetheless stubborn or "mulish" (her own word) in spurning direction from others and pursuing her own way. Choosing allies and spotting rivals, weighing and measuring talent and position, she cared about status, power, and social circumstance. Finally, as her jousting with President Butler in December 1910 suggests, she could defend her own interests with exceptional skill, or else she received deft advice. Virginia's greatest asset, as she contended, was her education at Barnard and Columbia, and her commitment to the goal of liberal arts education, "to broaden and develop evenly our minds." In the next decade, Barnard further shaped her character and she, in turn it, shaped the institution.

CHAPTER TWO

The Insider

1911 Through World War I

"Just twenty-five years ago on a Wednesday afternoon I entered a train on the Sixth Avenue Elevated railroad at the Rector Street station," recalled Nicholas Murray Butler, Columbia's president, as he described the start of Virginia's career.

> I found my seat to be next to an old and distinguished friend and frequent golfing companion and an outstanding representative of our best citizenship, Judge Henry A. Gildersleeve. I said to him: "Judge, if you can keep a secret, I will tell you something that will interest you." He said: "Of course, I can keep a secret. What is it?" I said: "Tomorrow afternoon at 4:00 o'clock I am going to appoint your daughter Virginia to be Dean of Barnard College." "Oh," he said, "I knew that." "But," I said, "my dear Judge, you cannot know it[.] I have not mentioned it to a living soul; I haven't yet spoken to a Trustee of Barnard College." He said: "That makes no difference—I was perfectly certain you would only appoint the best fitted person." So the dear Judge and I came to agreement without elaborate discussion.[1]

Butler's salient recollection, with its hint of an arranged marriage—an alliance forged by the Columbia president and his old friend, the judge—suggests Virginia's edge as a competitor for the Barnard deanship: she held the inside track. Her inauguration in 1911 as the college's third dean made her the youngest of a tiny group of women college leaders in the nation (she was thirty-three) and the highest-ranking woman administrator at Columbia. It also began a decade of intense achievement, in which Virginia molded Barnard as an institution, saved the college from some of the problems that might have beset it, shaped its role in the university, developed a highly effective administrative style, strove to enlarge women's opportunities, acquired a longtime partner or "intimate" companion, and settled on the fields of endeavor in which she would wield influence for decades to come. The most significant era was that of World War I, the "Great War," which opened new paths of action and led Virginia into world affairs.

Throughout her first decade, Virginia faced challenges. She had to manage the college, its trustees, faculty, students, and alumnae, and at the same time to represent her institution in the larger university and the world of higher education.

TAKING CHARGE

"Miss Gildersleeve Now Heads Barnard," announced the *New York Times* on February 17, 1911, the day after Virginia's inauguration in the auditorium of the Horace Mann School. Teachers, alumnae, and friends of Barnard had thronged the event; hundreds of undergraduates crowded the balconies; and a procession of "capped, gowned, and hooded students, professors and trustees" filed into the ceremony, the *Times* reported. All rejoiced "at the choice of one of their own college family as dean." Joining the Barnard audience were deans and presidents of other colleges, including Bryn Mawr, Radcliffe, Mount Holyoke, Adelphi, and two local colleges, Normal College (which would become Hunter in 1915), and the College of the City of New York. "In the twenty years of her existence, Barnard College has at last educated a leader for her work," declared Silas Brownell, head of the Board of Trustees, "a dean born and bred in New York, a graduate of Barnard, who has won in our own Columbia university the highest degree for women and has been promoted through the various ranks to her present leadership."[2]

Virginia's inaugural ceremony presaged an impressive first decade as dean. She took office with advantages. She knew the college and its place in the university; she had spent the past fifteen years at Barnard and Columbia. She knew the Barnard faculty, which included her colleagues and former professors, and which looked on her, as she saw it, "with a kind of paternal pride." Unlike previous deans, who had been, of necessity, "selected from the outside," noted Virginia's one-time instructor, Provost William T. Brewster, "She brings to her new duties an intimate knowledge of the ideals and the needs of the college." She was at home in New York City, where her father—who used his contacts to support her career as dean—had won respect and admiration; she knew the trustees, who had just hired her, and the alumnae, among whom her friends were active and who had scorned her predecessor. "We are all united in the esteem we feel for her fair-mindedness, sanity, and unselfish devotion," declared alumnae president Alice Chace in a statement of congratulation. Students voiced rapture. "We have heard that the side door of the Dean's Office is always to be left open," a student representative announced, "and Miss Gildersleeve has made us feel that we are all welcome there."[3]

Virginia also profited from the four years of difficulty that the college had faced in finding the right candidate, and, as the alumnae president suggested, from the negative precedent set by Dean Gill, to whom Virginia could now compare herself. In contrast to Laura D. Gill, Virginia from the start claimed an excellent rapport with Nicholas Murray Butler, one that she would maintain for decades and on which she relied.

That cordial link proved invaluable. Without Butler's favor, as everyone had just seen, a dean might flail and sink. As soon as Virginia was chosen, some of the older trustees, probably including George A. Plimpton and Elizabeth Anderson, warned the young dean to watch out for the university president, a potentially formidable foe. But Virginia knew that her relationship with Butler was secure, not least because he was her father's friend. Fellow Centurions (members of the exclusive Century Club), President Butler and Judge Gildersleeve (or "Murray" and "Alger," as they called one another) met on weekends when they drove to golf games with assorted companions. Virginia, in turn, took special interest in the Butlers' daughter Sarah, who had attended Barnard from 1911 to 1915. She later visited Sarah in England when the president's daughter married, and telegraphed Butler to report on his new grandson. Butler praised Virginia often. When he sent her a book to celebrate her first quarter century as dean, he claimed that the gift carried "a much heavier weight of real affection." Always solicitous, he made efforts to include her in professional events, and even to shift venues if meeting places like private clubs excluded women. "The bar association lets women enter its sacred portals," Virginia advised.[4]

The wary trustees who had tried to warn Virginia about Butler, of course, had a point. Much as he appreciated the new dean, President Butler continually sought to expand Columbia by absorbing adjacent institutions and never quite gave up the hope of acquiring Barnard, too. As soon as the college proved that it could stay afloat and thrive—and especially once Virginia took charge—it seemed an appealing target for takeover. "The corporate absorption of Barnard would be an extremely simple matter," Butler told a Columbia trustee in 1914. "Miss Gilder-sleeve's tactful handling of administrative problems has done away with all the friction which her predecessor carefully developed and whenever the Barnard trustees feel that they have carried their separate responsibility long enough, that college could be taken into the university without the slightest difficulty or embarrassment." Still, though he longed for Columbia to swallow up Barnard—to annex the college and put it under his own control—Butler held back and never did so, a tribute to Virginia and her management style. That style fused deference and compliance, collegiality and independence. Virginia liked to view Butler as a mentor and role model. Ignoring his effort to deprive the dean of authority and give it to the provost, she restored power to the deanship. After William T. Brewster resigned as provost in 1923 and returned to the English Department, the position of provost vanished.[5]

A second crucial mentor that Virginia inherited, a legacy from Barnard's early days, was college treasurer George A. Plimpton, publisher, book collector, philanthropist, critic of Butler, and major figure in her own appointment. Devoted to the college, as well as to his own alma mater, Amherst, Plimpton had been a member of Barnard's first Board of Trustees and treasurer since 1893, when he replaced financier Jacob Schiff. He assumed responsibility for fundraising, thus relieving Virginia of that onerous job, and at once started a two-million-dollar fundraising campaign. Happily, the multitalented Plimpton shared many interests with Virginia, starting with Shakespeare and Chaucer; well-traveled, he was especially involved with the Middle East and passed his avid interest on to Virginia. As with the Butlers, Virginia became a family friend as well as godparent to Plimpton's son, Francis, who remembered her as an indulgent figure. Not least, George A. Plimpton kept the funds pouring into college coffers.[6]

Plimpton's success reflected his expert tactics. An experienced salesman, he visited men of wealth at home or office. Starting out with solicitous letters of introduction, he first sought "to inquire if I might call upon you," as in the instance of financier and philanthropist George F. Baker, who had just funded Columbia's football field. "You have been so generous to Cornell and to Columbia that I wonder whether you would not like to do something for the education of the women of New York City." Plimpton followed his inquiries with personal visits, sometimes accompanied by a woman trustee such as Caroline Choate, and sought to depict college strengths in terms that would appeal to each donor, even if somewhat fanciful. "At Barnard, girls of every nationality meet—the rich as well as the poor," Plimpton assured one potential donor. "I wish you could see these girls, for they represent every type of New York life," Plimpton told Mrs. Russell Sage, founder of the Russell Sage Foundation and contributor to liberal causes. "There isn't a race or nationality that is not represented here."[7]

The outcome: Plimpton swayed donor after donor. He impressed heiress Elizabeth Milbank Anderson, whose gift helped buy college property uptown in 1895; as trustee, she gave further funds, for Milbank Hall, an administration and office building; Brooks Hall, a dormitory; and additional land. Plimpton extracted several hundred thousand dollars from John D. Rockefeller and his son. At Plimpton's urging, financier Jacob Schiff, recruited to the Board of Trustees by Annie Nathan Meyer, gave $250,000 for a student activities building, now Barnard Hall, which opened in 1917 as Students' Hall. In a major coup, Plimpton befriended California real estate financier Horace W. Carpentier, who owned most of the Oakland waterfront. He urged Carpentier to serve as board member twice and to make several big gifts; in 1916, when he retired, the elderly financier gave Barnard $500,000 in honor of his mother and left the college another a million dollars (half his estate) in 1918. Overall, the dynamic Plimpton secured far more in big donations than any president of a small college could have been expected to raise. Virginia helped Plimpton by writing an annual letter that set forth all the college's financial needs and that he could use for fundraising, by seeking out opportunities among rich alumnae, and by appreciation of his effort. "Like most colleges, the more students we have the poorer we are," Virginia explained in her dean's report for 1913. "To educate each one costs about $125 more per year than she pays in tuition fees. The difference must be made up by income from endowment or gifts."[8]

While working with Plimpton, Virginia also coped with trustee Annie Nathan Meyer, so pivotal in the founding of Barnard. A decade older than Virginia, Meyer had been a trustee since the college started in 1889 and would remain one until mid-century. She was the daughter of a distinguished New York family of Sephardic Jews whose roots went back to the seventeenth century, a family that had founded its own synagogue, Shearith Israel (1654); held a seat on the stock exchange; and would in 1932 boast a Supreme Court Justice, Annie Nathan Meyer's cousin, Benjamin Cardozo. In 1887, after her brief involvement with Columbia's "Collegiate Course" for women, Annie Nathan had married Alfred Meyer, a German Jew, pulmonologist at Mount Sinai, and leader in the treatment of tuberculosis, an ailment widespread among new immigrants of the era. Foe of woman suffrage and prolific writer, future historian of the college and always a crucial figure in that history, Annie Nathan Meyer had long made a practice of advising Barnard deans; almost daily letters to Virginia, as to previous deans, conveyed her views on details of college administration. Virginia found herself in continual correspondence to answer Meyer's questions and address her many concerns. These might involve the back net of the tennis court, which Meyer had offered to fund; or how to invest a legacy that the college had received; or whether the managers of the Brooks Hall dormitory had spent too much on a table. Annie Nathan Meyer also turned to issues of admission, finance, curriculum, and college policy on student activism, as in the area of women's suffrage, which she opposed, perhaps out of concern that woman's vote would "double the ignorant vote." Her boundless concern for the college and countless interventions, though at many times a burden for the dean, had an impact.[9]

Some of Virginia's initial work, beyond placating Annie Nathan Meyer, was campus housekeeping, with special attention to rules, regulations, and insignia, which always interested her. She discussed rules that applied to the college seal, for instance, with lawyer Silas B. Brownell; checked with the college law firm about whether the minutes of the last executive committee meeting were in proper order; reported to the local police precinct about the theft of two silver cups from the sports trophies shelf; and complained to the New York City police commissioner about nearby loiterers whose noise disrupted classrooms, rubbish that blew in from 119th Street to a college garden, and nursemaids with charges who congregated outside college buildings ("Surely this should be contrary to some city ordinance"). In these and other details of campus life, Virginia had the aid of her father, the now-retired Judge Henry A. Gildersleeve, who still ran an office, practiced law, and connected with colleagues, and who used his contacts to aid his daughter. Indulgent as ever, Virginia's parents gave up their brownstone on West Forty-Eighth street and in 1912 moved to an apartment at 404 Riverside Drive at 113th Street to live with Virginia. According to Virginia, her mother's failing health (a sense of vertigo) called for a daughter's care and spurred the family move; it is likely, too, that her parents made the move to accommodate Virginia and to give her a home near her job.[10]

From the outset, Virginia forged links with college constituencies such as alumnae. She consulted a college lawyer about rules for the election of an alumnae trustee, to help repair relations with those alumnae alienated by Laura D. Gill, and steered potential donors among alumnae into service as trustees. Mary Harriman Rumsey, '05, sociology major and KKG sister, for instance, served as trustee from 1911–1934; Virginia urged her to pressure her mother, wealthy widow Mrs. E. H. Harriman, who had inherited a railroad fortune, to offer money to fund the sciences; this effort soon led to a $100,000 donation. Virginia also informed treasurer Plimpton that the new alumnae trustee—sociologist Elsie Clews Parsons '96, who served from 1911 to 1915—was another potential source of family funds, "very much interested in getting us a gymnasium" and in fundraising for the current building campaign. To publicize alumnae activities (and her own), Virginia wrote the first issues of the alumnae magazine, started in 1912. Finally, the new dean joined forces with alumnae clubs of other women's colleges to found a Bureau of Occupations for alumnae; the joint effort was one of several that prefigured the Seven Sisters of the 1920s.[11]

Like heads of other colleges, Virginia sought to leave her imprint on curriculum. She ended compulsory Latin, introduced physical education, and started a system of student advising by faculty, "as elastic as possible," for juniors and seniors in their majors. Her changes to undergraduate education also relied on options available only at a coordinate college. Though opposed to vocational training as part of the liberal arts curriculum, Virginia sought to galvanize ambition and steer students into professions beyond teaching, currently the dominant occupation of women college graduates. "We have been making some efforts to enlarge the opportunities for professional training," she wrote in her dean's report for 1912. A Barnard senior might now take several courses at the New York School of Philanthropy (in 1917 to become the New York School of Social Work) or the Columbia School of Architecture. A two-year program began that led to two years of "purely professional training" in the new Columbia School of Journalism, founded in 1912. As historian Rosalind Rosenberg points out, Barnard still lacked a class in government, which the nine prospective journalism students needed, so Virginia hired Columbia professor Charles Beard to teach one. According to Barnard recruitment literature, "able students" in their senior year might take advanced courses in the Graduate Faculties (Columbia's graduate program in arts and sciences), or in architecture, business, education, journalism, philanthropy (social work) or religion. An older two-year program, already in progress, prepared students to transfer to Teachers College.[12]

In some ways, Virginia's tasks as dean of Barnard resembled those of the "dean of women" at any large university; she coped with whatever problem involved women on campus. In 1913–1914, for instance, the Columbia Dames (wives of male graduate students) needed a campus room for their monthly meetings of sixty to seventy—in what place would the wives' presence and their children's racket least disrupt academic life? The dean placed them in 301 Philosophy Hall, a room on the ground floor. More important to Virginia, the dean of Barnard, as "Advisor to University Women," took charge of all women graduate students at Columbia. In 1912–1913, out of a total of 636 women students, 136 were graduate students at Teachers College, forty-five more came from the Graduate Faculties, and two studied at the New York School of Philanthropy. Virginia dealt creatively with her graduate student assignment. As historian Andrea Walton relates, she shifted her advisory role to a new committee, the Committee on Women Graduate Students, started in 1914, whose distinguished members included historian James Harvey Robinson, philosopher John Dewey from Teacher's College, Ida H. Ogilvie in the Barnard Geology Department, and Barnard economist Emilie Hutchinson. The committee considered questions that had been raised since 1895 by the Women's Graduate Club of Columbia University, such as where on campus women graduate students might live. The committee's work, Walton points out, led to the building of a Columbia residence hall, Johnson Hall, for graduate students, which benefitted from a million-dollar investment by Columbia trustees.[13]

Virginia also found a vital role at Columbia, as member of the Columbia University Committee on Educational Policy, which made decisions on appointments and promotions, prepared the budget, and considered new educational proposals. On this all-important advisory committee, run by President Butler, Virginia gained access to campus decision-makers, her fellow deans. These included, at the outset of her deanship, Frederick Keppel, Columbia '99, who had been her fellow editor on the college magazine; Harlan Fiske Stone, dean of the law school, to be appointed to the Supreme Court in 1925; and James Earl Russell, who led Teachers College until 1927. Virginia was active and cooperative, one dean of engineering, George Pegram, remembered; she was "'just as good a man' as anybody," he recalled, and "respected and admired by all." Always willing to take on responsibility, Virginia perfected her strategy of "working from within"; she fused service to the committee with policy initiatives of her own. Her initiatives expanded women's opportunities in academic life, not only for Barnard juniors and seniors but for women graduate students in general. When the Columbia Journalism School began in 1912, funded by a 2.5 million donation from publisher Joseph Pulitzer, Virginia insisted on women's admission; she then won admission of women students to the school of business in 1916 and the medical school in 1917. The law school remained out of reach until the 1920s—and the engineering school until even later.[14]

"Working from within," Virginia's crucial strategy for achieving administrative goals at Columbia—that is, in a work environment dominated by men—was a complex, multistage process, laden with the hallmarks of her brand of women's politics. The first stage was to be an attentive but inoffensive participant at meetings of administrators, that is, to begin "very gently"—to listen for hours and hours while everyone else talked, "speaking rarely and briefly, to comment on the business, to ask intelligent questions, occasionally to make a suggestion." The woman who wanted to make headway on campus, in Virginia's account, had to strike her male colleagues as "no trouble but rather a help." Such nonconfrontational and supportive tactics, Virginia found, led to results: "The men can then turn to her in any puzzling questions regarding women, perhaps enjoying her protection in warding off attacks by militant feminists from outside, and in time will lend an attentive ear to her own projects." Virginia's "own projects" included acceptance of women throughout the university, or most of it, in advance of what happened at comparable institutions. The woman administrator, in Virginia's account, did not "lean in" (to use a modern expression) but awaited her moment.[15]

The strategy of "working from within" had limitations, which Virginia analyzed in her autobiography of 1954:

> This technique of mine, which I drifted into naturally because of my own temperament, was a slow-moving one, not at all spectacular in its results. It required patient months to win the confidence of male colleagues. Meanwhile, the militant feminists outside sometimes accused me of feebleness or indifference or treason against "our cause." In one sense perhaps they were right, for I would always, I think, have placed the welfare of the whole institution above the present advancement of our sex.
>
> My technique would not, perhaps, have been effective for the pioneers in seeking opportunities for women. Probably they had to batter at the doors rather violently and spectacularly, before I could get in and sit there peacefully in a friendly atmosphere, "boring from within."[16]

This passage on campus politics, with its adroit concession to "militant feminism," is one of Virginia's major contributions to the women's movement and the gist of her effort to exert leadership. Her concession is important: Virginia concedes that a relationship exists between militant feminism and the backdoor, in-house, low-key, and nonconfrontational strategy that she found so effective; the latter depends on the former. A second and sudden concession follows: the "present advancement of our sex" was not her supreme goal.

Virginia's stance on "militant feminism" suggests her relation to the U.S. women's movement. In the pre-World War I decade, the movement encompassed two loosely defined wings, temporarily united under the umbrella cause of women's suffrage. Egalitarian suffragists, the minority wing, led from 1915 on by Alice Paul, became, once the vote was won, the National Woman's Party, which strove for an agenda of equal rights and for an Equal Rights Amendment, first proposed in 1920. Most activists in the women's movement, Virginia among them, adopted a less demanding posture; suspicious of militancy or confrontation, they stood apart from calls for equal rights, which they saw as potentially injurious to women's interests. Instead, like Virginia, they sought advances in women's status and gave priority to other women's causes such as labor reform, the settlement movement, or advances in higher education. The type of position that Virginia took is sometimes, though retroactively, called "social feminism." But labels rarely fit perfectly. Virginia's credo is perhaps best called "anti-militant."[17]

Finally, Virginia grasped the mantle of educational leadership in another way; she found her strong hand in the defense of a liberal arts education. In 1917, she published her credo in the *Educational Review*, the journal founded by Nicholas Murray Butler in 1891. Virginia disparaged "free electives," the system of curriculum associated with Charles William Elliott at Harvard, under which students selected most of their courses (feasible only at a large university). In Virginia's view, the student should not shape the curriculum. Rather, "the faculty should develop what is productive." Liberal arts courses must offer "tools which the educated being is to use in the process of life." What were these tools? Students should acquire, Virginia wrote, "a reasonable stock of information" and habits of learning ("good habits of accuracy, concentration, thoroughness.") A "trained mind," she argued, was "valuable in any field of life." Virginia believed that "a liberal curriculum should widen and multiply a student's field of interest, should make the world . . . a more interesting place." She also believed the curriculum should improve "the student's power of judgment," and meet "ethical and spiritual needs." Ideally, the liberal arts curriculum that she envisioned followed progressive tenets. It provided "varied fields of interest in the world; judgment with which to view the complexities of life; sound ideals of character and conduct: and finally some exhilarating zest in life."[18]

Not least, Virginia reiterated her stance against vocational training in the liberal arts curriculum. Vocational *ambition*, she believed, held value. But "vocational training in the narrower sense has, I believe, no place in the collegiate course." Conversely, a liberal arts education itself had vocational worth: anything that developed a student's intellect, personality, or spirit, Virginia argued, "is of real vocational value."[19]

By the time Barnard celebrated its twenty-fifth anniversary in 1914, its new dean had left a positive imprint on the college, won support among its various constituencies, empowered the deanship, and capitalized on the college's relationship to Columbia. Barnard finances soared, and by 1918, the college's grand new building, Students' Hall, opened, funded by Jacob Schiff, with its gym, library, lunchroom, and alumnae center. The building was not named for its benefactor; but its benefits to the students, said the dean's report, "will seem to its generous donor an adequate return for his noble gift."[20] Virginia also tackled some special challenges, including the loaded issue of "fraternities," the six or so exclusive societies (soon to be called sororities), to which about a quarter of Barnard students belonged.

FRATERNITIES, SUFFRAGE, AND WORLD WAR I

When Virginia took office, a movement to limit fraternities was already underway; in 1910, the college had ended the rush process among freshmen. In 1912, a student antifraternity campaign arose. Freda Kirchwey, class of '15, daughter of law professor George Kirchwey, who had served as dean of the Law School from 1901 to 1910 and was thereafter Kent Professor of Law, wrote an editorial in the *Barnard Bulletin* that attacked fraternities; exclusive and discriminatory, such groups defied democracy. President Butler's daughter, Sarah, joined the protest. Such "insider" critics carried weight. The dissenting students asked the dean to form a committee to investigate fraternities. Thereafter, Virginia's skill at crisis management prevailed. The first step: She appointed a fourteen-member investigation committee: four students and four alumnae (with mixed views on fraternities, pro and con); four faculty members; and the dean and provost. The committee would investigate the evils and advantages of fraternities.[21]

On May 14, 1913, the committee adopted two reports. The majority report, which Virginia wrote, declared fraternities on balance beneficial to the college but argued that they should be more transparent. The minority report, written by the provost, William T. Brewster, said fraternities should be abolished; their evils trumped their advantages. In her dean's report for 1913, Virginia, tried to sum up the committee's work. Assuming the role of an impartial judge, she reviewed at length the advantages and disadvantages that committee members weighed. Fraternities were valuable in order to give as many students as possible "experience in managing organizations and conducting meetings," the report stated; students learned to act, debate, and participate in sports, and they shaped "a varied and cosmopolitan community." Fraternities also promoted "helpful and stimulating friendships" and developed "lasting loyalty to the college." But fraternities also failed in many ways. Committee members noted:

> These organizations often cause snobbishness by overemphasizing lines of social cleavage, especially race lines [the reference to "race" meant discrimination against Jews] . . . that they cause pain to some people who are left out; that "rushing" and "pledge day" often produce confusion, distractions and bad manners; and that the element of secrecy is especially harmful, in that it inspires suspicion in outsiders and gives the organizations a morbid appearance in the eyes of young students.

Moreover, the scholarship of fraternity members was "somewhat inferior to that of non-fraternity students." Virginia ended her dean's report with a bland statement: "Our problem now is to preserve, so far as we can, the good features of our social organizations and make them available for all who desire them, while eliminating harmful characteristics." But events had already surged ahead of this vague conclusion.[22]

The minority report, which sought to end fraternities, drew support on campus, especially from faculty. The Faculty Committee on Student Organizations endorsed it, and on May 26, 1913, the faculty voted overwhelmingly to end fraternities. Faculty members resolved that for a three-year term, beginning October 1, 1913, no fraternity could elect new members; the resolution to ban recruitment equaled a death sentence, though fraternities still existed. A student referendum of 1915 asserted by 255 to 159 that fraternities should end. A second student referendum of 1916 endorsed that view by 244 to 30. Virginia summed up what had happened in her dean's report for 1916. "On the recommendation of the Committee on Social Organization, the faculty voted on May 29 to abolish fraternities," she declared. Under the supervision of the faculty committee, as the minority report of 1913 had provided, students were "encouraged to experiment with new forms of organization."[23]

To what extent did Virginia endorse the end of fraternities? She probably would have appreciated a different outcome. Virginia had always valued her own fraternity experience and often mentioned her KKG membership along with her membership in Phi Beta Kappa. Unsurprisingly, she voiced some regret about the end of fraternities, especially in 1915, when the dean's report again reiterated the pros and cons, although the Greek system was fast fading. Virginia also voiced regret in the press. The dean told the *New York Times* that Barnard students who wanted to pledge sororities (as they were now sometimes called) "go over to Columbia," and their social life became "less centered around Barnard." The reporter who covered the story, too, missed the sororities. "The students who are working to get the sororities reinstated to full standing are finding solace in Miss Gildersleeve's report," the *Times* reported. "Many predicted that sororities at Barnard will again come into their own next year." By 1915, this resurgence was highly unlikely. However, "contrary to the expectations of the Faculty," according to the *Times*, "no new organizations have grown up to take the place of fraternities" and students were "still casting about for some form of social organizations." Virginia told a fellow dean at Swarthmore in 1915 that "in many ways we miss the fraternities very much. . . . They were very useful in getting hold of certain students and helping to interest them and adjust them to college life. On the other hand these secret societies caused . . . bad feeling and suspicion. Life has certainly been more peaceful since they have been given up."[24]

A distinctive facet of the clash over fraternities is the way that Virginia kept an explosive campus issue from igniting. She seized control through administrative tactics—an investigative committee, reports, and referenda—and never allied herself with a public stand either way. Woodrow Wilson, as Princeton president, had recently had a different experience. A foe of Princeton's eating clubs, Wilson in 1906 had denounced the exclusive clubs as "peculiarly hostile" to intellect; the eating club system, he charged, "divides classes, creates artificial groups for social purposes and renders a wholesome university impossible." Wilson sought to replace the eating clubs, which were in fact residential clubs, with a quadrangle plan of college residences; as his political stance turned more progressive, his critique of club snobbery sharpened. But Wilson underestimated the clout of his foes. The fate of his quadrangle plan, never popular with any campus faction, became entwined with a yet more heated battle over where on campus to place the graduate college; after a two-year feud, the quadrangle plan failed, eating clubs survived, and Woodrow Wilson moved on to state and national politics. His attack on eating clubs had totally collapsed. Virginia, who, in contrast to Wilson, seemed ready to tolerate exclusive student institutions, fared better; she managed campus conflict more adroitly, survived a contested issue rather than starting one, and remained unscathed. However, it can be argued Wilson, in this instance, had a firmer grasp of democratic principles and progressive ideals.[25]

As with the feud over fraternities, Virginia sought to stand back from the feud over women's suffrage. Unlike her predecessor Gill, who had supported the College Equal Suffrage League, Virginia held a position closer to that of a previous dean, Ella Weed, who had cautiously avoided issues of controversy. Virginia did not preclude activism in women's suffrage at Barnard, but she did not encourage it either. Rather, she sought to evade the pressure exerted by the College Equal Suffrage League, which arose on campus around 1909, and kept up this escapist posture through 1917, when New York State enfranchised women.

The issue arose in her first year as dean, in April 1912, in reference to student participation in a suffrage parade that the College Equal Suffrage League had planned for May 4. Might Barnard students wear Barnard caps and gowns at the parade? Invoking the always-useful Faculty Committee on Student Organization, which had just formed to deal with fraternities, Virginia offered a student member of the Equal Suffrage League a qualified response. "As an individual, any student has, of course, a right to march," the dean confirmed, although that was not the point at issue. But students might wear caps and gowns only "if they appear merely as individuals with the other College Women in the parade, and wear or carry . . . no Barnard insignia of any kind," Virginia stated. "No group of students should appear to represent the college on such an occasion . . . the name or insignia of Barnard should not be used for what might be considered partisan purposes." For good measure, Virginia rejected the offer from the league president of a box at Carnegie Hall, where the suffrage march was supposed to conclude. "I do not think that the college ought to participate officially in the matter," she wrote. Thus, Virginia sought to insulate the college from the threat of controversy.[26]

By staking out an indeterminate, uncommitted stance Virginia sought a point midway between two clashing arguments: one was the objection of trustee Annie Nathan Meyer, who opposed the suffrage campaign and had long been embroiled in the issue with her sister Maud Nathan, head of the New York City Consumers League, activist in the National Council of Jewish Women, and women's suffrage exponent at international meetings. "I feel strongly that our students should not march in processions through the streets," Annie wrote to Virginia on the occasion of the 1912 event. "I am not speaking because I am opposed to suffrage [though she was], but because I am opposed to publicity for very young women." To pacify Mrs. Meyer, Virginia agreed that freshmen "should be discouraged from participating." A competing argument came from suffragist Barnard students. One, for instance, Iphigene Ochs '14, daughter of the publisher of the New York Times, noted in her memoir that she became a suffragist after hearing Annie Nathan Meyer give an antisuffragist speech at Barnard; such students pressured the dean for commitment. By 1915, Virginia had given way on the issue of identifying Barnard in suffrage parades—marchers from the college that year carried a banner that blared out "Barnard Equal Suffrage Society." Ever reluctant to concede a point, however, Virginia now argued that student marchers needed parental approval in order to march; the faculty committee did not seek to "interfere with family jurisdiction." The Barnard Suffrage Club, meanwhile, claimed that it had become "a feminist club." No longer concerned solely with the vote, the members turned to "the whole problem of the economic, social, and moral advance of women." Once suffrage was enacted, Virginia claimed to have not stood in its way. Choosing to avoid the fray, she endorsed the cause in retrospect.[27]

World War I presented another sort of challenge: Patriotism, in contrast to conflict over fraternities or women's suffrage, provided safe space. Unwilling to join the suffrage campaign, Virginia became a model of patriotic activism during World War I; she used the entry of the United States into war in 1917 as a bridge from campus life to public affairs and especially to international affairs.

Since she started out as dean in 1911, Virginia had seen the deanship as a local power base from which she reached outward through organizations. In the World War I era, her affiliations included the New York Women's City Club, a nonpartisan civic pressure group formed in 1915 (her friend Alice Duer Miller was the first club president); the American Council on Education, a federation of pressure groups in higher education, formed in 1918; and its offshoot, the Institute of International Education (1919). Joining or chairing committees was one of Virginia's skills; often inviting local contingents to meet at Barnard, she proved able to draw a plan of action out of even the most chaotic or conflicted gathering. Three days after the United States ended relations with Germany in 1917, President Butler asked Virginia to chair Columbia's Committee on Women's War Work, which determined what jobs women might perform in wartime and appointed Barnard/Columbia women and graduates to fill such posts. Virginia also joined the New York City Mayor's Committee of Women in National Defense (the current mayor, John Purroy Mitchell, had been a classmate, Columbia '99) and the American Council of Education's Committee on War Service Training for Women College Students; the latter brought her to Washington for three days in September 1918. These positions advanced her standing in civic life and, as historian Christy Jo Snider points out, steered her toward the goal of international cooperation once the war had ended. Also, for Virginia, U.S. entry into World War I meant new options for educated women (as would later be the case in World War II). First, she used U.S. entry into war to press for acceptance of women at Columbia's medical school. As male applicants for admission dwindled, Virginia urged the admission of a Barnard graduate; thereafter the College of Physicians and Surgeons accepted women. Moreover, the government urgently needed "greater numbers of women with the general all-around training of mind and character given by the liberal college course," Virginia argued in a dean's report. "Every single subject taught in our curriculum—except perhaps one or two—had at the moment a direct, practical value to the country."[28]

One of Virginia's routes to wartime public life in 1918 seemed briefly to be as sponsor of "farmerettes." Under the aegis of the Mayor's Committee of Women on National Defense, the dean led a committee that promoted neighborhood gardens in New York City and set up agricultural camps, or "units," in the countryside to train women for farm work (abandoned by men who joined the armed forces). Women residents of the units, eleven by 1917, worked under contract for local farmers or estates. The agricultural camp in Bedford, New York, in Westchester County, recruited women wage earners, or in Virginia's words, "working girls," who had graduated from the Manhattan Trade School, to live in an old farmhouse and work in the community. Students and alumnae from Barnard, plus three students from Teachers College, joined the Bedford unit, as did Barnard geology professor Ida H. Ogilvie, who led the group; another unit flourished at nearby Mount Kisco. Overall-clad, the farmerettes won applause. By the summer of 1917, Virginia wrote in the *New Republic*, "the demand for units has been greater than the Committee can fill." Virginia saw the rural gambit as both a popular experiment and a learning experience for its managers: "The Committee hopes to profit from its mistakes as well as its successes."[29]

Another way to win recognition in public life soon proved more important: Virginia used her connection to the Association of Collegiate Alumnae (ACA) to create a route into international affairs. Founded in 1882, the ACA enabled women graduates to continue their collegiate ties and share common concerns. In 1899, the year Virginia graduated from college, the ACA had welcomed Barnard to membership; in 1917, when the United States entered the war, Virginia pressed the ACA to start an International Relations Committee, formed in 1918, which she headed. The committee sought transatlantic roles for itself in war relief and especially in education. It strove, for instance, to gather data on women's higher education in nations roiled by war and also to help French students whose training had been disrupted by war to come to the United States for study. Virginia's position as committee chair put her in place for further achievement. One mission of the committee would be "to work out a plan for an International Association of College

Women," as Gertrude S. Martin, the ACA's executive secretary, wrote to Virginia in her appointment letter of May 1918. "Doubtless under your chairmanship, the Committee will find other fields of usefulness that we cannot at present foresee," Martin added. The committee became one of Virginia's fiefs; she would dominate its meetings (often held at Barnard), even when she was not chair, throughout the 1920s. Her first mission as committee chair, foreseen by Gertrude S. Martin, soon took firmer shape.[30]

FOUNDING OF THE IFUW

In May 1918, in her role as chair of the ACA International Relations Committee, Virginia secured a prestigious appointment. The U.S. government chose her to serve on a government-sponsored reception committee, full of academics—including, significantly, Columbia's President Butler; the committee was assigned to greet a small contingent of visiting British academics. Appointed by the British Foreign Office, the British group had been invited by the U.S. government to visit forty-six American universities and to propose plans to enhance transatlantic exchange. Under pressure from the Americans to include women in its British Educational Mission, the British Foreign Office had reluctantly added two women academics, Caroline Spurgeon, a Chaucer scholar from Bedford College, a women's college at the University of London, and Rose Sidgwick, lecturer in ancient history, from the University of Birmingham, to the five-man crew of visitors.[31]

After meeting with the welcoming committee, Caroline Spurgeon and Rose Sidgwick traveled together to universities across the North American continent—to the northeastern women's colleges, to the universities of Michigan and of Texas, and into Canada to visit McGill and Toronto. They sought relationships with the American institutions, pressed Oxford and Cambridge to welcome women students, and urged scholarships to send U.S. women abroad for graduate work. For Spurgeon and Sidgwick, these were heartfelt goals. Spurgeon said that British women graduate students, like their American counterparts, needed "the broadening and widening experience of travel and of life in countries other than their own." More important, to open British universities to American women graduate students, significantly, meant that those same universities would have to admit British women graduate students as well.[32]

To Virginia, the two British visitors were kindred spirits. At Caroline Spurgeon's instigation, the three women conceived the idea of a transatlantic alliance of academic women to work for international fellowship and cooperation; this mission had indeed been mentioned in Virginia's letter of appointment from Gertrude S. Martin a few months earlier. Alarmingly, in December 1918, Rose Sidgwick died, a victim of the Spanish flu epidemic; the death drew transatlantic attention, not least among women academics. "The grief for Miss Sidgwick is universal," as a Wellesley English professor assured Caroline Spurgeon. Virginia cared for Spurgeon, also sick, for several weeks, and the two scholars of English literature bonded. They founded a new organization, the International Federation of University Women, in London on July 11, 1919.[33] From then on, both Caroline Spurgeon and the IFUW became central facets of Virginia's life.

On many future occasions, Virginia—who would be the last survivor of the founding trio—described the moment when the IFUW began. 'It started for me, while I was sitting on a steamer trunk in Professor Caroline Spurgeon's bedroom at the old Women's University Club on East 52nd Street, New York, one evening in the autumn of 1918," Virginia wrote.

> Rose Sidgwick was there, too, on a chair. The two were members of the British Educational Mission then in the USA. . . . World War I had just—apparently—ended, & ended right. So life seemed full of possibilities. "We should have," said Miss Spurgeon, "an international association of university women; so that we shall at last have done all we can to prevent another such catastrophe." Miss Sidgwick & I looked at each other, & I said "Well, I guess I must rally the Association of Collegiate Alumnae," and she said, "We must consult the British Federation of University Women." So it was done.[34]

The meeting at which Virginia and Caroline had probably first bonded had occurred a few weeks earlier. On December 6, 1918, after their whirlwind tour of colleges and universities, the two British visitors joined American scholars from the ACA and the National Council of Education at a Radcliffe conference to discuss modes of international cooperation. Here, a connection between Virginia and Caroline Spurgeon took root. The topic at the Radcliffe meeting, chaired by Virginia: How could each nation offer opportunities to women graduate students of the other? In the most dramatic moment of the meeting, Caroline Spurgeon, speaking at length and extemporaneously, in her idiosyncratic and irrepressible train-of-thought manner, on problems American graduate students might face in English universities—such as the inability to earn doctorates—faced an interruption. Professor William Allan Neilson of Smith, Virginia's former instructor, "very much" disapproved of Spurgeon's remarks. "I don't believe it is true that our best students are degree hunters," Neilson declared, with indignation. The students that the United States sent to England, he claimed, would show "disinterested interest in learning," not hunger for doctoral degrees. The discussion veered off into whether doctorates had "commercial value." But Virginia, who defended her British colleague, kept control of the debate and forced the committee to reach conclusions on international exchange, or else imposed such conclusions ex post facto. Among the group's resolutions: that degrees in British universities, if open to American women, would be open to British women; that British universities would not be asked to modify their degree requirements for U.S. women; that the country of origin would supply exchange students with "a money stipend" and receiving countries pay board and tuition; and that an Institute of International Education would be established, in which women's college representatives would be part of management.[35]

The new federation held its first meeting on July 12, 1920, at Bedford College in London, Caroline Spurgeon's home base. The inaugural gathering of the IFUW involved thirty-two official delegates from fifteen nations, plus individual women members of the eight women's associations represented (Britain, Canada, Denmark, France, Norway, Sweden, and the United States). IFUW goals, explained Caroline Spurgeon, the first president, were to promote internationalism, commit to a "world community" (the League of Nations), form bonds of friendship, strive for peace, secure women's access to higher education and academic advancement worldwide, and foster international exchange and contact among students, teachers, and researchers. According to its first declaration of purpose, the new federation sought "to promote understanding between university women of different countries, to promote the exchange of lecturers and scholars of different universities, to co-operate with the national bureau of education; and by these means to strengthen those foundations of international fellowship which must form the basis of the League of Nations."[36]

Where did the IFUW fit into the women's movement of the time? On one hand, it joined a roster of international women's groups that had been campaigning since the 1890s, if not longer, to press for specific causes—for socialism, for labor, and especially for peace. Examples included the International Council of Women (1888), the International Alliance of Women (1904), and the Women's International League for Peace and Freedom (1915). The federation also joined a spate of women's international groups that arose in the wake of World War I, including the International Congress of Working Women, which first met in Washington, D.C. in October 1919. In the context of women's politics, the IFUW claimed an exclusive space for women academics, somewhere on the right wing of the international women's movement.[37]

The new federation served a special professional purpose for women who sought careers in academic life: Few nations eased a woman's path to an academic career. In the United States, for instance, the women's colleges and state universities furnished ample space for undergraduate work, but options for graduate study were scarce; in European nations, the reverse situation might apply; and for British women, graduate work in Britain was almost impossible and graduate degrees unavailable. In consequence, international connection and exchange were more vital for women academics than for men.

The IFUW embraced a second educational mission. "We believe that this is the beginning of the organized training of women to be citizens of the world," Caroline Spurgeon told the first meeting in London in 1920. The covenant of the League of Nations did not bar women from service as delegates or staff, though few served; the league provided no channels through which women of different nations could interact with one another. Although Spurgeon saw foreign policy as an enterprise shared with men, a separate institution, she believed, would best prepare women to serve on an equal basis with men in international affairs. The IFUW would provide channels through which women might interact and achieve recognition. Or, as Virginia explained to the first conference, with some cogency, "Even the men who have the greatest sympathy with the work and aspirations of our sex occasionally forget that we are there."[38]

Finally, and most crucially, the new federation saw itself as a proponent of peace: it strongly supported the just-formed League of Nations (1919), which sought to preclude another conflict like the recent world war. To preserve peace was indeed the foremost goal of the IFUW, though usually cloaked in some combination of subordinate goals. Virginia explained the goal of peace with most clarity retroactively, when looking back from midcentury at the formation of the IFUW. "Of course our most important aim was world peace," she wrote. "We had already found, however, that it is better not to talk about peace. It is, indeed, a highly controversial subject that can stir up belligerency in almost any international gathering. The best way to work for it is to work together for definite, concrete ends on the value of which we agree, & thus get to know one another as comrades."[39]

Thus, in IFUW-speak, women's friendships would prevent war. Virginia's reluctance to focus more explicitly on peace perhaps reflected a need to separate the new federation from prewar U.S. women's groups of the left that also focused on peace, such as Jane Addams's Woman's Peace Party (1915). Still, her own work in IFUW, as Virginia would see it in the coming years, was to move beyond the turmoil that had generated World War I; to prevent resurgence of ill feeling that might start another war; and to reconcile the family of nations that war had divided, even to reach out to former enemies. International links among women would achieve these ends. In Caroline Spurgeon's view, the IFUW would even compete with the League of Nations in its role as peacekeeper: as she told the federation conference in 1922, the women's group could do more to advance peace than the league. To preserve world peace, both agreed, was the federation's fundamental goal. The IFUW gave Caroline Spurgeon and Virginia a common purpose and an international field of operation among educated women.[40]

VIRGINIA AND CARA

Just as important, the two women formed a life-changing relationship. A child of empire, Caroline Spurgeon had been born in India in 1869; her father was a captain in an infantry regiment from Herefordshire that was stationed in India from 1863 to 1875. Her mother died in childbirth when she was born. Her father, who remarried, died in 1874 and left Caroline to be raised by her stepmother; emotional neediness pervaded her youth. Educated at first in Europe, in France and Germany, Spurgeon attended Cheltenham Ladies College and then King's College for Women in London. She studied English literature at Oxford and passed her examinations in 1899, but Oxford did not grant doctoral degrees to women until 1920 (and Cambridge not until 1948); ambitious British women went abroad for graduate degrees. Spurgeon earned a doctorate in medieval literature from the Sorbonne in 1911 at age forty-two. Her dissertation was on the history of Chaucer criticism. Meanwhile, in 1901, she joined the faculty of Bedford College, became a lecturer, and in 1913 won a chair in English literature; she was the first British woman to achieve such status. "No woman has ever been elected to a Professorial chair in any British university," Spurgeon wrote to her aunt in March 1913 while still a candidate for the Bedford chair. "[I]t is the chance of my life time. Even with all this I am very doubtful about getting it—though for once—I quite agree with you that I ought to get it." Facing an interview with the board that would select her and vying with four male rivals, she reported to her aunt on the competition: "[T]he men looked ghastly—with their teeth chattering." Caroline Spurgeon was formidable.[41]

Installed at Bedford (an institution that Virginia viewed as a British counterpart to Barnard), Spurgeon amassed honors. The British Federation of University Women, formed in 1907, awarded her a research fellowship in 1912; the Royal Society of Literature elected her a Fellow in 1916. Long an enthusiast of things American, Spurgeon had pressed the British government to start its transatlantic educational mission of 1918. She saw a chance to improve the career prospects of British women academics, who faced, as she had, high hurdles. To "undertake research or advanced independent study was almost impossible," as Caroline Spurgeon's classmate Edith Morley noted in 1914. "There are scarcely any fellowships or post-graduate scholarships." Apt to get caught up in the "whirl of teaching," women lacked the chances that men enjoyed to qualify for "higher university appointments." Despite all the barriers, Caroline Spurgeon achieved distinction. By the time she first met Virginia in 1918, Spurgeon was well known in her field as a Chaucer specialist; a scholarly society had published her dissertation in sequential segments, and she enjoyed prestige as a professor. Though much of her achievement in English literature lay ahead—her work on Chaucer criticism would not appear in English as a book until 1925—she was already an academic star.[42]

An intellectual live wire, engaging and original, Caroline Spurgeon had wide experience in education and great interest in the teaching process. She did much to steer the concern of English departments away from philology and toward literature. Spurgeon excelled in the classroom; like Virginia, she was attached to the tenets of progressive education. To both, as to educational philosopher John Dewey, the purpose of education was more education, or, to learn how to learn. According to her notes on teaching in an extension program for working-class students in 1915–1916, Caroline Spurgeon involved each student in original research on manuscripts from the British Museum and invited students to join a scholarly community. She shared her lecture notes with classes and urged students to link what they learned with what they already knew. All students, she argued, needed "a knowledge of how to use their own language and an introduction to the riches of their literature." University students, she posited, learn from tutors and from one another, and start a lifetime of assimilating new knowledge. Critical of the British educational system, she extolled American practices and voiced concern for the needs of "industrial populations."[43]

Beyond her skill in every facet of academic life, Caroline, called "Cara" by her friends, radiated intellect and charm. Academic Edith Morley, who had been a student with Cara at King's College for Women in the 1890s and later became a professor of English language at the University of Reading, described Cara in her twenties: "Miss Spurgeon at that period of her life seemed to have been visited by fairy godmothers who had endowed her with every gift," Edith Morley remembered. "Attractive and possessed of great personal charm and a delightful speaking voice, she also excelled in everything she undertook." Artist, pianist, and tennis champion ("she excelled in every form of athletics then open to women"), Cara left an intense impression on all around her. "Her step-mother had done her best to curb her interests lest they interfere with her social success," Edith Morley recalled, "but by 1894 she had inherited a small independent income and thus became free" to carry out her own plans. Initially bent on science or philosophy, with no attraction to English, Caroline Spurgeon adapted her goals to focus on one of the few academic fields at all open to women.[44]

An anonymous friend captured Cara's impact on others in 1920, soon after she met Virginia and embarked on the United States phase of her career. "Her personality is extraordinarily attractive," the friend wrote in the British magazine *Time and Tide*. "In spite of her success in life and all the honours which have been showered upon her, she retains a positively childlike power of enjoyment, and never fails to be genuinely surprised and delighted when her own achievements are praised. She is apparently just as pleased when the least intellectual of her friends ventures to express approval of her lectures as when she wins the sincere admiration of those whose opinion is of value. . . . She has the most astonishing trick of finding amusement and pleasure in everything, and has probably never been really bored in her life, except perhaps when attending committees." To this admirer, Cara, "one of the simplest and most easily pleased of women," had "a jolly, good-natured manner, which makes it very difficult to realize that she is rapidly becoming an intellectual celebrity." It is easy to see how Cara—optimistic, joyful, and always adulated by her entourage—inspired friends and audiences as well as captivated Virginia. She and Virginia formed, in Virginia's words, an "intimate friendship."[45]

By the time she met Virginia, however, Cara, with her radiant popularity, already had another intimate companion. Lilian Mary Clapham (1871–1935) had lived with Cara since 1896. They had met in the 1890s at King's College for Women as hockey players. "It was the Hockey Club which cemented our closest friendships," recalled their teammate Edith Morley; the team's navy blue serge uniforms, blue straw hats, and the annual hockey dinner created "a real sense of belonging to a corporate body." A leader in athletics, Lilian was active in the start of the English Women's Hockey Association. Interest in sports linked together the new threesome, too—Virginia, Cara, and Lilian. So did their serious career paths.[46]

Lilian Clapham first found occupation after college at a settlement venture, the Women's University Settlement in Southwark, started in 1887 by women who had attended college. Thereafter, as a civil servant,

Lilian worked at the British Ministry of Labour under the Board of Trade, the branch of government that controlled commerce and collected statistics. Lilian took charge of women's affairs at the employment exchange, the public agency that sought to match job openings with possible hires and distribute unemployment benefits. In World War I, when Lilian was at the Board of Trade and Cara teaching English at Bedford College, MI5 approached both women to recommend potential employees; as the intelligence agency sought to hire educated people of means who would work for low pay, it was no doubt requesting the names of women to employ. In 1917, later in the war, the Ministry of Labour sent Lilian Clapham on a wartime assignment as Principal Officer in the Women's Section of the National Service Department. Lilian and Cara were living together in a London flat when Cara traveled to the United States in 1918 as a government appointee and met Virginia.[47]

When Virginia joined Cara in England, then, in mid-1919, she became the interloper, the rival for Cara's affection, and the challenging third party in a romantic triangle. Lilian still remained at the center of Cara's affection; Lilian and Cara continued to live together in England, as they had for years, whenever Cara was in the country, until 1935, when Lilian died. Only after Lilian's death did Cara permanently leave her native land. In 1936, illness—and no doubt loss of Lilian—began to keep Cara in the United States. During all the years when Virginia visited England to be with Cara—every summer from 1919 into the mid-1930s—Lilian was in residence, too. To their British admirers, Lilian and Cara were the *real* couple, life partners of long standing, and Virginia merely a recent addition, an arriviste. Virginia presents a competing narrative, in which Lilian is barely a minor character. In real life, Lilian and Virginia, if not friends (as Virginia claimed), were regular coresidents. They were also rivals; the trio centered on Cara. Her power of personality forced both relationships to coexist. Though distinctive, such a trio was not unique.[48] Nor was it ideal: Virginia, in her memoir, introduces Lilian as Cara's "friend and comrade of many years," "of old Yorkshire stock," and as "gentry"; but otherwise, beyond a perfunctory expression of affection, Virginia ignores her.[49]

In Virginia's view, the "Cara and Virginia" narrative dominates: From 1919 until Cara's death in 1942, Cara and Virginia became a devoted couple, as Virginia portrays them—and as all who coexisted with Virginia at Barnard seem to agree. Virginia began a pursuit of Cara just as Cara returned to England after the British educational mission of 1918. Writing to Cara in January 1919, Virginia spoke of "the indefinable electric connection" she felt between them and of the "odd combination of affection and intellectual exhilaration" that Cara inspired in her. In February, referring to "our increasing desire to see each other," Virginia brought up her idea for a "grand . . . scheme" of academic exchange that would facilitate their continued relationship. The "scheme" led to a transatlantic arrangement for cohabitation that prevailed through the 1920s and after. Cara visited Virginia for half the academic year, sometimes teaching at Columbia as in 1920–1921 or at Barnard; every June Virginia took the first vessel of the Cunard line to sail for England, where she spent the summer with Cara (and perforce Lilian). By the early 1930s, Virginia resembled her partner in appearance, with her tweed suits and walking stick. Only a few samples remain from the 1930s of what must have been a devoted correspondence between Virginia and "my own darling." Virginia, in her signature, even echoed the type of baby talk ("loves you *very, very* dearly, darling") that Cara had long used within her circle of old friends.[50]

Interpersonal relations flourished in the transatlantic space carved out by the international women's movement. International women's organizations offered a special realm to fuse careerism and public service with personal attachment and romantic friendship. IFUW activists shared a vision of international networking—in Spurgeon's words, "weaving together these individual strands of friendship to form indestructible bonds." Even M. Carey Thomas, firmly convinced of Anglo-Saxon superiority and terrified of Catholic influence or Jesuit manipulation, reveled in meeting with counterparts from Spain and France under IWUF auspices. Historian Leila J. Rupp describes the role in the international women's movement of women who made their "personal and political lives with other women." Virginia and Cara Spurgeon, so deeply involved in the formation and success of the IFUW, were a leading example.[51]

Long-term, single-sex relationships such as that of Virginia and Cara were commonplace among faculty and administrators at U.S. women's colleges at the start of the twentieth century, when Virginia was starting graduate work. At Bryn Mawr, M. Carey Thomas, dean and then president (1894–1922), had well known relationships with Mary Guinn and later Mary Garrett, who left her a large estate. At Mount Holyoke, Mary Woolley, president from 1901 to 1937, had a long partnership with English professor Jeanette Marks, whom Woolley had met while teaching at Wellesley; Marks was class of '00. Both M. Carey Thomas and Mary Woolley were in office when Virginia became dean at Barnard and, like her, remained in their posts for decades. Similar relationships pervaded the Wellesley faculty. English professor Katherine Lee Bates and economics professor and dean Katherine Coman became a couple in the 1890s. Caroline Hazard, the college president, who in 1910 had suggested a few candidates for the Barnard deanship, had close relationships with both partners. Social worker and English professor Vida Scudder and author Florence Converse formed another Wellesley couple. In Chicago, lawyer, professor, and labor reformer Sophonisba Breckinridge, head of the Chicago School of Civics and Philanthropy (whose name had been proposed but rejected for the Barnard deanship in 1910), had romantic relationships with two colleagues at the University of Chicago, Marion Talbot, dean of women, and Edith Abbott, dean of the social work school. The British contingent of women academics, in which Cara Spurgeon was embedded, showed similar patterns. At the time that Cara and Rose Sidgwick visited the US as part of the British Educational Mission, Cara, though living with Lilian Clapham, was involved as well in a relationship with Margaret (Meta) Tuke, principal of Bedford College (1907–1929), where Cara taught. Rose Sidgwick had established a partnership with Margery Fry, whom she had met while both studied at Somerville College, Oxford; Fry had moved with Sidgwick in 1904 to Birmingham to become warden of a women's college, and, when chosen for the British Educational Mission, had recommended that her partner go in her place.[52]

Women in single-sex couples at colleges and universities may or may not have had sexual relationships; they did not see themselves as lesbians, at least early in the century. But by the 1920s, the fluidity of categories waned. Thus, during the course of Virginia's early professional years, perceptions of sexual identification or orientation were in flux. Virginia and Cara began their partnership in an era of transition in the norms of sexual categorization and terminology. "Between the 1880s and the 1920s, the historical record is filled with women who intervened in a wide variety of public policy issues and who remained unmarried but sustained intense, sometimes lifelong partnerships with other women," write two scholars, Elizabeth Clement and Beans Velocci. "Before the development of homosexuality as a category, intense relationships between women had gone largely unremarked upon. . . . the privacy afforded to middle-class white women . . . makes it very difficult to know exactly what these relationships were. Were they romantic, sensual, sexual, or something outside our modern relationship categories?. . . . While these women did not call themselves lesbians, and while what they did in their long-term committed relationships remains shrouded in private domesticity, by the 1920s a particularly virulent form of homophobia had emerged." When Virginia and Cara began their partnership in 1918, it is unclear how they viewed their relationship; they were cautious about revealing its nature. By the 1930s, women in partnerships with women were more aware of a lesbian identity: "the homosexual and heterosexual had each become a type of person."[53]

Still, female partnership remained "shrouded in private domesticity" for decades longer. In her autobiography of 1954, where Virginia describes her partner Cara as an "intimate" companion, she notes that in her younger years many women in the academic world "led celibate lives." Persisting with her discussion of celibacy, Virginia does not seem aware of *other* women couples. "My colleagues, the heads of other colleges for women . . . never married, and it was considered perfectly natural and proper that they should lead their active and useful lives in celibacy." Virginia also protests the "particularly cruel and unwholesome discrimination against *unmarried* women for some teaching and administrative posts." Attacking bias in the teaching profession, she segues into a wider critique. "Less responsible psychologists and psychiatrists of the day . . . voice disrespect for spinsters in the teaching profession as 'inhibited' and 'frustrated,'" Virginia charges. "After all, many of our sex can never marry; women outnumber the men."[54] The question remains: How did Virginia view her relationships, first with Cara and later with Elizabeth Reynard? She chose not to answer the question. As writer Francesca Wade suggests, in a recent study of some of some of Virginia's British contemporaries, "In public, women tended to present their relationships vaguely."[55] In the instance of Virginia and Cara, as in many others, it is difficult to navigate definition with accuracy, to categorize women who were alone but not alone, to identify the precise motives for lives lived outside marriage, and just as difficult to grasp how subjects perceived themselves. Some clues exist, however, such as Virginia's reference to an "immediate electric connection;" the evidence is suggestive more than definitive.

One clue that Virginia leaves is that she never sought a heterosexual partnership, although she alluded elusively in her memoir to a long-ago courtship. The same holds true for Caroline Spurgeon, though, like Virginia, she enjoyed long-term friendships with men; still, the brilliant though oddly childlike Cara, with her penchant for infant talk, had always been a center of female attention since her school days, admired and sought after, and continued this pattern in adulthood. As recent work by scholar Natalie Francesca Wright suggests, Cara excelled at forming networks of female friendships, at shaping institutions that welcomed such friendships, and at using coded language to refer to women's relationships.[56] A second clue: Virginia's two major partnerships, as she presents them, first with Cara and then with Elizabeth Reynard, fill the place in her life of long-term romances. In her memoir, Virginia depicts the ongoing relationships as de facto marriages, full of joint social lives and travel, shared friendships and entertaining, banter and chats. A third clue involves inheritance and transference of property: like other members of couples, women in extended relationships with women left their estates to their partners in whole or part, as did Virginia and her two life companions. Continual movement of funds and real estate characterized each of Virginia's partnerships. Finally, Virginia's lifelong spirit of defiance, which she saw as embedded in her character as a toddler, may have roots in a defiant if unlabeled or unrecognized sexual orientation that emerged only later in life and very gradually.

Looking back on the crucial moments of her life, as she prepared to write her autobiography, Virginia recalled the start of her partnership with Cara with the type of attention given to romantic attachment. She focused on a March afternoon in 1921, a few years after their relationship had begun, when she and Cara, embarked on an eight-month trip to North Africa and Europe, visited an Arab village in the Sahara Desert. The moment signified, in retrospect, the start of two intense connections, one with Cara and the other with the Arab peoples and the region of the Middle East, to which Virginia would be devoted for the rest of her life.[57]

Virginia awoke to a passion for the Middle East in the World War I era, though earlier influences fed her enthusiasm. Barnard treasurer George A. Plimpton had long supported Middle East volunteer groups, including the American College for Girls in Istanbul, an institution founded and funded by U.S. backers. Incorporated in Massachusetts in 1890, the school granted its first BA degrees in 1891; its longtime president, May Mills Patrick, who often visited New York, impressed Virginia, who began to serve on the school's board. A still-greater influence was Charles R. Crane, wealthy Illinois industrialist, sometime diplomat, and leading promoter of Arab interests in the Middle East.[58]

Heir to a family business in plumbing parts, the eccentric Crane held diverse gifts and vast interest in global affairs. First known as an expert on Russia and China, he rose to prominence in 1919 when he cochaired the King-Crane Commission of Inquiry, a five-man group that Woodrow Wilson sent to the Middle East. The commission, set up before the Senate rejected the United States' participation in the League of Nations, sought to grasp—in the interest of self-determination—the political goals of former subjects of the Ottoman Empire, which had controlled Palestine and which Britain and France had broken up by World War I. In its report, not published until 1922, after Wilson was out of office, the (divided) King-Crane Commission supported Arab nationalism, new allocations of power in the region, and limits on the arrival of Jews in the Middle East. The last provision defied the British government's Balfour Declaration of 1917, which urged a "national home" for Jews in Palestine and sought continued British influence in that territory. Charles R. Crane's pro-Arab views, which shaped the King-Crane Commission's report, failed to affect US policy, but held sway with Virginia in years to come.[59]

Crane had started public life as a political progressive, one who supported local good government groups and national politicians with progressive credentials. Serving Woodrow Wilson's two presidential campaigns as finance chairman, Crane joined progressive organizations such as Chicago's Municipal Voters' League and Senator Robert La Follette's National Progressive Republican League. The recipient of honorary doctorates, Crane endowed a pioneer program in Russian studies at the University of Chicago. He maintained friendships with prominent Americans, including Henry Ford, George Westinghouse, John Dewey, and lawyer Louis D. Brandeis; among women, his friends included the settlement leaders Jane Addams and Lillian Wald and muckraking journalist Ida Tarbell. But progressivism was just the start.[60]

Crane's opinions, always forceful, sometimes veered in clashing directions; he swerved and reversed himself. In 1917 a foe of the Russian Revolution, he changed his mind decades later after a 1937 visit to the USSR. In the World War I years, Crane spoke to President Wilson with concern, he wrote, about "the situation of Jews in the world" and "what we should do for them when peace comes." In 1933, his concern for Jews had ebbed; he spoke of "the race's enormous capacity for mischief." By the 1930s, according to a recent article, Crane "worked in Europe and the Middle East to support Hitler and opposed the 'Jewish menace' to the Christian and Islamic worlds." Dropping progressivism, Crane embraced Nazism. Support for Nazi policies and a 1933 meeting with Hitler, whom he declared similar in manner to Theodore Roosevelt, shattered Crane's reputation in foreign affairs, though it is possible that his anti-Semitism and attachment to Nazism swayed Virginia.[61]

To Virginia, looking back from the 1950s, Crane's "peculiar genius" was "piloting the minds of men into new channels of experience." In her own instance, Crane inspired an awakening to Arab culture and causes that lasted a lifetime. "In the troubled and confused times after the First World War," Virginia recalled, "when I began to think about this history of their past, the Arab nations, having been for centuries under foreign rule, were trying to emerge as modern states, deplorably poor . . . groping toward some new social organization, but intensely proud of their ancient culture."[62] Her sense of affiliation with the Arab nations, which took hold in the wake of World War I, brought her into new networks and generated new public commitments.

Virginia's acquaintance with Charles R. Crane began "shortly after" she became dean, as she remembered it; their interchanges intensified in the 1920s, when he returned from a stint as U.S. ambassador to China in 1920–1921, at the end of Wilson's second term. Crane then settled in New York and founded the New York-based Institute of Current World Affairs (1925). Virginia visited him in his apartment on Twelfth Street, where they listened to singers from the choir of the Russian church, one of Crane's interests; she welcomed Crane at her Barnard office, where he dropped in in between trips to China or Istanbul. Under his influence, Virginia explored Arab intellectual life and educational history; she looked into the ancient Near East and the history of Persian art. In the next decade, she appreciated *The Arab Awakening* (1938), a study of Arab nationalism by George Antonius, a friend of Crane's and activist in his institute, and James H. Brested, *The Dawn of Conscience* (1933) on Egyptian culture. According to Charles R. Crane's son John, Virginia was "a vital influence" on his father's Institute of Current World Affairs "because Crane consulted her constantly." "My father always spoke in the most flattering terms of Dean Gildersleeve," John Crane stated. "Father was always interested in outstanding women, and counted many of them among his close friends, but to him the dean topped them all."[63]

While involved with Crane and with his enthusiasm for the Middle East, Virginia also learned about the American missionary movement in that region and its adherents, in Virginia's words: "American preachers and teachers who for a hundred years had been working in the Middle East with unselfish devotion." In part, writes historian David A. Hollinger, the missionary community in the Middle East represented an "ethnocentric desire to make the world over in a Protestant image." In part, it represented a religious impulse "to help suffering people" throughout the region and to "end poverty and injustice." Near East Relief (1915–1930), the first pressure group or nongovernmental organization to embody the missionary spirit of Near East advocates, sought to raise funds to help suffering Armenians of 1915 and soon other groups in the region. Organizations that the missionary community inspired sought to ward off, in Hollinger's words, "any anti-Arab prejudice that would disadvantage the Palestinian population." Increasingly, the network of Middle East enthusiasts took an interest in U.S. foreign relations; descendants of the missionary community, the Arabists, would fill posts in the U.S. State Department and other government agencies.[64]

Though hardly inspired by missionary zeal, as were many of her associates in the Middle East support community, Virginia—who was totally secular—shared their passion for the region. Several new affiliations reflected her Middle East enthusiasm: In 1924 she joined the Board of Trustees of the American School for Girls in Istanbul, to which George A. Plimpton had long belonged, and in 1944 became its chair, a position that Charles R. Crane had previously held. Run by its American trustees, who met in New York, with an American head of schools, a Turkish assistant head of school, and a mainly American faculty, the college was in part an exercise in Americanization. U.S. trustees supervised every aspect of the college, from its preparatory school, designed to bring applicants up to par in English, to its faculty, curriculum, and buildings and grounds. Still, this long-lived and successful school saw itself in a "delicate balance" between two cultures and two educational systems, Turkish and American. Virginia's concern for the education of young women of Turkey, some of them invited to study at Barnard, extended forward through the decades. Through her service to the American School for Girls and its Board of Trustees, Virginia secured an enduring place in the circle of American Middle East supporters.[65]

Virginia extended her influence among supporters of Middle East education by joining the board of directors of the Near East College Association. This group (1928–1943) raised and helped manage endowment funds for institutions in Greece, Turkey, Lebanon, Syria, Bulgaria, and Iraq. Original executive committee members included George A. Plimpton and minister Henry Sloane Coffin, an influential future colleague; Allen W. Dulles, another influential future colleague, headed the association from 1946 to 1951. Tapping the coffers of U.S. corporations that did business in the Middle East, board members channeled funds into the region's American colleges. Like the American College for Girls, one of its prime constituents, the association absorbed Virginia's attention for decades to come. She also became interested in the American University at Cairo and traveled to Egypt in 1930 with Cara and Meta Tuke. Virginia's volunteer work of the 1920s thus brought her into the world of Arabists and into a connection with the Middle East support network that would have future import in her career.[66]

Since World War I, the American missionary community in the Middle East had been preoccupied with competing Arab and Jewish claims to land in Palestine. Virginia shared this concern. Involvement with the post-World War I Middle East made her alert to the threat of Zionism, as she saw it, "a plan to convert Palestine into a 'homeland' for the Jews." Arising in the late nineteenth century, Zionism surged in support after the war. Originally home to three religions, Virginia wrote, the Middle East now seemed imperiled by a scheme to enlarge one of them. In her view, only turmoil lay ahead; the Zionist movement, in retrospect, would "plunge much of the region into war, sow long-lasting hatred, and make Arabs consider America not the best liked and trusted nation of the West . . . but the most disliked and distrusted."[67]

Virginia's awakening to the Middle East after World War I left her with a commitment to education in the region, an interest in Arab culture and history, an involvement in American pro-Arab networks, and a sense of commitment to the Arab peoples. "Surely, I thought," she wrote in the 1950s, looking back, "it was worthwhile to try to keep in friendly touch with the Arabs, to watch the rebirth of their world, to learn from it, and even perhaps, in a very humble way, to help some of them on their new path."[68] Her post–World War I attachment to the Middle East also left Virginia with suspicions about Zionism that she had yet to fully express. Only as her employment at Barnard neared an end would she commit herself in public to the anti-Zionist cause. In her first decade at Barnard, in contrast, Virginia was absorbed with the college's local concerns.

CAMPUS AND COMMUNITY

By the time Virginia became dean in 1911, New York City had become a city of immigrants. Since the 1880s, an influx of southern and eastern European newcomers had settled on the Lower East Side, in the outer boroughs, and even in Harlem, on Columbia's doorstep and since 1900 home to a Jewish community. To face the sea of newcomers presented Columbia with exactly the challenge it had hoped to avoid: in a trustee's words, "one of our most dangerous problems, viz: the Hebrew question." Columbia officials braced for an onslaught of applicants. "You know as well as I that we are in danger of being overwhelmed by the number of Jewish students who are coming to us, and who are certain to increase in number," trustee John B. Pine wrote to President Butler in 1902. Barnard officials perceived a danger, too. "Personally I am discouraged," Barnard's bursar, Mrs. N. W. Liggett, confided to treasurer Plimpton in 1906. "Every year we are drawing less and less from the private school element and from the well-to-do classes." Repelled by the "sort of material coming to us," Mrs. Liggett feared that Barnard attracted "a very large percentage of Hebrews, and others of foreign extraction. . . . Already Hebrews are coming to us from other sections of the country. . . . all history proves that any cause which attracts a large number of Hebrews is a losing cause in the end"[69]

By 1910, half of New York City's public school students were immigrants or children of immigrants. Immigration gradually began to affect the student body on Morningside Heights; both Columbia and Barnard accepted a large proportion of Jewish students before World War I. By 1917, Columbia was at least 25 percent Jewish; at Barnard by 1910, at least according to the vigilant bursar, Jews filled 40 percent of the freshman class. Officials at both institutions feared that they had lost access to the clientele that they deserved. In 1914, Frederick Keppel, dean of Columbia College, worried that Columbia had become "socially uninviting to students who come from homes of refinement."[70]

Anti-Semitism flourished unapologetically in New York in the early twentieth century, as Nicholas Murray Butler's biographer, Michael Rosenthal, observes, and President Butler shared such views. So did other Columbia administrators. Butler, however, was circumspect; he did not want to invite a public relations disaster, his biographer points out, and he avoided discriminatory statements. He also avoided the blatant prejudice of a quota system in admissions. Virginia, a member of the university-wide admissions committee, followed Butler's lead. Her public statements were circumspect. Her other role models were the heads of women's colleges, such as M. Carey Thomas at Bryn Mawr, who made her distaste for immigrants clear. Thomas sought to exclude Jews—"a most terrible set of people to my thinking"—from both the Bryn Mawr faculty and the student body. In her view, feminism required discrimination. "If the present intellectual supremacy of the White races is maintained, as I hope that it will be for centuries to come," the Bryn Mawr president declared to the college's opening ceremony of 1916, "I believe it will be because they are the only races that have seriously begun to educate their women."[71]

When Virginia took office as dean in 1911, concern about rising numbers of Jewish students was well in play. The labeling of the new building that opened in 1917, Students Hall—instead of using the name of the building's donor, financier Jacob Schiff—reflected the college outlook. That fraternities, until their abolition, excluded Jewish students, was another part of the picture. When publisher Adolph Ochs, a parent—father of Iphigene Ochs (Sulzberger) '14—complained about such exclusion in 1912, treasurer Plimpton sought to reassure him, "With you and all other thinking people I deplore the social prejudice which causes this discrimination."[72] But Plimpton functioned in the world of fundraising; Barnard did not share the tolerant stance he presented to Adolph Ochs, nor did most of its trustees or administrators.

Mrs. Liggett, who had run the college in Virginia's first year as a student, was always a staunch fount of anti-Semitism. "Mrs. Liggett was the chief executive officer of Barnard College from 1891 on," wrote Annie Nathan Meyer in 1931. "I am not sure what was her exact title at first, but later on she was our bursar until her retirement in 1924." Meyer appreciated her "fresh breeziness and common sense." A Vassar graduate of 1880, Mrs. Liggett had been briefly married and soon widowed; she taught at Packer Collegiate Institute before finding work at the new college at 343 Madison Avenue. "Ella Weed was a Vassar woman and so was I," Mrs. Liggett recalled. "At first I was Secretary, Registrar, everything." Mrs. Liggett patrolled the college community for less favored entrants, as suggested in her correspondence with Plimpton, to whom she turned often for financial advice, and with the deans. In 1901, for instance, "Miss Meyer left a most unsavory girl, named Fox, who took the examinations for Barnard College," Mrs. Liggett reported to Dean Gill.

> Her name and locality where she lives [Fall River, Massachusetts] persuaded me that she was made of Saintly Puritan stock. . . . She turns out to be an unwashed (I crave pardon for the word but it requires a strong one) Jew! She has friends living on the lower east side of Third Avenue, with whom she proposes to live. I gave her almost an hour of my time, and wished heartily she would betake herself to Radcliffe.[73]

Most Barnard personnel, unlike the bursar, voiced their objections to Jewish admissions in code. Former dean Laura D. Gill, in response to Mrs. Liggett's concerns of 1906, argued that Barnard should favor applicants from private schools "who regarded higher education as chiefly ministered to general intellectual ends" as opposed to public school applicants who were "looking to self support professionally." Her successor, William T. Brewster, later provost, agreed in principle. "We have also to deal with a good deal of inferior stock," he wrote to President Butler in 1909, "and with women for whom present and prospective economic pressure is the prime motive." These were veiled anti-Semitic references. Jewish applicants, in the view of Barnard administrators, put social and economic mobility ahead of "general intellectual ends." They were climbers, they sought footholds in Barnard degrees, and they would degrade Barnard's status as a rival of its sister schools.[74]

Barnard had always admitted a portion of Jews, as in Virginia's class of '99, which had five Jewish members (of twenty-two students). In Barnard's view, and as Virginia saw it, the college stance was welcoming. Such early students were German or Sephardic Jews, from families with longtime New York residence or who had arrived in the mid-nineteenth century. Virginia hoped to discourage more recent arrivals, Eastern European immigrants, those who attended New York City public schools, and whose numbers as applicants rose—in contrast to the type of middle-upper-class applicant whom Virginia found desirable. By the start of the 1920s, the college found it hard to appeal to "conventional middle class students" from New York City, as Virginia told a staff meeting, because of the public perception "that we have a large proportion of Jews and Radicals." The college needed students "of every creed, group, and race," Virginia argued, "but not too many of any one" kind, so that "all may be assimilated." Restricted admission would thus, in her view, support a greater goal, "assimilation."[75]

Several factors fused in Virginia's first decade as dean to make local applicants more threatening to Barnard administrators. The New York State Regents Examination provided scholarships for high scorers; by 1913, as historian Robert McCaughey points out, sixty of 184 Barnard entrants joined the freshman class on the basis of Regents exams, many on state scholarships. Barnard, however, sought the sort of students who attended its rival colleges, the "country schools." To attract such applicants, the college built a dormitory; Brooks Hall had opened in 1907. But the expensive rooms, unfilled by Barnard undergraduates, most of who commuted, failed to lure the clientele that Barnard expected. The college then took further steps to limit local applicants. It raised tuition, steered its prestigious Pulitzer fellowships to out-of-town applicants, and sought to expand links with New York City private schools; in 1915, Virginia reported, she made arrangements with the Spence School (run by a favorite trustee, Clara Spence), so that it might guide able students into taking Barnard exams. Virginia also turned to director of undergraduate admissions for the university, Adam Leroy Jones. A philosophy professor at Princeton, Columbia, and then Barnard, where he remained, Jones ran admissions for all three undergraduate colleges—Columbia, Barnard, and the engineering school—from 1909 to his death in 1934.[76]

Virginia and Jones steered Barnard's admissions committee, which met every few months, at times with other faculty members. In 1913 Virginia pointed out to Jones the need for tighter standards. She cited the case of an ill-starred Barnard applicant, Anna Gold, who had taken the college entrance tests multiple times in English and Latin and even with four or five attempts had failed repeatedly. "There is no apparent reason for her failures except stupidity," Virginia claimed. "In conversing with her personally, I felt that she was just the sort of person who ought not to come to College. . . . What do you think of her case?" Virginia then veered, in discreet language, "to another question, one of the most important which the college is now facing, that we ought to discuss very carefully within the next few months. It will evidently be necessary for us in future to restrict the number of our admissions. How can we do this so as to select the students most desirable in scholarship and personality?" Use of the word "personality" was often a code for non-Jewish attributes. Virginia recommended that undergraduate deans on the admissions committee confer, along with President Butler, to review current standards. "It seems to me a very delicate question, but one vitally important to the University. Of course the two undergraduate colleges are the point where it has to be faced."[77]

Columbia College faced the question at hand; it soon took steps to revise its admission requirements and to reduce the number of less-desired applicants. The college's revised requirements—beyond secondary school grades, subject tests, and recommendations—included an elaborate application form with extensive data on race, religion, and family background; an intelligence test, called "the psychological test"; nonacademic criteria such as character and leadership; and personal interviews, in which qualities of character might be discerned. The Columbia admission office intensified efforts to recruit nationally and to establish channels with private schools. It also employed "conditional" admissions, the acceptance of candidates with academic deficiencies—who had failed one or more of the tests or other requirements but who fulfilled other criteria and, in Columbia's judgment, might profit from the college experience. With all the new tactics in effect, Columbia College managed to reduce acceptance of Jewish applicants from 40 percent in 1910 to around 22 percent in 1921. Its competitors—Harvard, Yale, and Princeton—to which the New York applicants that Columbia really wanted increasingly applied—excluded Jews at still-higher rates. Frederick P. Keppel, Columbia College dean from 1910 to 1917, put the best face he could on Columbia's predicament, as he saw it. "What most people regard as a racial problem is really only a social problem," Keppel declared in 1914. "The Jews who have had the advantages of decent social surroundings for a generation or two are entirely satisfactory companions." Herbert Hawkes, his successor, was more of a hard-liner.[78]

Virginia monitored admission tactics at both Columbia and the rival sister schools; her dean's reports reflected a shift away from exam results toward more malleable standards. In 1914, she mentioned the need to consider "school records, health certificates, testimonials regarding character and personality, and wherever possible, personal interviews." The college would choose "those best qualified to profit from a college education." Candidates needed "not just intellectual qualities," Virginia stated again in 1918; just as relevant were "their general character and powers as shown in the confidential school reports, in letters of recommendation." The college sought "those who seem as the best fitted to profit from the college course" or, as in 1920, "candidates who show most promise of future ability and usefulness." In 1920 Barnard favored the "New Plan," adopted by rival women's colleges. Instead of using subject tests, the college now relied on College Boards and/or Regents exams, in use since 1913, when New York State began a Regents Scholarship program. Barnard considered the "psychological tests Columbia has used in the past year," Virginia wrote, and looked at evidence "on health, character, personality, and all round promise." Exams alone were not enough, she reiterated. There were "other important qualifications for college work and future usefulness." Like Columbia, Barnard shaped its standards to expand its realm of discretion—and to support rejection of whomever it hoped to exclude.[79]

Anti-Semitism, then, to Virginia, was part of the lingua franca of Barnard, a sentiment that had long prevailed at the college before she arrived as dean, that she had absorbed throughout her life, and that she expressed with a combination of caution and fluency; she had no problem with it. It was also, in part, a way of bonding to a university community in which she sought security, even as an insider. Although Barnard had a slightly later start than Columbia in restrictive admissions, Virginia and Adam Leroy Jones worked together in the next decade to put its precepts into effect. As gatekeepers, they used conditional acceptance to excel at Jewish exclusion.

CHAPTER THREE

Gatekeeping

The 1920s

"In September 1925, two years after the death of my parents," Virginia wrote, "it was with deep appreciation and hope that I returned to Barnard to live in a new official residence for the Dean, a duplex apartment on the campus with an entrance of its own and an open terrace facing green grass, trees, and Broadway over the fence." Built into the northwest corner of Hewitt Hall, an elegant new dormitory designed by Charles Rich at McKim, Mead, and White, the Deanery, as it was called (the term usually refers to the residence of an Anglican dean, in charge of a group of parishes, or to that of the head of an Oxford college), suggests Virginia's affirmed value to the college. The place was impressive. The formal dining room, spare and elegant, enabled the dean to hold meetings of colleagues and committees in her home; at teas in the book-lined living room, students clustered around the fireplace. With trustee approval, Virginia had planned the new residence, overseen its furnishing, and scattered her possessions throughout. "It gave me the feeling of living in the heart of my College," Virginia wrote. "At last I had found harbor."[1]

The opening of the Deanery marks the midpoint of a peak decade for the dean and the college. With its enlarged residential capacity, Barnard entered a new era—expansive, ambitious, and competitive. Virginia extended her influence in the university and ramped up her power in the college. As her position at Barnard grew secure, she channeled her spirit of rivalry in new directions. She sought to steer Barnard into a shape she envisioned—one closer to that of its country counterparts, the other women's colleges in New England towns and the Middle Atlantic states. To gain sway—or even primacy—among the sister schools took some maneuvering. To shape Barnard's role meant not only to mobilize alumnae, trustees, and faculty but also to control admissions—to increase enrollment among those applicants who formed the constituency of the "country schools" and to curtail it among a growing pool of local contenders, daughters of New York City immigrants, whose numbers as applicants skyrocketed. "Gatekeeping" was not Virginia's sole role of the 1920s; she was busy beyond Barnard in civic affairs and, insofar as she could, foreign affairs. But even as she forged a path in local and international circles, Virginia sought to reconstruct Barnard to meet the competitive new era of the 1920s.

AT THE DEANERY

When the 1920s began, Virginia lived with her parents, Henry A. and Virginia Gildersleeve, at 404 Riverside Drive, where they had moved in 1912. Life with the elder Gildersleeves was a formal affair, Virginia recalled. "We were as polite to one another in the home as we were to guests or strangers." Home life with her mother, she found, curtailed access to others. "For many years before the death of my parents my mother's unwillingness to have guests in the home limited for me, as well as for my father, the normal give and take of friendships," she wrote. The elder Gildersleeves died within months of one another in 1923. Virginia and Alger shared their estate, which gave Virginia great financial security. The estate enhanced her ability to take charge of Cara, who seemed to depend on solicitude from others. Virginia first used her inheritance to give Cara time off from teaching and enable her "to finish her monumental work on Chaucer," as Virginia told Dorothea Setzer. "She had tremendous intellectual drive, which is extraordinary among women, as very few have it as men have."[2]

As the 1920s began, Cara took the fall term off from Bedford College to pursue scholarship. When the Deanery opened in 1925, Virginia and Cara gained a residence. "Cara Spurgeon stayed with me from October to January and worked at the writing of her books, in the little upstairs study," Virginia writes. Virginia dictated "letters and statements" in the downstairs library. College students "grew accustomed to the sight of the two good friends, followed by a pair of diminutive terriers, pacing the boardwalk between the fields for archery and field sports," recalled Barnard historian Marion Churchill White '29. Virginia and Cara spent their summers traveling to IFUW conferences in European capitals. Virginia also stayed with Cara in England, at Cara's rented London flat, 19 Clarence Gate Gardens, near Bedford College; in a country cottage that Cara owned at Ralph's Mill, in Westleton Heath, Suffolk; and then in Alciston, East Sussex, where Virginia bought the Old Postman's Cottage in 1925. Cara had been living with Lilian Clapham since 1896, but by the 1920s Virginia had more firmly encroached on the household arrangements.[3]

To what extent did the start of Virginia's connection with Cara overlap with the last years of the elder Gildersleeves? Were Virginia's parents aware of her new friendship or its intensity? Virginia carefully writes her way around these questions, without addressing them. Overlap between Cara and the elder Gildersleeves seems unlikely. After meeting one another in 1918, Cara and Virginia had each crossed the Atlantic to spend time together, first for the inaugural IFUW conference in London 1919 and then on other voyages. A crucial step forward in their relationship was the eight-month trip begun in early 1921, when Virginia took a year-long leave from Barnard; the two women sailed for North Africa on a French steamer. Starting out in the Sahara Desert, they traveled through Algeria and Tunisia, and then to Naples and Rome, "where Mussolini had begun to muster supporters," Virginia noted, and on to the French Riviera, where she felt the presence of Crocheron ancestors. Upon her return, during the following academic year, 1922–1923, when Virginia resumed the deanship, her parents died, her father in February 1923 and her mother in August ("More than any other single person she influenced my life"). Only then did Virginia shift to Cara as the focus of her life and companion-in-residence; as narrator, she glides smoothly into the relationship: "In Caroline Spurgeon I had found a delightful companion of like pursuits and since we had worked and traveled together and she also had no close family ties, we decided that we might in future share a home to our mutual advantage and pleasure for as much of the year as our duties would permit. (If it is at all practicable to avoid it, I believe that women, single or widowed, should not live alone.)" Clearly, when Virginia declares that Cara lacked "close family ties," she ignores the existence of Lilian, not family but indisputably a close tie, as Cara's British friends attested. In retrospect, when she wrote her memoir in the 1950s, as at the time, in the 1920s, Virginia did not let Lilian stand in her way.[4]

Cara was by habit the center of attention, and, as Virginia observed, encircled by friends. She took her popularity for granted, as did her admirers. Apart from her successful scholarship, where she wielded authority, Cara radiated a childlike charm—that she had referred to herself as "Childie" in letters to her aunt, written as a young woman, seems fitting. Virginia—among others—found her delightful. Cara was eight years older, but Virginia "frequently felt the elder, for her ebullient spirits and runaway enthusiasms frequently needed curbing." Virginia never forgot Rose Sidgwick's "canny comment" about Cara, "made in those first days of our acquaintance when the two had just arrived from England. 'A voyage with the distinguished professor,' said Miss Sidgwick, 'is not what I expected. It is more like traveling with a sturdy, curious, eight-year-old boy.' " Cara's lifelong precocity and joyful stance evoked transatlantic praise. "She enjoys her popularity and success quite honestly and frankly but has no desire for notoriety," exuded a British admirer in 1920. Her "jolly, good-natured manner . . . makes it very difficult to realize that she is rapidly becoming an international celebrity."[5]

The 1920s was a decade of achievement for both Virginia and Cara, who became an enthusiast of all things American. Cara had little to say on political issues. In her youth she had attended meetings among Fabians; decades later, whatever political ideas she may have held seemed to settle into an endorsement of Americans. In a 1922 article in the *Atlantic Monthly*, an attack on the English education system, Cara celebrated "the eager and thrilling vitality of the United States" and urged class-ridden Britain to emulate the democratic principles of the United States. She tore into the elitism of the English system, extolled American educational practices, and voiced concern for the needs of "industrial populations." In words redolent of progressive educators in the United States, Cara offered her own interpretation of progressive education principles. "True education, the 'drawing out' and training of already existing faculties, is really guidance in the acquiring of experience," Spurgeon wrote. "For the gaining of experience . . . is the one thing that matters; it is in this continuous gain that life itself consists."[6]

After publishing her major work on Chaucer in 1925, Cara shifted fields in English literature to focus on Shakespeare. Generous support from American donors, recruited by Lucretia Perry Osborn, wife of paleontologist and director of the American Museum of Natural History, Henry Fairfield Osborn, enabled her to take many leaves from Bedford College and to retire entirely in 1929. Throughout the 1920s and into the next decade, Cara committed all her time to work on Shakespeare, to master the field and develop an original line of exploration. In 1935, when she published her definitive work, *Shakespeare's Imagery and What It Tells Us,* Spurgeon thanked the donors who supported her scholarship for "practical and generous help." Her major acknowledgment was to Virginia: What she owed to Virginia, Spurgeon wrote, "from the very inception of this book to the final reading of the proof sheets," was not possible "adequately either to describe or to acknowledge."[7]

While Virginia's first decade in the Deanery centered on Cara—at least for part of the academic year—it focused as well on the college.

COLLEGE LIFE

Exuberance pervaded memories of college life at Barnard in the 1920s. "We belonged to a generation of young women who felt extraordinarily free," remembered anthropologist Margaret Mead '22. "We had more than the equivalent of Women's Lib in the twenties," recalled Eleanor Rosenberg '29, English professor. "We believed that we *were* the New Women, fully liberated!" Administrators sought to harness the appeal of campus culture that students celebrated by appropriating rites and rituals; in Barnard's case, Virginia turned to the freshman/sophomore Greek Games, "our strange perennial festival . . . which blossoms afresh each year, under the stimulus of Greek myth and art." Dating back to 1906, the Greek Games were no longer on the cutting edge; still, Virginia valued the hold of recent versions of college life on 1920s students. The Anglo-American tradition of higher education, distinctively, as Virginia saw it, provided "a period [of] common residence, a mingling of social life and human experience that makes the common denominator more powerful and richer than it would be if confined to the casual contacts of laboratory and classroom." Students would be bound more firmly to their institutions by their "common body of memories and ambitions."[8]

Memories of Virginia from 1920s alumnae were restrained. Eleanor Rosenberg, so impressed with the culture that Barnard students of her era created, saw Virginia more critically: "She was respected, admired, somewhat feared, and seemed almost completely detached."[9] But if aloof from students, Virginia was a totally involved, hands-on administrator—highly controlling, unable to delegate, and more than agile in wielding her authority as dean.

Virginia solidified the power of the deanship, as historian Andrea Walton shows. With William T. Brewster's withdrawal in 1923 from the job of provost and abolition of that position, the dean now dominated the college and its faculty. She put her stamp on the Board of Trustees by appointing new members, whose allegiance lasted for decades; these included classmate Alice Duer Miller, who served from 1922–1943, and Columbia trustee Gano Dunn, engineer and head of the New School, 1922–1953. A gift for alumnae relations further boosted the dean's power: Alumnae became a loyal power base. Women's college graduates had already joined forces in 1911 to form a New York City vocational bureau for alumnae; confident of Virginia's favor, Barnard alumnae served steadily as her cheering section. Each issue of the *Barnard Alumnae Bulletin* announced the dean's achievements on campus and her "wider activities." So did the college publicity office, which supplied the local press with college news. Each issue of the annual dean's report made its way to New York newspapers, which gave the college and Virginia attention. With her shrewd sense of publicity, the dean was always ready to give an interview. Among her associates were prominent women of the press: Helen Rogers Reid '03, owner of the *New York Herald Tribune*, had been a trustee since 1914. Iphigene Ochs Sulzberger '14, daughter and wife of owners of the *New York Times*, and Agnes Meyer '07, wife of the publisher of *The Washington Post*, would serve as trustees in the 1930s and 1940s. Barnard, as Virginia knew, could count on "the friendly interest of these distinguished papers."[10]

Extensive publicity made Virginia a local celebrity. In November 1928, Democratic Party officials swept her downtown to a campaign rally at Madison Square Garden for Governor Al Smith, then running for president. "Hustled up to the speakers' platform," where she was introduced by Mayor Jimmy Walker, Virginia addressed twenty-three thousand cheering Democrats, until hustled *off* the platform to make way for the next speaker, Franklin Delano Roosevelt, then a candidate for governor. A few days later Smith lost the presidential election (though FDR won the governorship). Virginia, who recounted the event with humor, seemed happy to return to decisions about curriculum changes and faculty appointments.[11]

Barnard in the 1920s pursued its own path in curriculum design, apart from Columbia, which, introduced its Contemporary Civilization program after World War I. Barnard instead focused on the disciplines and on introductory courses in each discipline. Under the direction of botany professor Louise L. Gregory, the college began a system of student advising. Virginia acceded to the end of requirements in Greek and Latin, dropped before she became dean, though with regret. The curriculum grew under her watch with the introduction of government, fine arts, music, and the social sciences. Overall, Virginia valued the process of learning more than the material learned: "I came to believe that it did not matter greatly which subjects a student studied." Her main goal was to keep the liberal arts curriculum intact. Barnard never offered a gender-specific program such as that begun at Vassar, with its interdisciplinary School of Euthenics (1925), devoted to the development and care of the family. Relentlessly, Virginia promoted training in the liberal arts, unsullied by vocational taint. She used her dean's report for 1927 to lash out at "the idea that women should be educated as women only." Women, she argued, should not be "cut off from a full and undiluted share, for all who desire and can absorb it, in the treasures of the natural and social sciences, the humanities, and the arts" and their "right to a part in the intellectual heritage of the race."[12]

Virginia took an active role in faculty appointments and promotion. "She controlled the faculty, most of whom seemed fearful of disagreeing with her," Agnes Meyer recalled, "but they all admired her." The dean held one card unavailable to heads of rival women's colleges: she was able to borrow Columbia faculty, who sometimes preferred Barnard. Columbia's leading anthropology professor, Franz Boas, in Virginia's tenure, shifted his undergraduate teaching to Barnard. Virginia also hired visiting professors, starting with Cara in 1920. Her appointments included impressive women. Chilean poet Gabriela Mistral took a visiting professorship in 1930–1931. Historian Eileen Power, lecturer at the London School of Economics and author of *Mediaeval People* (1924), arrived in January 1930 and won great popularity. With much acuity, Virginia offered Power a well-paid professorship. Although Power returned to the London School of Economics, the dean's recognition and weighty offer helped her career.[13]

Such an offer stands out. With a faculty almost half female by the 1920s, historian Robert McCaughey reveals, women at Barnard occupied the lower end of the professorial scale. They earned less than the men, won promotion more slowly, had less professional mobility, and usually remained at Barnard for their professional lives. Male faculty, in contrast, better paid and more quickly advanced, were more likely to move on to other institutions. "We could, as a rule, secure for an assistantship a better quality of woman than of man," Virginia recalled. Promotion from below, however, would lead to a predominantly female faculty. "Was this a good thing?" she asked. "I was inclined to think that it was not and for this some feminists blamed me." Instead, Virginia claimed, she sought to "provide the best professors we could secure for our students irrespective of sex." To bring in a new professor, "we were more likely to try to bring in a man."[14]

Favoritism toward men prevailed on college faculties, even at women's colleges. At Smith, women faculty members, again about half the faculty, complained that President William Allan Neilson favored men in salary and promotion. "Every salary is an individual bargain," Neilson declared. "The fact that there are more men at the top is due to two things, first—that there are more men of superior ability and equipment in the profession, and second, that such men are in more demand than the women, and consequently, through receiving calls, have often more rapid promotion." Remarkably, as Robert McCaughey observes, college presidents discussed bias in hiring and promotion with resounding clarity. At the same time, historian Rosalind Rosenberg points out, Virginia pursued progressive policies on maternity leave for faculty members. With the support of Helen Rogers Reid and Alice Duer Miller, Virginia swayed trustees to provide one semester off at full pay or a full year at half pay. Economist Clara Eliot, who had just started teaching at Barnard, was the first to receive maternity leave in 1926.[15]

Barnard followed a path carved out by Bryn Mawr to set up a special summer program that involved the labor movement: the Barnard Summer School for Women Workers in Industry. The Bryn Mawr model, started in 1921, was residential, but Barnard ran a day program. Two activists in the National Women's Trade Union League—Hilda Smith, the guiding spirit of the Bryn Mawr Summer School for Women Workers, and her assistant, Ernestine Friedman, a professor at Wheaton College—urged Virginia to make Barnard space available without charge to about forty students and their instructors. Opening in 1927, with alumnae financial support, the Barnard summer school lasted until 1934. Virginia, who spent every summer in Europe, still appreciated the chance for Barnard to claim credits in the women's movement by hosting the women workers' program and set up an administrative board to run it. The school, she said, would be an experiment in adult education and in "friendly cooperation between the Labor groups and the university."[16]

"We have every reason to be proud of this experiment," Barnard economist Emilie Hutchinson boasted in the *Barnard Alumnae Bulletin* in 1928. Enthused working-class students that summer, all but four immigrants, provided a wealth of national backgrounds—Russia, Italy, Poland, Romania, Czechoslovakia, Germany—and a cross section of industries, "the garment trades, millinery, upholstery, electrical," Hutchinson wrote. "Every branch of the labor movement" was represented. On campus from 9 a.m. into the evenings, diverted with programs in sports and music, the summer students took classes in economics, English and general science. They studied economic problems "such as unemployment, the meaning of industrial democracy, changes in the cost of living, etc." said Hutchinson. "Economic questions are enriched by the students' practical experience and their first-class knowledge," declared Ernestine Friedman. Most summer students lacked high school education, but they had intelligence, breadth of interest, and intellectual curiosity, the instructors reported: "Every bit of new knowledge was absorbed." Summer participants left behind a trail of publications, full of stories, essays, and tributes; one noted "the cells of our brains are beginning to open."[17]

Virginia also resolved the lingering problem of admission of women to Columbia Law School. Compared to the medical school, the law school had always been "a far more difficult proposition," in her view. Back in November 1915, when she had corresponded with law school dean Harlan Stone, progress had been impossible. The law school faculty had firmly resisted admission of women, and Stone found the proposition "inadvisable"; he preferred, he said, an "independent" law school for women, an improbable notion. But Dean Stone, who had tired of what he called "administrivia" and of President Butler, whom he antagonized, resigned in 1923 to join a law firm. He became U.S. attorney general in 1924 and an associate justice of the Supreme Court in 1925. His successor as dean, Huger Jervey, proved more amenable. The law school faculty still rejected admission of women, but Jervey offered a concession. On December 10, 1926, in response to petitions for women's admission from Virginia and the Barnard faculty, Jervey declared that as of September 1927, students and graduates of Barnard would be accepted. Virginia, who credited her faculty with the victory, at once recommended a Barnard student for admission. Jervey intended the concession solely as an exception to an overall policy of rejection. The law school had in no way decided, he said, to "admit women equally with men." But somehow it had done just that. Two graduates of Smith and Vassar, respectively, each armed with a Columbia graduate degree, applied at the same time as the Barnard applicant, and could not easily be refused. At last, in October 1928, the law school faculty, so long opposed, voted to admit women on the same terms as men. The staunch resistance of law school professors and the "slowness of the process," points out scholar Barbara Black, a future dean, suggests "the tenacity, the ferocity, with which these men clung to the world they knew."[18]

To Virginia, the law school victory represented a capstone achievement. Exuberantly, she recalled in her memoir how she and the Barnard faculty outmaneuvered the law school faculty; the decision to admit women was "the most significant change in the position of women in this university within the last few years," as Virginia wrote to a fellow dean in 1929.[19] With the law school triumph in progress, Virginia turned to the long-term issue of college finance. At the same time, she moved toward a second long-held and elusive goal: to bring Barnard into the fold with its competitors, the other leading women's colleges.

Presidents of the leading eastern women's colleges had been meeting for one purpose or another before 1920, informally or under the aegis of the Association of Collegiate Alumnae, but Barnard had not always been among the schools involved. At the "four-college conference" of 1915, organized by Vassar's president Henry Noble MacCracken, the heads of Mount Holyoke, Smith, Vassar, and Wellesley met to discuss common problems and procedures, mainly admissions. William Allan Neilson, Smith's president as of 1917, recalled proposing the addition of Bryn Mawr to the mix. Other occasions drew college heads together, too. When the United States entered World War I in 1917, the presidents of Bryn Mawr, Wellesley, and Mount Holyoke formed a War Service Committee; in 1918 leaders of several women's colleges, including Barnard, met at Radcliffe to discuss "After-War Problems in the Higher Education of Women," joined by Caroline Spurgeon and Rose Sedgwick; and after M. Carey Thomas's retirement from the Bryn Mawr presidency in 1922, women's college heads convened at the inauguration of her successor, Maud Wood Park.[20]

The end of M. Carey Thomas's reign at Bryn Mawr enabled Barnard's dean to move forward among fellow administrators. In 1926, Virginia saw a chance to both join with the rival women's college presidents and to seize a leading role among them. At her instigation, as she told the story, heads of seven eastern women's colleges met in New York on September 15, 1926 at the Cosmopolitan Club to start a joint publicity campaign. The goal: to raise endowment funds and awareness of a need to finance women's education. According to Virginia, the joint effort arose from a recent conversation held by herself and Wellesley's president, Ellen F. Pendleton, with philanthropist Anson Phelps Stokes at a meeting of the American Council of Education. The leaders of Wellesley and Barnard then, in Virginia's account, assembled "five of our friends, who were heads of the other colleges of women for a lunch in New York City." Other college presidents seemed to accept Virginia's role as initiator; she had know-how about public relations and contacts with New York foundations that all hoped to share. After several meetings at the Cosmopolitan Club, the Seven College Conference rolled out a lively publicity campaign, starting with a statement of collective purpose.[21]

"The Question of the Women's Colleges," written by the seven college leaders and published in the *Atlantic Monthly* of November 1927, called for funds to raise endowments. "The women's colleges must parallel the education offered, not by the mediocre colleges for men, but by the colleges which train men most efficiently," the college heads declared. However, compared to elite men's colleges, the women's colleges lacked endowments and had to charge high fees to compensate for lack of income from endowments. Their needs were many. They needed to increase faculty pay but "expected to have our best men drawn from us by our wealthier brothers." They needed "first-rate faculty" ("first-rate women" as well as men) to keep up the level of intellectual life at their institutions. They needed income for scholarships "to retain our clientele even among the daughters of teachers, ministers, and doctors, and other professional men on moderate salaries." Students from such backgrounds, the writers claimed, were vital "to maintain the intellectual quality of the colleges." The colleges needed, too, "their still poorer sisters to maintain the democracy which has always been a valuable element in our intellectual life." But currently, the women's colleges faced financial crises. When making donations, wealthy men and their widows favored "the alma mater of a husband or son" over "a college for women." The seven colleges called for "fair play." "Do Americans believe in educating women or do they not?" the college presidents concluded. "If they do, the question is one of justice rather than of chivalry."[22]

The argument of the *Atlantic* plea, which moves backward, exudes a stilted vagueness, as if some unseen censor robbed the writers of clarity. It is unclear how elite men's colleges were run more "efficiently" than other men's colleges or in what way the education that the women's colleges "must" provide was "parallel" to that offered to men; and it is especially unclear why donors should support women's education by contributing to a select group of private colleges rather than to public coeducational institutions. Though the writers claim to foster democracy on campus, they voice concern with rank, status, and social class to an extent that might jolt modern readers. But the document undoubtedly spoke to the moment. As the college presidents declared, they enabled the spirit of cooperation to trump that of competition; they planned to divide any gifts bestowed in response to their effort on the colleges jointly. Most important, they challenged the powerful sway held by elite men's colleges, already well financed, over gifts from foundations as well as from wealthy patrons.

Each of the women's college presidents reiterated the new credo of the Seven College Conference, as did Virginia, in her dean's report for 1928, where she spoke solely to a Barnard audience. Barnard's attention had been drawn to the problem of finance "in acute form" the previous spring, Virginia announced, when Columbia had adopted a new salary scale; it was "obviously essential to follow Columbia's example at once." Virginia also explained how the public profited from the existence of the women's colleges, a point on which the *Atlantic* article had been foggy. "The problem of financing a college for women will probably always be more difficult than that of financing a college for men," she posited. Women "do not control much of the money of the world." After college, they worked for no pay or low pay; they became homemakers or child-rearers or teachers or social workers, or they gravitated to the "public health side of medicine." But graduates of women's colleges brought "trained intelligence" and "spiritual force" to the work they did, Virginia claimed. Thus, their "vital occupations 'pay' the community a thousand times over for the cost of the higher education that developed them," she concluded. "The college women rely on public-spirited citizens of both sexes to appreciate the real value of this service we render and support our work."[23]

The college presidents bolstered their appeal in the *Atlantic* with an intense publicity effort, or what William Allan Neilson called the "agitation." The Seven College Conference opened a New York office, hired an administrator, and announced its goal of raising fifty million dollars. The seven presidents, alone or in pairs, visited potential donors and foundations, such as the Commonwealth Fund and the General Education Fund, set up by John D. Rockefeller. The conference held a series of dinners, addressed by the college presidents, to which it invited prominent citizens, opinion-makers, and likely contributors. "Those joint dinners made quite a dent on public consciousness," Virginia recalled. "We found that whereas one college president arriving in Chicago or St. Louis might not achieve much of a headline, seven of us together distinctly seemed something worth photographing and writing up." Alumnae of the seven colleges held similarly successful events in a dozen major cities, attended by the college presidents, individually or in groups, and potential donors, in Neilson's words, "several hundred carefully selected guests." Virginia recalled distinguished outside speakers, including future chief justice Charles Evans Hughes; banker Thomas Lamont of J. P. Morgan; and journalist Walter Lippmann. In 1932, the seven colleges formed a financial advisory board of prominent executives to develop fundraising plans.[24]

Joint efforts by the seven-college alumnae, helped by their presidents, suggest the main tactic: to assemble men with financial expertise among whom to solicit advice—with the goal of extracting donations. Virginia appeared often on the podium with visiting experts in this effort. In February 1930, when banker Lamont spoke to a Philadelphia dinner on how to raise endowments, Virginia followed up with a declaration of need. The total endowments of seven leading men's colleges, she stated, was $318.5 million, a figure that far surpassed the $36 million total endowments of the seven women's colleges. When Walter Lippman joined the seven presidents on the rostrum at a lively session in St. Louis in November 1933, Virginia again found an audience. Lippmann tackled the question that had hung over the Seven College Conference agenda unanswered since its start: *Why* support the elite women's colleges? "Why, if there is to be higher education for women, should we make specific efforts to support the private colleges, of which the seven women's colleges represented in this group are the foremost?" asked Lippmann. "Why not rest content with the tax-supported co-educational universities?" His answer: To preserve educational freedom, to "maintain the full vigor of private initiative," to deprive government of "monopoly of education," and to make educational experimentation possible, "for no one knows what is the best education for every one forever." Lippmann hoped his words would prod some millionaire in the audience "to the point where he reaches for his checkbook." In her own talk at St. Louis ("Why Not Stenography and Domestic Science?"), which followed, Virginia defended the liberal arts tradition in women's education, as exemplified by the sister colleges, and began to focus on the value of "trained brains"; that theme would be central to her arguments of the 1930s and 1940s.[25]

Even as the nation sank deeper into the Great Depression in 1933–1934, alumnae and college heads forged forward with the campaign.

Lunches and dinners that year attracted scores of trust officers and lawyers, alumnae claimed. In New York in December, 1933, after speeches on the needs of colleges by Virginia and Vassar's President MacCracken, forty-five trust officers offered suggestions on how to build endowments. In Buffalo, New York, in March 1934, a talk by Mary Woolley of Mount Holyoke impressed executives from trust companies and law firms, who proposed further fundraising tactics. In May, President Neilson of Smith fielded fifty guests at a private club in New Haven ("the enemy's camp, so to speak," according to Vassar alumnae) plus fifty more at a similar venue in Brooklyn, and Virginia hosted thirty trust officers and lawyers at a lunch in Indianapolis. At year's end, to supplement a report prepared by the financial advisors, the joint alumnae promised a pamphlet listing the needs of each college, plus forms of bequest that patrons might make. Alumnae leaders reveled in their achievements. The "ability to submerge individual interests in a higher common cause," they concluded, "is a great tribute to college training."[26]

In Virginia's recollection, the excitement of the seven-college campaign faded after about a decade. Several of the sister colleges—Wellesley, Smith, and Bryn Mawr—hesitated to share their donor lists with the common pool. Nor did the campaign reel in corporate donations or score with most of the big foundations, though it did win a Carnegie Foundation grant. But from 1926 to 1935 the seven-college group excelled at publicity. In a spectacular coup at the start of 1930, Paramount News ran a clip of a formal dinner held at New York's Astor Hotel and attended by the new chief justice, Charles Evans Hughes; New York State's first lady, Eleanor Roosevelt; and the seven college presidents. The conference met regularly after 1935 as well. Student recruitment drew its attention in the 1940s. In 1943 Virginia helped run a Seven College Conference College Scholarship competition for students from states in the Midwest, Southwest, and Far West that did not "normally send them" to the eastern women's colleges, followed by a publicity campaign. The colleges thus adopted a collective recruitment tactic to seek applicants from what admissions officers would later term "sparse country." The conference continued to support schemes to attract corporate funding, though it collected mainly rejection letters. Virginia headed the scholarship committee until she left for her stint at the UN charter meeting in 1945. By then, her attention had been drawn away from the seven-college collaboration to a new field of competition in foreign affairs.[27]

The start of the Seven Sisters remains among Virginia's major triumphs of the 1920s. The dean had found a way for the seven colleges to win favorable attention and for Barnard to claim a common identity with its competitors. Far from accepting a future as a commuter school that enrolled a big share of local public high school graduates, Barnard could now profit from the company of its more glamorous sister-rivals, with whom it would permanently share a thriving brand. That brand, in turn, had an enduring life of its own, first academically, as a source of highly successful graduates, who excelled in field after field, and also socially, as a counterpart to elite men's schools. The Seven Sisters connoted status, privilege, exclusivity, and entitlement.[28] As Virginia had always understood, publicity counts; moreover, a group gains sway both by whom it includes and whom it leaves out.

Both principles—of course—applied to college admissions.

ADMISSION AND EXCLUSION

In October 1922, Rebecca Grecht, a recent NYU graduate, *cum laude*, claimed in a letter to the editor of the *Nation* that anti-Semitism had deprived her of admission to Barnard. In June 1918, charged the writer, she had applied to the college from her New York City public high school, with a record of "high scholarship," an average grade of 92, excellent references, and a high rank on the list of winners of State Regents Scholarships. But in July, Barnard had turned her down, without apparent cause. When she visited the college for an interview, after her rejection, "I was assured that my rejection had not been due either to scholarship, character, or health," the rejected applicant reported. Just as telling, she claimed, "non-Jewish applicants had been admitted from the school [her high school], with records appreciably lower, as was well known." The only possible explanation for her exclusion was anti-Semitism: "What then could have been the cause but my race, my religion?" Despite her bad experience, which "left rankling a bitter antagonism," the writer made two more tries to enter Barnard, both futile ("Nothing prevailed, however").[29]

Two months after Rebecca Grecht's letter appeared, Virginia, in a letter of response to the editor of the *Nation*, defended Barnard's admissions policy. "As we explained at the time, the only reason we had for rejecting this applicant was that, in the judgment of our Committee on Admissions, she did not seem as promising a student as the others whom we admitted," the dean contended. To invoke the judgment of a committee, Virginia had learned, solved many problems. Sometimes the college made mistakes, she conceded, "but we have to do the best we can." Virginia then moved on to the heart of Barnard admissions policy. "We are particularly anxious to have Barnard a college where New York girls, of every class and creed, can meet girls from other parts of the country and other nations," she declared. Like other colleges, Barnard had "found that the mere ability to pass a certain set of examinations with high marks is not necessarily the most important evidence of scholarly promise and general future usefulness," Virginia wrote. "Personally I am deeply interested in the problem of getting Jew and Gentile to live together helpfully as useful fellow-citizens in our country." She was motivated, she claimed, by her "friendship and admiration" for the late Jacob Schiff (who had donated the funds to build Barnard Hall and for whom the building had *not* been named). Virginia concluded that "it frequently strikes me that the chief reward of labor in this field is blame and reproaches from both sides."[30]

The startling exchange of views in the *Nation* in 1922 reveals two versions of Barnard's "Jewish problem" of the 1920s—the stance of aggrieved applicants and the official Barnard version of the situation, as set forth by Virginia. The exchange also marks a shift in patterns of college admission. Until recently, the elite colleges admitted students on the basis of academic standards, though with a built-in class bias; few public schools prepared their graduates for all college entrance requirements. Still, admissions were meritocratic, after a fashion. When Nicholas Murray Butler sent two applicants to Virginia at the start of her deanship, in 1911–1912, his messages reflected both the role of social status and the need to keep up academic standards. In the case of a Livingston descendant and trustee's daughter, the prominence of an old New York family long connected to Columbia ensured admission. The applicant looked forward to entering Barnard, Butler noted to Virginia, and "I am sure you will be glad to assist her to that end." In the second case, that of a good friend's daughter, Butler was alert to the need to meet academic criteria. The applicant—a weak candidate, he feared—might show "infirmity of purpose or lack of ability," as well as "unwillingness to prepare." In such an instance, Butler assured Virginia, he would not force the issue.[31]

At that point, in 1911–1912, Butler and the new dean supported an admission system based on grades and tests. But during Virginia's first decade as dean, admission standards at Columbia and Barnard began to shift. Objective criteria comingled with subjective ones, such as character and personality; decisions on admissions rested not merely on academic requirements but also on personal interviews and letters of recommendations. As applications from Jewish students surged, colleges sought to preserve their status and identities. Administrators of elite schools feared being overrun by Jewish applicants, alienating their traditional or favored clienteles—white, Protestant, and privileged—and losing the most desirable potential students to rival institutions.[32]

Although Barnard admitted most of its applicants in the 1920s, it turned down disproportionate numbers of Jewish applicants, even those with impressive academic records, as the rejected applicant charged in 1922. This policy was underway before World War I but accelerated in the 1920s as pressure rose. Many factors shaped Barnard biased admissions policy. Higher numbers of applicants and rising competition played a role, as did demographic change. "A larger proportion of Jews go to college than of any other race in America," as the *Nation* observed in 1922. Antagonism to Jews dominated higher education generally. "I have seen college administrators exchanging in whispered conferences their ideas as to the best method of 'controlling' the Jewish invasion," as a professor declared (under a pen name) in a *Harper's Monthly* article. "The deans went into an anxious huddle. Keep down the Jewish percentages, but do not *seem* to be doing so was the order." Columbia policy, which followed the "do-not-*seem*" principle, affected several institutions; since 1909, admissions director Adam Leroy Jones had guided admissions in all undergraduate divisions. Admissions restriction was not as effective at Barnard as at other elite women's schools; at the same time, Barnard faced a far greater demand for admission from Jewish applicants than did the rival women's schools. Still, Barnard's critics had a point. Virginia in the 1920s acted to reject disfavored Jewish applicants and to preserve the power of an entitled class. Throughout the decade, she strove to strengthen "college life" and to make Barnard more like its rivals, the socially elite and prestigious "country schools."[33]

Following the lead of President Butler and admissions committee chairman Adam Leroy Jones, Virginia never referred to a quota or made public remarks that were overtly discriminatory. Her public statements followed an easily discernible code; each of her dean's reports that discussed admissions mentioned slightly different but equally vague criteria on which candidates might be judged, such as "attitudes." The goal for Jewish admissions, established by the university-wide committee on undergraduate admissions, and therefore the same for Barnard and Columbia, went unstated. In practice, Jewish admissions hovered around 15–20 percent. Each college reached its destination independently. Through the 1920s, as before, while working on the undergraduate admissions committee, Virginia kept track of Columbia's progress.[34]

Herbert Hawkes, who succeeded Frederick Keppel as Columbia College dean in 1918, proved an effective gatekeeper. "I believe we ought to carry at least 15 percent of Jews and I do not think 20 percent is excessive for Columbia College," Dean Hawkes told a correspondent, an MIT professor with inquiries about admission procedures, in 1922. Still, the gatekeeping policy under Hawkes proved more restrictive than that of his predecessor. "What we have been trying to do is to eliminate the low-grade boy," Hawkes declared to his correspondent, in one of the more forthright if still baffling statements on Columbia admissions in the 1920s. "It turns out that a good many of the low-grade men are New York City Jews. It is a fact that boys of foreign parentage who have no background in many cases attempt to educate themselves beyond their intelligence. Their accomplishment is over 100 percent of their ability on account of their tremendous energy and ambition. I do not believe however that a College would do well to admit too many men of low mentality who have ambition but not brains. At any rate this is the principle on which we are going."[35]

Columbia tried various ploys to limit Jewish admissions. President Butler endorsed an idea that had simmered in Columbia circles since World War I: to set up a university outpost in Brooklyn, a Columbia-run institution with some collegiate cachet, that might attract ambitious high school graduates and deter them from applying to Morningside Heights. In the fall of 1928 Seth Low Junior College, a two-year liberal arts institution, funded by and affiliated with Columbia, opened in a part of Brooklyn Law School's premises on Pearl Street. Intended to prepare students to apply to medical school and law school, or so Columbia claimed, Seth Low enrolled some four hundred in 1928–1929. Junior faculty trekked to Brooklyn to teach the classes. The two-year college closed in 1936; by then half of those enrolled, disillusioned, had withdrawn. The real goal of Seth Low, as its disappointed students grasped: to absorb applicants unwelcome at Columbia College, those of "foreign parentage," and to preclude their arrival "uptown." A misconceived fiasco, Seth Low Junior College sank from sight. Barnard never tried anything as bizarre.[36]

Beyond watching Columbia, Virginia monitored the other elite women's colleges. These rivals faced less of a challenge than Barnard; they kept Jewish admissions low without apparent difficulty. Before World War II, Wellesley held to a Jewish limit of about 10 percent. In 1946 Wellesley denied any "absolute quota of Jewish students" but referred to "a conscious effort on the part of the Board of Admissions to keep the percentages of Jewish students small enough so that segregation and prejudice will be at a minimum within the college." Virginia had made a similar argument at Barnard as early in 1921. By administrators' Swiftian logic, curbs on Jewish admissions would limit bias on campus. After World War II, a change in Massachusetts law, opposed by Wellesley's president, made enforcement of ethnic limits more challenging, though not impossible; in the 1950s, the proportion of Jewish students rose to 15–20 percent. In the late 1930s, however, at some of the women's colleges (Mount Holyoke, Wellesley, Vassar, Smith) the percentage of Jewish students enrolled still hovered around 10 percent, a figure to which Barnard may have aspired but could not quite achieve.[37]

Barnard's restrictive policy was well underway before 1920, as Virginia's dean's reports suggest. She clearly set forth in her reports the gist of the new system of Barnard admissions and the tactics to be employed. In the 1920s, Barnard reached out to its desired clientele. The college developed contacts with private schools, whose seniors might be funneled into the application process. It favored the College Board Entrance Examination (which charged a fee) over New York State

Regents Examinations (which were free); made dormitory space available to out-of-town entrants; and asked for detailed family information on application forms, such as where each parent were born and attended school, and what the father's occupation was. The form also requested a photo of the candidate. To these tactics, Barnard added the new psychological test, the Thorndike Test for Mental Alertness, devised by E. L. Thorndike at Teachers College. Introduced in 1918 at Columbia, the test purported to measure capacity to learn. It supplemented tests already in use—the New York State Regents and College Boards—and would, colleges hoped, foil overachievers by identifying character defects. By 1927, Virginia reported to Barnard alumnae, academic standards had risen ("Better work is demanded"). But, as she reiterated often, the college did not rely on academic prowess alone. It also considered, as the dean's reports stated, *other* standards: "general character and powers"; "future ability and usefulness"; and "character," "personality," and "all-around promise," attributes that were hard to describe with precision but that admissions officers could ostensibly discern and assess.[38]

Virginia relied on Barnard professor Adam Leroy Jones, who had assumed his post as director of admissions for Columbia in 1909 and proved a valued colleague in the Barnard admissions office until his death in 1934. Loyal to the college, where he taught American philosophy, he was married to a Barnard graduate, Lily Murray '05, member of Kappa Kappa Gamma and officer of the Barnard alumnae association. Jones was adept in the lingo of admissions, as suggested in an article of 1913 on admission methods, published in Nicholas Murray Butler's scholarly journal *Educational Review*. Jones recommended that colleges rely on a detailed school record and on an entrance examination, graded by committee, "as a means of testing for 'power' more than information" and "to test capacity and not merely memory." "What we all want is a body of students prepared for what the university can give," Jones stated.[39]

Adam Leroy Jones and Virginia formed a two-person committee on admissions; occasionally other faculty members joined their meetings. An efficient duo, Jones and the dean chose the next class in the spring and issued a major report on admissions in September, close to the start of the fall semester. In addition, from time to time during the academic year, they announced small groups of additional admitted candidates, freshman and transfer. Jones and the dean relied on the use of conditional admissions, which they applied as a form of triage. Their tactic: to separate candidates for admission into three categories: "Admitted," "Admitted With Conditions," and "Rejected." By admitting a large group of non-Jewish applicants in the "Admitted With Conditions" category and placing a large number of Jewish applicants on the "Rejected" list, the two admission officers could shape the class and limit its Jewish members.[40]

The class of 1926 provides an example. In September 1922, when the Office of Admissions announced members of the class, the college accepted 77 percent of applicants. Competition, in short, was muted. Jones and Virginia listed the names of sixty-two "Admitted" applicants. Another sixty-two applicants were "Admitted With Conditions," and so was a second batch of twenty-five "Candidates with Irregularities in their Records," who received credit for various courses they had failed to take or pass, mainly French, Latin, and Math, or were granted extensions to complete the work. The "Rejected" list was forty-three. Thus, the Office of Admissions filled much of the class of 1926 with conditional admits who met whatever standards the college sought to impose on them. Subsequent classes of the 1920s differed in number and the size of the components varied, but conditional admissions played a role in all. In 1925, for the class of 1929, for instance seventy were "Admitted Without Conditions"; twenty-seven "Admitted with Conditions," and forty-four "Rejected". "I don't think that Barnard accepted any considerable number of Jewish girls from New York," recalled future economist Mary Dublin (Keyserling) '30, daughter of Russian immigrants. "Most of my friends were from around the country." Yet the proportion of commuters at Barnard remained high.[41]

Did at least some applicants with roots in Eastern Europe, like Mary Dublin, get by the gauntlet of admissions officers? Of course. Many leading academics of the future, in particular, attended Barnard in the 1920s. Sociologist Mirra Komarovsky '26, later a Barnard professor, had only recently arrived with her family from Baku, in the Caucasus; political scientist Pearl Bernstein (Max) '25, from nearby Harlem, another prize-winner, served at CUNY and on New York City's Board of Estimate. But Barnard's bias under Virginia and Jones remained notable. Two investigators of 1931 found the percentage of Jewish students at Barnard slightly lower than that at Columbia.[42]

Barnard alumnae, who wrestled (gingerly) with admission questions, voiced steady support for Virginia's mode of restriction. The alumnae invented their own subtle form of code. "Should any new methods of selection be adopted in sifting out the applicants?" asked an article in the *Barnard Alumnae Bulletin* of December 1923. Should the college expand? What proportion of students should spend their college years "in residence"? Alumnae responses to such questions stressed the importance of "college life." "The girl who misses it misses the best of college," as an article of May 1924 declared. Overly intellectual applicants, in the alumnae view, threatened "the best of college." To alumnae, preservation of "college life" was tied to the to the type of students that Barnard admitted—to the "delicate matter of the bases for admission and rejection." On what grounds, alumnae asked, should the college discriminate? "Without restriction, there will be an ever increasing number of students who come to choose what they want of the intellectual bill of fare, who are interested not at all in college life and but little in the making of friendly ties." Such a development would make Barnard a "famous center of learning" and "provide a brilliant scholarly atmosphere," the alumnae concluded. But, "It would not be the Barnard that we knew and loved."[43]

Virginia clung to the admissions tactics of the 1920s into the next decade. Even when enrollment declined in the 1930s, Barnard sought to keep the number of Jewish entrants low. The class that entered in 1935, writes historian Robert McCaughey, resembled that of the 1920s. Virginia remained circumspect in her explanations for college policies. "Barnard has not been able for some years to accept all the good students who apply from New York City," she explained to a fellow educator, the founder of a Westchester private school. In her dean's reports, where she discussed Barnard's method of "selective admissions," Virginia reiterated that Barnard criteria for admission involved not merely grades but intangible qualities that only the college could discern or assess. Its modern methods of "selective admissions," she declared, "lay great stress on teachers' estimates of the candidates and on each candidate's interests, abilities, and attitudes." Continual reference to the intangible, un-measurable, and impressionistic justified whatever decisions the admissions office made.[44]

Virginia was less guarded in her correspondence with Annie Nathan Meyer, to whom she confided her bias against East European immigrants. "The immense influx during the years before the war of a particularly crude and uneducated variety of Jew from Russia gave rise, as you know better than I, to the strangest misconceptions of the nature of all Hebrews," Virginia wrote to Meyer in the early 1930s. "Many of our Jewish students have been charming and cultivated human beings," Virginia posited. "On the other hand, as you know, the intense ambition of the Jews for education has brought to college girls from a lower social level than that of most of the non-Jewish students." Such applicants through the 1920s, typically graduates of New York City public high schools, filled the pages of the Barnard Admissions Office's "Rejected" lists.[45]

Virginia's confidence that Annie Nathan Meyer (another multi-generation American) grasped her opinion on the "Jewish problem" was not misplaced. Meyer shared a suspicion of recent newcomers from Eastern Europe, a suspicion common in the long-established Jewish communities, German and Sephardic, which found the presence of the new arrivals threatening. Indeed, in her earlier correspondence with the very sympathetic former dean, Emily James Smith, Annie Nathan Meyer discussed tensions that arose *between* Sephardic and German Jews, who, she noted, "mix as easily as oil & water." Annie Nathan Meyer's vision for Barnard's ideal clientele resembled Virginia's. Meyer wanted Barnard to admit "the desirable type of Jewess," as she wrote to Virginia in 1921. She favored Jews who represented "excellence of conduct" and objected to "the hordes of Jews who are without manners or business or professional standards" and those "whose behavior exacerbated prejudice." Like Virginia, who opposed Zionism, Meyer opposed support for a Jewish state; such a state, she believed, would weaken the position of American Jews. But Annie Nathan Meyer's stance differed from Virginia's, too. Meyer had long acted to assist members of the Jewish community who appealed to her for help with entry into schools and colleges, as far back as the1890s. As the years passed, her essential generosity and liberal streak found new forms of expression. Meyer wanted the "educated person" to "refuse to lump [together] any people or group," as she wrote to Virginia, and to treat each person as an individual. She also wanted the public to integrate Jews into the mainstream of American educational and cultural affairs. Meyer came politically to life in the 1930s in ways that might have distanced Virginia when she confronted Madison Grant, advocate of "scientific racism," in a series of public letters and denounced pro-Nazi theories.[46]

Virginia defended her stance on admissions in the 1920s and 1930s in response to a critique from her former professor in graduate school, William Allan Neilson, who had recently retired from his long stint as president of Smith College (1917–1939). Neilson had played a part in Virginia's life in many salient instances; in the 1920s, he had worked with her at the Seven College Conference. Fifteen years later, in 1941, Neilson wrote a report for Barnard trustees to assess college procedures, including admissions. Two-thirds of recent Barnard applicants came from New York City, Neilson stated, and the proportion of Jews in that group far exceeded that in the population at large. Neither the college nor the "racial" group in question, he argued, "wishes to see Barnard become a predominantly Jewish college." (Here, Neilson treated Jews as a "racial" group, an anachronism that Virginia used, too, and that in World War II went out of use). But the Barnard admissions office, Neilson charged, "limits arbitrarily the number of any one group admitted." Barnard, he stated, accepted students with relatively weak records and rejected those with superior credentials. William Allan Neilson urged "more liberal and flexible" quotas. Virginia responded that Barnard did not have any quotas—in the sense of any "precise and rigid figure"— and that in any case quotas were impossible, as it was impossible, she claimed, to determine who among applicants was Jewish.[47]

Neither facet of Virginia's defense, though each in part true, was quite on the level. Neilson's accusation was more accurate than not. Over two decades of anti-Semitism in college admissions, barely concealed, much resented, and often criticized, undercut Virginia's record as an innovative administrator and proponent of women's modern roles. Virginia's "modernism," as historian Lynn D. Gordon points out, "was thus flawed by her failure to appreciate cultural diversity."[48] Of course, "diversity" holds many meanings. Virginia would claim diversity as her goal: She sought a student body that represented not just New York City but the nation, if not the world. "We wish to give the New Yorkers a chance to meet girls from all the other states in the Union, and from foreign countries as well," as the dean explained to alumnae in the 1930s. "This is an immense educational advantage."[49] Virginia's admissions policy, though saddled with bias, bears the hallmarks that distinguish contemporary admissions policy—the search for a "cosmopolitan" student body and for geographical distribution so that students from diverse regions would be represented. Virginia's pursuit of out-of-staters paved the way for the more recent type of search waged by admissions officers for students from varied locales. An avid participant in the admission process, Virginia was at once blatantly discriminatory and in advance of her time.

Annie Nathan Meyer, oddly, though laden with old fashioned if not retrograde tenets, such as her anti-suffrage stance, was in her own way also ahead of her time. By the 1920s, as an arts patron and philanthropist, Meyer had become a supporter of campaigns for African Americans. She worked with the National Association for the Advancement of Colored People (NAACP), founded 1909; donated books on Black history and literature to Hunter College, which was building a collection; and in the 1920s began to write a play opposing race prejudice, "Black Souls." The play's plot concerned "the visit of a distinguished Northerner to a school in the Black Belt something like Tuskegee," as Meyer described it in 1932 to W. E. B. Dubois, whom she had just met at the funeral of reformer Florence Kelley. The remarkable drama, endorsed by Meyer's friends from the NAACP and praised by author James Weldon Johnson ("one of the most powerful and penetrating plays yet written on the race question ") opened at the Provincetown Playhouse on March 30, 1932, in a performance that Annie subsidized.[50]

Annie Nathan Meyer also sought a role as patron in the Harlem Renaissance, a cultural event that took place at Barnard's doorstep and one that Virginia ignored. In her earnest and determined way, Meyer integrated Barnard by race. In 1925 she arranged for the admission of Zora Neale Hurston (1891–1960), the college's first Black student, and coerced Virginia into tacit acquiescence. Though occasionally a naysayer, Virginia stood back at a distance and did not interrupt Annie Nathan Meyer's plan. Neither trustee nor dean could have expected Hurston's exceptional gifts. If Virginia was the consummate insider at Barnard, Zora Neale Hurston was her counterfoil, the ultimate outsider. Irreverent and unintimidated, Hurston excelled at defying boundaries, disrupting categories, and transcending difference, whether of race, class, or gender. Reveling in her singularity and embracing novelty, she invented a new collegiate self.

"I suppose you want to know how this little piece of darkish meat feels at Barnard," Zora Neale Hurston wrote to her friend Constance Sheen at the start of 1926. "I am received quite well. In fact I am received so well that if someone would come along and try to turn me white, I'd be quite peevish at them." A recent arrival in Harlem, Hurston had won second place in a writing contest run by *Opportunity* magazine. Encouraged by the magazine's founder, Charles S. Johnson, Hurston traveled to New York to attend the award dinner in May, 1925. There she mingled with luminaries of the Harlem Renaissance, including first-place prize winner Langston Hughes, who became a friend, and Alain Locke, who had been her teacher at Howard University in Washington, D.C. She also met some future white patrons—Carl Van Vechten, impresario of the literary revival; author Fannie Hurst, who would be pivotal in her career; and Annie Nathan Meyer, arts advocate, philanthropist, and Barnard trustee, who arranged for Zora Neale Hurston to enter Barnard and sought funding for her expenses. "I am striving desperately for a toe-hold," Hurston wrote to Meyer in May 1925. "You see, your interest in me keys me up wonderfully, I must not let you be disappointed in me."[51]

Zora Neale Hurston had grown up mainly in Eatonville, Florida, an all-Black community, to which she would return often in print. She attended high school in part at Morgan College, the secondary school branch of Morgan State University, a Black institution in Baltimore, in 1917–1918, and then entered Howard. In 1920 she received an associate degree from Howard and five years later, after varied work experiences (including manicurist, waitress, and housemaid), won the *Opportunity* contest. When Annie Nathan Meyer requested Barnard admission for Hurston, Virginia obliged though, characteristically, with reluctance. "Ordinarily we would not admit a transfer with this record," Virginia wrote to Annie Nathan Meyer in June 1925. But Zora Neale Hurston's status as a literary prizewinner carried weight. "10 terms at Howard University—probably 2 years to go," wrote Barnard's Committee on Transfers as Hurston entered. At the time she became a Barnard student, Hurston, born in 1891, was about thirty-four, though she claimed to be twenty-six. On the Barnard "Record of Freshman Interest" form, where she listed a birthdate of 1899, she presented her career goals.

"I have had some small success as [a] writer and wish above all to succeed at it," Hurston wrote. "Either teaching or social work will be interesting but consolation prizes."[52]

While Annie Nathan Meyer sought donors who would cover Hurston's tuition, Virginia interviewed the new student. The dean quibbled again about Hurston's qualifications and, as she would continue to do, qualified whatever favorable comments she made. Though she found Zora Neale Hurston an "interesting person" and "distinctly promising," Virginia told Annie Nathan Meyer in October 1925 she felt that Hurston's less-than-stellar record at Howard did not support a scholarship. She advised Meyer to seek funding "from some outside person interested in the Negro race." To Virginia, simply admitting Hurston was enough of a concession to Annie's whims. Barnard admission, in the case of its first Black student, did not include access to residence in a college dormitory; Zora Neale Hurston lived in a rented room in on West 139th Street in Harlem.[53]

Within weeks, Meyer found the new student some financial support. In mid-October, as Hurston ran out of funds, Annie wrote to novelist Fannie Hurst, who had attended the *Opportunity* awards dinner back in May. Hurst invited Zora Neale Hurston to move into her apartment on West Sixty-Seventh Street and to do secretarial work in exchange. Zora Neale Hurston's stay with Fannie Hurst and her labor as a personal assistant—running errands, answering the phone, and reading copy— lasted only about a month. But Fannie Hurst's patronage continued; she saw Hurston as "awash in splendor." Once Hurst's support became known, Hurston found that the attention of her classmates rose. The famous author's friendship "made both faculty and students *see* me when I needed seeing," Zora Neale Hurston wrote to Hurst. Pursued by the student government president and "the social register crowd," Hurston became, in her memoir, "Barnard's sacred black cow." Hurst's patronage brought another benefit, too, as Zora Neale Hurston's biographer Valerie Boyd points out: The dean's interest rose. Virginia now told Annie Nathan Meyer of a student loan fund available to Hurston and raised the possibility of a scholarship, which she had previously dismissed. Thus, Hurston used her important connections to advance her standing at Barnard. Virginia, meanwhile, doled out mini-rewards only as other authorities weighed in.[54]

Virginia's response to Zora Neale Hurston was almost always distant—she used Annie Nathan Meyer as an intermediary—and uneven. Virginia would take one step in Hurston's favor and then find something to criticize. In February 1926, after Hurston had received some financial aid, Virginia voiced doubts that Hurston belonged at Barnard at all. Hurston had missed a recent history exam and had trouble completing the registration process for spring semester. "I wonder whether we really ought to encourage her to remain in college," Virginia wrote to Annie Nathan Meyer. "Does she get enough out of it to compensate for the difficulty and annoyance of trying to fit into the administrative machine? We have given her a grant from the scholarship fund but I feel a little uncertain about her."[55]

Zora Neale Hurston felt otherwise. "Just finished the History exam and feel quite all right about it," Hurston wrote to Annie on February 22, 1926. Living once again in a Harlem room, as the new semester began, Hurston was totally engaged, with both college life and with Harlem life—with her Barnard friends; with her patrons, white and Black; with short fiction and plays; with her part-time jobs, to meet expenses; and with social events in Harlem. Her play "Color Struck" was scheduled to be produced, and her prize-winning story "Spunk" would be published in Alain Locke's book, *The New Negro*, published in December, 1925, a classic collection that defines the Harlem Renaissance. She wrote for small journals, joined circles of writers and artists, mixed with celebrities, starred at parties, and seized center stage at every gathering. Zora Neale Hurston was an "original," said artist Arna Bontemps. "In any group she was the center of attention." To her friend Constance Sheen, in a letter of February 1926, Hurston wrote that she was "just running wild in every direction, trying to see everything at once." Hurston fell into feuds as easily as she created friendships. She eventually fought with her friend Langston Hughes, attacked Alain Locke as "intellectually dishonest," and took issue with W. E. B. Dubois, with whom she dealt in the 1920s on the production of her plays and whom she later labeled "Dr. Dubious."[56]

By the spring of 1926, Hurston, still an English major, had became totally absorbed in the field of anthropology and part of the circle around Professor Franz Boas, who, with his protégés, such as Ruth Benedict, Melville Herskovits, and Gladys Reichard, staffed Barnard courses. Boas, father of cultural anthropology in the United States (a label popularized by his students) had begun his affiliation with Columbia in 1896; three years later, President Seth Low appointed him professor and chair of the anthropology program. Boas split his time between Columbia and Barnard, and preferred the Barnard students. Virginia, who valued the teaching that Boas did at Barnard, may have welcomed him initially as a relative of her favored friend, Marjorie Putnam Jacobi, through Marjorie's father, Dr. Abraham Jacobi, who had fostered Boas's career in Germany and then the United States. Virginia never lost her admiration for "our brilliant genius, Franz Boas."[57]

Convictions about white superiority prevailed in the Progressive Era, but Boas dissented. He taught his students "to consider diversity without hierarchy," writes scholar Charles King. He explored the science of race to debunk its claims, such as the inferiority of immigrants. In 1917, Boas published a critical review of Madison Grant's *Passing of the Great Race* in *The New Republic*, and later, in the 1920s, stood against "scientific racism" and restrictive immigration laws. When Boas opposed World War I, Butler cut his salary and research budget but Virginia provided an academic home at Barnard, which self-identified as a pioneer in social science instruction. Margaret Mead, Barnard '22, an admiring undergraduate and later a Boas graduate student, found Boas "a surprising and somewhat frightening teacher." His lectures were "polished and clear," she recalled; his face marred by "a long dueling scar from his student days in Germany. . . . But seen from the other side, his face showed him as handsome as he had been as a young man."[58]

In the mid-1920s, when Zora Neale Hurston arrived at Barnard, Boas disciple Gladys Reichard led the Barnard introductory courses in anthropology. Joining the admirers of "Papa Franz," Hurston became a disciple, as well. "I began to treasure up the work of Dr. Reichard, Dr. Benedict, and Dr. Boas," she recalled in *Dust Tracks on a Road*, her memoir of 1942. "We all called him Papa, too." Never losing the zeal for writing that had propelled her into a literary career, Hurston added social science scholarship to her repertoire. Her first class was with Melville Herskovits, Boas disciple. "I am being trained for anthropometry," she wrote to Annie Nathan Meyer. Her class project: to stop pedestrians on a Harlem street and to measure their skulls with calipers. Hurston voiced reluctance to focus on race in her research, at least in retrospect. "Negroes were supposed to write about the Race Problem," she wrote in *Dust Tracks*. "I was and am thoroughly sick of the subject." But race became the focus of her work, nonetheless. When she was still an undergraduate, in 1927, Boas sent her on a field expedition to Florida and arranged for a fellowship to cover her costs. Her assignment: to explore stories—folk tales, tall tales, jokes. Returning to Eatonville, Hurston applied what she had learned in her anthropology courses. She remained ensconced in her Florida research and within the circle of "Papa Franz" for the rest of her time at Barnard and Columbia.[59]

After graduation in 1928, Zora Neale Hurston pursued her research in anthropology with many stops and starts. She interspersed her Florida forays with stints at running a catering business, producing musical reviews, and starting a novel for Lippincott, *Jonah's Gourd Vine* (1934). This was "the novel that I have wanted to write since 1928," Hurston told Charlotte Osgood Mason, the patron whom she called "Godmother." The story, about a Black minister, takes place in an all-Black town like Eatonville and reflects Hurston's field work in anthropology. In January 1935, Hurston enrolled as a doctoral candidate at Columbia, supported by the Julius Rosenwald Fund. A patron of the National Urban League and other causes, Rosenwald provided Hurston with a grant to pursue studies with Boas on "special cultural gifts of the Negroes." In fall 1935, Lippincott published her study of Black folklore in Eatonville, Florida, *Mules and Men*. Hurston thus used her Eatonville roots to generate both fiction and scholarship.[60]

Lippincott began to promote *Jonah's Gourd Vine* by making a list of influential readers to whom advance copies would be sent. All were white; "no Negro names were on There," Hurston complained to James Weldon Johnson. As Hurston recruited support among her patrons, white and black, Virginia—included on the list of white opinion-makers who received copies of the book—responded to Lippincott's advance copy with passive aggression. The dean sent the publisher a less-than-enthused review. She had been interested in Hurston "for a number of years," Virginia began, "and delighted that she has been able to publish this novel." She then launched into an unsolicited critique of the book. "I confess that I do not think as highly of it as do some of the critics," Virginia wrote." The novel was "interesting and convincing as a picture of Negro life but I found a good deal of it rather hard reading—largely because of the dialect—and I do not feel that it quite succeeds in its more tragic moments."[61]

Virginia's critique—a swipe that Hurston was unlikely to have seen—did not deter Lippincott from publishing Hurston's next book, *Mules and Men* (1935), also based on her Florida research. The center of Hurston's legacy in scholarship, the book was a study of Black folklore in Eatonville, examined through "the spyglass of anthropology," with a preface by Franz Boas and dedicated to Anne Nathan Meyer. The book met mixed reviews. Hurston's rendition of folk culture, some critics said, bypassed the oppression that shaped southern Black life. "*Mules and Men* should be more bitter," one reviewer wrote, "it would be nearer the total truth." As the book achieved notice, Hurston kept Rosenwald Fund officials informed about social events in her honor. On Sunday, February 10, 1935, she wrote, "Mrs. Annie Nathan Meyer, 1225 Park Avenue, is giving a tea for me. Pearl Buck, Fannie Hurst, Robert Nathan, the British Ambassador, and 35 other notables are coming, I am told," Hurston wrote. "Really, I am cold all over." The next day, she reported "the Literary World is taking due notice of me. . . . The Annual Writer's Tea at Barnard College has me for the guest of honor."[62]

After these events of the mid-1930s, Hurston's contact with Barnard—and her intense correspondence with Annie Nathan Meyer—faded; a final letter to Meyer went off in 1941. Did Hurston cultivate Meyer's indulgence—and that of other patrons—only to advance her career? No doubt she did. But as biographer Valerie Boyd explains, Hurston had a sophisticated understanding of patronage and relationships. Nor had she ever dissembled about her motives. She had entered Barnard solely for professional goals, as she had declared to Annie in 1925: "The time I spend at Barnard will enhance my reputation considerably and boost my earning power."[63]

Zora Neale Hurston's interlude at Barnard marked a change in Barnard admission policy. In 1926, wrote W. E. B. Dubois in the *Nation*, Vassar had graduated one Black and "did not know it at the time." Bryn Mawr and Barnard "have tried desperately to exclude them." The elite women's colleges of New England behaved differently. "Radcliffe, Wellesley, and Smith have greeted them with tolerance and even cordiality." By the 1930s, Barnard had improved its record, if only slightly.[64]

Several, though few, Black students followed Hurston in the 1930s and 1940s. Belle Tobias and Vera Joseph entered in 1928, the year that Hurston graduated. Belle Tobias, who graduated Phi Beta Kappa in 1931 and earned an M.A. in botany at Wellesley, was the daughter of the prominent civil rights leader Channing Tobias, officer of the Black branch of the National Council of the YMCA, the first African American to serve as director of the Phelps Stokes Fund, and a member of the NAACP National Board. A friend of Eleanor Roosevelt, Channing Tobias also spent time with Virginia on an international affairs committee of the late 1940s, where she ignored his presence. Vera Joseph, from George Washington High School in Harlem, where Black businessmen and educators provided funds for her college costs, also graduated Phi Beta Kappa in 1931 and then attended Columbia's College of Physicians and Surgeons. It was only after the New York Barnard Club failed to invite her join, she told historian Caroline Niemczyk in an interview, "that I recognized I was being discriminated against and resented it." Black women graduated again in 1932 and 1935. New England's elite women's colleges, meanwhile, in contrast, steadily admitted several Black students a year.[65]

In 1943, Harlem minister James Robinson accused Barnard and Vassar of racial quotas in a speech at an interfaith conference at Columbia's Teachers College. Virginia, in response, denied that Barnard had racial quotas in admissions. "We always have some Negro students at Barnard," she said. "This year our most valuable graduate fellowship is held by a Negro." To assuage Robinson, Virginia offered privately to take in a deserving student, tuition-free; his choice, economics major Charlotte Hanley '47, later became a trustee. Publicity about Robinson's speech also spurred Barnard to make efforts to attract Black students. By the time Virginia retired in 1947, Charlotte Hanley recalled, "the number of Negro students attending Barnard . . . had risen to eight—the largest number in her history." Through the mid-century, however, Barnard barred Black students from living on campus in college dormitories.[66]

One tool that Barnard used to keep Black enrollment minimal: entrance requirements. Few African American students attended secondary schools that provided the academic courses to meet Barnard's entry prerequisites. Future lawyer and civil rights pioneer Pauli Murray explored Barnard admission in 1926, when, as a young high school graduate, she moved to New York to be part of the Harlem Renaissance. Murray first sought admission to Columbia College, which, she found, did not accept women; many barriers, she discovered, precluded Barnard as well. The cost was too high—$300 for tuition plus more for living expenses. Moreover, the stringent academic requirements excluded graduates from schools in the Jim Crow South, including Murray's high school in Durham, North Carolina, where she had graduated first in her class; excelled in athletics and at debating; and served as editor in chief of the student newspaper, as a class officer, and as president of the literary society. But the school had not offered all the courses needed for Barnard admission. Pauli Murray had to return to high school in New York for two and a half years to meet similar academic requirements at Hunter. For many potential Black applicants, therefore, Barnard remained beyond grasp. Those who met the requirements probably found more welcoming elite schools to attend.[67]

Barnard Administrator Jean T. Palmer, Barnard General Secretary and former director of admissions, commented on Black admissions in 1954, the year of the *Brown v. Board of Education* decision that integrated public schools. Palmer, in the tradition established by Virginia, first denied that Barnard had any racial quotas; the college's application form did not list race. New York state law by now precluded such a question; photographs, however, were required. Barnard received only about three Black applicants a year, Palmer stated. Most of these applicants needed scholarships and their secondary school records did not warrant academic scholarships. One likely reason for this judgment: the secondary schools attended by Black applicants, like Pauli Murray's high school in 1926, did not offer the full load of academic courses that Barnard required for entrance. Thus, the few Blacks who applied in the 1930s and 1940s, as Palmer explained, often ran into problems. A history of Barnard commissioned by the college and published in 1954, to which Virginia contributed her additions and corrections, had no reason to mention either Black admissions or Black attendance. Nor did it mention Zora Neale Hurston, in whom revival of interest awaited author Alice Walker's rediscovery in the 1970s.[68]

While her role as gatekeeper consumed part of Virginia's effort in the 1920s, she managed to spend even more time and energy on gate-crashing—that is, on breaking down barriers for herself in the field of international affairs. Her tactics: resume-building, ambitious committee work, and relentless conference-going.

INTERNATIONALISM

World affairs began to attract Virginia's time after World War I. Newly absorbed by the Middle East, she joined the circles that supported Arab peoples. This effort involved visits to Charles R. Crane's Institute of Current World Affairs, from 1925 on. Virginia was "a vital influence in this organization," Crane's son recalled, because his father "consulted her constantly." In the mid-1920s Virginia joined the board of trustees of the American School for Girls in Istanbul and that of the Near East College Association, with her friends George A. Plimpton and Henry Sloane Coffin; she also served in Near East Relief (1915–1930), which provided food distribution, schools, and humanitarian aid to refugees of the Ottoman Empire (Armenians, Greeks, and Syrians). Developing networks in the world of support for the Middle East, the dean began methodically to shape a second career in foreign affairs.[69]

Virginia's first effort to build up a record in diplomacy in the 1920s centered on her crucial chairmanship of the new International Relations Committee of the Association of Collegiate Alumnae, a post she took on in 1918 and held through the decade. Month after month, she dominated every International Relations Committee meeting, often held at Barnard and after 1925 in the dining room of the Deanery. The committee's efforts at mid-decade included the following: to raise funds for fellowships; to send speakers on international topics to AAUW (American Association of University Women) branches; to reappoint committee officers; and to welcome Theodora Bosanquet, London-based executive secretary of the IFUW from 1920–1935 (known as critic, literary editor of *Time and Tide*, and secretary to author Henry James), who arrived for a visit to the United States. Committee members also appointed subcommittees for various purposes, such as in October 1924: to manage Latin American and Asian ("Oriental") scholarships; to select a woman delegate to the next Pan-American conference; to coordinate activities with IFUW centers abroad, Crosby Hall in London, and the "Paris Club House" (soon called Reid Hall); to forge links with the League of Nations International Committee on Intellectual Cooperation; and finally, to raise funds to continue its own activities.[70]

Virginia's International Relations Committee was never at a loss to generate activities for itself, but this achievement, as Virginia saw it, was the very purpose of the committee. The group's main function was to create tasks for its members, to enable them to collaborate with one another, and to continually reinvent new obligations and assignments, all of which served, in Virginia's words, to "extend and develop international work." The *process* of committee business, in short, *was* the purpose. Adept at motivating committee members and at prodding meetings forward, Virginia excelled at imposing conclusions on even the most rambling or perfunctory of discussions. The committee, in turn, gave Virginia a base from which to promote her policy objectives. She also seized a pivotal position as a link between U.S. academic women and the International Federation of University Women, where she created yet another leadership role.[71]

The founding meeting of the IFUW in London in 1920 had initiated an era of growth. In 1921, the American branch, the ACA, changed its name to the American Association of University Women, to fit in more closely with its admired British counterpart—in Virginia's words, "to conform to British and world practice." Moreover, as she noted in her memoir, "We had found to our surprise that outside the United States, no one knew what a 'collegiate alumna' was." By 1922, the number of member organizations in IFUW had leapt from eight to twenty-two. By 1930, the thirty member organizations, mainly but not exclusively European, involved 24,000 women affiliated with colleges or universities. Not least, the IFUW held summer conventions in various European cities—Paris in 1922; Oslo (then called Christiana) in 1924; Amsterdam in 1926; and Geneva in 1929. Virginia found the frequent conventions "a kind of power house of energy." These, plus annual meetings of the IFUW Council, a small group of leaders, gave the dean a reason to cross the Atlantic as soon as the spring semester ended. "Gildersleeve Goes Abroad," as the *New York Times* reported in June of 1924, invariably on the Cunard Line, in that instance on the *Aquitania*. The same year, Virginia won the IFUW presidency to replace Caroline Spurgeon, who had served two terms. Virginia's success elated her constituents at Barnard. "The whole world now looks to our Dean for leadership," the *Barnard Alumnae Bulletin* announced.[72]

When Virginia spoke at the second IFUW conference of September 1922 in Paris, she discussed two years of IFUW achievement—the founding of clubhouses, the exchanges of professors and students, the start of fellowships and traveling funds, and the role of friendship in international affairs. But rumblings arose of what she called "knottier" issues. From that conference onward, IFUW officials became embroiled with German academic women who avidly sought membership in the new international group. As the German women had not yet organized a national federation, a prerequisite for membership, IFUW officers found reason to stave them off; the recently ended world war had left women of the Allied nations, who had founded and dominated the IFUW, with a legacy of distaste for all things German. In 1922, Caroline Spurgeon, then president, voiced the IFUW suspicion of the German applicants: "None of us would wish to have them unless their presence was likely to contribute to international good feeling rather than the reverse."[73]

Virginia held a more conciliatory stance toward the academic women of defeated Germany, or at least held great hope for pacifying German women. In her view, the major IFUW goal, to promote international peace, started with cordial relations among university women; as IFUW president from 1924–1926, she took a guiding role in the formation of a German federation that would enable German women to join the IFUW. In 1924, at Oslo, the IFUW extended a tentative invitation to the German women. In 1925, Virginia conferred with the formidable Dr. Agnes von Zahn-Harnack, historian and spokeswoman for German university women, who, as Virginia explained to the AAUW International Relations Committee, organized themselves by profession, unlike the American contingent in the IFUW. In 1926, as Virginia concluded her term as IFUW president, the German women, peeved at prior rebuff but still pressing for admission, formed a national federation, the Deutscher Akademikerinnenbund (DAB), and the IFUW accepted the new group as a member. As IFUW president, Virginia formally welcomed the new German federation, along with those of Poland, Hungary, and Estonia, at the IFUW Conference in Amsterdam in 1926. The welcome occurred a few weeks before the League of Nations accepted Germany as a member.[74]

But IFUW problems with its new German contingent lay ahead. The large German federation (it had almost 4,000 members, most of them holders of advanced degrees) at once submitted a request to the IFUW for the acceptance of the German language in federation proceedings as a third official language—in the German view, German should rank the same as English and French as one of the federation's official languages. The demand evoked a major dispute over "the language question," a confrontation that, as historian Christine von Oertzen shows, pitted nationalism against internationalism and pervaded IFUW proceedings for the rest of the decade.[75]

Language was a sensitive issue. IFUW founders had assumed that English and French—and mainly English—would be the official languages. As two AAUW officers observed happily in their official account, as they described the initial IFUW conference and early IFUW meetings, "There was no babel of tongues." The sudden German demand struck many members as preposterous. To accept the Germans at all, in their view, had been a major concession. Moreover, the German contingent was not timid; its members, as historian von Oertzen observes, were "anything but quiet joiners." The second-largest national federation in the IFUW, next to the Americans, the German group included not merely college graduates—as did the U.S. and British national federations—but also professional women—doctors, lawyers, philologists (degree holders in language and literature), and other academics. The Deutcher Akademikerinnenbund was itself a federation of German professional associations; it acted with professional authority and its members, in their view, held academic qualifications superior to those of other federation members. To Agnes von Zahn-Harneck in Amsterdam in 1926, the educational standard of the many American women at the conference "was in many cases far below what one generally understands by an academic educational background." Virginia, too, was impressed with the German contingent. "We realized almost at once that a great people had come amongst us," she recalled.[76]

Virginia's hope to pacify German members persisted, as did the "language question"; the clash over whether the German language might achieve official status pervaded IFUW proceedings for the rest of the 1920s into the 1930s. IFUW officers who sought to narrow the gap between German demands and their own met rebuff, as in 1929, when the German contingent, unable to accept a compromise proposal, threatened to leave. British professor of physiology Winifred Cullis, an IFUW colleague "with a genius for organization and for friendship" (in Virginia's opinion) who became IFUW president in 1929, staved off this possibility. Virginia tended to downplay Cullis's role, but it was significant. A founder of the British Federation of University Women (1907), Cullis engineered talks that at last led to a tentative rapprochement with the dissident Germans in 1932.[77]

While the "language question" smoldered, the IFUW made strides in real estate. Virginia led a drive to found a new international center in Paris, Reid Hall, to add to the current centers—the AAUW headquarters in Washington and Crosby Hall in London. The Reid Hall property, a stunning sixteenth-century mansion on the rue de Chevreuse, in the heart of the fashionable Montparnasse district, had drawn the attention of Elisabeth Mills Reid, daughter of a California financier and wife of publisher Whitelaw Reid, owner and editor of the *New-York Tribune* and U.S. envoy to France 1889–1892. When a school on the rue de Chevreuse property went bankrupt, Elisabeth Reid founded a center for visiting American artists and in 1913 bought an adjacent property, once a porcelain factory. A concurrent development in the Reid family involved Barnard. Alumna Helen Rogers became private secretary to Elisabeth Mills Reid and in 1911 married the Reids' son Ogden, who by then owned and ran the *New-York Tribune*. A Barnard trustee as of 1914, Helen Rogers Reid persuaded her mother-in-law to support the start of an international residence for women graduates (the "American Girls' Club"). When the United States entered World War I, Elisabeth Reid created a French-American officers' hospital and in 1919–1922, turned the properties over to the American Red Cross.[78]

In 1922, the same year that the first IFUW dealings with German women arose, Virginia began a process that enmeshed Reid Hall with the AAUW and the IFUW. A group of AAUW educators, led by Virginia and M. Carey Thomas, sought to use the premises as a residential center for the AAUW's Women's Paris Club; the French Association of University Women, a branch of the IFUW, shared the terrain. In 1927, Elisabeth Reid gave the property to her daughter-in-law, Helen Rogers Reid, later president of the *New York Herald Tribune*, who named the place Reid Hall in honor of Elisabeth. In the 1920s and 1930s, Reid Hall served as a residence for over fifty women visitors a year and an international social and cultural center; the property offered a safe and welcoming space for U.S. women scholars and expatriates to mingle with French counterparts. "It is a charming old house with courtyard and garden," the *Barnard Alumnae Bulletin* reported in 1923, "and well equipped with steam heat, baths, electric lights, and other modern conveniences." In 1928, the lease to AAUW members became a right of use with no time limit. Reid Hall was now an IFUW stronghold and a visible monument to Virginia's goal, "the international cooperation of the university women of the world."[79]

Virginia would probably have liked to rest her reputation on the acquisition of Reid Hall. Instead, as both IFUW president and as leading negotiator, she remained ensnared in the "language question," a barrier to her goal of international cooperation. But, as with her leadership of the AAUW International Relations Committee, Virginia valued the process of collective enterprise. Her speech to the IFUW Fifth Conference in Geneva in the summer of 1929, closing a decade of achievement, fused two of her favorite themes, the primacy of peace as a goal and the importance of process in international affairs.[80]

Virginia's speech at Geneva directly followed a twenty-minute talk (in German) by the intimidating president of the German federation, Dr. Agnes von Zahn-Harnack, who summed up the efforts of her nation. "In thinking of the aims of the IFUW, I naturally think back to ten years ago, when I remember sitting with Professor Spurgeon in her cottage in Suffolk, and drafting the first constitution of the IFUW," Virginia began, in one of her many self-congratulatory commemorations of the federation's founding.

> Well, we had in mind and tried to express . . . our wish above all else to achieve through [the IFUW] this social purpose of mutual understanding, friendship between the nations, world peace. That I know has always been uppermost in my own mind. Now the last way to achieve friendship and peace is to talk about it. Peace is, I think, the most controversial and belligerent subject I know. I have hardly ever known any group to try to discuss peace without almost coming to

blows. I am sure this international friendship, this world peace, will be a by-product, not the thing we come to work at directly, but the thing we achieve through contact, through acquaintance, through understanding. But we must not talk about it. . . .

Virginia then veered into a sub-theme, the need to appreciate "difference" in international relations, no doubt to remind delegates how to cope with the challenging stance of the German federation and its demanding members. "In a most interesting way these contacts [made through the IFUW] help us first to tolerate, and then to like differences," Virginia posited. Nations, similarly, had to learn to tolerate, like, respect, and admire the differences among themselves. "None of us want to force on any nation anything contrary to its genius and desires," she argued. "We want each country to develop in its own way, according to its own special genius." By the end of the speech, Virginia had circled back to the role of process in international affairs. "One of the best ways of coming into contact, in order to achieve friendship and peace, is to work together," she told the delegates. "I do not so much care what they work on; the great thing is to have pieces of work which we do together."[81] The specific purpose of the joint activity was less relevant, Virginia insisted, than the very act of collective endeavor, the "by-product." The focus on process that Virginia announced in her Geneva talk resembled the priority that she gave to the process of learning over specific subject matter (that is, it did not matter what discipline a student studied). That focus on process had served her well in the AAUW International Relations committee and in the IFUW and would do so again as the federation entered the hazardous 1930s.

All of Virginia's efforts in the international women's movement through the 1920s and into the 1930s anchored her relationship with Cara, which depended in turn on the time they spent together in Alciston. Here the two friends took part in an innovative women's community.

ALCISTON

Engaging, exuberant, and admired, Caroline Spurgeon remained at the center of Virginia's life in the 1920s. Virginia especially valued the time spent with Cara in the summer, when they traveled together to wherever that year's IFUW conference was held—or to where the IFUW council met—and also settled in for a time at their shared home in East Sussex, where they welcomed friends and colleagues. Located near the southern coast of the United Kingdom in the village of Alciston, a tiny hamlet, the Old Postman's Cottage was a local landmark. A home had first been built on the site around 1750, but only its chimney remained after World War I. Since then, a bungalow, shed, and stables arose on the property, which Virginia bought on September 29, 1925. Cara spent eight months a year at Alciston with Lilian Clapham, her companion since 1896, and Virginia joined them for part of the summer.[82]

Soon after Virginia purchased the Alciston property in 1925, the Old Postman's Cottage became an impressive piece of real estate, with added-on wings and modern improvements. "The original cottage, like the kernel of an almond, lies embedded in the additions which have gradually grown up around it," said an article in *Homes and Gardens* in January 1931, "(a long wing to the west and additions to east and north), though all weather-boarded and under similarly thatched roofs." A photograph shows Cara in the library (once a granary), at her desk, surrounded by papers and books, under a vaulted ceiling and in front of a multipaned window. Other photos show the dining room, with its old brick fireplace; varied views of the house and its additions; the garden full of tulips; and the ample entertainment space. "The newly-added sitting-room, with its long windows looking south and west, is in harmony with the older portions of the house," said *Homes and Gardens*. On October 24, 1931, Virginia, who had financed all the renovations, turned the property over to Cara on the latter's sixty-second birthday. Whatever love Virginia professed in her memoir for Lilian (to whom she referred, in passing, as one of "the intimate friends whom I had loved best in England"), that affection did not extend to the conveyance of real estate.[83]

Virginia never tired of relating the joy of life in Alciston. She "lived in a thatched cottage," she told a reporter for the alumnae magazine (journalist Emma Bugbee), and became one of 207 villagers; "our village consists only of a big manor farm with its laborers' cottages, and three other houses, peaceful and rural and remote." The manor had had two owners since the Norman conquest, first the Battle Abbey; when Henry VIII dissolved the monasteries, he gave the property to Sir John Gage, in whose family it remained. "How do I pass the time?" Virginia continued; she found country life irresistible. "Well, I walk on the Downs and dabble in archeology. I take the dogs out, I work in the garden, and I drive a car on the left side of the road." She could go up to London, sixty miles away, for lunch with friends. "It is a great change from New York and I love it."[84]

Above all, for the many years that Cara, Lilian, and Virginia occupied it, the Old Postman's Cottage welcomed guests, who seemed to flock there, especially in the summers. The trio of residents, mainly Lilian, with Cara chiming in, recorded arrivals and departures, including their own, in the cottage's Visitors Book (1927–1936), along with dates of visits and occasional comments. Cara's friends and associates dominated the visitors' list. A frequent presence was Meta Tuke, the impressive principal of Bedford College, who worked with Cara for part of the academic year and often shared the cottage with the three main residents. IFUW visitors included Winifred Cullis, cofounder of the BFUW and IFUW and one-time president of each, who visited in July 1935, and Theodora Bosanquet, longtime IFUW executive secretary and literary editor of *Time and Tide*, who arrived in August of 1929 and 1930. Edith Thompson (or "Edif," in Cara's special language), an old friend of Cara and Lilian from Kings College and the hockey team, fixture in their social circle, fundraiser for Bedford College—and not an admirer of Virginia, according to Theodora Bosanquet—was also a frequent guest. A. W. Pollard, head of the British Library, longtime friend of Cara, called often to discuss Shakespeare research. Mary Aeldrin Cullis ("M.A.C."), Cara's secretary/assistant, similarly a frequent arrival, would later follow Cara to both New York and Arizona. Edith Morley, Cara's classmate from the 1890s and since 1908 a professor of English language at the University of Reading, came to lunch in September 1932 and again in April 1935. Various Spurgeon relatives visited, as did some former students. "Seven old students down for the day," Cara noted in June 1930.[85]

When Virginia discusses Alciston in her autobiography of 1954, she mentions only one pair of British visitors by name, economist John Maynard Keynes and his wife, the Russian ballet dancer Lydia Lopokova, who intrigued Virginia with her skill of mental choreography or what Keynes called "Lydia dancing in her mind." The couple ("brilliant and delightful people") lived in nearby Tilton and called often, according to Virginia, with their dogs; the resident terriers at the cottage had to be locked up "to avoid combat." Curiously, the Visitors' Book, which takes such scrupulous note of comings and goings, makes no mention whatsoever of the Keyneses. But that is only part of a larger mystery. A well-known group of Keynes's friends held properties within miles of Alciston. Virginia and Leonard Woolf spent time at Monks House in nearby Rodmell. Vanessa Bell and Duncan Grant lived not far away at Charleston Farmhouse, near Lewes. Half of Bloomsbury, it seems, arrived in East Sussex whenever they could, especially to get together at Charleston. Virginia Gildersleeve, however, usually such a name dropper, ignored the existence of the Bloomsbury contingent (and vice versa). Perhaps, to Virginia, the nearby existence of a rival Virginia—esteemed, accomplished, well-connected, avant-garde, and unconventional—*and* a celebrity—was anathema.[86]

Cara, however, sought a connection with Virginia Woolf. In November 1929, while in residence with the dean at Barnard, Cara wrote to Virginia Woolf to praise *A Room of One's Own*, which had just been published in September. The book, based on two lectures that Virginia Woolf had given in 1928 at the Cambridge women's colleges, Newnham and Girton, defended the needs of women artists: money and a place to work. After telling Woolf about her own illustrious career, Cara, most appreciatively, invited a response. "I should so much like to meet you if you ever had half an hour to spare," she wrote, and gave her address in Alciston. But Virginia Woolf did not reply. The worlds of Alciston and Bloomsbury (save for the Keyneses) had no overlap, in fact or in print.[87]

Beyond the British visitors to the Old Postman's Cottage, scores of Virginia and Cara's American friends made their way to Alciston. Virginia's brother Alger stayed for four days in August 1931, without his spouse ("sans conjoint"), Cara pointedly observed. Virginia's Brearley companions Bessie Coffin (now Thomassen) and Alice Castree (now Williams) arrived together, with their husbands, for tea in September 1932. Formidable M. Carey Thomas, longtime Bryn Mawr president and IFUW stalwart, visited in August 1928 and again in October 1931 ("to tea only," noted Cara or Lilian, perhaps with relief). Dorothy Leet, Barnard '17, who directed Reid Hall in Paris, as of 1924, and would do so for four decades, arrived in July 1930 and August 1932. Several relatives of Nicholas Murray Butler appeared, including his sister Eliza Butler, a Columbia administrator and frequent visitor of the 1930s, and a niece. Barnard generated a large coterie of guests. Treasurer and trustee George A. Plimpton, who had been so pivotal in Virginia's tenure as dean, visited with his wife and son, for the day in June 1930. Minor Latham, founder of the Theatre Department and overseer of dramatic productions at Barnard from 1914 to 1948 (in Margaret Mead's view, "our most popular professor, vivid, colloquial, and contemporary-minded"), came in September 1930 and July 1932. Mabel Choate, trustee (1918–1936) and philanthropist, and daughter of founding trustee Caroline Choate, visited in January 1931. Philosophy professor Helen Huss Parkhurst came for tea in July 1934. Economist Elizabeth Faulkner Baker arrived in September 1934, as did William Pepperell Montague, whose history of philosophy course "brought enlightenment to many Barnard students," Virginia recalled.[88]

The visit of Charles R. Crane, former diplomat and Virginia's admired guide to the Middle East and foreign affairs, proved a memorable occasion. Arriving in July 1934, Crane, who spent much time with Virginia in the 1920s and early 1930s, brought with him his friend George Antonius, future author of *The Arab Awakening*. Mysteriously un-introduced by Crane, Antonius admired some plants in the garden and left his card with Virginia and Cara; when asked where his home was, Antonius (Lebanese-born and Cambridge educated) responded, just as mysteriously, "Jerusalem." By the time of that visit to Alciston, Crane, a recent traveler to Germany, had become a supporter of Nazism and admirer of Hitler, whom he had interviewed on October 5, 1933, a set of circumstances that Cara either ignored or knew nothing of. Virginia did not comment on Crane's pro-Nazi stance either. Concern with current events or world politics in the early 1930s, even with the steady stream of visitors from near and far, seemed remarkably distant from the haven in East Sussex.[89]

To Cara, always the pivot of activity at Alciston, the place was idyllic. "This has been a perfect summer, one to remember always," she jotted down as a note in September 1928. "I have been here from beginning of April to now, with a fortnight's interval in London in early June, Virginia with a week's absence in mid-July has been here from June 19–September 8. We have all enjoyed it greatly. We have had some lovely bathing, we have been drenched in sunshine, we have gardened." In August, 1933, she noted, though "rather dogged by ill health," she had finished up her years of work on Shakespeare. How did the trio of Virginia, Cara, and Lilian get along in Alciston? Typically, Cara alternated companions—between Virginia and Lilian—on the occasions of her local outings. "Paid two visits to Harrogate, one with VCG [Virginia] in July, again with Lilian in Sept-Oct," as she noted in 1933.[90] That some form of distancing separated Lilian and Virginia seems likely, though on occasion the two went on trips or vacations together; in one instance, Virginia drove Lilian home from a medical visit.[91] It is also likely that Cara and Lilian's old friends in England lacked appreciation of Virginia and that Virginia's friends and associates in the United States knew little or nothing about Lilian. Significantly, Cara seemed well aware of her central role in this romantic triangle. In a letter to Lilian in 1931 from New York, where she was living with Virginia in the Deanery, Cara referred (perhaps with some cruelty) to her "2 little friends with racing hearts."[92] Still, the precarious trio endured. One photograph in Cara's large collection captures Virginia, Cara, and Lilian together at Alciston, sitting outdoors in front of a wall of rocks, with Cara, as might be expected, in the center. Each of the others stares straight ahead, looking at neither the camera nor one another.[93]

Enthralled with Cara and their time together, Virginia commemorated the Old Postman's Cottage and Alciston in her autobiography, with special attention to her own role in village life. One freighted recollection includes a vivid soliloquy on class and rank, concerns that—to Virginia—were never far from the surface. In this instance, the main actor, Virginia-of-the-1920s (an avid class-climber, always calculating her own social status vis à vis that of others) and the more distant narrator, decades later (equally class-conscious as well as tone-deaf on all nuances of interpersonal relations), jostle for dominance. "The old social structure of England still survived in my bit of Sussex," Virginia begins, in her narrator's cap. The circumstance delights her. "Lord Gage was the chief landowner and the great personage," she recalls, though his estates produced little revenue. Still, he served the community: "The residents of his villages felt through him a direct connection to the Crown." At the other end of the social scale, two servants came with the Old Postman's Cottage, "like the ancient serfs of the Middle

Ages, connected to the soil. They were comfortable and self respecting in their allotted niche."[94] Where did Virginia fit into this hierarchical scheme?

> As a stray American I had of myself no social rank, no niche in the hierarchy. I took my color from those with whom I lived, and they were "gentry": Caroline Spurgeon, of an old East Anglian family with a small estate in Norfolk, and her friend and comrade of many years, Lilian Clapham, of old Yorkshire stock. (Cara assured me that being a university professor, as she was, gave one no social standing whatsoever!) The Old Postman's Cottage was the only household of "gentry" in Alciston, and that brought various responsibilities upon us.[95]

Sailing forth to assume her purported social responsibilities (this story changes tone with each word, as the narrator steers herself into the ranks of the British class system), Virginia is impressed into public service by "dear Mr. Stacey, tenant farmer at the manor house." Her assignment: to welcome Lady Gage to a village fête and to escort her for the day. "Being an innocent American, eager to do anything to help him . . . I took on the task cheerfully, and found it a pleasant one, for Lady Gage was a beautiful young Englishwoman, one of the Grenfell family, charming and friendly." By now, the innocent American has the hang of things. Next, the residents of the Old Postman's Cottage hold their annual garden party for the Women's Institute, assisted by the vicar and his wife, an event that attracts all the women of Alciston and nearby Selmeston. "Making a speech to our Women's Institute was about the hardest job I ever tackled in the field of oratory," the visiting American recalls; as she proceeds, Cara, Lilian, and Meta Tuke sit in the front row, calling out "Hear, Hears." But the speaker, addressing an audience of whom, Virginia writes, most had never seen an American and some had never been to London, rises to the occasion. "Odd though my dialect was, I in some way belonged to them." Thus, Virginia first hobnobs (upscale) with Lady Gage and then steals the show (downscale) at the Women's Institute, cheered on by her entourage. The upshot: actor and narrator alike were entranced with the English class system.[96]

Lilian's death of cancer on December 21, 1935 brought the Visitors Book to a close. The final visitor listed in its pages, in April-May, 1936, was Meta Tuke. Soon after that, no doubt profoundly shaken by losing Lilian, Cara moved to Arizona. She last saw the cottage, after the move west, when she and Virginia visited England in the summers of 1937 and 1938. But the property continued to play a role in the drama of Virginia and Cara. At her death in 1942, Cara bequeathed the property to Virginia, who sold it in October 1946, twenty-one years after she had purchased it and just before she retired from Barnard. After Virginia left East Sussex that year, she never went back. But she returned to the days at Alciston in the 1920s and 1930s in her autobiography, when she thought of all the visitors to the Old Postman's Cottage from America, England, and further afield. "So the little place served well in the work of international liaison," Virginia wrote. "But its great value to me lay in what I had learned from the village itself, from being immersed part of every year in its atmosphere, from getting there the *feel* of England."[97]

For Virginia, the 1920s had been a decade of achievement, personal and professional. In the Deanery, on campus, in New York and abroad, success followed success. Moments of triumph from the 1920s pepper Virginia's autobiography—the trip to the Middle East with Cara in 1921, the address to Democrats at Madison Square Garden, the experience of outmaneuvering the law school faculty or of mobilizing the Seven Sisters or of escorting Lady Gage at the village fête—all were mini-peaks of personal narrative. In the 1930s, as Virginia coped with Cara's decline, with the Great Depression, and with the onset of war, new concerns eclipsed the victories of her earlier years.

Henry A Gildersleeve. Full of ambition, Henry Alger Gildersleeve gave up hope of college to join the Union army in Dutchess County, New York. A major in the 150th New York State Volunteers, Gildersleeve was mustered out in June 1865. A year later, he began to practice law in New York City. Photo courtesy of the New York Public Library.

Barnard College on Madison Avenue. When Virginia entered Barnard in 1895, the college was housed in a rented brownstone at 343 Madison Avenue, between Forty-Fourth and Forty-Fifth Streets, not far from her home at 28 West Forty-Eighth Street. Photo courtesy of Barnard College.

Kappa Kappa Gamma. Virginia, second from left, with four friends in her "fraternity" at Barnard in the late 1890s. Her good friend (and sometime rival), the accomplished Alice Duer, is third from the left. Photo courtesy of Barnard College.

Class of '99. Barnard transformed Virginia from a diffident entrant, "shy, snobbish, solemn," to a class frontrunner, entrenched among admirers. Self-conscious and self-congratulatory, the graduating class of 1899 declared itself dignified, studious, full of "social-mindedness" and fortified with "armor against prejudice and bigotry." Photo courtesy of Barnard College.

Class Day, 1908. After Barnard dean Laura D. Gill resigned at the end of 1907, Virginia, who earned a doctorate at Columbia in 1908, saw an opportunity to join the faculty at Barnard, where she had once taught freshman composition; she returned as a lecturer in English. In this photo: the sophomore class marches through the college gates. Photo courtesy of Barnard College.

The Dean in 1912. When Virginia Gildersleeve took office as dean in the academic year, 1910–1911, Barnard College had 497 regular undergraduates enrolled and fifty "special" students, non-degree candidates who registered for less than a full course load. By the mid-1920s, the college would double in size. Photo courtesy of Barnard College.

Gildersleeve and Butler, 1914. The patronage of Columbia University president Nicholas Murray Butler proved invaluable to Virginia's career as Barnard College dean. Here, Butler joins the dean on campus to celebrate Barnard's twenty-fifth anniversary in 1914. Getty Images.

Armistice Parade, 1918. Barnard student activism on behalf of US forces during World War I culminated on November 11, 1918, when French and American officers visited the campus to celebrate the war's end. For Virginia, the war era was a turning point. "The First World War had a profound effect on my life," she concluded. "It sent me out from my College Halls into public affairs," especially international affairs. Photo courtesy of Barnard College.

Five U.S. Delegates, 1922. The American Association of University Women (formerly the Association of Collegiate Alumnae) sent five delegates in 1922 to the IFUW conference in Paris; they could vote on issues such as the admission of new members to the federation. Virginia is in the front row, left. Wikimedia Commons.

Virginia and Cara. Virginia and Caroline Spurgeon on the Barnard campus in the 1920s. Their international partnership led to a two-continent annual schedule. Typically, Cara took the fall off from teaching at Bedford College in London to stay with Virginia in New York; Virginia spent the summers in Europe and the UK with Cara. Photo courtesy of Barnard College.

The Dean with Terriers. Virginia on the terrace in front of the deanery, her on-campus residence as of 1925, with her dogs, Jean and Culag Beag. Photo courtesy of Barnard College.

Greek Games, 1927. The Greek Games served Barnard since 1906 as a traditional annual rite, comparable to college-wide ceremonies at Barnard's sister schools. Here, sophomores of 1927 stage an offering, "Bacchae and Youths Revel." Photo courtesy of Barnard College.

Eleanor Roosevelt With College Presidents. Alumnae events to publicize the Seven College Conference, or "Seven Sisters," founded in 1927, drew prominent guests and press attention into the early 1930s. New York State's new first lady, Eleanor Roosevelt, and soon-to-be Chief Justice Charles Evans Hughes attended this fund-raising dinner of January 1, 1929 at the Astor Hotel in New York City. Vassar president Henry Noble MacCracken stands in the back (right) with Hughes. Those seated, from the left, are Eleanor Roosevelt; Marion Edwards Park, president of Bryn Mawr; Josephine Sheldon Edmonds Young (Mrs. Owen D. Young), Radcliffe '96, an alumnae leader; Ada L. Comstock, president of Radcliffe; Virginia Gildersleeve, dean of Barnard; and Mary E. Woolley, president of Mount Holyoke. GettyImages.

IFUW Conference, Amsterdam. Virginia, who had won the presidency of the
International Federation of University Women in 1924, chaired the Fourth Conference of
the IFUW at the end of July, 1926 in Amsterdam. Here, officers welcomed to membership
the German women's federation, which had sought admission since 1922. Once admitted,
German delegates began at once to press for acceptance of German as one of the IFUW's
official languages. Vereemigde Fotobureaux, Collection IAV-Atria, Institute on Gender
Equality and Women's History.

Zora Neale Hurston. Entering Barnard in 1925 at the invitation of trustee Annie Nathan Meyer, published author Zora Neale Hurston—over a decade older than her classmates—lived off-campus in a room in Harlem and for a time with novelist Fannie Hurst, for whom she performed secretarial work. A graduate of 1928 and a devotee of anthropologist Franz Boas, Hurston became a graduate student in anthropology. Virginia, who interviewed Hurston when she entered Barnard, remained distant. This portrait of Hurston, by Carl Van Vechten, patron of the Harlem Renaissance, is from 1938. Photo courtesy of the Library of Congress.

Three Friends at Alciston. Virginia Gildersleeve, Caroline Spurgeon, and Lilian Clapham pose outdoors near the Old Postman's Cottage sometime in the 1920s or early 1930s. Cara beckons one of the resident terriers; her companions stare straight ahead. A fourth figure that can be seen, barely, between Virginia and Cara, is probably Meta Tuke, head of Bedford College in London, where Cara taught. Photo courtesy of the East Sussex Brighton and Hove Record Office, with the permission of the owner.

Virginia and Cara, Alciston. The *Barnard Alumnae Magazine* for October 1935 ran this photo of Virginia and Caroline Spurgeon in the garden in front of the Old Postman's Cottage at Alciston. "How do I pass the time?" asked Virginia, addressing alumnae. "Well, I walk on the Downs, and dabble in archeology. I take the dogs out, I work in the garden, and I drive on the left side of the road." Photo courtesy of Barnard College.

The Old Postman's Cottage. Purchased by Virginia in 1925 and extensively renovated, the Old Postman's Cottage in Alciston became an impressive local landmark. When Virginia mentioned living in a cottage with a thatched roof, she did not convey the imposing size of the place. Photo courtesy of the East Sussex Brighton and Hove Record Office, with the permission of the owner.

Inside the Old Postman's Cottage. The dining room of the Old Postman's Cottage, also on display in the *Barnard Alumnae Magazine* for October 1935, contained the fireplace of the original dwelling that came with the property. Photo courtesy of Barnard College.

Fiftieth Anniversary Committee. Members of the committee to organize Barnard's College's fiftieth anniversary in 1939 join Virginia just outside the deanery. Trustee Helen Rogers Reid (Mrs. Ogden Reid) '03 is third from the left, just behind the dean. Trustee Iphigene Ochs Sulzberger (Mrs. Arthur Sulzberger) '14, is second from the right. Photo courtesy of Barnard College.

Mirra Komarovsky. Mirra Komarovsky, class of '26 and later a distinguished sociologist, began teaching at Barnard in 1934 as an instructor. Much admired and widely honored, Komarovsky attained tenure only after Virginia retired and was replaced as dean by Millicent McIntosh. Photo courtesy of Barnard College.

Seventh IFUW Conference in Cracow, 1936. When the IFUW cancelled its original plan to hold the 1936 summer conference in Berlin (the Nazified German contingent of academic women had by then left the international organization), IFUW leaders moved the event to Cracow, Poland. Photo by Mucha Stanislaw, Collection IAV-Atria, Institute on Gender Equality and Women's History.

Elizabeth Reynard in Uniform. A Barnard graduate of 1922 and specialist in American literature and folklore, Elizabeth Reynard taught English at the college. In World War II, on leave from Barnard, Reynard served the U.S. Navy; she participated in the start of the WAVES, ran an innovative training program for its volunteers, charmed the officers who worked with her, and left the navy as a lieutenant. After Virginia retired from Barnard in 1947, the two women lived together in Reynard's house in Westchester, "Navarre." Wikimedia Commons.

The Dean with Students, 1940s. Barnard students of the early 1940s would soon constitute the "trained brains" that Virginia promoted for wartime employment in all fields. Photo courtesy of Barnard College.

At the UN Charter Conference, 1945. Virginia addresses guests at a lunch in her honor given by the women of San Francisco at the Mark Hopkins Hotel on May 26, 1945. Days and nights at the UN Charter Conference, according to Virginia, filled up with "dinners, luncheons, receptions, meetings with the consultants, special small conferences with representatives of foreign nations, some important radio broadcast, interviews with journalists—lots of them—and with visitors of all kinds." Photo courtesy of the United Nations.

An AAUW Tea, 1945. Women's groups were among the non-governmental organizations (NGOs) that interacted with delegates at the UN Charter Conference. Here, the American Association of University Women, in which Virginia had long been involved, hosts a tea for women attached to the US delegation, May 5, 1945. Photo courtesy of the United Nations.

Bertha Lutz Speaks. Delegate from Brazil and leading advocate of equal rights for women at the UN Charter Conference, Bertha Lutz addresses a committee meeting on June 15, 1945. Joining forces with delegate Minerva Bernardino of the Dominican Republic and other Pan-American feminists, Lutz voiced dismay that Virginia Gildersleeve and her British allies took a contrary stance: that women's rights were implicit in human rights and did not demand separate attention. Photo courtesy of the United Nations.

Middle East Lunch, 1945. Virginia meets with Middle East delegates to the UN Charter Conference and other diplomats from the region at a lunch in May 1945. On her right, the prime minister of Syria. On her left, the delegate from Turkey, and next to him, the delegate from Saudi Arabia. On the far left of the photo is Charles Malik, minister to the US from Lebanon. Photo courtesy of Barnard College.

Signing the UN Charter. Virginia rises from signing the UN charter to shake hands with President Truman. The memorable moment, in June 1945, at the conclusion of the San Francisco Charter Conference, delighted the dean; her fellow delegates, smiling and applauding, seem to appreciate her presence among them. Standing next to the president is the US delegation chair, Secretary of State Edward Stettinius, whose civility toward Virginia eased her path at the UN meeting. Photo courtesy of Barnard College.

The Dean in 1945. Even before she retired from the Barnard deanship in 1947, Virginia Gildersleeve began her post-retirement career as a fervent anti-Zionist. Her first steps, in 1945, were publication of two letters in the *New York Times* opposing partition of Palestine. In 1948, she served as nominal leader of the Committee for Justice and Peace in the Holy Land, an anti-Zionist pressure group. Photo courtesy of Barnard College.

Dorothy Thompson. Well-known journalist Dorothy Thompson brought to anti-Zionism her longtime credentials as an anti-fascist and proponent of democratic values. In 1950, chosen to lead American Friends of the Middle East, the major anti-Zionist organization, Thompson replaced Virginia Gildersleeve as the leading woman in US anti-Zionism. Here, in 1940, Thompson awaits a meeting with FDR. Photo courtesy of the Library of Congress.

Students from Abroad, 1947. Virginia's global vision affected Barnard through foreign visiting faculty and an International Affairs program. The international student program that the dean founded after World War I grew steadily. In 1947, Virginia's last year in office, a record-setting seventy-four students from thirty-two nations were enrolled. Photo courtesy of Barnard College.

CHAPTER FOUR

Emergencies

1930–1947

"In Twenty-Five Years Miss Gildersleeve Has Built Up Her College and Changed the Pattern of Women's Education," announced the *New York Times* in February 1936, as Virginia celebrated her twenty-fifth anniversary as dean. The *Times* reporter hailed her both as an educational conservative (a "doughty champion of the classics") and as a progressive who made Barnard the first of the elite women's college to drop its Latin requirement, who imported foreign faculty, and who insured that every graduate "had taken a course in economics or sociology." Most important, in Virginia words, Barnard used New York City as a "laboratory," as its rivals among sister schools could not. "Where students in a country college sometimes feel 'out of it' and frequently regard their instructors as mossy old persons in cloistered halls, our students get a constant stimulus from the pageant around them," the dean declared. "They love to see their own professors taking a real part in economic and political affairs."[1]

Through the Great Depression and World War II, Virginia pursued bifocal goals. She held "the most interesting and worth-while position open to women in the academic world in this country," as she told alumnae. At the same time, the deanship provided a platform from which to engage in public life, to take "a real part in economic and political affairs." In the 1930s and 1940s, Virginia claimed a second career outside the college, both through the international women's movement and also through continuous commentary on policy questions, domestic and foreign. When World War II began, Virginia's extra-academic engagement became more intense, directed, and methodical; she began to shape her role as an internationalist. The peak of this effort came in the spring of 1945, when she served as the only woman member of the United States delegation at the charter meeting of the United Nations. All her prior experience had led up to the crucial moment of her appointment, as she saw it, "and helped fit me to play some useful part."[2]

ON CAMPUS: THE 1930S

The stock market crash of 1929 eroded campus life. Enrollments, endowment, and budgets shrank; gifts declined and deficits rose. Special projects like the Summer School for Women Workers folded. Dorm rooms emptied and the proportion of new students who commuted increased. Classrooms grew shabby; the student yearbook, *Mortarboard*, almost failed. By mid-decade, half of students worked part-time, one hundred of them for instructors or administrators to earn support from the Federal Emergency Relief Administration (FERA), which gave states funds to run relief programs. Virginia met challenges of the Depression with ingenuity. The college practiced "humble" economies, and even achieved a small budget surplus one year, in 1933. The dean resisted merger with Columbia to solve Barnard's monetary woes; to cede financial independence would disadvantage Barnard, she stated. Moreover, as Columbia focused on its graduate students, Barnard provided better undergraduate teaching; it thus had "something to bargain with in its relation with the university." The college coped with the death in 1936 of its devoted treasurer George Plimpton who had been, in the dean's words, "so wonderful at money-raising"; Virginia and trustees raised funds from the Carnegie and Harkness foundations. Not least, the college found low-cost ways to enhance the curriculum; in the late 1930s it started interdepartmental programs in medieval studies, which united the efforts of six departments (English, French, Italian, fine arts, philosophy, and history) and in American studies, an "integrated study" of economics, literature, government and history, according to the dean's report, that explored the "American way of life which we are saying we wish to defend and preserve." A third interdisciplinary effort, international studies, followed in 1943.[3]

Virginia used the press coverage she received on college occasions—anniversaries, class days, graduations, and alumnae events—to boost Democratic party initiatives, women's movement goals, and the interests of educated women. She supported FDR's reelection in 1936 and backed FDR's foreign policy thereafter. She endorsed a favorite cause of New Deal women, working wives, and slammed a proposed law to bar married women from work for pay. She derided any call for "dilution" of standards in women's education and trashed teacher-training programs at state normal schools as a "racket"; prospective teachers, she argued, needed training in the liberal arts. Finally, as early as 1932, Virginia began to publicize the nation's need for the "trained brains" of educated women, a theme she would promote yet further in World War II. In the Depression (as later in war), according to Virginia, a demand for highly qualified women workers prevailed; educated women of the 1930s were needed in government and public service, she argued. "Having trained brains, they will think straight," she declared in reference to 1932 graduates. "They will know a fact when they see it. . . . They will know whose opinions to value. . . . They will feel a devotion to the general welfare."[4]

Some of the troubles that Virginia and Barnard faced in the 1930s reflected financial constraint; others were legacies of prior problems. Promotions lagged; no one became a full professor from 1930–1940, according to historian Robert McCaughey. Salaries remained uneven; married professors who supported families (mainly men) held priority with Virginia over single scholars (mainly women), among whom earnings languished. Distinguished faculty members like Elizabeth Faulkner Baker in economics, hired as an instructor in 1919 and untenured until 1939, and Mirra Komarovsky in sociology, hired as a part-time lecturer in 1934 and untenured until 1948, found that academic mobility took decades. Virginia always fared well with men, noted the observant Gano Dunn, head of the New School and Barnard trustee. "She was an exceptionally competent judge of men, illustrated by the prominent part she took in the selection of men for the Barnard College faculty, and by the satisfaction reported of her dealings with male members of the trustees, faculties, and other officers," Dunn told an interviewer. "And it was common knowledge that the men would rather deal with Gildersleeve than anyone else."[5]

Bias in admissions persisted. The college, said the dean, followed modern methods of "selective admissions," focused on each candidate's least measurable qualities. The "character" requirement had been growing more and more important, as Virginia told alumnae in 1939; so were "personality" and "general promise." As pressure from local applicants rose, the goal of geographic distribution gained sway; the ethnic composition of the 1935 entering class resembled that of a decade earlier. Virginia's relationship with Annie Nathan Meyer deteriorated. "As the years went on, Mrs. Meyer's dynamic energy became a bit crabbed," Virginia wrote. "She grew eccentric and difficult and somewhat over-possessive towards the college which she had helped to found. So people who knew her only in the evening of her life sometimes did not realize that essentially she was a first-rate human being, sound and fine."[6]

Among her troubles of the 1930s, Virginia was ill and on leave at the start of the decade, 1930–1932. She referred in later years to heart problems. Thereafter, through mid-decade, she and Cara followed a version of the routine they had established in the 1920s; they spent the academic year at Barnard (Cara retired from Bedford College in 1929) and summers at Alciston. Cara's outstanding scholarship on Shakespeare appeared in England in 1935 and the next year in the United States. *Shakespeare's Imagery and What It Tells Us* unveils clusters of images in each of the plays (such as illness and injury in *Hamlet* or clothing images in *Macbeth*); the images led to the playwright's thought processes. The book brought rave reviews for originality and insight. Spurgeon had revealed the "mind behind the plays," one admiring reviewer (a friend and IFUW official, Theodora Bosanquet) wrote; capitalizing on modern interest in psychological process, in "pre-consciousness or fore-consciousness," the author used imagery as key to Shakespeare's "personality, temperament, and thought." Over the decades, Caroline Spurgeon won a widespread following. Russian film director Sergei Eisenstein, who applauded her use of body and plant images, found the book inspirational.[7]

But Cara was aging. She suffered from asthma, plus rheumatoid arthritis, high blood pressure, and arterial sclerosis, and by 1936 had to move to a dry climate for her health. Virginia first rented and then bought property in Tucson, Arizona, where Cara remained and Virginia visited continually. She hired a companion for Cara, a graduate of Smith '17, Catharine Weiser, called "Bunter" by Cara and then by Virginia, too. (This was no doubt an homage to the Dorothy L. Sayers novels about Lord Peter Wimsey, aristocratic sleuth, and his loyal friend/servant Mervyn Bunter. Sayers was one of the first women to earn an Oxford degree; her first novel about Lord Peter, *Whose Body?*, had appeared in 1923, with many more to follow.) Weiser, who had studied nursing at Columbia Presbyterian Hospital in New York, described herself as "nurse, housekeeper, secretary, bookkeeper, and general factotum" and remained in those jobs for the rest of Cara's life. A lively third member of the household, Weiser referred to her employers as "the professor" and "the dean." Both women had a marvelous sense of humor, said Weiser, "but the dean never sparkled as did the professor."[8]

The last phase of Cara's life challenged Virginia. "She must many times have been torn apart in those latter years," recalled Columbia University secretary and Barnard trustee Frank Fackenthal, "for Miss Spurgeon was an autocratic, demanding person, and drained Miss G. in more ways than one."[9] Catharine Weiser confirmed Fackenthal's assessment. "The professor was demanding, and would fly off the handle over nothing at all," she recalled. "Just as quickly, she would change and become all sweetness and light." When not in Tucson, Virginia sent continual messages to Catharine Weiser, full of directions, concern for Cara, and regret for her absence. "The poor British Lion!" Virginia wrote in September 1942 from New York. "I'm so sorry she is roaring and snapping, but I don't wonder; I should do it worse in her circumstance." Cara lived until October 24, 1942, her seventy-third birthday. In her final years, Catharine Weiser noted, Cara especially enjoyed letters from Virginia. "The professor just lived for these letters," said Weiser, "and I am sure that without them she could not possibly have carried on."[10]

Several letters from August, 1939, during Virginia's final prewar summer voyage to Europe, convey the affectionate bond between Virginia and Cara that had endured since 1919. "Own Darling," wrote Virginia from London on August 1 to Cara in Arizona. "I have just had your cable . . . it was lovely to feel in such close touch. Loves you *very, very* dearly, Darling." Virginia was then abroad to attend the triannual IFUW meeting, that year held in Stockholm; the impending war in Europe cast a pall over all that occurred (World War II would begin in Europe on September 1, 1939, when Germany invaded Poland). "Own darling," Virginia wrote from Gothenburg, Sweden on August 4. "A big zeppelin passed over us flying very low—a sight with its swastikas." "All my love to you, my darling," Virginia wrote from Stockholm on August 7. "My Darling," she wrote to Cara from Helsinki on August 18. "It is rather thrilling being way up here on the northeast edge of Europe, next door to Russia." "London seems calm and cheerful," Virginia telegraphed on August 24. "In case of war will stay with Meta [Tuke]. Sailing Wednesday." And finally, en route back to New York, "My Own Darling," Virginia wrote on August 31. "Here we are streaming along briskly on the Queen Mary. . . . Lots & lots of love, my Darling." The smattering of letters, omitted by accident from obliteration when Virginia destroyed her correspondence with Cara in the 1950s, suggests her devotion to her companion in the couple's last years.[11]

Cara's sickness elicited messages of sympathy from the couple's friends and colleagues. "I have been thinking so much of you and Miss Spurgeon in the last few days," wrote Winifred Cullis, the British president of the IFUW, to Virginia in July 1942. "You two have had such a marvelous friendship and I know what it means to you to have Miss Spurgeon anything but her own brilliant self." When Cara died in October, the dean received more reflections on the two women's long connection. "I well know how dear she was to you and how close and valuable your friendship," wrote Nicholas Murray Butler to Virginia, with whom he maintained a lifelong and indulgent relationship.[12] For Virginia, the last years with Cara in Arizona were taxing. The politics of the IFUW presented another set of challenges; these arose each summer of the 1930s as Virginia sailed off to federation meetings in Europe.

INTERNATIONAL AFFAIRS IN THE 1930S

Conflict over language, which had gained velocity in the 1920s, continued to roil the IFUW in the 1930s. After German admission to the federation in 1926, as Virginia's first term as president ended, a feud about the role of Germany festered. Historian Christine von Oertzen suggests the questions that federation leaders confronted. Would the IFUW put the German tongue on a par with its official languages, English

and French, as German members demanded? At the IFUW 1929 convention in Geneva, delegates approved German as a third conference
language but second in status to English and French; any statement
made in German would have to be translated into English or French.
German delegates spurned this outcome, and in 1930 German members
posed an ultimatum to the IFUW: either "to place the German language
on an equal basis with English and French in every respect" *or* the
German contingent would withdraw until a satisfactory solution was
found. Blindsided, IFUW leaders weighed their options. What if the
Italian or Spanish delegates came up with similar demands for language
equality, as Italy, urged by its leader Benito Mussolini, had threatened
to do in 1927? Talks among IFUW leaders in 1931 in Berlin (in German)
addressed the problem. The German contingent then proposed a modified resolution to the 1932 IFUW convention in Edinburgh. German
members, under the new resolve, would accept Anglo-French dominance
but win a concession: the IFUW would make promoting the German
language a "cultural task." Though the German federation had not won
equal status for the German language, the concession pacified German
delegates, who at once offered to hold the next international conference
in Berlin in 1936. In the context of international women's politics, the
IFUW had been accommodating.[13]

Dispute had hardly abated at the IFUW in 1932—only six years since
German delegates had begun to press their demands—when Germany
underwent profound change. In January 1933 Hitler became chancel-
lor; thereafter National Socialism prevailed. The German women's
contingent—the German Federation of University Women or Deutscher
Akademikerinnenbund —ousted its Jewish members, quashed its lib-
erals, and, in May 1933, endorsed the Nazis; membership plunged from
3,100 to 400. How would IFUW leaders respond to the transformation of the German federation into a Nazi auxiliary? Division ensued,
especially as the twenty-nine-member council convened in Budapest
at the end of August 1934. The meeting was "most dramatic," reported
Virginia, who led it, and the moment in history perilous. "Any day, we
felt as we started for Hungary, Central Europe might burst into flames."
The British contingent of IFUW urged expulsion of the Nazified
German federation; the U.S. group—that is Virginia and her allies—
sought to maintain relations with the Nazi member group as long as

possible. German women, according to Meta Glass, president of Sweet Briar College, former president of the AAUW, and ally of Virginia, were "torn between trying to do what Hitler wanted, and at the same time conform to the policies of the Federation. This was an emotional concern with which the Dean coped successfully." Virginia was able to control the meeting and prolong the status quo; she was, at this moment, Glass noted, "a person who instinctively commands deference from others." Relations with the German contingent continued, if precariously. Meanwhile, strategically, the IFUW Council shifted plans for its next international conference, intended for Berlin, to Cracow. The IFUW also changed its constitution to state that no federation would be "admitted or retained" if it disbarred qualified women "by reason of their race, religion, or political opinions," though without rejecting the German contingent.[14]

As late as the summer of 1936, when the IFUW held its seventh conference at Cracow, the IFUW Council, which Virginia dominated, sought to preserve an alliance with the German contingent; the Council wished the head of the German federation "success in the speedy rebuilding of the federation in such a way as to strengthen its relation with the IFUW." In October 1934, right after the Council meeting, however, the DAB had restructured itself as the Reichsbund Deutscher Akademikerinnen (RDA), a part of the Nazi establishment, and in January 1936, before the international federation announced a policy, German women seized the initiative: the RDA left the IFUW. The reason for the departure: RDA found IFUW support for Jewish academic women incompatible with the current German "race and political outlook." Italy withdrew as well, the 1936 IFUW convention in Cracow reported.[15]

Rebuffed, though now liberated from the "German question," the IFUW resumed its original arrangement of Anglo-French dominance: English and French remained the official languages. Virginia regained the IFUW presidency in 1936 and held that post until 1939. The withdrawal of the German federation still seemed, in her view, a source of regret; she had hoped that academic women could maintain peaceful international relations among themselves, even as the rest of the world did otherwise. "For Dean Gildersleeve, elected president for the second time, the apparent destruction of so much for which she had striven must have been particularly hard to endure," writes Edith C. Batho, historian of the IFUW. As she welcomed federation members in 1936, Virginia urged them "not to judge too harshly your sister university women in other countries." Instead, Virginia counseled understanding: "You must realize that they are in the grip of political powers which make them almost helpless." In her second term as president, the federation sought ways to assist refugee scholars from late-1930s Europe. It established a two-year emergency fund for refugees and in 1938 an ad hoc Refugees Committee to which it referred individual cases. Virginia presided over these efforts; all links between the IFUW and the Nazified German federation were at an end.[16]

In the early 1930s, however, in the period between the Nazi rise to power in 1933 and IFUW's loss of its German members at the start of 1936, Virginia voiced sympathy with Nazism in venues beyond the IFUW. Her statements reflected at least several factors, beyond the bonds with German women that she had developed through the IFUW. First, she maintained an enduring friendship with her longtime mentor Charles R. Crane, who had shaped her commitment to the Middle East, who made no secret of his support for Nazis or his 1933 visit to Hitler, and with whose Institute for Current World Affairs Virginia was involved at least until his death in 1939; "during the last ten years of his life, he never had an important gathering without her," Crane's son John recalled. Second, Virginia moved at Columbia in the shadow of Nicholas Murray Butler, friend of Mussolini since the 1920s, who made no secret of his own fascist sympathies or his involvement with Germany and all things German from 1933 to 1937; as usual, Virginia catered to Butler's views and followed his lead. Thus, both of Virginia's major advisors held fascists in esteem. In addition, leaders of the other eastern women's colleges voiced profascist sympathies in the 1930s. The Seven Sisters, as historian Stephen Norwood shows, "shared a sanguine view of Nazi Germany and enthusiastically participated in academic and cultural exchange with the Third Reich." Visiting professors and exchange students voiced pro-Nazi views. Finally, to continue business dealings with counterparts in Nazi Germany through the mid-1930s was commonplace in New York boardrooms, banks, and law firms; heavy investment in Germany fed a vested interest in the new regime. Still, the rise of fascist dictators in Europe alarmed Americans; few U.S. friends of fascism in the mid-1930s had positions as prestigious as that Virginia occupied or the level of foreign policy expertise that she claimed. In that light, her flirtation with fascism in the mid-1930s is notable.[17]

Virginia embedded her apology for Nazism in neutral themes, such as the need for mutual understanding among nations, the right of free speech in academic life, or hope for world peace. At the same time, she condoned Nazi policies, spoke well of developments in Germany under the Third Reich, promoted German and Italian expansionism, and found benefit in the Nazi law of 1933 that rid German universities of their Jewish populations. In some instances, she attributed the fascist-friendly views that she espoused to others ("a few individuals" or "far-sighted persons"). But this was a transparent effort at camouflage.

By spring of 1933 Germany fell to Nazi rule; in April 1933, most ominously for students and educators, the Nazi "Law Against the Over-crowding of German Schools and Universities" targeted Jewish students in schools and colleges and also imposed a quota on women students, whose numbers sharply fell. Virginia entered the ranks of apologists for fascism as a defender of forbearance and international understanding. In a speech of April 29, 1933 to one hundred alumnae at the Barnard Women's Club, in which she called the new Nazi government "discon-certing," Virginia declared the current German regime "a tragic 'Alice in Wonderland.'" Other nations should try to grasp the psychology and emotions of alien peoples, she argued. "We must stop thinking of other nations as if they were ourselves acting eccentrically," she claimed. "In many instances, could we know the circumstances in which seemingly unreasonable actions take place, those actions would seem reasonable. Perhaps if we knew more of the facts we could understand what the German people are feeling and trying and wanting to do."[18] Virginia reiterated her public reluctance to take issue with Nazi Germany in private correspondence. At the end of 1933, when Annie Nathan Meyer urged Butler and Virginia to protest the Hitler regime and to end cooperation with the Nazis that allowed pro-Hitler Germans to lecture at Columbia, Virginia refused. She said that "formal protests against the actions of the Germans just stiffen the back of the German Government and make things harder for those who are being persecuted."[19]

In 1934, Virginia's account of the IFUW council meeting in Budapest in August grew into an apology for Nazi policies. At the meeting, DAB head Friederike Matthias, the new president of the German federation and a Nazi party member since 1929, defended the German federation's mission to expel non-Aryans, and at the same time claimed a policy of nondiscrimination on the basis of race, religion, or political opinion. Matthias's contentions, like her promises of German state funding for the IFUW, were duplicitous. But not to Virginia. "We found her [Matthias] a charming person to deal with," the dean reported to AAUW members in the fall of 1934, "sincere, enthusiastic, a gentle spirit, and eager to have her country cooperate effectively in our international work."[20] Virginia repeated the "gentle spirit" analysis to a Barnard interviewer, author and educator Cornelia Geer le Boutillier, class of '17, who publicized Virginia's "brave push into Central Europe" to attend the Budapest meeting in the *Barnard Alumnae Bulletin*. "The Status of University Women in Germany was a special topic for the Council's discussion," wrote le Boutillier, in a paraphrase of Virginia's words.

> The new president of the German Federation, an ardent Nazi but a charming, gentle soul withal, assured the meeting that women would have excellent educational opportunities under the Hitler regime and that such changes as had been written up by correspondents were greatly exaggerated. It was, however, quite apparent that there *had* been changes, and that the position of women in Germany was still in process of development. Dean Gildersleeve saw much of the German delegates, and found much to interest her in their attitude toward international problems.[21]

As this article appeared, Virginia reiterated her sympathy for fascism in another campus context. In October 1934, the Italian consul general in New York conferred an award on Peter M. Riccio, a leading member of the Barnard Italian Department, former Columbia graduate student, and ardent fascist, at a Casa Italiana ceremony. The impressive Casa Italiana, the center for Italian Studies, built in the 1920s, had been funded by Italian fascist contributions. Antifascist students picketed the ceremony for Riccio's award. "Is the Casa Italiana a fascist haven?" a student poster asked. Citing concerns about academic freedom, Virginia, in a short introductory address, defended Riccio. "I don't care about what Professor Riccio is," she stated. "One should not inquire into the political beliefs of our professors." But as historian Stephen Norwood points out,

Virginia defined academic freedom narrowly: It did not apply, in her view, to student protesters such as those who picketed the Casa Italiana ceremony.[22]

In April 1935, Virginia again took issue with student protesters, this time with Barnard students who challenged her "unwillingness to participate" in a demonstration "against war and fascism." Virginia voiced her stance in a letter to the editor of *Barnard Bulletin*, the student newspaper. "Though I am opposed to fascism as a form of government for this country ["for this country" was a salient qualification], I am just as much opposed to communism," she wrote. "To single out fascism as the chief enemy seems to me to imply, rather vaguely, perhaps, that it is worse than the other "isms," and I do not believe this is necessarily true. Moreover, this singling out of fascism as the chief enemy gives me an uncomfortable suspicion, probably unfounded, that the Communists are, in the main, controlling the demonstrators and using the rest of us for their publicity purposes." To conclude, Virginia fell back on the shared goal of peace: "I have often observed how hard it is to conduct a peace movement without stirring up a lot of ill feeling," she wrote, "but I still hope that we at Barnard can differ about methods of working for peace, without hurling insults at one another."[23]

Five months later, Virginia plunged further into an apology for fascist policies. In September, 1935, returning from her annual summer trip, she told the *New York Times* of her belief that Italy and Germany had legitimate need to colonize new land in Africa. "There is strong feeling in England that Italy and Germany should be given colonies; that the world cannot ignore natural expansion and expect Italy and Germany to sit back and be satisfied with no chance for expansion," she said. President Butler had voiced a similar position as he returned from a summer trip to Europe a few weeks earlier. Virginia also defended the Nazi law of 1933 intended to prevent the alleged "overcrowding" of German universities, a goal achieved by expelling Jews (and women). She told the *Times* that "she had been pleased to learn, unofficially, that Germany would permit women to attend universities." "While the total number of students has been reduced, she said she understood that one-fifth of the total could be women, and that a certain proportion of Jews also could attend universities." Virginia went on to endorse the Nazi rationale for reducing school and college attendance: "She said she would not blame universities in Germany for cutting down on enrollments [wrote the *Times*] because professions apparently were overcrowded."[24]

Virginia's assertion was an apology for fascism. "Overcrowding" was a myth; the argument that hordes of graduates led to overstuffed professions was a feeble excuse for German universities to cut student populations by evicting Jews. (Within a few years of the Nazi law of 1933 enrollment at German universities indeed fell dramatically. "Membership in some Nazi organization is practically a prerequisite for university admission," as a German scholar reported in 1937.) After her assertion of overcrowding, Virginia then shifted the topic of her *New York Times* interview strategically. "The German university, she added [wrote the *Times*], is different from the American college; is more advanced and intended for professional training. There never will be any reason for limiting college attendance in this country, where a liberal education is designed to prepare students for life in general."[25]

Virginia repeated her defense of Nazi policy in an interview with *New York Herald Tribune* reporter Emma Bugbee, a Barnard graduate, class of '09, who had been sent in 1933 by her paper to Washington to cover First Lady Eleanor Roosevelt and her press conferences. Published in the October 1935 issue of the *Barnard Alumnae Bulletin*, Virginia's interview with Emma Bugbee returned to the rationale for expansion. "In some quarters [in London] there was a good deal of feeling that the surface of the globe would eventually have to be redistributed," Virginia stated.

> Far-sighted persons saw that England and France, having all the land they wanted, could not forever deny Germany and Italy the same chance to expand. A few individuals were saying, "let's get together and have a re-allotment of territory giving everyone room for legitimate expansion". . . . Whether this will ever be possible or not I don't know, but at least the mere discussion shows the growth of the international outlook and the sense of community responsibility for the world as a whole. . . . When England and France seized their colonies, nobody paid much attention. Now everybody has his eye on everyone else.[26]

After 1935, Virginia's public support for Nazi policies ended. What caused her retreat from a role as apologist? Perhaps the resignation of the German contingent from the IFUW in January 1936 was one factor. When Virginia regained the IFUW presidency in the summer of 1936, although she urged friendship with all academic women regardless of politics (a way of reiterating her regard for the ousted Germans), the federation remained antifascist and Virginia catered to that stance. Another possible factor: Perhaps the Nuremberg laws on race in late 1935 and their publication in 1936 made the Nazi regime too difficult to defend. Also, by 1937 Nicholas Murray Butler had dropped his own outspoken support for fascism; in September 1937, Butler condemned "the military dictatorships of Japan, Italy and Germany." Perhaps most important, President Roosevelt invited Virginia and Caroline Spurgeon to a small White House dinner on March 3, 1936; other guests included the Sulzbergers and the Morgenthaus. It is possible that the impact of the meeting with FDR, and with Eleanor Roosevelt, also present, along with pressure from prominent families with influence in New York and Washington, brought Virginia's few years of vocal sympathy for fascism to an end.[27] Still, as Stephen Norwood points out, German exchange students at Barnard continued to issue pro-Nazi statements to the *Barnard Bulletin*. "We love our leader," declared a visitor of 1936–1937; a German student of 1937–1938 argued that anti-Jewish discrimination was justified because Jews had acquired too much control over money.[28]

By the late 1930s Virginia, like her mentor Nicholas Murray Butler, sought in public only to preserve peace. In 1938 Virginia urged Butler to use his influence to prevent German expansion into Czechoslovakia, "to try to get over to Germany more definitely the fact that . . . in the event of war the whole weight of America—moral, economic, industrial—would be thrown against Germany," she wrote to Butler on September 27, 1938, just before the signing of the Munich Pact, in which Britain, France, and Italy agreed to Germany's occupation of Czechoslovakia's Sudetenland. If Butler "could make this point vigorously clear," Virginia insisted, "that would be by far the best way of getting the idea across to Hitler's advisors." In 1939, when the IFUW held its conference in Stockholm, Virginia took issue with the rest of her IFUW colleagues. The dispute by now was semantic. The IFUW in Stockholm confirmed its principles of nondiscrimination. Its goals, the federation reiterated, were to "promote understanding and friendship among university women of the nations of the world, irrespective of their race, religion, or political opinions." It would accept only those national federations whose aims meshed with its own; nations that discriminated by race or religion remained excluded. But Virginia argued for her own twist on IFUW goals. She hoped that the IFUW would make "every effort to keep in touch with all university women in the world, irrespective of their race, religion, or political opinion." Always a lawyer's daughter, Virginia put her emphasis on "keep in touch" and "irrespective of . . . political opinion."[29]

U.S. colleges in the 1930s faced questions on how to hire scholars who might be rescued from fascism. "Like other American colleges, we were eager to give shelter to the refugees from the Hitler regime in Germany," Virginia declared, in retrospect. But such eagerness arose less intensely than she recalled. U.S. colleges and universities "were more likely to hire refugee scholars who were not too old or young, right or left, or female," reveals historian Laurel Leff. Administrators preferred non-Jewish refugees; they voiced concern that adding European scholars would make American faculties "too Jewish." Concern arose, too, about "how Jewish the candidates seemed," and on whether such candidates threatened jobs for U.S. scholars. Hiring exiled academics, Virginia told the *New York Times*, aggravated "our problem of placing women in teaching positions."[30]

The refugee scholars that Virginia hired, both in art history, fulfilled the "not too Jewish" requirements that U.S. colleges preferred. Classical archeologist Margaret Bieber, an IFUW colleague and professor at the University of Giessen, considered herself Catholic. Dismissed in Germany in 1933, Bieber, well advanced in her career, left for Somerville College at Oxford. Hired as a lecturer by Barnard in 1934, Bieber visited at Columbia in 1936 and received tenure at Barnard in 1937. Rembrandt expert Julius Held, much younger and forced out of a museum job in Berlin, became a lecturer at Barnard in the mid-1930s on a year-to-year basis, and did not receive tenure until 1950, after Virginia retired and only after an offer from Yale. Virginia "was a powerful woman and had a national name," Held told an interviewer, and his early years had been uncertain. "I was never sure I would be hired again."[31]

Historians differ on how to interpret Virginia's statements that condone Nazi policies in the early 1930s. To some her apology for fascism is of a piece with her anti-Semitism in college admissions, and perhaps also with her steadfast anti-Zionism; to others her brief-lived fascist sympathy is only one part of a complex personality profile.[32] Did the apology for fascism constitute a clueless misstep or a critical failure of empathy? Did it spring from the goal of preserving peace or represent a veering toward the pro-Nazi views of longtime mentor Charles R. Crane? Or was it simply an instance of "trying it on," a testing of limits, and the indulgence of a contrarian inclination, or what Virginia called her "mulish" disinclination to listen to others? None of the interpretations really invalidates the others. By the time World War II began in Europe, Virginia's favorable statements about fascism had ended, not to be mentioned again—by either her critics or by reporters. Nor did Virginia ever refer in public remarks to her one-time tolerance for Nazi policies of the 1930s. Instead, she sought to revise history so as to write such a viewpoint out of the record. Looking back from midcentury, in revisionist mode, Virginia repositioned herself as a staunch antifascist. As in her autobiography of 1954, she claimed that "when Hitler perpetrated his persecutions and massacres I felt a wave of horror sweep over me." This sense of horror at Nazi persecution had not been so clear to her in 1933–1935. Still, as United States entry into World War II approached, Virginia adjusted quickly to the war era, embraced the options it offered, and supported the administration. By 1939, she had become an interventionist. "We want England and France to win this war," she told a Barnard all-college assembly. "We want to do something to help."[33]

In short, at some point during her second term as president of the IFUW, 1936–1939, probably in 1936, Virginia shifted gears; the condoning of Nazi initiatives that she had previously voiced disappeared. Her activism in World War II—her organizational ties plus her support for women's education, jobs for educated women, and administration policy—showed deft choice of commitment and mastery of public relations. She also profited from the start of a second close relationship.

VIRGINIA AND "THE SKIPPER"

By the time Caroline Spurgeon died in 1942, Virginia had met a new romantic interest, Elizabeth Reynard, an English professor at Barnard. A Barnard graduate of 1922, Reynard began teaching part-time at the college; by 1939, with two years of graduate study and a limited record of publication, Reynard became chair of Barnard's new American Studies Program and personally involved with the dean. Philosophy professor Joseph Brennan noted "the way the aging dean wore her heart on her sleeve, giving her beloved friend the privileges and preferences of a court favorite." Such favoritism did not endear the Gildersleeve-Reynard connection to faculty members; instead it fed feuds in the English Department, which fermented until Reynard finally departed from Barnard in 1949, amid much tumult. But the relationship buoyed Virginia, ever smitten, through the war years and beyond.[34]

Born in 1898 in Boston, twenty years younger than Virginia and a distant relative through the Algers (some of the ancestors of Henry A. Gildersleeve), Elizabeth Reynard took pride in her maritime background. "We came from a seafaring family," she wrote in a memoir; one grandfather was a sea captain, Captain Bob, and she loved all things nautical. In later years, Virginia would refer to Reynard in correspondence as "the skipper." Reynard had an indirect route to college. She never attended secondary school, and barely any school at all. In her teenage years, Reynard relates, she went to Europe with her parents, and, during World War I, served in a hospital in Belgium, for which she received a medal, the Cavell De Page medal for war service. After the death of her father—a cotton broker who retired young, suffered a nervous breakdown, and spent his time thereafter collecting shipping news from distant ports, which he cut and pasted—Reynard moved from Fall River, Massachusetts to New York with her mother, impoverished. Reynard described her family's status as among the "socially effaced ranks of the shabby genteel."[35]

Reynard entered Barnard in 1918 as a nonmatriculated special student with no credentials save a few courses in Columbia's extension division. "The dean had a soft spot for Greek," which she had studied for three months, Reynard later told a reporter. While an undergraduate, she supported herself as a copywriter. She also reveled in college life; she made friends with Robert Frost's daughter, a classmate; met poet Edna St. Vincent Millay, whom college women adulated; and kept company with a well-off Columbia boyfriend, "W. J.," who had a roadster and access to speakeasies. A double major, in geology and English, Reynard embraced both science and humanities. When she graduated with honors, one of her instructors, Ida Ogilvie, professor of geology and a longtime associate of Virginia—Ogilvie and the dean had served together on the committee to further women's graduate school admission around 1912—recruited Reynard to teach. To do so, Reynard postponed graduate work at Oxford, where she later studied English (Somerville College), where she received a B. Litt. in 1927, and where, Virginia reported, Reynard was "the first woman ever to be nominated by the English school of Oxford University 'to petition for the D. Litt.'" Oxford had only recently begun to award doctorates to women; it did not do so before 1920. Reynard never received a D. Litt., however; her obituary, dictated to the *New York Times* by Virginia, refers only to "post-graduate study" at Oxford, not to a doctoral degree. As a teacher of literature, Reynard made a powerful impression on her students, who appreciated, in the words of a former student, "the provocative and challenging mind that she brought to her teaching." And as an instructor, as in all else, Reynard seemed—to Virginia—outstanding. "Long before we became personal friends," wrote Virginia, "I knew her well as one of the most brilliant and promising young scholars on our staff, and a teacher of quite exceptional ability, original and ingenuous in her methods, tireless and self sacrificing."[36]

Always something of an oddball, or so she portrayed herself in her madcap memoir, a stylized remembrance of her teenage and college days, Reynard had a flair for self-dramatization. The protagonist of her memoir, a spunky naïf, full of whimsy and histrionics, enjoyed pranks, scrapes, hijinks, escapades, derring-do, and her own live-wired eccentricity. As suited her distinctive persona, Reynard had a distinctive *curriculum vitae*. A specialist in eighteenth-century British and American literature, she gained a reputation in the field of folklore, a subject she had first studied with anthropologist Franz Boas at Barnard. In 1934 Reynard published a book of folk tales told over generations by settlers of Cape Cod; the stories in *The Narrow Land*, dating back to Icelandic sagas, dealt variously with witchcraft, whales, ghosts, giants, and pirates, with Wampanoag lore and sea yarns. Cape Cod denizens and vacationers would not soon forget characters like Goody Hallett, "The Witch of Wellfleet," who, banished for pregnancy, haunts the dunes, hurling curses at the wreckage of the pirate ship of her one-time lover and betrayer, "Black Sam" Bellamy. Virginia, in her will, financed a new edition (Houghton Mifflin, 1968); the book reappeared in two further editions, 1978 and 1985. *The Narrow Land*, over time, found rapt readers and a wide audience. Reynard would return to the story of Goody Hallett and Sam Bellamy in a novel, *The Mutinous Wind* (1951). Her achievement, as she saw it, derived from Boas. Franz Boas taught his class "how to 'read' folktales, how to collect them, how to study them, what their scholarly uses can be," Reynard recalled. "When I came to collect and study the folktales of Cape Cod, I knew that in most instances, I was not dealing with folk tales at all, but with hybrid forms of popular history and theology often cloaked in allegory."[37]

According to Elizabeth Reynard, she first met Virginia Gildersleeve, unaware of her identity ("that dark-eyed girl?"), on entering Barnard in 1918. Virginia would "be my boss for twenty-five years and for fifteen years a constant comrade in work and play and retirement," Reynard wrote. "I took a dislike to her at once." Virginia remembered approving the admission of the less-than-credentialed Reynard, but knew little, she claimed, of Reynard's outstanding undergraduate career: "We did not become close personal friends—though cousins through the New England Alger line—until World War II loomed and our simple, old-fashioned instinct to serve our country drew us together for patriotic efforts." In Virginia's account, the friendship took shape at the end of the 1930s with the start of Barnard's American Studies Program, the first of several shared endeavors. Reynard chaired the faculty committee of 1938 that shaped the interdisciplinary program. Historians and economists, specialists in government and literature, would join forces to explore American society and culture, its ideals and institutions. Virginia envisioned a multimedia endeavor that included film, recordings, and folk craft; reflected "great diversities in racial, cultural, and economic background"; and used New York City life "as a proving ground for the more theoretical parts of the course." Students appreciated the escape from disciplinary requirements, the imaginative spirit that shaped the curriculum, and the aura of creativity that infuses new academic enterprise. One of Elizabeth Reynard's courses in the 1940s, American Sources for Creative Writing, for instance, focused on primary source material used by selected writers in fiction and nonfiction; each student, who would find source material of her own, would be "assisted in using it in creative writing." The goal: "to attract gifted young writers to American Studies."[38]

In World War II, Elizabeth Reynard and Virginia collaborated to establish a branch of the navy, the WAVES (Women Accepted for Volunteer Emergency Service), an acronym that Reynard invented, and also to propose one another for various posts connected to the WAVES. When the navy, which expected a manpower shortage, started to consider recruiting women in 1942, it contacted Virginia for suggestions. Virginia recommended Elizabeth Reynard to assist Rear Admiral Randall Jacobs, chief of the Bureau of Naval Personnel, to develop guidelines for the WAVES. As soon as she took this post, Elizabeth Reynard organized a Women's Advisory Council, made up of academics and headed by Virginia, to make suggestions to the navy about recruiting and training women. The advisory council proposed a director of the WAVES, Wellesley president Mildred McAfee [Horton], who served with distinction from 1942 to 1945. Reynard, on leave from Barnard and appointed a lieutenant in the WAVES in 1942, became assistant director. In 1943, Reynard moved on to yet a third important post in the navy; she directed the six-week training program for WAVES at Hunter College in the Bronx (now Lehman College). There, at the U.S.S. *Hunter*, she lectured recruits on naval traditions and tactics; her lectures featured visual aids and nautical devices that she collected from helpful naval officers. Her leadership, talent, and interpersonal skill impressed the enlistees. "The Navy needs you—thousands of you—and it needs you fast," Elizabeth Reynard, now a lieutenant commander, wrote in the energetic and chatty scrapbook she compiled for women recruits.[39]

The start of the WAVES helped open the wartime military to women; with 86,000 members, the WAVES was the largest women's military unit next to the Women's Army Corps, started slightly earlier. Distinctively, the WAVES was a *part* of the navy, not an auxiliary entity. Officers of the WAVES had attended or graduated from college and were trained for command at Smith and Mount Holyoke; their group photos resembled collegiate gatherings. "Elizabeth Reynard, Dean Gildersleeve, and the advisory council spearheaded a campus Blitzkrieg," wrote *Time* in 1945. "For their key officers they were frankly looking for the best product of the colleges . . . No glamor girls." Many officers, like Reynard, came straight from professions. "A fairly high percentage of women who first joined the services came from positions of considerable responsibility and established reputation," according to Mildred McAfee Horton.

Enlistees, or "apprentice seamen," trained for six weeks at Big Ten university centers (as at Madison, Wisconsin or Bloomington, Indiana) as well as at Hunter, which became the main training center; many recruits moved on elsewhere for further training. Their labor, as radio operators, weather forecasters, stenographers, cooks, and lab technicians, among other jobs, freed men in the navy for combat service. The first WAVE that the U.S. government decorated for war service (1944), Reynard excelled as "Commandant of Seamen" at Hunter. Recruits voiced enthusiasm about the WAVES. "It is truly a most broadening experience," an officer wrote to her mother from the Pearl Harbor Navy Yard, "and I shall never outlive it."[40]

Virginia, meanwhile, won attention in wartime not only for her own role in the navy but also as a commentator on foreign affairs, an exponent of the nation's need for educated women ("trained brains"), and a supporter of postwar internationalism. With her new companion, who enlivened her every experience, and with new opportunities, which the home front provided, Virginia had a very "good war."

THE UNITED STATES AT WAR

Virginia used the war years to add credits to her growing resumé as a leader in higher education, civic activism, and international affairs. Her support for FDR's foreign policy in the war era boosted her credit with the administration and among its foreign affairs experts. Before the United States entered World War II, Virginia had endorsed United States efforts to arm Great Britain, to support the allies, to end isolationism, and to defeat the Axis powers, without declaring war or committing U.S. troops. In 1940 she joined the Committee to Defend America by Aiding the Allies, an interventionist pressure group that urged the United States to take action in the European war ("steps short of war"), as opposed to neutrality, nonintervention, or the America First Committee. In 1941, she denounced the anti-interventionist stance of Charles Lindbergh as "near to treason." Her reputation among foreign policy experts rose when the United States declared war. At the same time, as war began, she claimed a public foothold on more familiar ground: education and women. A member of the American Council on Education's Committee on College Women Students and the War, started in 1940,

Virginia compiled data on college women's potential contribution to the war effort. Chaired by her friend Meta Glass, the committee involved a network of women leaders in education on whom Virginia would draw in future wartime projects. Committee members, Virginia wrote, "were concerned with the same old questions—the need and use of woman power. . . . From time to time we drew up reports."[41]

In 1942, Virginia enhanced her reputation in public life with her service on the Women's Advisory Council to assist the navy as it began the WAVES. "The Navy has suddenly come to life," as Virginia wrote to Catharine Weiser in Tucson, in July 1942. The eight members of the Women's Advisory Council included, among others, Ada Comstock, Radcliffe president; Alice Crocker Lloyd, a dean at the University of Michigan; Harriet Elliott, dean of women at the University of North Carolina; and household engineer Lillian Gilbreth, whose family life would captivate generations of readers in the 1948 bestseller *Cheaper by the Dozen*, written by two of the twelve Gilbreth offspring. Steered by Virginia, the council persuaded Mildred McAfee Horton to serve as director of the WAVES. "It was Barnard's determined Dean who talked Miss Mac into it," wrote *Time* in 1945. After her work for the navy, Virginia secured a prime invitation. In the summer of 1943, she began a five-week visit to see how England faced the impact of war; she reported to a radio audience from London, "the very heart and brain of the free world." Eleanor Roosevelt had in 1942 made a similar trip to England, accompanied by radio talks. Finally, the dean used her speeches at Barnard, to alumnae, and to women's groups to invoke aspects of world affairs, whether the value of solidarity with Britain, the need to exterminate "poisonous elements" in Germany, or the expectation of a postwar United Nations. All of these activities—the navy experience, the visit to Britain, and foreign policy commentary—underscored Virginia's growing status as an expert in international affairs.[42]

The visit to England in 1943 was impressive: Invited by the British Ministry of Information, Virginia crossed the Atlantic in a two-engine plane, a two-day trip. Her companions in transit included anthropologist Margaret Mead, Columbia sociologist Robert S. Lynd, and Brooklyn College president Harry Gideonse; the guests enjoyed the ministry's consent to do whatever they wanted. Beyond visiting the Wrens (members of the Women's Royal Naval Service) and the Queen (fifteen minutes),

Virginia served the function of expert observer: she heard R. A. ("Rab") Butler, president of the Board of Education, a precursor to the Ministry of Education, defend his White Paper on Educational Reconstruction. Butler proposed reforms in primary schooling and a hike in the age for leaving school from fourteen to fifteen and eventually sixteen. The proposal, which became the Butler Education Act of 1944, marked a turning point in British history. "Cara Spurgeon used to tell me that in England nobody ever wanted to talk about education," Virginia recalled, but the gifted Butler, her lunch partner, proved otherwise. The visit to England gave Virginia the fodder for broadcasts and speeches for the rest of the war.[43]

At home, Virginia promoted the role of educated women in the war effort. "There is already a serious shortage of trained personnel," she declared in a college address as 1942 began, and that shortage would only become more acute. For the dean, as historian Rosalind Rosenberg notes, the war was "an opportunity to be exploited." The nation's need for trained personnel, as Virginia announced in speeches, broadcasts, interviews, and news releases, made hiring educated women imperative. As vocational options for women rose, she urged Barnard students to remain in college, not to take jobs—even when government campaigns pushed women to do so—and, if they married, to stay in school rather than to follow husbands to far-off military bases. She prodded Columbia's school of engineering to accept women, which it started to do in 1942, though not with much enthusiasm. Beyond Barnard, Virginia pressed employers to hire women graduates, and touted the options open to educated women. "[T]he country acutely needs and will continue to need in the future citizens trained to think," Virginia told a radio audience, "and also doctors, social workers, physicists, chemists, bacteriologists, statisticians, and a hundred other kinds of highly trained workers." The end of war, Virginia foresaw, would end some of the new opportunities that women enjoyed. "Competition will again become more severe as the war time demand for workers slackens," she warned, and the standards of professional schools would rise. But that only made the "the best possible preparation" for women graduates more imperative; they needed to retain a competitive advantage.[44]

The feminism of Virginia's wartime demands was pragmatic and opportunistic; she did not urge women to pursue "top jobs"—though she often edged toward egalitarian ends. She made her case for educated women most explicitly in a speech of 1942, "The Shortage of Trained Brains," in which she resurrected the "trained brains" phrase that she had introduced a decade earlier. The nation needed "not only the top officials who take responsibility," Virginia declared, "but thousands of assistants with trained brains, honest scholars who can collect, weigh, and interpret facts and hand on to their chiefs the conclusions they must have in order to make their decisions." Judging from the calls that came into a woman's college like Barnard, she claimed, there was "a tremendous demand—to mention a few outstanding examples—for chemists, physicists, engineers, statisticians, economists, physicians, bacteriologists, and educated secretaries;" the last, she explained, meant "trained brains *plus* the technique of typing and stenography." Trained brains were also needed to shape public policy, to develop "a sound public opinion . . . a grasp of the facts of the war and the aims of the peace." One "fact of the war" that Virginia began to consider was possible inclusion of women in a military draft. Women should "bear a definite responsibility for service as men do," Virginia stated in 1941, though she did not favor conscription of women at that moment because no one had proposed "a practible plan" to deal with it. In February 1943, Virginia opposed any "draft" of women into wartime civilian jobs, which was a separate, if related, issue. In August of 1943, however, at a Barnard press conference on her return from England (where women had been registered to serve in the army, government agencies, or industry), she stated that she "saw no reason why women should not be drafted for the armed forces or for any work in the national war effort." By the fall of 1944, the Seven College Conference supported the inclusion of women in required military service as "preparation for total war."[45]

Finally, from the start of the war, Virginia focused on preparation for peace. In 1940 she joined the Commission to Study the Organization of Peace, or Shotwell Commission, a research affiliate of the American Association for the United Nations. Supported by the Carnegie Endowment for International Peace, long chaired by Nicholas Murray Butler, the commission was a discussion group of about fifty (at the start), including fifteen women, mainly academics, "all students of international affairs." The commission chair, James T. Shotwell, an old friend, had been Virginia's classmate in James Harvey Robinson's course on medieval institutions; a Columbia historian, international affairs expert, and director of research at the Carnegie Endowment, Shotwell held great influence. Another longtime colleague, William Allan Neilson, the soon-to-retire president of Smith, chaired the commission's executive committee. Fellow members included lawyer John Foster Dulles, future secretary of state; civil rights activist Channing Tobias, board member of the NAACP and father of Barnard graduate Belle Tobias, '31; banker Thomas W. Lamont, chairman of the board of J.P. Morgan, who had worked with Virginia at Seven College Conference events in the 1920s; and Emily Hickman, Rutgers professor, peace activist, and part of the commission's founding group. Meeting one Sunday each month at the Murray Hill Hotel, for all-day sessions, often heated, commission members discussed a proposed text that had been precirculated. The commission "studied and analyzed the great problems of world organization," Virginia wrote. "Month after month and year after year we plugged along, until finally the horizon brightened, and victory appeared probable."[46]

With its news releases, speakers' bureaus, conferences, study groups, regional commissions, and academic affiliations, the Shotwell Commission was a pressure group for internationalism, a challenge to America First, and a stepping-stone to postwar world organization. Its four reports dealt with the principles of a lasting peace, convictions about economic interdependence, and a United Nations to carry out the principles of the Atlantic Charter; the reports envisioned an international court and an international declaration of human rights. The Shotwell Commission's recommendations influenced the Dumbarton Oaks Conference of 1944, which in turn shaped the UN Charter meeting of 1945, to which Virginia would be selected as a delegate. By 1943, participants in the Shotwell Commission numbered over 120. For Virginia the commission provided access to networks of scholars, lawyers, and businessmen, a thick web of contacts. Her involvement with the commission, and especially her link to Shotwell, would prove useful in her own postwar plans.[47]

Virginia voiced firm ideas about what should happen to Germany and its leaders once the war had ended. "I should like to see Hitler taken to a remote island and kept there while he lives—quite quietly," she told the *Herald Tribune* in February 1945. "This is the third time within the memory of persons now living that Germany has brought war to the civilized world, and now I am for demilitarizing Germany. If that is a hard peace I'm for it. . . . I assume that the armies of occupation will eliminate the most poisonous Nazis—somehow." Virginia spoke next of her prior experience with Germans: "You and I know there used to be Germans of virtue and merit," she stated to the *Herald Tribune*. "But even these good Germans have got to learn to take responsibility for their government and to choose the right kind of people to rule over them. Yes, I knew such people. I had friends in Germany before the war. They may be dead now." Finally, Virginia turned to the Yalta Conference (February 4–11, 1945), just concluded, where FDR, Churchill, and Stalin met to make final plans for German defeat and the postwar peace. She was thankful that an "Anglo-Saxon type agreement" had prevailed at Yalta—by which she meant, she explained, that views were exchanged, deals reached, and problems resolved. "We Anglo Saxons," she said, "are used to that kind of give and take. I was glad to see compromises arrived at. We got something out of that conference. It was wonderful to see so many running sores healed." This article conveys a valid point on the virtue of "give and take." The way the United States ended World II, Virginia believed, should not repeat mistakes made when ending World War I.[48]

At the same moment, as Yalta concluded, Virginia learned that a new appointment lay ahead. In mid-February 1945, newspapers announced that she had been chosen to serve as a U.S. delegate to a meeting to shape the United Nations. The process of selection had begun when her name had been placed on a list of 260 possible women candidates, selected by women's organizations, for public policy posts. The long list of women's names had been generated by a White House Conference of June 14, 1944, held under the auspices of Eleanor Roosevelt, titled "How Women May Share in Post-War Policy Making." Virginia assumed that the Washington office of the AAUW had urged her candidacy. A State Department official, Durward V. Sandifer, had drawn up a shortlist of a dozen women who were qualified to be a UN delegate; the new secretary of state, Edward Stettinius, Jr., who had replaced the ailing Cordell Hull in December, 1944, had just made the final decision, approved by FDR, at Yalta. That a woman would be chosen as a delegate to the UN conference came as no surprise. At Eleanor Roosevelt's insistence, it was now State Department practice to place one woman on each delegation to an international conference. Vassar economist Mabel Newcomer, for instance, had been sent to the recent Bretton Woods Conference in June 1944 to shape postwar monetary policy; Vassar dean C. Mildred Thompson had been chosen in April 1944 to serve as one of six U.S. delegates at an international education conference, where she had been the only woman delegate from any nation. But winning a spot on the UN delegation in 1945 was a truly extraordinary honor.[49]

Many factors fused to boost Virginia's candidacy for the momentous UN job, including her wartime support of the administration and her articles on the need for women in the peace process. Decades of prominence in higher education and long experience in women's organizations helped make her a top candidate. Her leadership role in the IFUW, especially, served as a springboard to the UN post; an even more crucial bridge was her recent participation in the Shotwell Commission, with its focus on world problems and its coterie of influential leaders. Such qualifications "added up to a good foundation," Virginia observed; in retrospect, she saw "how all my experience over many years had led up to this moment."[50]

At the Shotwell Commission, William Allan Neilson, chair of the commission's executive committee, fired off a press release to support her appointment. The selection of Virginia, he claimed, with some self-interest, represented the overcoming of prejudice against academics in politics; she was "a scholar and organizer of scholars." Second, her leadership in the AAUW had boosted women's interest in international affairs. Finally, and most importantly, Neilson underscored Virginia's expertise and professionalism. "For years Miss Gildersleeve has given time and energy to cultivation of understanding between peoples," he declared. "She is not an amateur."[51]

AT THE UNITED NATIONS: 1945

At the end of February 1945, two weeks after news of their appointments had reached the press, FDR asked eight Americans to represent the United States at a meeting to prepare a charter for the United Nations. "I take pleasure in inviting you to serve as a member of the Delegation of the United States to the United Nations Conference which is to meet at San Francisco on April 25th, 1945," wrote the president to Virginia and the other delegates. The current secretary of state, Edward Stettinius, led the delegation; handsome and genial, he proved solicitous ("Just call me Ed," he told Virginia, who had trouble saying his name). A bipartisan group, the delegates included Cordell Hull, the previous secretary of state; Senator Tom Connally, Democrat of Texas, chair of the Senate International Relations Committee; Senator Arthur Vandenberg, Republican of Michigan and internationalist since 1941; and naval commander Harold Stassen, former Minnesota governor, who impressed Virginia favorably. Lower on Virginia's approval scale were the delegation's two congressmen, Representative Sol Bloom of New York's "silk stocking" district on the Upper East Side, a Democrat and current chair of the House Foreign Affairs Committee, and Representative Charles Eaton, Republican of New Jersey, future chair of the House Foreign Affairs Committee. Each appointee, save Virginia, had experience in national politics as well as diplomacy. They had served in Congress, on other delegations, and in some cases at the recent Dumbarton Oaks Conference in August and September, 1944, which called for the start of the United Nations and from which women had been excluded, and at the Bretton Woods conference on postwar monetary policy.[52]

Called to Washington in March to meet her fellow delegates, Virginia looked forward to "sizing up these colleagues." Special attention went to the secretary of state, whom she first "sized up" as a lightweight but later came to appreciate. At the capital, the new delegates heard from State Department advisors and also from FDR, who reported to them on Yalta and elicited Virginia's concern for his health, according to her detailed notes. Back in New York, as she prepared to head west, President Butler voiced concern about *her*. "But who will be with you whom you know really well," the aging Butler asked, "and who will take care of you?" As she could bring two staff members, Virginia invited her secretary from Barnard, Martha Lawrence, '41, and, from the U.S. Navy, Lieutenant Commander Elizabeth Reynard, who served as aide and informant. In Virginia's view, Elizabeth had "exceptional qualifications for international relations of the sort in which we were engaged"; their relationship was now in full swing.[53]

FDR died on April 12, 1945, two weeks before the San Francisco conference began; his successor, Harry S, Truman, was "flying blind," a State Department official recalled. The goals of the new United Nations: to replace the League of Nations, which the United States had failed to join; to maintain international peace; and to focus on human rights, a focus that FDR and his advisors had hoped would preclude further conflict. The fifty delegations that convened in San Francisco, all from Allied nations, met for eleven weeks, into June 1945. Besides the official delegates and their staffs, representatives of many nongovernmental organizations—pressure groups—traveled to San Francisco from the nations involved. The NGOs sought to introduce provisions, sway delegates, and shape developments. The United States invited at least forty-two such organizations, including five women's organizations, among them the AAUW. Other NGOs invited themselves, as did journalists from around the world.[54]

When she accepted the invitation, Virginia vaulted from her career of activism in voluntary organizations to an official position on the world stage. She saw herself both as a representative of American women and of all Americans. "I feel I was appointed because American women made a drive for representation and my name was on the roster they compiled," Virginia told Agnes Meyer of the *Washington Post*. "Therefore I do represent our women but I hope I also represent my fellow citizens as a whole." She was still an outsider, however. Virginia was one of only six women delegates. Of the signatories of the UN Charter, she was one of only four. Even counting support staffs along with delegates, women constituted only 3 percent of the total. Virginia thus faced two overlapping challenges in San Francisco: First, accustomed as she was to "working from within," how well would she cope with the status of outsider? What would she contribute to the UN meeting and the UN mission? To compound this challenge was another: The feud between equal-rights feminists and their foes that had for decades pervaded the U.S. and international women's movements arose again at the UN conference, indeed at its outset. To what extent would "human rights" include equal rights for women? To what extent would Virginia support women's rights?[55]

"I was confident that I could serve my sex as well as my country by just being a good delegate," Virginia recalled. Installed with fellow delegates on the fourth floor of the Fairmont Hotel, she served on two committees, one to draft the preamble to the UN Charter, the other the Economic and Social Council. In each committee, questions of equal rights for women arose. The United Nations credits women delegates as a group with inscribing equal rights in the UN Charter, but this was not quite the case; women delegates clashed on equal rights. Virginia entered the fray in San Francisco as an antimilitant, averse to specific mention of equal rights for women in UN documents. Any such mention of women, she argued, "the idea of women as a separate group," would segregate women; such separatism would be discriminatory, unnecessary, and counterproductive. "Miss Gildersleeve does not think in feminist terms," as Agnes Meyer, an admirer, observed. As was common at the time, Meyer reserved the term "feminist" for supporters of equal rights.[56]

Conflict arose in the committee to create a preamble to the UN Charter. Latin American women present, led by Dr. Bertha Lutz of Brazil—scientist, lawyer, suffragist, Sorbonne graduate, and veteran women's rights advocate—strove to include specific references to equal rights for women in the Charter. Virginia saw Bertha Lutz as a "militant feminist in favor of what seemed to me to be segregation of women." She charged the Lutz faction with backing "an old militant feminism, which I thought had passed away" and with separatist goals. Opposed to a strident campaign, Virginia endorsed "a conception of women as equal comrades with men working for the same end and on the same basis." The Lutz faction won backing from the Australian woman present, Jessie Street, in Virginia's view "a zealous and very militant feminist"; the U.S. faction drew support from Canadian and British women present, including the British MPs Ellen Wilkinson and Florence Horsbrugh. To antimilitants, the equal rights advocates represented a sort of feminist nationalism, with Latin American roots, that sought to undercut the internationalist spirit of the moment—the very spirit that the new UN celebrated. Virginia's fellow U.S. delegates supported the stance she adopted—human rights for all without distinction of sex—but lacked interest in the preamble, so she pursued the battle over the wording of documents herself. "British and American men were bored and irritated by the repeated lengthy feminist speeches," Virginia wrote. "Some of the American staff bestowed on Dr. Lutz the nickname 'Lutzwaffe' as a humorous adaptation of the German Luftwaffe, which had been devastating Europe."[57]

Bertha Lutz, who arrived in San Francisco with the specific goal of advancing women's rights, understandably had a different version of events. At her first meeting with Virginia, at the start of the conference, when the U.S. delegate held a tea for women delegates in her sitting room at the Fairmont, an event that Lutz later saw as an ominous "prelude to subsequent happenings," the Brazilian feminist felt "condescension" on Virginia's part. The U.S. delegate, she recalled, grilled her with questions about her qualifications in an attempt to "place her." This observation was astute; the dean typically "placed" people in terms of background and status—or "sized" them up, as in the case of her fellow U.S. delegates—in order to control social situations. In response to the perceived or real slight (probably real), Bertha Lutz held her own reception a few days later at the St. Francis hotel, to which she invited women delegates and women representatives from NGOs, but not her three foes, Virginia, Wilkinson, and Horsbrugh. Lutz felt only disappointment, she claimed, to find that the trio sought to dissuade other women from supporting women's rights; she marveled that these three opponents, who had benefited from feminist movements in their own countries, were so eager to disassociate themselves from women's rights. Lutz concluded that Virginia voiced "a very old-fashioned anti-feminism." Jessie Street of Australia, who endorsed the equal rights faction, applauded her Brazilian colleague's interpretation and accomplishments. "Suffice it to say," she declared, "Without Bertha Lutz from Brazil we could not have got anything as satisfactory as we have for women in the Charter."[58]

A first version of the preamble, proposed by Field Marshal Jan Smuts, head of the South African delegation and the second prime minister of his nation (where the racist laws of apartheid, already in progress, would be fully imposed in 1949), stated a belief "in the equal rights of men and women." Claiming that the draft of the preamble was too long and clumsy, Virginia offered a revised version that deleted the reference to equal rights for women. The use of the word "women" segregated women, she claimed; she sought brevity and concision. But the original wording survived. The UN Charter was the first international agreement to proclaim the equal rights of men and women as part of human rights; the principle of equal rights would be repeated four times, each time challenged by Virginia. According to Norwegian diplomat Torild Skard in an article of 2008, "The United Nations reaffirmed faith in women's equality in the preamble not due to the efforts of Virginia Gildersleeve but in spite of them."[59] Bertha Lutz and her entourage of women's rights advocates would have agreed.

Virginia tackled the equal rights issue again in her second committee assignment, the Economic and Social Council. Once more, a feud simmered among women delegates, this time over the start of a Commission on the Status of Women, as proposed by Bertha Lutz of Brazil and endorsed by thirty-three of thirty-five delegates to the Council. Virginia and the United States led the opposition, supported by Wu Yi-Fong, the woman delegate from China. To its proponents, a commission on women's status was a tactic to enforce equal rights. Foes opposed the segregation of women in a separate commission apart from the already agreed-upon Commission on Human Rights, to be established in 1946, which, they posited, could handle any women's rights issue that might arise. A separate commission on women's status, they contended, defied the principle of nondiscrimination. Were women isolated in a separate commission, Virginia argued, in retrospect, "it might well happen that the men would keep them out of other commissions and groups, saying they had plenty of scope in their own organization. That would be contrary to what we were working for—no discrimination because of sex." The argument that Virginia supported, in short, vetoed gender as a category of analysis. "I am anxious that nothing should be done to isolate women," as Virginia contended in a September UN conference, where the clash persisted. "I hope that we shall rather insist on their being regarded as 'people,' as we have long tried to do in this country."[60]

Although the Commission on the Status of Women won majority support among UN delegates, and Virginia acknowledged her opponents' success ("Some of the men of other nationalities . . . spoke to me with admiration of the feminists, especially of Dr. Lutz"), the issue arose too late for a vote at the charter conference of 1945. Virginia could thus elude defeat, though only briefly. At the end of the conference, she stated in a broadcast of June 16, 1945, her belief that in the future, where women suffered from discrimination, the new Commission on Human Rights would take action. But proponents of a Commission on the Status of Women pressed the issue at subsequent, soon-to-occur international conferences. When the United Nations held its inaugural meeting in London in February 1946, the Human Rights Commission created a Sub-commission on the Status of Women. On June 21, 1946, the new entity became a permanent Commission on the Status of Women. In January 1947, when the Commission on Human Rights held its first session at Lake Success, New York, its members unanimously elected Eleanor Roosevelt chair. Appointed to the United Nations by President Truman in December, 1945, the former first lady had long been in the faction of women activists that voiced suspicion of demands for equal rights; at first, like Virginia, Eleanor Roosevelt opposed the idea of a separate commission on women's status but then—expediently—agreed to it. The moment of that concession represents a last gasp of international enmity to equal rights among women. As its foes suspected, the new commission *was* an instrument of equal rights; its stated purpose was "to achieve equality with men in all fields of human enterprise and to eliminate all discrimination against women in statutory law, legal maxims or rules, or in interpretations of customary law."[61] So in about a year Virginia lost the battle she had waged at the United Nations.

Bertha Lutz and her allies had their own versions of the skirmish at the United Nations over a Commission on the Status of Women. To its proponents, the commission was a logical conclusion to their victory on the preamble; the League of Nations had already formed such a commission, in 1938, led by U.S. lawyer Dorothy Kenyon, though it had ended at the start of the war. The resolution to start a similar commission at the United Nations represented "the culmination of a campaign lasting several weeks, to get article 8 into the charter," wrote Jessie Street. It was "regrettable," in her view, that "the woman delegate from the US—Dean Gilderleeve [and her allies] refused to take any part in this campaign." Bertha Lutz disputed as "untruthful" the account of the fight over the commission that Virginia later published in her autobiography. Virginia, Lutz claimed, had deprived Lutz of credit for her role at the UN conference, diminished the role of Latin American feminists, and "fallaciously wrote that the conference had voted down the commission on the Status of Women." As Lutz concluded (in Portuguese) in the margin of her copy of Virginia's book: "much biased and wrong information." Ironically, as historian Katherine Marino points out, U.S. women dominated the new commission on women's status, where they sought to limit its impact to issues affecting solely the General Assembly. But the feminist pressure exerted at the 1945 conference, Marino shows, insured that the

Declaration of Human Rights, approved by the General Assembly in 1948, referred to "all human beings."[62]

While she was coping with Bertha Lutz and the equal rights issue in committee sessions, Virginia dealt with yet another segment of the women's movement: the women's press corps. Few weeks went by in San Francisco without an interview with a woman reporter, typically for an article that would run on the women's page of a U.S. newspaper on the sole woman member of the U.S. delegation. Topics discussed, all non-controversial, included why the dean had been appointed, what talents she brought to the assignment, what goals she espoused, and how ably she had represented the rest of U.S. women. Virginia had hoped to be "a good delegate, competent and not too troublesome," as she explained to Margaret Parton of the *New York Herald Tribune*. "She smilingly calls herself a 'progressive conservative,'" wrote Edith Efron in the *New York Times Magazine*. "Beneath her august façade, the dean conceals a quiet whimsy." As the conference concluded, Virginia urged ratification of the UN charter. "So far as I have had a mandate from women, it was a mandate to get a world organization to stop war," she declared to a reporter in June. Virginia did not share the equal rights issue with the women's press corps or discuss the battle that had arisen over it.[63]

Beyond the clash over equal rights for women, a dispute that she did not invite or expect, tried to avoid, sought to ignore, and could not win, how did Virginia fare as a U.S. delegate? Was she a "good delegate," as she had intended?

"JUST BEING A GOOD DELEGATE"

Like Virginia, who began to compose an account of her stint at the UN Charter meeting in August, 1945, to save for future reference, other participants, too, sought to preserve their UN experiences for posterity; after the historic conference ended, they discussed their own roles in the event through memoir, interviews, or oral history. Just as Virginia summed up her impressions of fellow delegates and other colleagues, so did her colleagues, on occasion, recall their impressions of her, some favorable and some otherwise.[64]

Virginia's fellow U.S. delegates and male members of the U.S. support staff could be disdainful, if not hostile. "Gildersleeve only showed up for ceremonial occasions and sometimes droned out the speeches we wrote for her," recalled the State Department's leading economic advisor, Leroy Stinebower, in an oral history of 1974. When interviewed in the early 1950s by Virginia's potential biographer, Dorothea Setzer, Stinebower had given a more balanced report. Gildersleeve was one of the hardest workers at the conference, he stated, a team player, always available and ready to cooperate. More accomplished than "Big Bertha," Stinebower said, Virginia showed "a genius for cutting through irrelevancies," impressed foreign delegates with her dignity, and did a better job "than any other woman he could think of who might have replaced her." These were careful observations, laced with nuance. But Stinebower had been dismissive as well. Dean Gildersleeve lacked experience, he claimed; with no political or technical background, she depended on advisors. Intimidated, she was too eager in seeking advice and too passive in taking it. Resigned to having a woman on the delegation, her colleagues in the U.S. delegation gave her short shrift. Overall, said Stinebower, and this was his most crushing blow, Dean Gildersleeve knew she was "window dressing."[65]

A self-interested observer, Leroy Stinebower both shared in and conveyed (one suspects accurately) the sexism of the U.S. delegation and his State Department colleagues. His statements suggest the condescension that Virginia faced, not so much from foreign delegates, among whom she often won applause, but from Americans. Each meeting of the U.S. delegation featured not merely the interplay of the U.S. delegates but also the many interjections of the lively corps of State Department advisors that participated in such meetings, a competitive group that included John Foster Dulles, Archibald MacLeish, Adlai Stevenson, Abe Fortas, Averill Harriman, and Nelson Rockefeller. In this challenging context, U.S. delegates and their advisors remembered, variously, that Virginia was either not assertive enough or else too assertive.

Compared to the leading members of the U.S. delegation, for instance, she "was never very aggressive in her role," a State Department official recalled. The scheduling of her committee work proved unfortunate: both groups to which she was assigned, inexplicably, met at the same time. When she did not attend the Economic and Social Council, Leroy Stinebower did so in her place, and, in his recollection, he performed the brunt of *her* work. Yet when Virginia seized the initiative, as occurred on occasion in other accounts of the conference, she again ran into criticism. Her efforts to revise the preamble by mentioning the word "education," for instance, antagonized the rest of the U.S. delegation, though her fellow delegates finally upheld this change. ("Oh, have it your way," said Senator Vandenberg). A message that Virginia conveyed about Charter revision to consultants from Jewish groups seems to have alarmed if not misled activists in several U.S. NGOs, including the NAACP, who feared that the revision of the Charter then underway would mean a retreat on human rights. So, whether she was either less than aggressive or, alternatively, more aggressive than expected, problems arose; Virginia did not always satisfy her U.S. colleagues. This was a taxing situation.[66]

In her own account, in contrast, Virginia underscored her diligence, resourcefulness, and accomplishment. Here, in her own words, was the "good delegate" she had hoped to be. She left her imprint on the preamble, for instance, in which her fellow U.S. delegates took "not the faintest interest," she contended, by replacing Field Marshal Smuts's awkward words, "the High Contracting Parties," with "We the peoples of the United Nations," a big improvement. Revising the preamble, Virginia noted, "was much like attempting to warm over someone's flat soufflé," but by doing so she carved out a role for herself. Harold Stassen, whom Virginia had always liked, remembered her contribution favorably. Diplomats had "ridiculed" her proposal, he recalled, but eventually she prevailed, "and eloquence overcame diplomatese."[67]

Virginia also attended five-power conferences (United States, China, USSR, United Kingdom, France) at plenary sessions in a penthouse of the Fairmont Hotel. The conferences decided challenging issues such as the right of veto on the Security Council. ("We did not conceive of it being used so often by the Soviet Union," Virginia recalled). A careful observer, she noted the role of State Department officer and secretary general of the conference, Alger Hiss, seated up on the dais ("No one dreamed of the tragic developments which were to send him to prison within a few years"). After full days of delegate meetings, committee conferences, radio broadcasts, and interviews with reporters, she dealt with visits from foreign delegations, especially those from the Near East. Foreign delegates proved, in Virginia's account, more receptive than their disparaging U.S. counterparts. Unlike the rest of the U.S. contingent,

Virginia paid attention to the Arab delegates, as when she attended a dinner in their honor (the only U.S. delegate present) and discussed with Egypt's minister of foreign affairs the future of the Middle East. She strengthened ties with the Arab league, whose members, ignored by the United States, voiced "disillusion" with Britain and France. By failing to "give any guidance to the Arab League," she argued, the United States missed an opportunity for leadership. Not least, Virginia made use of her two-woman support system, especially Elizabeth Reynard, who stayed at another hotel, the Francis Drake, among other staff members from whom she could elicit information and who attended committee sessions Virginia had to miss.[68]

Throughout her daunting schedule, however, Virginia explained, she faced a slew of obstacles, from the unexpected enmity of the Lutz faction to bare tolerance of her fellow delegates, who, from their first meetings in Washington, seemed to ignore whatever she proposed. She coped with the critical brigade of State Department advisors, men of ambition who sought to shape diplomacy themselves. She had, she explained, become accustomed to this sort of competitive if not disparaging conduct by "long experience with male colleagues at Columbia." Still, her resentment simmered, along with some pathos: "I thought how disappointed all these men must have been to have a lone woman speaking for them." Virginia never reached the conclusion that became clear to her foe Bertha Lutz, who, in a letter to U.S. suffrage leader Carrie Chapman Catt, declared the UN conference a "living hell;" according to Lutz, she spent fifteen hours a day "listening to men talking, talking, talking endlessly." Virginia, less outraged, longed for the approval of her U.S. colleagues, a forlorn hope that pervaded her final memory of the conference: the occasion when a photographer captured each of the U.S. delegates signing the UN Charter. As Virginia rose up to shake hands with President Truman, all of her fellow delegates beamed at the camera. At this moment, Virginia observes, the delegates seemed "to approve of me and like me," which had hardly been clear-cut previously. Virginia's commentary—her wish to be an "equal comrade," her hope for approval, and her ongoing sense of rebuff—adds depth to her detailed, vivid, and much-cited account of the UN Conference in her autobiography of 1954. In her own account, she met a challenging situation with self-confidence and resourcefulness.[69]

As soon as the UN conference ended in 1945, Virginia began the long process of shaping her United Nations experience for the historical record and showing her role as the "good delegate." Any issue over "the position of women," she insisted, had been merely "a matter of prolonged discussion," not a source of conflict. Any votes that she had cast on the issue in committees, as she explained in a radio talk, had represented the opinion of the U.S. delegation, not "the private view of Virginia Gildersleeve." And finally, the U.S. delegates had treated her "with complete fairness as well as good comradeship," as she explained to the General Federation of Women's Clubs." "We all worked together as a united team."[70] As Virginia began shaping the record, however, another event intruded. President Truman suddenly chose a second woman to join the U.S. delegation to the UN.

Appointed in December 1945, Eleanor Roosevelt did not at first elicit high expectations. Diplomats initially found the appointment unwise. The former first lady, they feared, lacked experience in foreign affairs; she was too voluble and might blunder into controversy. But these critics were wrong; Eleanor Roosevelt defied adverse expectations to win over her UN colleagues, grasp a leadership role, and preside over historic achievement in human rights. By 1948, as the *New Yorker* proclaimed in a series of articles, Eleanor Roosevelt had become "first lady of the world." She also eluded the challenge posed by equal rights feminists at the United Nations by deftly and strategically giving way to their demands, though always with caution or even with an occasional sideswipe. "I can see that perhaps it does add a little to the position of women to be declared equal before the law and equal politically and in whatever work a woman chooses to undertake," Eleanor wrote in her "My Day" column in 1951. The UN Commission on the Status of Women had just endorsed such a position at its last meeting, she explained. "There is one thing to remember, however, and that is that when you put things on paper you haven't actually accomplished anything." This was the social feminist speaking! Bertha Lutz had made a similar observation, a few years earlier, though from the opposite perspective. "[T]he United Nations have written beautifully sounded words into the Charter," she told Carrie Chapman Catt in 1945, "but have no intentions of carrying them out."[71]

The contrast between the experiences of Virginia and of Eleanor Roosevelt in the male-dominated arena of the UN is also salient. The two women had encountered one another as far back as the 1920s when Eleanor Roosevelt entered women's groups and Democratic politics in New York City. They undoubtedly met at a Seven College Conference dinner in January 1929 at the Astor Hotel, where a photographer captured the meeting. They met again in 1935 when Eleanor Roosevelt spoke at Barnard on the absurdity of entitlement; the first lady decried "any sense of superiority" based on family roots or social status. They met yet again at the White House dinner of March 3, 1936. Two more meetings took place in the early 1940s, at a New York social event of 1942 and again when Eleanor visited Barnard in 1943. Virginia was scheduled to have lunch with the first lady in April 1945, before leaving for San Francisco, or so Eleanor announced at what would be her final press conference, on April 12, 1945, the day that FDR died. The lunch of course never occurred; at the end of the year, in December 1945, President Truman appointed Eleanor Roosevelt as a delegate to the United Nations. Eleanor replaced Virginia in effect as the sole woman among U.S. delegates to the United Nations (though Virginia had not yet formally resigned). Finally, the two fellow Democrats shared the same suspicious stance on women's demands for equal rights. Eleanor Roosevelt, however, handled the issue with much greater finesse. By far the more experienced politician—and hence diplomat—the former First Lady knew when to take a loss. She also brought to her UN assignment years of wielding political power, as she had done in Washington and as she continued to do in her years at the United Nations and after; this was a skill set and an advantage that Virginia simply lacked.[72]

Eleanor Roosevelt expressed regret that Virginia turned down a UN post in 1947. "I am sincerely sorry, for I was proud that our delegation had two women in the last session," ER wrote in "My Day" on September 15, 1947. But a chasm separated the two women. ER overshadowed everyone in her path at the United Nations. Threatened by rivalry, Virginia had reason to resent the former first lady's prominence. Her response was to exclude Eleanor Roosevelt almost entirely from her autobiography.[73]

Eclipsed by Eleanor Roosevelt on the U.S. delegation to the United Nations in 1945, Virginia rebounded in 1946 with an offer from General

Douglas MacArthur to join a twenty-six-member committee to revise the educational system of defeated Japan; her colleagues, mainly educators, such as school superintendents, also included Mildred McAfee Horton of Wellesley and former New Dealer Emily Woodward. Touring Japan for six weeks in the spring of 1946, led by New York's commissioner of education, George D. Stoddard, committee members clashed on what stance to adopt toward the former enemy, became embroiled with one another, and barely churned out a final report. The report urged replacement of the Japanese education system with one based on American values; it recommended easier access to higher education for students of all social and economic classes and inclusion in university curricula of lectures in world history and international relations. Above all, the report promoted progressive goals, such as coeducation, vocational education, an end to memorization and conformity, retraining of teachers, and decentralization. "A highly centralized educational system, even if it is not caught in the net of ultra-nationalism and militarism, is endangered by the evils that accompany an entrenched bureaucracy," the final report declared, in its convoluted and ponderous style. The committee also proposed reorganization of Japan's written language— an effort to facilitate the nation's transition to political democracy. "It is recommended that some form of Romanji [representation of Japanese in Latin script] be brought into common use," the final report said. The Japanese language, in its current form, the committee charged, impeded expression of democratic concepts. "Language should be a highway, not a barrier . . . for the transmission of knowledge and ideas." At first the U.S. suggestions had some effect, but within a few years Japanese reluctance to accept the committee's educational credo stymied efforts at implementing reform. Asked by the press about the future of Japanese education, Virginia said, "it would be necessary to wait twenty-five years to see."[74]

Even to an experienced traveler like Virginia (now sixty-nine), the trip to Japan was a challenge. Arrangements capsized, officials blundered, committee members seemed trapped in Guam interminably, and once in Japan, at last, found "air reeking with bacteria and viruses." Like her companions, Virginia battled sore throats, sinus and ear infections, coughs, and fevers. "Classes were crowded. None of the schools were heated," a committee member recorded. "In the afternoon

Jerry got a movie of General MacArthur leaving his office to go home for lunch." But worst were the battles with one another. From the start, "we were handicapped by profound differences of opinion among us," in Virginia's view. It became clear "that if we discussed until Doomsday," no accord would arise. Virginia discerned two factions: On one side were the "Supra-Americans," who "had no friendly feeling for the Japanese people or regard for their culture and no desire to aid them," and who wanted to impose "American education in its entirety" (or "what they thought to be American education") on Japan. Her own faction, in contrast, the "Live-and-let-Live" contingent, respected "the ancient culture of the Japanese." But dispute prevailed, and Virginia's foes dominated the panel's report. Democratization of postwar Japan would have to follow other paths.[75]

In the fall of 1945 Virginia turned to yet another issue in foreign affairs, one with which she would spend much time in the coming years: the future of Palestine. She began with two letters, one to the *New York Times* on October 9, 1945 and another, on January 10, 1946, to the Anglo-American Committee of Inquiry on Palestine, a group just formed by Prime Minister Clement Atlee and President Truman, to consider Palestine, Jewish immigration, Arab resistance, and international security. Both letters warned against admitting Jews in any numbers "to a section of the world where they will have as neighbors many millions of enemies." As an American citizen "deeply interested in the Near East," Virginia wrote, she sought "a peaceful solution of the Palestine Question." Her solution: to end the inflow of Jews to Palestine. She opposed "imposing by force on Palestine the political domination of a minority of its citizens [Jews], against the will of the present majority [Arabs], or changing forcibly the present majority by compelling Palestine to receive unlimited immigration of Jews." To enable Jewish immigration, Virginia contended, "would make Palestine a Jewish political state" and "would not further the interests of the Jews. It would place the Palestine Jews among millions of hostile neighbors, a position which could be maintained only by force, presumably in large measure the force of our American arms. It would arouse much ill feeling against the Jews in the public opinion of the world." Such a move would damage U.S. interests, inspire resentment, create enemies, "turn these peoples away from us and from the Western world," and harm the United Nations, which sought to build international understanding. She urged admission of 200,000 Jewish refugees to the United States, above the usual immigration quotas, to ease the influx to Palestine.[76]

The letters were an opening salvo in Virginia's postwar anti-Zionist campaign, and more than that. Anti-Zionism had been a long-term part of Virginia's arsenal; she had shared such sentiments in the past with her allies among the Barnard trustees, such as George A. Plimpton and Rev. Harry Emerson Fosdick, pastor of Riverside Church since 1930, and with the larger community of Near East aficionados and benefactors. But now, in 1945 and 1946, concern with refugees from war-torn Europe had arisen, the Middle East was in transformation, and anti-Zionism faced a more challenging future. Virginia chose this moment to find a public venue for what was bound to be a divisive stance.

Preoccupation with the future of Palestine shaped Virginia's final interchange with the United Nations. In July 1947, Secretary of State George Marshall invited Virginia to serve as an alternate U.S. delegate at the second session of the UN General Assembly. The timing was good: Virginia had just retired from Barnard. But she declined, due to pneumonia. The illness was temporary; her refusal, in contrast, was final. Why did she turn down the invitation? Eleanor Roosevelt had by then set a standard of achievement at the United Nations that Virginia could not equal or even approach; to accept the appointment would have meant to be upstaged. But that was not why Virginia declined the UN offer. A far more pressing reason existed: her convictions on U.S. Middle East policy. As Virginia stated, the vote on partition of Palestine would have come up and it would have been impossible for her to vote with the U.S. delegates.[77] In any case, the moment passed; the state of Israel was created in 1948. Further work at the United Nations, in Virginia's view, was not a possibility.

TOWARD RETIREMENT

Virginia had mentioned her own prospects for retirement from Barnard in the early 1940s. On December 1, 1941, six days before Pearl Harbor, she had told President Butler of her hope to retire on June 30, 1943, when she would be sixty-five. "Why in the world do you want to retire?" said Butler. "I don't understand it. Why, if I should retire, I'd be dead within six months." But the U.S. declaration of war on December 7, 1941 delayed Virginia's plans. President Butler and the Barnard trustees asked her to stay on as dean during the war. She remained.[78]

Virginia watched President Butler totter through his last years in office, "when his powers faltered." By 1941, Frank Fackenthal, former university secretary and now provost, helped out with university administration; the president was blind and half deaf. University trustees sought Virginia's help to ease Butler's exit, though she had no success. The president resisted leaving; as he had told the press at age seventy-nine, "They'll have to give me fifty million dollars before I approach retirement." His last days in office were trying, in Virginia's view, due to his second marriage in 1907 to Kate Lee Montagne. "Outwardly the perfect wife for a President, a perfect hostess for a great university, the second Mrs. Butler was in the home a jealous, hysterical tyrant," Virginia wrote. "She even tried to cut him off from his daughter by his first wife, his dearly loved and only child, Sarah Butler, "Barnard '15." Finally in the spring of 1945, as Virginia left for San Francisco, a few trustees gained the courage to ask Butler to depart. The trustees accepted his letter of resignation in April. Butler retired in 1945 at age eighty-three—he had served since 1902. Two years later, in June 1947, the trustees appointed his successor, General Dwight D. Eisenhower.[79]

Across Broadway at Barnard, ever since Virginia had first mentioned the possibility of leaving the deanship, college trustees had sought a replacement and formed a special committee to do so. By 1942, the trustees had settled on a favored candidate who was not quite ready to consider the offer. Meanwhile, as Virginia advised the navy, flew to England, praised "trained brains," and built up her foreign policy resumé, her problems at Barnard mounted. Charges of discrimination in admissions had been hurled at the college, notably by William Allan Neilson's report to the trustees in 1941 and then by Harlem minister James Robinson's accusations of 1943. Such charges of bias, though nothing new, in Virginia's experience, were now more trenchant; wartime changes in public policy and popular conviction—a tilt toward democracy—gave the accusations more political heft. Virginia, under pressure, responded defiantly. At the same time, her long-term anti-Zionism surged into public view; her letter of 1945 to the *New York Times* opposed to Jewish migration to Palestine rattled the Barnard community. Just as defiantly,

Virginia sought to interrupt the trustees' search process and to settle the choice of her own replacement.[80]

By 1945, as it became clear that the trustee search committee had a first choice. Virginia submitted to the committee her personal list of candidates and urged the appointment of her favorite, Elizabeth Reynard, her loyal lieutenant and current partner. Such a proposal, irregular and inappropriate, begged for rebuff. "As the time for her retirement drew near, Miss Gildersleeve became obsessed with the notion that Reynard should be her successor as Barnard head," recalled philosophy professor Joseph Brennan. But the trustees rejected Elizabeth Reynard. In their view, she lacked the skills in administration and fundraising that they sought. As Brennan put it, when it came to Reynard, "the trustees were unwilling and the faculty did not like her style at all." Members of the Special Trustees Committee awaited their opportunity. In November, 1945, six months after President Butler's retirement, Virginia asked again to retire, this time by June 30, 1947. This time, the Barnard trustees accepted. "As I happen to be feeling particularly well and vigorous," Virginia told the press, "it seems a good time to plan to go." A year later, in the fall of 1946, the trustees' committee formally announced its choice of a replacement for the dean. The winning candidate differed greatly from Virginia.[81]

"Headmistress of the Brearley School, Mother of Five, Will Succeed Miss Gildersleeve," said the *New York Times* on November 26, 1946. Millicent Carey McIntosh—"Mrs. Mac"—had been the head of Brearley since 1930 and had been under consideration for college posts since the late 1930s. A niece of M. Carey Thomas, Mrs. Mac was a Bryn Mawr graduate of 1920. She studied at Newham College, Cambridge and received a PhD from Johns Hopkins in 1926. After teaching for a year at Rosemary Hall in Greenwich, Connecticut, Mrs. Mac taught English at Bryn Mawr, where she was appointed freshman dean in 1928 and acting dean in 1929. In 1932, a few years after arriving at Brearley, she had married a prominent doctor and begun her large family. Mrs. Mac would become Barnard's first president in 1952. Her administration, though not trouble-free—at first Virginia loyalists griped and finances sagged—lasted until 1962. Admired and talented, Mrs. Mac proved an exceptional leader. And though Virginia left reluctantly, Mrs. Mac always extended a hope of friendship. "Certainly you and I have a right to be friends, whether I am the Dean or not!" she wrote to Virginia in December 1947.[82]

Virginia, in her autobiography, took credit for the Mrs. Mac appointment: she claimed to have submitted a list of potential successors with Millicent McIntosh near the top of it. But her claim covered up a demoralizing clash with the Board of Trustees. Mrs. Mac had been the trustees' choice, not her own; her advocacy of Elizabeth had been scorned. The pivotal trustees in the decision, moreover, had been Virginia's longtime friends and allies Helen Rogers Reid and Agnes Meyer. Virginia put the best spin she could—in retrospect—on an appointment she had opposed. At the moment, in contrast, rejection stung. Mrs. Mac's appointment followed yet another moment of transition. On a final visit to Alciston in the summer of 1946, Virginia had packed up the books, had them carted away to Bedford College, called on the vicar, and finally, deposited Cara's ashes, which had been sent from Arizona to Sussex, in the Alciston Parish churchyard next to Lilian Clapham; the dean then left England forever. She also confronted the inevitable: "[M]y long term at Barnard was drawing to a close."[83]

Mrs. Mac won the type of national publicity Virginia had always sought. "At Barnard this week as they prepare to celebrate her inauguration, Barnard students are looking forward to their new dean," reported *Life* magazine in October 1947. "For as long as they and most of their mothers can remember, brilliant Dean Virginia Gildersleeve has ruled Barnard. In her thirty-six-year term she made the rules and planned the course efficiently and effectively, with an awesome lack of foolishness," *Life* declared. But Mrs. Mac, in contrast, the parent of four sons and a daughter, occasionally wore slacks around the campus, projected an up-to-date aura of success, and seemed to delight her new clientele.[84] Next to her successor, the former dean looked (to *Life*) like a relic.

Virginia's departure from the deanship was probably long overdue. She had no doubt stayed on too long, as historian Robert McCaughey suggests; by the mid-1940s, coteries of students, faculty, and trustees awaited her exit. But the dean had her partisans, too. "I just don't know what would have happened to Barnard if Miss Gildersleeve hadn't stayed [through the war]," recalled Frank Fackenthal. "As it is [looking back from the 1950s], there has been a deplorable change there [at Barnard] since her retirement. Even our [the trustees'] relieving Mrs. McIntosh of many of her routine committee meetings, and functional affairs that the dean always had to cope with, things don't seem to get done as they were when she was at the helm."[85]

As she prepared to leave, Virginia accepted many tributes. On April 27, 1947, Barnard alumnae and trustees hosted the dean at a luncheon at the Waldorf Astoria where the French ambassador, Henri Bonnet, offered the retiring dean the Legion of Honor Award in recognition of her support of France during the occupation and her role at the United Nations. Barnard trustee Gano Dunn gave Virginia the title of Dean Emeritus and use for life of Barnard facilities. Former Secretary of State Edward Stettinius praised her achievement, as did trustee Agnes Meyer, who cited the dean's "integrity, reason, objectivity, and moral tenacity." A representative of Kappa Kappa Gamma bestowed a $1,500 gift, which Virginia said she would use to buy library books for the American College for Girls in Istanbul. "There are now 7,500 alumnae of Barnard," the dean declared in her acceptance speech, her last official talk. "Of these all but 875 have been graduated during my deanship. So I have a large family." Before leaving campus Virginia accepted plaudits of the college staff—cooks, porters, gardeners—at a Buildings and Grounds department celebration. "Some families," she noted, "Irish and Negro, have had members on the staff for two or three generations." As she left the campus, the staff sang "Auld Lang Syne."[86]

Elizabeth Reynard retired two years after the dean, amid conflict with colleagues who disputed Reynard's academic value and claimed that the program she ran was falling apart. "Circumstances and personalities" in the English department, according to Virginia, "blocked the development and advancement she [Reynard] deserved." By then Elizabeth and Virginia had moved from Morningside Heights to Bedford, New York, from where they sent letters of recrimination to college administrators about the circumstances of Elizabeth Reynard's departure. Virginia would visit Barnard only once more in her lifetime.[87]

Another Gildersleeve legacy faded in the late 1940s: the biased admissions policy that had prevailed until the war. Challenges to discrimination in college admissions reflected a postwar surge in liberalism. In New York State in 1945, the American Jewish Congress challenged Columbia's tax-exempt status on the grounds that state tax laws barred discrimination on the basis of race or religion, and that patterns of discrimination existed. State courts ruled that only individuals could press a challenge to a university on admissions bias; a pattern of discrimination was invalid for redress. The same year, legislators who had just passed New York's Fair Employment Practices Law turned to antidiscrimination legislation applicable to private colleges and universities. An early draft, which spoke of a "predetermined pattern of admission," would have barred discriminatory admissions practices at colleges and universities statewide. The law that passed in 1948, the Fair Educational Practices Act, was much weaker; it enabled the commissioner of education to investigate the complaints of a rejected applicant but left college admissions criteria, such as geographical distribution goals, in place. In state law as in private lawsuits, a "pattern of discrimination" remained irrelevant. New Jersey and Massachusetts passed slightly broader versions of the same law.[88]

State efforts to reform college admissions in the late 1940s had mixed impact. As the New York law had been enfeebled en route to passage, opportunity for bias remained. "Selective admissions," as historian Harold Wechsler shows, had become the accepted mechanism of college admissions. New York's law of 1948 left that mechanism in place; colleges like Columbia and Barnard remained free to focus on geographic distribution—to pursue their "national aspirations." But a college's criteria for admissions now came under closer scrutiny. Blatant discrimination by race or religion *could* now be challenged, if only by an individual whose application had been rejected. In response to the new laws, some colleges removed obligatory mention of race, religion, and nationality from their application forms. Most important, the postwar legislation reflected rising awareness of the hazard of bias and exclusion. "It was thought that since the colleges set the moral tone and climate for the nation," as a New York City official of the 1940s recalled, "discrimination in the campus might lead to further discrimination elsewhere." "Limitations of Jewish admissions ceased to be an issue by the mid-fifties," Wechsler states. By the time Virginia left Barnard, professionals ran its admission office.[89]

"Had it not been for the strong leadership of Virginia Gildersleeve in the first half of the century, it is likely that Barnard would have disappeared as an independent college for women long ago," wrote Joseph Brennan in the 1970s. "Under her firm hand Barnard grew from a barely tolerated morganatic adjunct of Columbia to a university college, respected and autonomous, within Nicholas Murray Butler's scholarly imperium."[90] His assessment resonates. Virginia had pursued dual goals with success; since 1940, especially, she had shaped a remarkable career. The 1930s and 1940s, however, had enmeshed her in difficulty, too. She had dealt with her own illnesses, at first heart disease and later pneumonia; she had faced Cara's decline, financial woes on campus, and ultimately rejection by the trustees of her chosen successor. Most grievously, she had condoned Nazism when she should have attacked it; her interlude of apology for fascism in the 1930s undercuts her record of achievement. Still, as admirers and detractors all recognized, Virginia had created Barnard as they knew it—its curriculum, faculty, student body, and alumnae, its values and its distinctive nature. Through her decades in office, no one had questioned her devotion to a liberal arts education for women or her concern for the college and its constituents. With that part of her career in the past, the former dean now severed herself almost completely from Barnard and, with Elizabeth Reynard, began a new life.

CHAPTER FIVE

Embattled

After Barnard, 1947–1965

On an icy day in January 1947, Elizabeth Reynard drove Virginia to see a property that Reynard had bought in Westchester County, about forty miles north of New York City. They looked at "a shabby old house in Bedford Village," Virginia wrote. "It stood at the top of snow coated terraces, looking small and deserted but with an air of elegance and dignity." The house had been built around 1800 for John Jay, the first chief justice of the United States Supreme Court; the façade, with its columns and portico, exemplified Federalist style. Virginia moved in on June 19, 1947, just as she retired from Barnard. She and Elizabeth agreed that Virginia would occupy the house in exchange for "contributing some improvements," and that Elizabeth, still teaching, would stay on weekends. The two women had the original fireplaces restored and new pipes installed; they called the property Navarre, one of its former names. Elizabeth began a full-time residence two years later when she stopped teaching at age fifty-two. "Since I retired from Barnard, and Elizabeth resigned for reasons of health," wrote Virginia, "we have cast our lot in together, as most academic people must do to make their pensions stretch."[1]

Navarre became the backdrop of their relationship and of the next decade's activities. There, at Navarre, Virginia came to terms with disengagement from Barnard, her academic home for over half a century. Pursuing her interest in international affairs and especially in the Middle

East, Virginia embarked on a campaign against Zionism to which she devoted abundant energy. Finally, both Elizabeth and Virginia became authors and memoirists. In 1951 Elizabeth published her novel, *The Mutinous Wind*, about a folktale from Cape Cod, where she and Virginia had begun to buy and renovate properties. Elizabeth also worked on some chapters of an autobiography, which Virginia later circulated among friends. In 1954, seeking a larger audience, Virginia published her impressive autobiography, *Many a Good Crusade*, in which she sought to shape—and reshape—her role in history.

AT NAVARRE

During the first few years in Westchester, Virginia adjusted to separation from Barnard. But disputes arose at once, at first over the role of Elizabeth Reynard at the college and of Barnard's American Studies Program. Elizabeth had bought the historic Bedford property, Virginia noted, as a place for students in her American Studies courses, "but American Studies at Barnard underwent changes in organization, which made this plan no longer possible."[2] The fate of the academic program, to Virginia, was linked to Reynard's failing health and to the resignation that ended Reynard's academic career.

"She would have succeeded me as Dean of Barnard College, I often think, had she chosen, as others did, *not* to volunteer to serve her country," Virginia wrote in 1954. "When she left us for military service she was admired, loved, and trusted by her colleagues." The war era, in Virginia's version of events, disrupted this era of rapport.

> When she [Reynard] returned, at the end of four years, there was not a student left who had studied under her. An unusually large number of senior officers had been retired. There were many new appointments, often due to wartime expediency. There were sharp struggles for power among those who coveted advancement, an unfortunate human habit that arises in every institution from time to time. So when, after four years, Elizabeth Reynard returned to her College, she found it greatly changed—as so many G.I.'s found their former posts—and life in it far more difficult for her. Tired by her strenuous war service, her health soon broke.[3]

Virginia's statement, though defensive, included some unrefutable facts: the war years had indeed brought changes in personnel to the college, as Virginia had observed at the time. "There is an appalling lot for me to do!" the dean had informed Catharine Weiser ("Bunter") in September 1942. "So many of the staff have left or are leaving that many readjustments are needed and new people must be found." Departure, death, and retirement made an impact in wartime, and postwar hiring brought yet more changes—perhaps spurred by newcomers who sought career advancement. Old-timers, too, of course, sought advancement, which Virginia had withheld for years.[4]

But Elizabeth Reynard's very presence at Barnard, after her return from the navy, also posed some problems for her colleagues. Virginia's demand that Elizabeth succeed to the deanship caused consternation and drew critics; although the plan of succession sank, a sense of resentment among faculty lingered. Faculty newcomers in the English Department, at the same moment, faced a sensitive situation: a colleague with authority over an important program was closely tied to the not-yet-retired dean. "I think that I was timorous about the fact that Miss Reynard was so much Dean Gildersleeve's lady," as cultural critic John Kouwenhoven, a new arrival of 1946, recalled, "and that Elizabeth was in charge of the American Studies program." Virginia's particular brand of tone-deafness, as in this instance, applied to everything that involved Elizabeth Reynard.[5]

Just as important, when she resumed her old college position in 1946, Reynard proposed a new plan for the American Studies Program, one that reflected her current interest—and Virginia's longtime involvement—in international affairs. From now on, American Studies would enable students to focus not only on the "character of the United States," its traditions, ideals, and institutions, but also on "its relation to other nations and its place in world affairs." Elizabeth Reynard's plan for the program, as it veered into international waters, put a burden on the pivotal course she had created, The Legend of America. Thus far, the course had been a survey of American literature with a historicist edge. Imbued now with an international thrust, the revised course focused on "our country as others see us," as Elizabeth wrote to Helen Rogers Reid in 1947; it provided "some insight into America's place in world affairs." Under the new plan, students learned about "significant literary and cultural traditions . . . which have influenced foreign conceptions of America."[6]

The enlarged goals of the American Studies program—with its new international spin—may have alarmed some faculty participants or else provided an excuse to defy Elizabeth Reynard. Critics charged that Reynard lacked experience in international affairs and challenged her ability to teach The Legend of America. Virginia came to Reynard's defense; in a letter of May 1948 to her replacement, Dean Millicent McIntosh, Virginia lashed out at Elizabeth Reynard's assailants. "This criticism touches me rather closely, for I warmly encouraged her to develop the course and I think her excellently fitted to give it," Virginia wrote. Elizabeth, Virginia posited, combined "unusually extensive concrete experience in the international field with the brains and scholarly training to use this experience, and with the gift of effective teaching." To cite concrete international experience, Virginia summed up Elizabeth Reynard's life abroad with her family.

> She grew up in an international atmosphere, for her father was concerned in international affairs, and they travelled and lived abroad during a large part of her youth. She worked in a hospital in Belgium during the First World War and was afterwards decorated by the Belgian Government for her service. She studied for two years at Oxford, where she was the first woman invited to candidacy for the D.Litt. in English. During this period she spent all the vacations on the Continent, in Belgium, France, and Italy.

Reynard's further achievements, Virginia continued, included her assistance to Virginia at the UN Charter conference of 1945; her help with materials for Virginia's educational mission to Japan in 1946; and her record of distinction at Barnard and Oxford, which showed "first rate brains and scholarly equipment." Finally, Virginia conveyed her conviction—in response to the charges of critics—that Reynard "would never teach or write superficially . . . that the content of her *Legend of America* was thoroughly sound." Voicing regret that Elizabeth would probably not teach The Legend of America again, Virginia hoped, she wrote, that her testimonial to Elizabeth Reynard's skills might "help clear up any misunderstanding about the past."[7]

Virginia's defense was not enough, however, or else just compounded Elizabeth's problems with her colleagues. In 1949, the American Studies program collapsed, and at the end of 1949 Elizabeth Reynard retired from teaching. In her letter of the resignation to the Board of Trustees, arguing that she had brought "something new in college leadership and college service," Elizabeth listed the administrative posts she had filled for the college, including head of a wartime national service training program, director of the American Studies program, and creator of the ill-fated Legend of America course. "I regret that my immediate health makes it impossible for me to teach this year," Reynard wrote to Helen Reid, chair of the Board of Trustees, in December 1949. "I feel that I must sever now all connection with such unpleasant academic memories as might too gravely shadow the future." As a parting gesture, Reynard sent the trustees $2,000 to fund faculty projects "to enable the college to support the community." The substantial donation, worth ten times as much today, suggests Elizabeth Reynard's personal wealth. In May 1950, the *New York Times* announced Elizabeth's retirement for reasons of health.[8]

Virginia's assessment of Elizabeth Reynard's postwar problems at Barnard brought up the issue of friction over Elizabeth among faculty members, though with no grasp of her own role in generating such friction. Although Elizabeth Reynard was "one of the most successful teachers our college has known," Virginia declared, the academic environment had grown hostile and enmity among English professors had prevailed. "Unfortunately," wrote Virginia, "circumstances and personalities in her department seriously blocked the development and advancement she deserved and post-war academic chaos helped shatter her health and cut short her active career as it neared its peak." In the decade that followed, Elizabeth Reynard's health declined. According to Virginia, by 1954 Elizabeth suffered from crippling spinal arthritis; had endured three attacks of cancer, grim operations, and long hospitalizations; and was allergic to all drugs. Barnard faculty, meanwhile, in 1952 revived the American Studies program, at first called "American Civilization," under a five-year grant funded by the Carnegie Corporation. Led at the outset by a historian, Basil Rauch, the program enjoyed enduring success. Virginia, however, retained hostility toward its chairman. Six years later, when she and Elizabeth Reynard left directions in their wills for establishment of a Columbia chair, the "Navarre" professorship (never established), Virginia specified in a memorandum her personal wish that "Dr. Basil Rauch should never be appointed to this chair."[9]

Elizabeth Reynard's retirement was just one issue of several. Virginia's annoyance at Barnard grew when she learned that her successor, Millicent McIntosh, as of July 1, 1952, was granted the title of president as well as that of dean. Barnard trustees sought the change of title at the suggestion of the Ford Foundation in order to underscore Barnard's independent role in relationship to Columbia so that Barnard might compete for and receive funds on the same basis as other independent colleges. To Virginia, however, the honor of the new title should have gone to her, rather than to Mrs. Mac, her successor. "The sad part about this is that Millicent McIntosh never wanted to have the title changed from Dean to President," Barnard administrator Jean T. Palmer later wrote to Virginia, in response to a "blast" from the former dean about the issue. "I know this because I was General Secretary [of Barnard] at the time the change was made, and it came as a recommendation of our fund-raising consultant," Palmer stated. Foundations and corporations claimed that that their gifts to Columbia included Barnard, Palmer explained, and could "see no reason to make Barnard any additional gifts." Thus, Barnard needed its own president—as well as its own trustees and faculty—in order to raise funds. "I hope that you will always feel free to send us your 'blasts,' " Palmer added.[10]

By the end of 1952, Virginia's rift with Barnard had become a gulf of grievance. Dorothea Setzer, the freelance writer who helped Virginia compile notes and records for her autobiography in the early 1950s, summed up Virginia's sense of alienation after five years of retirement. "As of this date [February 1953] Dean Gildersleeve has not once been invited to return to Barnard College to participate in any activity other than that of the Finance Committee, who have asked her to help them raise funds for the college," wrote Setzer, who had, in the past few years, been interviewing Virginia's associates, gathering tributes to the former dean, and collecting biographical material. "She has never been asked to address the student body as a whole or by classes so that the girls who have come to college after her retirement have not even been privileged to see the great dean who put their institution on the map." It was Virginia, Setzer claimed, who had raised funds for the college after her successor took over; it was through Virginia's efforts that Mrs. John

D. Rockefeller had donated a million dollars to the college; and it was Virginia's friendship with Mrs. Thomas Lamont (wife of the banker) that had resulted in a bequest to the Seven Sisters. But the students no longer heard Virginia speak, Setzer charged, and the alumnae ignored her: "The dean was dropped out completely from the academic life of her college."[11]

To what extent Virginia shared the resentment that Dorothea Setzer so strongly voiced is unclear. Subsequently, some tentative interchanges arose between the former dean and her successor. "It seems a very long time since I have seen you," wrote Mrs. Mac to Virginia in September 1953. "My best to Elizabeth." In November 1954, Virginia visited Barnard for the last time to promote her new memoir, just published; the reception included trustees who had foiled her plan for a successor seven years earlier. In June 1955, when the United Nations toasted the tenth anniversary of its Charter, Virginia sent regrets through the Barnard public relations office. Two years later, the college established an annual visiting lectureship in Virginia's honor. "As you can guess, we are all much excited about the Virginia C. Gildersleeve Professorship," Mrs. Mac wrote to Virginia in September 1957; the former dean expressed appreciation.[12] Meanwhile, during the early years away from Barnard, Virginia found another arena in which to exert her influence.

THE ANTI-ZIONIST CRUSADE

Virginia had resigned from Barnard in 1947 with many international concerns in play. She continued her link with Reid Hall, in Paris, as it reopened for the postwar era, and remained chair of its board of directors, as she had been for thirty years, until 1952. The longtime Reid Hall president, Dorothy Leet '17, became president of the International Federation of University Women, "another of the enterprises I helped to create," Virginia wrote. Virginia also continued to lead the Board of Trustees of the American College for Girls in Istanbul and brought Elizabeth Reynard onto the board; she remained vice president of the board of directors of the Near East College Association, in which she had been active since the 1920s. But Virginia's overriding concern was the transformation of the Middle East, the region that had absorbed her interest since World War I; the rise of Zionism, which she had found a threat to Arab people through the interwar years, she claimed, and which had accelerated during World War II; and the movement into Palestine "of many thousands of Jewish immigrants, against the wishes the Arab majority of the population, whose ancestors had held and tilled (the land) for over a thousand years."[13]

Virginia's sympathy with anti-Zionism had a long history; as a disciple of Charles R. Crane, she had been involved with the Middle East and Arab peoples since the 1920s. Her campaign against postwar Zionism had begun before her retirement. She had used her time in San Francisco in 1945 to befriend delegates from Arab nations, who shared her opposition to the founding of a Jewish state. She had written public letters of 1945 and 1946 protesting the arrival in Palestine of Jewish refugees from Europe. When offered a job on the U.S. delegation to the United Nations in the summer of 1947, she had declined, as she sought to avoid the General Assembly vote on partition of Palestine, which the United States backed and which she opposed. To what extent the State Department grasped Virginia's stance on the Middle East when it offered the UN job is unclear; but a few months later, she restated her views. "The partition of Palestine will fertilize the soil for another world war," Virginia declared in a group letter to the *New York Times* in 1947. Dismissing the UN offer, she claimed, had freed her "to do what I could for what seemed the cause of justice and well-being for the whole Middle East." The partition plan that the General Assembly approved on November 29, 1947 would have created independent Jewish and Arab states, ended the British mandate that governed the area, and arranged for staggered withdrawal of British troops. Arabs rejected the plan, never implemented, and on May 14, 1948, when British forces left, the state of Israel began, amid Arab-Israeli armed conflict.[14]

To campaign against Zionism in 1947–1948—just as Israel came into being—meant reaching out to like-minded allies, to others who opposed the creation of a Jewish state. "Almost all Americans with diplomatic, educational, missionary, or business experience in the Middle East fervently believed that the Zionist plan is as directly contrary to our national interests, military, strategic, and commercial, as well as to common justice," Virginia declared, discussing the postwar era.[15] In fact, U.S. sentiment and policy now tilted strongly toward Israel. Nazi genocide and compassion for surviving victims of fascism, now refugees, ensured such a tilt. Still, anti-Zionism had a core of support among State Department Middle East specialists (or "Arabists"), ministers and educators with experience among missionaries to the Middle East, and members of pro-Arab interest organizations; these were overlapping constituencies.[16] Some anti-Zionists joined national pressure groups that arose during or after the war.

At the end of February 1948, Virginia joined in the founding in Washington of the Committee for Justice and Peace in the Holy Land (CJP), a pressure group to reverse partition of Palestine. Virginia chaired the new group, as "I no longer had much to lose from Zionist threats and attacks." Her fellow officers included Dr. Henry Sloane Coffin, president emeritus of the Union Theological Seminary, vice chairman, and, as executive director, Kermit (Kim) Roosevelt, grandson of Theodore Roosevelt and during World War II a member of OSS, the forerunner of the CIA; to Virginia, Kim Roosevelt was a "gifted and energetic young man who has done so much with the Palestine question." Behind the CJP leaders stood a council of one hundred "well known Americans, churchmen and educators," reported the *New York Herald Tribune*, some of whom had lived in the Middle East. The CJP's goals: to urge the General Assembly to reconsider partition, to secure a cease-fire in Palestine, and to find homes for displaced persons. The leaders visited with Secretary of State George Marshall, whom Virginia found "in sympathy," in contrast to President Truman, who, in her view, "did not follow the advice of his own Middle East experts but acted contrary to it."[17]

In March 1948, as CJP chair, Virginia conferred with Warren Austin, head of the U.S. delegation to the UN to urge a truce in Palestine, a temporary UN trusteeship, and a plan to "return the unity of the Holy Land." The same month, as an individual, she resigned from the American Committee for the United Nations because of the U.S. stance on partition, which, she charged, endangered "the prestige of the UN," and misinterpreted its charter. Its board and executives, she charged—and this included her former mentor James Shotwell—had become "a tool of Zionist propaganda."[18]

The CJP, meanwhile, found an ally in another anti-Zionist bastion, the American Council for Judaism (ACJ), the leading U.S. Jewish anti-Zionist group. Formed in 1942 by Reform Jews of German origin who saw Judaism as a religion, not a nationality, the ACJ defied the ascending trend of Zionism. Arising in the nineteenth century, Zionism made gains in the United States during World War I; the endorsement of Louis D. Brandeis, who took over leadership of the American Zionist movement in 1914, legitimized it. This was a turning point: Brandeis, writes his biographer, Melvin I. Urofsky, turned the American Zionist movement "from a moribund organization into a powerful political presence." He also showed that Zionism was compatible with patriotism. The Nazi menace of the 1930s increased support for Zionism, and World War II solidified it. By the war era, anti-Zionism was a minority view in U.S. Jewish politics, the remnant of a once-dominant stance. By 1948, writes historian of religion Martin E. Marty, the ACJ "had itself become largely isolated within Judaism and could no longer attract the support of notables such as it had a few years before."[19]

As the founding of Israel loomed, the ACJ welcomed an alliance with the CJP, and vice versa. Each group served the other; they shared a common cause. Cooperation prevailed. The CJP invited a prominent ACJ officer, Morris S. Lazaron, to join its national council, which Virginia led; Elmer Berger, another ACJ activist and executive vice president, participated in meetings of the CJP executive board and helped plan publicity; leaders of the two groups corresponded, addressed one another's gatherings, and worked together to thwart the start of Israel. To the CJP, cooperation with the ACJ reduced its own vulnerability to charges of anti-Semitism. "How comforting it is to discover the large number of fine non-Zionist Jews who appreciate our position," wrote Henry Sloane Coffin to Virginia in March 1948. Virginia shared the sentiment; the ACJ, in turn, appreciated *her*. To postwar anti-Zionism in general, Virginia brought her illustrious resumé, academic prestige, a reputation for expertise in foreign affairs, and impressive cooperative skills, nurtured over many years of service as board member or committee chair. Overall, as Elmer Berger wrote to Virginia in 1949, the ACJ respected "people of your stature in life." To the CJP, meanwhile, as historian Hugh Wilford suggests, a woman leader gave the impression that a group transcended "the masculine world of vulgar power politics."[20]

The last-gasp maneuvers to derail Zionism in 1948 failed: The Mandate ended, British forces left Palestine, and, wrote Virginia, "the Zionists proclaimed the State of Israel," which President Truman recognized. "The complete failure of our efforts to stem this tide of tragedy was a sudden blow to me," Virginia claimed. The only goals left to her, she believed, were to maintain rapport with peoples of the Middle East to whom she felt attached—the Arabs who fled their homes and farms as Jewish immigrants arrived and Jewish force prevailed. Up to 880,000 Arab refugees in 1954 lived in "tents, caves, and temporary shacks." "It has been difficult," Virginia observed, to get help for Palestinian refugees, "so little does the American public know about the Middle East and so efficient has been the Zionist control of media of communication." To be an anti-Zionist in 1949, as ACJ leader Elmer Berger told Kim Roosevelt of the CJP, resembled marching through the ranks of a parade "in the wrong direction."[21]

The CJP faded by the end of the 1940s due to shaky finances and, in Kim Roosevelt's view, in June 1948, to a "curious reluctance of the press to report our activities." Even as this happened, her prominence in anti-Zionist circles enabled Virginia to network among colleagues, such as Garland Evan Hopkins, minister and CJP executive vice president, and Kim Roosevelt. One effort of CJP leaders, to launch yet another anti-Zionist pressure group, the Holy Land Emergency Liaison Program (HELP), sought, in Hopkins's words, "to inform Americans about the serious refugee problem in the Middle East and to encourage large contributions for relief." The new group, its backers planned, would tap those funding resources—Arabs, oil companies, or the government—that seemed to elude the CJP. "I hope to have a talk with Allen Dulles both about refugees and about the importance of giving us help in setting up the new organization," Kim Roosevelt wrote to Virginia on September 13, 1948. Virginia knew Dulles from the board of directors for the Near East College Association. "The problem is to restore the friendship between the United States and the Arabs," Roosevelt told Virginia a year later, on February 21, 1949, as he pressed Dulles for assistance. "A week ago Garland Hopkins and I were informed (again) that financial backing for the new organization will be forthcoming." But the new organization did not materialize. As the scheme to start HELP sank, Virginia pursued her own efforts for the cause.[22]

Virginia contributed to anti-Zionism in the late 1940s by keeping in touch with Arab organizations and speaking at their gatherings; by her unending labor for American Middle East Relief, where she headed the executive committee and which after 1948 focused its efforts on aid to Palestinian refugees; and by her personal campaign of letter-writing, mainly to the *New York Times*. Virginia's opinions invariably stirred up responses, often among women. A letter to the editor in January 1948 that denounced the UN vote for partition—the American people were "shocked and alarmed by bloodshed in Palestine," Virginia wrote—elicited views among *Times* readers, pro and con. "I wrote to many of the leaders of Zionism to say that their propaganda would inevitably lead to a third world war," an appreciative woman reader responded to Virginia. In a letter to the *Times* of April 1949, Virginia's argument against the admission of Israel to the United Nations dismayed at least one reader. "You have forfeited our respect by your bigotry," this critic responded. "You are showing your true colors now more than you did when you had your biased quota system against Jewish applicants to Barnard."[23]

VIRGINIA AND DOROTHY

The founding of Israel—and its admission to the United Nations—did not end anti-Zionism; the anti-Zionist crusade persisted into the 1950s, and Virginia remained engaged. By 1950, Kim Roosevelt had recruited leading journalist Dorothy Thompson (1893–1961), a one-time Zionist. A 1914 graduate of Syracuse University, where she studied politics and economics, Thompson had won acclaim as both a print journalist and radio news commentator. Staunchly antifascist, Thompson had been the first U.S. journalist expelled from Nazi Germany, in 1934, when working for the *New York Post*. In 1936 she began a *New York Tribune* syndicated column and also ran a monthly column in the *Ladies' Home Journal*. At first in favor of Zionism, Thompson changed her mind about it in 1945 on a visit to the Middle East. She was shocked by the violence of Zionist fighting forces, then seeking a Jewish state, that challenged the British in Palestine. Her new views had professional consequences. In 1947 the *New York Post* discontinued her column, a loss she attributed to Zionist pressure.[24]

To anti-Zionists at midcentury, the involvement of Dorothy Thompson represented a major coup. By 1950, Dorothy had joined Virginia on the executive committee of American Middle East Relief and shared with her a zeal for the anti-Zionist cause. "There are so few people who know or care anything about the Middle East, and even fewer who have the courage to make known a few basic facts," Dorothy wrote to Virginia in March 1951. "I have greatly admired your courage and energy, and I am glad to stand by your side."[25]

On May 15, 1951, at a meeting in Dorothy Thompson's New York City home, Thompson and Kim Roosevelt, joined by twenty-four charter members, formed a new group, the American Friends of the Middle East (AFME). "Although still incipient our movement has met a truly remarkable response from all those who know at first hand the situation in these lands—scholars, educators, missionaries, journalists, and businessmen," Thompson declared in a press release; the new group absorbed the Committee for Justice and Peace in the Holy Land. The AFME goal: "To break through the curtain of obscurity and distortion by writing and publicizing material designed to broaden understanding in the United States of Middle Eastern peoples, problems, and progress." AMFE sought to defend Arabs and to promote U.S. interests in the Middle East versus the USSR. The charter members constituted a national council, on which Virginia served; the council elected a board of directors, on which she served as well. From the outset, historians contend, the CIA funded AFME, as did the oil consortium ARAMCO. The CIA connection, though not revealed until 1967, in *Ramparts* and then the *New York Times*, was known to AFME leaders, who exchanged views with correspondents at the CIA, including Allen Dulles, the new CIA director of operations, and in the State Department.[26]

CIA funding for AFME pumped up anti-Zionist efforts. Besides its annual meetings, the AFME held lectures, hosted Middle East visitors, ran student exchanges, issued annual reports and monthly newsletters, and published pamphlets and books. While the CJP had floundered, the AFME bustled with activity. AFME propaganda fused Cold War goals and anti-Zionism. The group sought to improve Arab views of the United States, to strengthen Middle East states against Communist penetration, and to advocate for Arabs and Muslims opposed to Zionism; that the Truman administration recognized Israel proved no deterrent. AFME also made its offices in Middle East nations available to CIA officers embarked on intelligence missions. Embedded in the national council, Virginia remained active in AFME networks. As of 1954, she hoped for more support from Eisenhower's incoming secretary of state,

John Foster Dulles, than anti-Zionists had received in the past from Democrats. Dulles, she noted, proclaimed a policy of "friendly impartiality" in the Arab-Israeli conflict.[27]

Though it is unlikely that Virginia knew about CIA funding for AFME, she had contact with AFME officers, who knew more. It is possible, too, that she fielded CIA requests to place agents or informants in Middle East jobs; the CIA enjoyed outreach among the interlocking directorates of the Middle East support network. Virginia, who served as head of the executive committee of Near East Relief as well as on the AFME national council, received one such request in 1953. According to a bulletin in her files, issued by a project called "Crafts and Tradework," Mrs. Alma B. Kerr, a CIA employee since 1948, sought work among refugees in the Middle East. A North Dakota educator and widow of a World War I army officer, Alma Kerr had an impressive resumé. When first widowed in the 1920s, she had found work with Near East Relief in Turkey; founded an orphanage in Sidon, Palestine; worked for the Ministry of Education in the kingdom of Iraq, then a British protectorate; and started a teachers' training school for women in Baghdad. In 1935, Alma Kerr directed the Women's and Professional Division of the Works Progress Administration in Minneapolis and in 1936 moved up to run the WPA regional office in Chicago; in World War II, she worked as a manager for the Red Cross in India and Burma. Postwar, Alma Kerr spent five years in "government research" (the CIA); she spoke Turkish and Arabic. "It is hoped that ARAMCO will pay her salary" and that of her secretary, the bulletin stated. Robert Long, deputy to Allen Dulles (whom Virginia knew from the Near East College Association, which he had headed from 1946 to 1951), asked Virginia to write to Dulles to request a leave of absence from the CIA for the accomplished Alma Kerr, who now sought work among refugees in Lebanon, Syria, or Jordan. Presumably, Virginia found a position in the ranks of Middle East Relief that could, for whatever purpose, use the executive skills of Alma Kerr.[28]

As Virginia pursued anti-Zionist goals in the 1950s, Dorothy Thompson, president of AFME and executive board member at Near East Relief, became a valued colleague and friend. Younger than Virginia and far better known, Dorothy Thompson replaced Virginia as the most important woman in U.S. anti-Zionism. Virginia had met Dorothy Thompson as far back as 1938 and had referred to her in a letter to Nicholas Murray Butler. The women began a correspondence of mutual admiration in the late 1940s; each praised the other's achievements. In November 1949, Virginia congratulated Thompson on a talk given to an ACJ audience and sent in return a talk of her own. "You are quite right that the one-sided Zionist propaganda has been successful because of a deplorable lack of knowledge of the Middle East . . ." Thompson responded. "But now I feel that they [Zionists] are seriously overreaching themselves. . . . Unfortunately, the slightest criticism awakens a violent reaction. Just now, as far as the USA is concerned, they are preaching 'cultural pluralism' as of John Dewey and interpreting it to justify the deepening intensification of 'Jewishness' in America—whatever that may mean. It perturbs me." In June 1951, when Virginia challenged a draft of Dorothy Thompson's first press release on behalf of the AFME—and even threatened to resign, Dorothy sent a revised draft, in "the hope that you might change your mind," and explained the challenges she faced. "I am sure you appreciate how extremely difficult it is to draft any statement which will not have our Zionist friends infuriated," Dorothy wrote. "I am also afraid that if we include the Israeli in any way within our range of tolerance, we will have all the other Middle Eastern people asking to be 'included out.' "[29]

To what extent were efforts to thwart "our Zionist friends" linked to anti-Semitism? Anti-Zionism and anti-Semitism were separate and distinct developments. U.S. anti-Zionists tried to steer clear of statements that connoted bias against Jews; they were cautious. Still, in the postwar era as subsequently, anti-Zionism might easily tip over into anti-Semitism or provide a vehicle on which anti-Semitic messages could ride. Dorothy Thompson, notably, who strongly repudiated anti-Semitism and denied any charge of it, voiced some anti-Zionist views that ventured onto precarious ground. In a problematic *Commentary* article of 1950, Thompson asked, "Do Israeli Ties Conflict with US Citizenship?" and answered, essentially, "Yes." "A Jewish nationalist, which means today the Israeli nationalist, will have to choose allegiances." To Thompson, Zionism meant split allegiances; it imperiled American Jews by casting suspicion on their loyalty to the United States. It was Hitler "who gave the greatest impetus to Jewish nationalism," Thompson declared. Although to equate anti-Zionism with anti-Semitism was dangerous, she stated, "Zionism made its foes into anti-Semites." In private as in public, however, though always a foe of anti-Semitism, Thompson continued to voice her exasperation with Zionism. "I am *seriously* concerned about the position of the Jews in the United States," she wrote to Virginia on August 2, 1951. "Everything on the surface seems to be going the Zionist way, but underneath this country is beginning to seethe with resentment . . . and [people] are asking themselves the question: Who is really running America?"[30]

Endorsing Dorothy Thompson's point of 1949 about the threat of Zionism, Virginia enlarged the attack on Zionism into an argument about Jews and culture. On May 25, 1950, Virginia addressed the New York chapter of the American Council for Judaism on the dangers posed by Israel and by those Jews who supported it. In "Self-Segregation of American Jews," Virginia assumed the stance of a welcoming assimilationist, a person astonished and affronted by the perceived desire of others, "some Jews," to remain apart from mainstream culture. "Some Jews are now telling us what Hitler told us and we denied, that Jews are a race apart, a nation apart, that they should live apart from the rest of us in their own state beyond the seas or, if here, in a community segregated from the currents of our American culture," Virginia stated. "The danger to our country is alarming."[31]

Zionists, according to Virginia, sought to segregate Jews into a political bloc concerned primarily with the well-being of a foreign country and tried, through "hidden censorship," to quash all opposition. "Anything suggesting that the state of Israel is ever wrong is either suppressed or the critic is violently deemed an 'anti-Semite,'" she charged; this argument appealed to the ACJ audience. Beyond its negative political impact, in Virginia's view, Zionism injured cultural life. Zionist acts to "self-segregate," she stated, sought not to preserve religion but Jewish culture. "What the advocate of this cultural segregation means by 'Jewish culture' is really 'Israeli' culture," she contended. Virginia's cultural argument, based, she said, on her reading of *Commentary*, posited a shift in Jewish attitudes. Jews had once been transmitters of European culture and contributors "to our special American culture," Virginia declared. "Now some of them threaten to withdraw even from that and express a strange desire to dominate or forsake it." These clashing charges—the desire to dominate or forsake—referred variously to recent trends that Virginia spotted in music and literature, when reading articles in *Commentary*. The "tendency to look at literature from an intensely Jewish self-consciousness," for instance, was "lamentable." Similarly, to "withdraw from western culture to Israel" was "threatening to our American way of life." Finally, "to instill in the minds of American Jewish youth the sense of being alien to our country," was reprehensible. Jewish cultural actors, in Virginia's analysis, were either too competitive in their fields or in retreat to some ethnic enclave, like Israeli folk music. The culprit in all instances was Zionism, which suppressed freedoms of speech, press, and discussion and was "a menace to our welfare."[32]

Virginia's charge of self-segregation—like her faux stance as champion of ethnic interaction and aggrieved observer of slights to American culture—is suspect, considering that she had sought for decades to limit Jewish presence in that portion of American culture under her control. Her charge also contradicted recent developments on the U.S. cultural scene; Jewish Americans of the 1940s strongly rejected cultural-identity politics, which they associated with totalitarians of recent decades. When Virginia repeated the self-segregation speech in June to the Baltimore chapter of the ACJ, her remarks reignited debate between anti-Zionists and their critics—as often happened after ACJ events. A local Zionist group attacked the ACJ as "a fanatical and reckless crowd" who set up "false contradictions between American Jewish helpfulness to the new state of Israel and loyalty to American life as a whole." The Baltimore ACJ, in turn, spurned the Zionist response as "McCarthyite character assassination." The ACJ position, its spokesman argued, was simple and clear. "It believes Judaism is a religion. It believes religion and nationality have no connection. It denies that any American has any responsibility or obligation to any foreign nation." One critique of Virginia's speech, in an article by the widely respected Unitarian minister John Haynes Holmes and passed on to Virginia's brother Alger by a correspondent, pointed more directly at the foremost liability of the address. "A person anti-Semitically inclined," said Holmes, "might well be tempted to talk as Miss Gildersleeve talks." Alger denied the charge. "Anyone knowing my sister and her work will recognize this as nonsense," he responded. But John Haynes Holmes had a valid point. "Self-Segregation" careened around the charge of dual loyalty, an anti-Semitic trope.[33]

Virginia continued her support for anti-Zionism through the 1950s, as the Eisenhower administration faced the Suez crisis, opposed Egypt's leader Gamal Abdel Nasser, and then reluctantly adjusted to Arab nationalism. She voiced her views in print and through contacts with anti-Zionist networks. In 1954, the AFME published a pamphlet by Virginia, "The Roots of our Crisis in the Middle East," based on twenty pages from her just-published autobiography, that went through four editions and drew praise from admirers in the region. "I beg to express to you the gratitude of the Arab people," wrote an officer of the Arab League from Cairo in 1956, "for your sympathetic attitude and your zeal in defending their rights and explaining the injustices to which they have been subjected." Virginia also kept up with allies from the ACJ. "I am much alarmed by the way in which American Zionists are succeeding in getting the United States politically involved in the affairs and international relations of Israel," she wrote in 1958 to Lessing J. Rosenwald, heir to the Sears fortune, Sears executive, philanthropist, and president of the ACJ from 1943 to 1955. "There seems to be some danger that the Zionist activities might even result in forcing us to go to war with Soviet Russia. Among all these ominous circumstances it is good to know that one of our distinguished Jewish fellow citizens, a man of your status in the community, is one of us."[34]

Virginia's cultivation of ACJ members reflected not just shared anti-Zionist goals but a new trend of midcentury: World War II had changed attitudes, increased tolerance, and made anti-Semitism less acceptable. Even with her retrograde views on "Self-Segregation," Virginia grasped that the ground rules on anti-Semitism had changed, and now tried to adapt in small part—to get on the right side of history. Looking back from midcentury, she sought to revise her own role in the IFUW so as to seem intensely concerned about the fate of Jews.

The "Scattered Reminiscences of the IFUW" that Virginia wrote in 1950, for instance (and saved in her files), featured a revisionist account of the council meeting in Budapest in 1934. Virginia now demoted Friederike Matthias, head of the Nazified German contingent, whom she had formerly characterized as a "gentle spirit," to (more accurately) an ardent Nazi: "[I]t was a little trying when Frau Mathias clasped her hands over her heart and in moving tones declared 'I *know* what my Fuhrer wants.'" This revisionist statement of 1950 moves far from the praise

Virginia had heaped on Mathias when she returned from Europe in the fall of 1934. Virginia also gave herself an enhanced role as a humanitarian who sought to protect German Jews. According to her new version of the 1934 council meeting in Budapest, she protested regulations that excluded Jewish women from membership in the German federation, the Reichsbund Deutscher Akademikerinnen; tried to "work out some plan whereby the German federation might have Jews as members"; insisted that Friederike Matthias confer with the [Jewish] president of the IFUW's Palestinian federation (admitted in 1932) to discuss "what could be done for the best with relation to the Jews"; and urged postponement of the proposed IFUW conference in Germany "until the German federation had grown again from its very depleted membership to something like its former strength." But Virginia discovered her proactive role in defending German Jews only retroactively. (German women would not be represented by voting delegates at an IFUW conference until 1953.)[35]

While Virginia pursued revisionist goals in history, she and Elizabeth Reynard began some writing projects on which they worked together or, alternatively, as in the past, each of them tried to advance the goals of the other. Virginia sought to expand the options of Elizabeth, who had retired from college teaching in her early fifties, just at an age when her career should have flowered. Using her contacts, Virginia promoted a new novel by Elizabeth, *The Secret Island*, which publishers returned. "It didn't come alive for us," wrote an editor at W. W. Norton in 1949. "You must try elsewhere." "Not sufficiently cohesive," advised the Charles Scribner's editor in 1950. "We can only hope that we will be proven mistaken in our judgment." Simultaneously, in 1950, Virginia sought to win for Elizabeth a place on General Electric's Board of Directors. Elizabeth, Virginia wrote to GE's chairman, in a less-than-convincing letter of recommendation, would be unthreatening; Elizabeth was "a small, quiet friendly person, with originality and vision but easy to work with." That odd ploy failed, too. The two women joined efforts to compile a short manuscript of eighteen excerpts from Virginia's speeches, intended as a public speaking textbook, with adulatory headnotes and introduction by Elizabeth. "She [Virginia] has never signed up with a Speakers' Bureau," Elizabeth declared, as if repudiating an unseen critic. "She has no parlor tricks. Untrammeled by allegiance to any ideological cult, her mind bites into each problem as it comes along." The manuscript title, *Merchants of Light*, came from a speech that Caroline Spurgeon had given to the IFUW in the 1920s. Submitted to Houghton Mifflin in 1951, the manuscript was never published.[36]

Through the early 1950s, finally, and with more success, Virginia and Elizabeth turned their energies to personal narrative. Elizabeth's short memoir of youth, privately printed by Virginia, recounts an exceptional college experience. Virginia's heftier and much-admired autobiography of 1954 became a leading record of her life and era.

SELF AND HISTORY: THE MAKING OF AN AUTOBIOGRAPHY

An autobiography is by definition an unreliable narrative. What happened in fact remains elusive; the writer continually selects and discards, embroiders and interprets, misremembers and distorts, and occasionally omits episodes entirely. All of this is the narrator's prerogative. Virginia brought many assets to the art of memoir, including a keen sense of self and clarity of expression. She had kept extensive records—of her activism in many organizations and of her long career as a college administrator. Most important, Virginia turned her main liability—she had never been strong on self-analysis—into an asset: a powerful, confident narrator, she seized command of her material, recalled whatever she wanted to recall, and sailed forward into her story, unhindered by self-doubt. Like any memoir, then, *Many a Good Crusade* (1954) reveals only a selective version of "truth," about either the narrator or her experience. A primary goal: Virginia wanted to publish *first*—before any biographer could distill the meaning of her life, in perhaps some less-favorable way.

Virginia had assistance. Her friend Dorothea Setzer coped with some of the preparation. Dorothea organized files and conducted interviews with many of Virginia's colleagues and friends; once the autobiography was published, Dorothea hoped, she might write a biography. Virginia's brother Alger, meanwhile, had long explored geneology; he had traced the history of the Gildersleeve and Crocheron families to the colonial era, saved clippings about distant relatives, contacted some of the living ones, and tackled difficult questions, such as whether the original Crocheron was really a Huguenot (yes). His ambitious work in family history included a study of the Gelb family on the Crocheron side. For the autobiography, Alger, or "Gildy," as he now called himself, offered a chart on "Forebears of Virginia C. Gildersleeve." "After the grandparents—I should say *before*," he told Virginia, "the congregation of ancestors becomes so great the individual is lost." Alger died in 1952, just as Virginia produced a first draft. Finally, Elizabeth Reynard helped by financing a strategic distribution of complimentary copies among Virginia's many contacts in the worlds of higher education and women's groups.[37]

Virginia found useful tactics to evoke the past and make sense of it. She began with notes of memories, organized into charts and diagrams ("Harry: His sunny charm, His brilliance, His generosity, His ambition, His love for me"). Using the present tense, she reconstructed scenes from the past ("The Barnard faculty is meeting in the Trustees Rooms at Low Library . . . [on] handsome wood-paneled walls hang portraits of former presidents of Columbia.") Further reflection generated a twenty-four-page typescript on concrete and detailed visual moments in specific places; these memories ranged from a childhood classroom, "A room on the fourth story of an old brownstone residence, October 3, 1884," to her last day at Barnard in 1947, when the caretaking staff sang "Auld Lang Syne." Finally, for the all-important UN story, which established her role as a witness to history, Virginia relied on a handwritten record she had foresightedly composed in August 1945, soon after the UN Charter Conference had ended. "While it is still fairly fresh in my mind," she stated, "I will write down some of the inside history of the San Francisco Conference—not to be published—at least not for a long time." This document, which included her impressions of her fellow delegates, provided the start of her chapter on the United Nations—and anticipated what historians might want to learn from her experience. Virginia also saved the verbatim minutes of a UN committee meeting of June 7, 1945, to preserve her own remarks on naming the UN the "United Nations," instead of a "league" or "union" as some nations preferred.[38]

By the end of 1952, Virginia had some chapters written and had also found a potential publisher, Macmillan, which agreed provisionally to consider the manuscript. Vice president and editor in chief J. Randall Williams III (a graduate of St. Paul's, Williams, and Oxford) oversaw the development of the book, along with his assistant, R. L. De Wilton, who handled line-by-line editing. Smart, smooth, experienced, and working in tandem with his assistant, the editor in chief proceeded cautiously; each editor mentioned continually the contribution of the other. "Mr. De Wilton and I both enjoyed very much having a chat with you the other day," wrote Williams to Virginia on November 24, 1952, when Macmillan received drafts of two chapters. Starting with some diplomatic "friendly thinking" on the "straightforward" and "highly readable" chapters Virginia had submitted, the editors looked forward to seeing more on Barnard as well as on the UN conference of 1945; they also looked forward to "expanded portraits of the more important men and women you have known." That is, they suggested, the book needed less on the narrator and more on her times. Virginia's new chapter on the UN conference, received at the start of 1953 and full of commentary on its participants, drew praise. The additional pages "provided a fine inside picture of a great moment in history," wrote Williams in January 1953. "They are also enlivened by anecdote and revealing, sprightly vignettes of the delegates."[39]

By August 1953, two anonymous outside readers had seen a complete manuscript; assistant editor De Wilton sent Virginia the challenging readers' reports on *Bright Journey to the Dark*, the original title of the book—one so ill-chosen that it was never mentioned again. Reader One, who got through seven chapters without incident, though using the phrase "defective in style," began thereafter to find the text "less satisfactory" and in need of "considerable reworking." An alternation of personal and "official" chapters annoyed Reader One. The personal chapters were often "discursive" and "sometimes deal with trivialities." Even in a later chapter, Reader One noted, "there is again the problem of what personal details are important and what aren't." The only chapter that Reader One appreciated was that about the UN conference of 1945.[40]

More seriously aggravated, Reader Two made one concession about style ("workmanlike") and one about content; in the chapter on the 1945 UN conference, said Reader Two, the author was "at her very best." Mainly, Reader Two attacked. Like Reader One, the second reader spurned those chapters that focused on the narrator. "I think that the book is weakest in what you might call its personal sections," said Reader Two. The chapters lacked "that intimate, warm, vivid touch." Anything that the author had intended as personal failed to reach the second reader: "There is too much about her parents, her dogs, her servants, her friends, her trips with 'Cara,' hither and yon, etc." Reader Two wanted more on educational problems and more on Barnard ("She was there, after all, for thirty-six years.") The chapter on the International Federation of University Women seemed "interminable." Reader Two called for more as well on the changing status of women. "It seems almost impossible for those who were involved in it to dramatize the women's movement, to make it seem other than a pretty dead duck," the second reader observed. "One doesn't need, or want, all those bright detailed accounts of the Federation's various conferences, of its principal leaders, etc. Not only is most of this material just plain dull, but it seems to have no relevance for the present." In conclusion, Reader Two directed Virginia to "minimize the personal trivia, say a little bit more about her actual work as an educator, develop her stand more fully on the issues of the day, [and] a more vigorous book would result. . . . It is this kind of thing that one wants to hear her talk about."[41]

To her credit, considering the hectoring tone of the outside reviews, especially the hostility of Reader Two, Virginia pared her manuscript and got rid of tedious detail, sometimes with scissors; she kept a file of excised material, mainly on travel and illness, even the discarded shreds of sentences. By the fall, Macmillan had received a revised manuscript. "You will surely want to take it easy for a while and let some of the rest of us do a little work," suggested editor in chief Williams, ever tactful, in October 1953. After a year of coping with Virginia, Williams was often out of the office, busy at a staff meeting, just returning from a trip, or falling a little behind, though his assistant pitched in. "Mr. De Wilton has put down on two sheets specific comments on each chapter and some general overall suggestions," Williams wrote to Virginia in November. On December 2, 1953, Macmillan finally offered a book contract; the publisher promised a large first printing, a world market, 10 percent royalties, and a price of five to six dollars (about fifty dollars in 2020). On the same day, editor Williams arranged with Elizabeth Reynard to pay Macmillan $7,000 in installments for a batch of about 3,000 half-price books, to be distributed by the publisher among Virginia's many contacts and associates. Reynard, in effect, bought out a big chunk of the first printing in advance; her purchase ensured a second printing.[42]

By the spring of 1954 Reynard was hospitalized with one of her many illnesses, spinal arthritis. "It's lonely here without Skipper," wrote Virginia to Dorothea Setzer on April 23, 1954. "Daily I expect the first batch of galleys, which do not appear." But they did. As publication approached, Virginia shared with her editor suggestions for book publicity: Macmillan could make use of her institutional affiliations. As of August 1954, she told Williams, she was vice president of the Near East College Association, member of the Board of Trustees of the American College of Girls (Istanbul), member of the national board of AFME, and on the boards of directors of American Middle East Relief and of Reid Hall. Virginia's plans for book promotion included, beyond these institutions, Brearley, Barnard, the Cosmopolitan Club, the International Federation of University Women, Kappa Kappa Gamma, the League of Women Voters, the American Association for the UN, the General Federation of Women's Clubs, the Daughters of the American Revolution (DAR), Colonial Dames, the WAVES, higher education periodicals, and finally, the American Council for Judaism.[43]

When *Many a Good Crusade* appeared in October 1954, Macmillan's mighty publicity machine surged into motion. The publisher sent publicity about the book to thousands of professionals—lawyers, college presidents, deans, professors of education, deans of teachers' colleges, educators at all levels, UN delegates, Barnard faculty, members of AFME, and Reid Hall personnel, in addition to colleges libraries. Macmillan mailed the book to women's organizations; all branches of the American Association of University Women had received copies, editor Williams assured Virginia in November 1954. Such gifts depended on Elizabeth Reynard's generous purchase of much of the first printing. Macmillan's publicity director lined up interviews with book editors and radio programs, such as with "Martha Deane" [Marian Young Taylor], a popular weekday news-and-talk show on WOR. The publicity department also hosted receptions for Virginia and the book at an AAUW gathering, at Barnard on November 10, 1954 (Virginia's last visit), and then in the spring, to mark a second printing, at Brearley. Working through Macmillan, Elizabeth Reynard bought an ad in the *Saturday Review of Books*. "I've just been autographing 48 copies for our local bookstore at

Mt. Kisco," Virginia wrote in October 1954 to Dorothea Setzer, whom she continued to encourage on a biography project. "This book is as I see the world," Virginia told Setzer in an undated note, "and I suppose the biography will be as the world sees me."[44]

Many a Good Crusade attracted a chorus of favorable reviews. Typically, reviewers offered words of praise and then stepped back to make some qualifying remarks—more pointed and critical. "Here is a serene and dignified account of a lifetime of scholarship and vision," declared reviewer Margaret Irwin in the *Worcester Telegram*. "It seems petty to criticize," Irwin continued, "but . . . the book has the faintly Olympian tone of an elder statesman. . . . There is an oddly non-committal quality." Reviews in major journals followed this two-step pattern. Two significant reviews underscored in different ways the book's distinctive static quality. Lewis Gannett in the *New York Herald Tribune Book Review*, found "crusade" an odd word to choose for a title; Virginia merely "drifted into Columbia University" and then "went on to apply her talents in other fields." "As she tells the story, things happened to her," Gannett noted. "She didn't go out to make them happen. The crusades are all off-stage. She happened to arrive, with particular talents, at a particular moment of history." Author Elizabeth Janeway (a future Barnard trustee from 1970 to 1981), in the *New York Times Book Review*, found "generalities," a "detached" tone, and a distancing effect. "For all its frankness and observation of reporting . . . this is not an intimate book," wrote Janeway. "It is the record of a full and active public life rather than a growing and changing personality." The narrator, in short, Janeway observed, did not learn through experience; she lacked both an interior existence and the capacity to expand. Virginia was "a woman whose talents are for action, not introspection."[45]

Few reviewers had the surgical skill of Gannett or Janeway. But others assessed *Crusade* with discernment, too. Harry Emerson Fosdick (a Barnard trustee, from 1931 to 1956), in the daily *Herald Tribune*, appreciated *Crusade*'s value as "biography by mirror," a record of three quarters of a century. "The book's style is that of intimate confidential conversation . . . with uninhibited candor and familiarity about every conceivable kind of personal and public recollection." Fosdick also valued the Columbia story, the "educational liberation of women as only someone on the inside could tell it." Journalist Robert W. Wells in the

Milwaukee Journal focused on Virginia's contribution to foreign affairs and to the UN Charter meeting, including her battle with Bertha Lutz. Mildred McAfee Horton, former Wellesley president, navy officer, and Virginia's colleague from the war years, turned in the *Saturday Review* to Virginia's role in the WAVES and, in an exceptional digression, to a personal conflict with the author over "the relative merits of the trustees of Wellesley College and Barnard" and over the truth of the narrative. "Memoirs chronicle the chronicler as well as historic events," declared Horton, with a jab at the author. Other reviewers focused on Virginia's achievements as an educator. "A lively record of personal, academic, and intellectual activity, rich in anecdote," wrote Millicent Taylor in the *Christian Science Monitor*. "Those interested in the higher education of women . . . will value her story." "A Lady Who Fell in Love With a College," announced a review in the *Washington Post*; "the story of Barnard College," wrote Emily Taft Douglas in *The New Leader*, conveyed a "sense of joyful intellectual pursuits." The *Selma* (Alabama) *Times Journal* had its own interest in *Crusade*. "Cahaba's Dead Glory Relives Through Author" reprinted Virginia's description of the town.[46]

Finally, Virginia drew responses from readers who had either received the book from Macmillan, courtesy of Elizabeth Reynard, or had bought it. The roster included a galaxy of people Virginia had known for decades, such as Columbia administrator Margaret Pickel; former classmate Marjorie Jacobi; Meta Glass, colleague in the IFUW and Sweet Briar president; and friends that Virginia had met more recently, such as Susan Brandeis, a neighbor in Cape Cod. "I feel from your autobiography that my own youth was being explained," wrote the younger daughter of Justice Brandeis. "It is a startling sensation." Trustee Iphigene Sulzberger wrote, "I felt as though I had been sitting in an easy chair opposite you. . . . The chapters on San Francisco and Japan were of absorbing interest." Some fellow Barnard emeriti commiserated. "I am much distressed to read how much you have suffered since your retirement," wrote art historian Margaret Bieber, ever loyal and now herself retired. Readers who found themselves in the text voiced special delight. "You can just imagine my enthusiasm and how anxious I was to open it and look for my place in that book," wrote an acquaintance from the 1930s who had been mentioned. The experience was "like seeking one's place at an important banquet."[47]

From around the nation, scores of readers unknown to Virginia responded spontaneously that they shared some aspect of her experience—as distant relatives, alumnae, or members of organizations that Virginia championed. "I am reminded that we have beyond doubt a common Crocheron ancestor," declared a reader from Charlottesville, Virginia who had visited Staten Island as a child. The book was "so replete with reminiscence for anyone who has been at Barnard," wrote an alumna, class of '17. "We know that you have made Barnard what it was for us." "Words cannot tell you the indescribable thrill I received from reading this book," confided a member of the AAUW, "Possibly, it was due to an academic background." "Your career touches the lives of all our family," declared another, who provided pages of information about herself. "I have digressed to say these few things of my own affairs." Readers did not avoid controversy. "Special interest was taken in your comments regarding women and their rights," wrote a California woman lawyer. "All my life I have been subject to discrimination on this score, and you are fortunate that you have not been."[48]

The Middle East evoked more heated commentary. "I think that you are entirely right about the Zionist Conquest of Palestine," wrote a former Columbia graduate student who remembered Virginia from decades earlier. Arab diplomats, fellow activists, and some former colleagues similarly appreciated Virginia's anti-Zionist stance. "Those Arabs like myself who have had the pleasure and privilege of knowing you always remember you and think of you as a fine example of America's greatest," wrote the permanent Iraqi delegate to the United Nations, Mohamed Fadjil Jamali. "I find myself sympathizing with your views on Zionism, which as being unusual must have taken some courage," confided Virginia's former mentor, retired English professor and one-time provost William T. Brewster. He and his wife had "always found the Arabs gentle, quiet, and courteous," Brewster wrote, "so much so that it is painful to see them thrust out by a cleverer and more articulate folk." Several correspondents disagreed. "I am truly surprised that a person of your fertile imagination was not fired by the accomplishments of the people of Israel," wrote a former WAVE from Hartford, Connecticut. "Had the Jews of Israel waited for the world conscience to do something about the Jewish problem there would not be a Jewish person left in Europe today."[49]

A welcome response came from Dorothy Thompson, to whom Virginia had sent a copy of the book with directions to see the section on the Middle East, "and also, in the last chapter of all, the account of the vain effort of the Committee for Justice and Peace in the Middle East to make a better adjustment of the Palestine tragedy." "I have always greatly admired you," Dorothy replied, "partly for your public work, but equally for your scholarly devotions and educational activities—rather wistfully, since I often feel I chose the wrong calling." On Dorothy Thompson's retirement in 1958, when Virginia voiced "gratitude for all you have done for our country," she claimed that "Zionist censorship" in New York denied her the privilege of reading Dorothy's column, which she had followed in her Cape Cod newspaper, the New Bedford *Standard-Times*. "During many years I have immensely admired your wisdom, your soundness, your courage and your vigorous English style," Virginia wrote. "From my own personal experience I can to some extent appreciate what you have suffered for standing up for what you believed. I hate to see such a valiant fighter leave the field! But you will not altogether do that, I'm sure . . . And occasionally, like me, you may aim a sniper's shot from the sidelines."[50]

Many a Good Crusade was in many ways an exemplary performance, vivid, detailed, and evocative. Virginia wrote in a conversational style. Though always at a distance from the reader, she assumes a tone disarmingly candid and straightforward. Striding forward swiftly, she conveys a barrage of experiences, personal and professional. She explains her tactics as an administrator, conveys her achievements as an internationalist, defends her challenging assignment as a diplomat in 1945, and stakes out her role in history. This meant on occasion readjusting history.

Claiming a lifelong interest in Jews, Virginia proceeds to underline, with honesty if perhaps inadvertently, the gulf between herself and a subject that she saw as troublesome; her statements about Jews distance the Jews. Repeatedly, she defends her Barnard admissions policy. Jews had been "an important element in the make-up of our student body," Virginia contends; they had "generally mingled with the others in the student body on friendly terms." Moreover, she had "regarded it as one of the chief obligations of Barnard to bring about understanding and friendly relations between the girls of different religions in our student body and especially between Christians and Jews." When it came to Barnard admissions policy, Virginia followed a precept announced at the start of her book, to tell "the truth, but seldom the whole truth."[51]

With even more startling honesty, Virginia reveals her sequential relationships to Cara and Elizabeth. Though she offers a few ostensible reasons for the relationships—that unmarried women should not live alone (in the case of Cara) or that retired teachers might want to pool their pensions (in the case of Elizabeth)—Virginia does not minimize or camouflage the long-term partnerships. Rather, she comes close to flaunting the relationships, though without explicitly labeling them or discussing their nature. For Virginia to disclose such connections at midcentury would have been self-immolating and destructive to every person and cause connected with her. But there, on the page, is Cara, with her childlike brilliance and transatlantic charm; there is the Skipper, jaunty in her naval uniform, assuming command of the training program for WAVES, and in 1945 accompanying Virginia to the UN Charter meeting. Reviewers, significantly, did not comment on the two couples; a genteel silence prevailed. "When it comes to lesbians . . . many people have trouble seeing what's in front of them," literary critic Terry Castle observes. "The lesbian remains elusive, vaporous, difficult to spot—even when she is there, in plain view."[52]

In some instances, readers found Virginia's assertions discordant with their own recollections. Barnard administrator Jean T. Palmer, for instance, a former captain in the WAVES in World War II, wrote on the flyleaf of her copy of the book that "the passages on the WAVES are not accepted as true";[53] Mildred McAfee Horton, similarly, discredited that part of the section on the WAVES that involved her own appointment; Bertha Lutz, in the margins of her copy, objected to Virginia's account of the UN Charter meeting of 1945. In other instances, Virginia puffed up her own role, as on the local social scene in East Sussex in the 1920s and early 1930s or by virtually ignoring rivals deserving of mention, from Lilian Clapham to Eleanor Roosevelt; or more often she simply glided past or failed to recount an event, position, or development that readers might find relevant. Thus, she fails to mention the intensity of the conflicts that arose over her college's biased admissions practices, or her condoning of Nazi policies of the early 1930s, or her egregious diatribe on alleged "self-segregation" of U.S. Jews, spoken under the auspices of the American Council for Judaism in the late 1940s. She also omits any mention of the later career or influence of her mentor Charles R. Crane as he became a supporter of Nazism and anti-Semitism.

Overall, Virginia's vision was limited; however earnestly she reconstructed one or another set of circumstances, she did not "see" herself with accuracy. At the same time, her inaccuracy of vision was in its own way accurate as self-reflection. Autobiography reveals the personality of the subject under scrutiny in ways that the narrator might not expect, control, or even discern; the unreliable narrator can thus be quite reliable. In writing, as in life, Virginia could be obtuse, self-deluded, tone-deaf, overbearing, stunningly self-confident, relentlessly self-involved, and unable to grasp the stance or emotions of others or to care that she did not. Most important, as critic Elizabeth Janeway so astutely observed, the narrator of *Crusade* does not grow, change, or learn from experience. Thus, at an early point, perhaps by the end of the 1920s, Virginia was herself out-of-date. Her immutable and intransigent persona, formed at the start of the Progressive Era (if not earlier), grafted to the anti-equal rights wing of the women's movement, shaped by a conservative outlook, and laden with cautious political instincts, plowed forward through the century with few adjustments to changes in her social or political environment. For its delusion as well as its defiant and self-serving consistency, *Crusade* remains a fascinating document.

HOARDING FOR WINTER

In October 1957, the *New York Times* reported that Virginia and Elizabeth Reynard celebrated their joint birthdays at Navarre with their butler and cook; born almost exactly twenty years apart, they were respectively eighty and sixty. The two retired educators had been busy since Virginia's departure from Barnard a decade earlier. Most recently, Virginia enjoyed the positive reception for *Many a Good Crusade*. Elizabeth, who was also writing a memoir, said the *Times*, had won national notice for her role in the navy in World War II. Now cultivating her longtime interest in New England folklore, she remained best known for her 1951 novel about Cape Cod, *The Mutinous Wind*.[54]

By the 1950s, Virginia and Elizabeth had themselves become part-time residents of Cape Cod, the locale of Elizabeth's research and where they presented themselves as cousins; they were in fact distant relatives. Reynard "devoted much time and energy to a favorite hobby of hers—buying and rehabilitating old houses on Cape Cod," Virginia wrote. The two women bought and renovated several houses in Chatham and Dennis, including adjacent houses on Eliphamets Lane in Chatham, where Elizabeth had written *The Narrow Land: Folk Chronicles of Cape Cod.* In 1955, Elizabeth bought the 1801 house of Emma Baker, a recently deceased relative, on a corner where South and West Dennis meet. She restored the paneling and plastered the walls, but, according to Virginia, abandoned her dream of living there and planned to donate the house to the town for use as a historical center. When Reynard died in 1962, town selectmen promised Virginia to care for the abandoned homestead; it became the Jericho Historical Center, run by the Dennis Historical Society.[55]

Virginia kept up her letters to the editor to voice opinions, and not always on anti-Zionism. In 1953, for instance, in a letter that catered to academic sentiment, she denounced McCarthyism. "The kind of haphazard and illogical persecution threatened by Messers. McCarthy, Jenner, and Velde will tend to drive students and teachers into conformity with a rigid concept of Americanism defined (think of it!) by such legislators," Virginia wrote. "We shall become a totalitarian state like the Fascist and Communist models, and our colleges and universities will produce frightened rabbits instead of scholars with free minds." As she approached eighty, Virginia braced for the future. "My will leaves all my personal possessions to my friend Elizabeth Reynard, with whom I have lived for the last eight years," Virginia wrote to Columbia historian Allan Nevins in 1956. "If I should suddenly depart this life, she can turn them over to you or to the Library of Congress, as you both think wise." Virginia also left directions at the Columbia library, to which she left a large portion of her papers, to destroy her correspondence with Caroline Spurgeon, so that, in the words of a staff member, "nothing would be left of it."[56]

In the early 1960s the idyll of Virginia and Elizabeth ended. Elizabeth Reynard died, age sixty-four, in January 1962. Her *New York Times* obituary, dictated over the phone by Virginia, stated that Reynard had been assistant director of the WAVES, with rank of lieutenant commander, and the first WAVE decorated by the government for war service. The obituary for Elizabeth also related that she had gone to Belgium at the start of World War I and worked in a military hospital, that she had studied at Oxford after college and specialized in New England folklore, and that she been Commandant of Seamen at U.S.S. *Hunter*, United States Training School, the Bronx, and Chair of the Barnard Faculty Committee that set up the American Studies Program in 1938. "She had shared quarters in recent years with Virginia C. Gildersleeve, Dean Emeritus of Barnard College and her close friend of many years," said the *Times*. A Barnard memorial service in February 1962 paid tribute to Elizabeth Reynard's achievements. English professor Eleanor Rosenberg, an admiring former student, spoke on Elizabeth's exceptional skill as a professor, and Jean T. Palmer, Barnard administrator and former naval officer, covered Elizabeth's equally exceptional navy career. Virginia sent a formal remembrance, read by Barnard's president, Mrs. Mac.[57]

At Elizabeth Reynard's death, Virginia established a $10,000 trust fund in Elizabeth's name at the Chatham high school library, with dividends to go for new books. She also provided in her own will funds for publication of a new edition of Elizabeth's book *The Narrow Land: Folk Chronicles of Cape Cod*, which appeared in 1968. Most important, Virginia privately published Elizabeth's unusual memoir of youth and college life, which, Virginia wrote, had been started in the late 1940s and which, by 1961, Reynard wished to circulate among fifty friends.[58]

Compared to the life of Elizabeth Reynard, Virginia wrote in the preface to Elizabeth's narrative, her own life was "jog trot and commonplace." Elizabeth's memoir was also a contrast to Virginia's. Elizabeth's narrator, speaking in the breathless and enthusiastic voice of a young woman of 1920, is somewhat scattered, always hopeful, and wildly ambitious. Elizabeth shows the effective use she made of a liberal arts education—she "explored science and humanities with equal gusto"—and also how her studies with Franz Boas trained her to excel as a scholar—to read folktales, collect them, and discern their scholarly uses. "When I came to collect and study the folktales of Cape Cod," Elizabeth wrote, "I knew that in most instances, I was not dealing with folktales at all but with hybrid forms of popular history and theology often cloaked in allegory." Elizabeth's youthful narrator manages to look both backward and forward simultaneously. In her equally interesting preface, Virginia suggests that something (unnamed) had gone fundamentally wrong in Elizabeth's childhood, some threat that kept her out of school and sent the family to Europe for all of her teenage years.[59]

In a final, posthumous act of partnership, just as Virginia made Elizabeth's memoir available to their friends, Elizabeth enabled Virginia to publish *A Hoard for Winter* (1962), a book of essays that the former dean had written between the ages of seventy-five and eighty-two. Funded by a bequest from Elizabeth that covered publication costs and distribution to alumnae, these occasional pieces, dedicated to her "7,000 daughters," targeted a Barnard alumnae audience. Elizabeth Reynard, wrote Virginia, had "thought other Barnard graduates of my time might also like to see what their Dean had been thinking about in her retirement."[60]

The essays in *A Hoard for Winter*, some previously published, suggest a search for relevance. In most instances, Virginia missed the mark, though she might come close. Would microfilm replace books, for instance? She hoped not. Would her recent conversations with Elizabeth Reynard ("We are both teachers, the Skipper and I") lead to productive social policies? Probably not. In one essay, preoccupied with issues connected to aging and care for the infirm, Virginia proposed a national service requirement for women, similar to the draft, that would provide a national nursing corps to help the elderly. In yet another essay, Virginia touched—if only accidentally—on a timely issue. Did college students possess the right to free speech? Not necessarily, Virginia posited; the college administration could control speech on campus. "The only right a student has *as a student*," she stated, "is the right to receive the best possible education that the college can give."[61] The issue remained a live one and would recur in the Berkeley Free Speech movement of 1964. Awareness of the impending civil rights movement, in contrast, did not enter Virginia's field of vision. She could not predict the Selma to Montgomery March of March 1965, a few months before her death, which skirted the nearby remains of the slave owners' haven of Cahaba that had so prominently figured in Crocheron history and in Virginia's memories and identity.

By 1962, when Elizabeth died, Virginia had no immediate family members left. Her parents had died in 1923 and Alger in 1952, at age 84. With no one to care for her in old age, a task that she had envisioned would fall to Elizabeth Reynard, Virginia moved in 1964 to a nursing home on Cape Cod, in Centerville, Massachusetts, not far from where the Witch of Wellfleet haunted the dunes, shouting curses at the sea. She died there a year later of a heart attack on July 8, 1965. A private funeral was held at St. Matthew's Episcopal Church in Bedford, New York, where she was buried next to Elizabeth Reynard.[62]

A substantial obituary in the *New York Times*, starting on the front page, gave primacy to Virginia's expertise in international affairs. A booster of the League of Nations and then the United Nations, she had insisted, said the *Times*, that "there is no conflict between true internationalism and true patriotism." But like the major reviewers of *Many a Good Crusade*, the (anonymous) *Times* obituary writer then took a step back. Virginia, the *New York Times* pointed out, had been a formidable, contrarian, and somewhat remote personality. "An excellent speaker and forceful writer, she championed many causes, some unpopular in the United States," declared the *Times*. "Until recent years, when bouts of illness confined her to home, she moved briskly about in her English tweeds and Queen Mary-like hats, like 'a well-oiled steam engine,' as one officer of Barnard once said of her." As an educator, the *Times* added, Virginia had been an innovator. She had abolished Barnard's compulsory Latin requirement, if reluctantly, allowed students to smoke, and started departments such as political science. Sprightly but bemused in tone, and focused on Virginia's role as a relic of an earlier generation, the *Times* obituary did not give full credit to her achievements in higher education.[63]

Barnard's office of public relations in a press release had more to say on Virginia's achievements. During the thirty-six years of her tenure as dean, the office stated, she had strongly influenced the development of Barnard: The curriculum had expanded, an academic advisory system was introduced, new buildings arose (Barnard Hall and Hewitt Hall), and impressive scholars joined the faculty. Providing leadership through two world wars, Virginia had overseen a growing interest in global affairs and a changing relationship with Columbia: "The success of her leadership was reflected in Barnard's increased academic and administrative independence of the University, as well as in its educational stature." The college established an annual lectureship in Virginia's honor; the IFUW set up a fellowship.[64]

Several of Virginia's admirers, interviewed in the early 1950s, bolstered the favorable view of her legacy. "To Miss Gildersleeve alone should be given the credit for the university attitude of taking women for granted, and on their own merits," declared Columbia administrator Margaret Pickel. "They are shown no condescension, and they do not have to waste time fighting for their rights." Then she concluded: "The dean has a tough hard-bitten mind that has brought her the highest respect, and she relied on this and not her sex to achieve a place in university life, and in the world."[65]

Endnote

"Working from Within"

In 1935, when Eleanor Roosevelt visited Barnard to give a talk, the first lady denounced the notion of entitlement, such as that based on family legacy or rootedness in American history. "The idea that you are entitled to more consideration just because you are more native than others is something to get over," Eleanor Roosevelt told the students.[1] For Virginia C. Gildersleeve, in contrast, to be "more native than others" was part of her role as "Insider." The insider identity involved family roots, status, and connections; access to educational and cultural resources; and life-long membership in an establishment class that provided options and advantages. Benefits of that identity pervaded Virginia's career as an administrator, bolstered her drive to enter foreign affairs, and shaped her sense of her role in history.

But the insider identity was only part of Virginia's story. As much as she disclaimed ambition, at least in her younger days, Virginia was a striver and an achiever. In the tradition of progressivism, she valued expertise and sought to obtain and make use of it. Her impulses were transactional; she excelled as a committee chair or board member in a professional setting or voluntary association. At any given time in her career, she served as a member of multiple councils, boards, or directorates—in educational circles, in women's organizations, or in groups that bolstered Arab causes in the Middle East; at Columbia alone, she served on scores of committees, including the all-important Columbia University Committee on Educational Policy. In women's international politics, especially, Virginia managed multiple commitments with what her colleagues saw as exceptional deftness. "She let the discussion go on until everyone had his say, and they were all exhausted, and then she quietly took the floor and came up with the solution," said one admirer, Meta Glass, Sweet Briar president and IFUW colleague. "It was her theory that one top notch woman in the right place could do more than all the talking in the world and she herself was top notch every time, in every position." To Meta Glass, Virginia "instinctively" exuded authority, won esteem, and commanded "deference."[2]

Along the way, as she developed an administrative style, Virginia built up her resumé. She moved swiftly to adapt to the rules in place, in every instance; to make the right contacts; and, especially, to amass the right credentials.

At the very start of her academic career, in the few years after Laura Gill had antagonized President Butler and tumbled out of favor, Virginia acted methodically and strategically to pile up some credits in the English Department—to cater to the undergraduates and to join a prestigious faculty committee; to revitalize her contacts among alumnae; and not least to teach a graduate course at Columbia, the winning blow, in President Butler's view. Thus, she was prepared at the crucial moment when all other candidates fell by the wayside and opportunity finally turned in her direction. Virginia followed this pattern of preparation thereafter, as in her long and dogged route to a foreign policy role. She began collecting international affairs credentials in women's voluntary organizations, the AAUW and IFUW; moved on to foreign policy interest groups—to Charles R. Crane's Institute for Current World Affairs in the 1920s, then to James T. Shotwell's Commission to Study the Organization of Peace in the 1940s, and also to the navy when it needed a woman academic to head its advisory board. She was thus in place to be chosen for the all-important UN appointment of 1945. Not merely an "Insider"—or an Episcopalian with advanced degrees, though that counted, too—Virginia was a planner, a player, and a competitor.

Chance served a purpose as well—each of Virginia's major appointments rested in part on some development that she could not have predicted and for which she could not have prepared. That women's groups in 1944 demanded a role for women in postwar planning and that Eleanor Roosevelt called for a woman's presence on every diplomatic delegation, for instance, were not events that Virginia could have anticipated. Much like her father, she was often the right person in place at the right time. But preparation was just as important. Virginia's system of professional progress worked exceptionally well, especially when she capitalized on the role of "Insider," as at Barnard, or served as prime mover and institution-founder, as at the IFUW.

Virginia shared her strategies for career mobility in academic life with readers of her autobiography. At Columbia she learned to endure and persist while her fellow deans and male colleagues talked on and on; she took notes, kept records, cooperated with the other administrators, and waited for the right moment to push forward with some request. Eventually, the university president and her fellow deans catered to her demands, inevitably for some policy to raise women's status on campus or win for women admission to a university program. Virginia preferred "working from within" and waiting it out to militancy, stridency, or reference to women's rights. Although "militant feminists sometimes accused me of feebleness or indifference or treason," as she noted, such tactics suited her purposes. Here, Virginia described her stance in the women's movement in general: circumspect, strategic, deferential, and antimilitant.

She also favored "process" as both an educational tool and public policy tactic. In higher education, she contended, it did not matter what academic subject a student studied as long as the process of intellectual engagement occurred. Never wavering from her devotion to the liberal arts curriculum, Virginia kept enlarging the options for such engagement to take place. In the field of internationalism, "process" took on salience as well. As chair of the AAUW International Relations Committee, a post that served Virginia as a launching pad to further achievement, she sought to involve her members in a continual round of projects, reports, and campaigns; unlike the discussion of peace, which could go on forever, the process of communication and interaction *was* the purpose. The process of communication among women similarly held importance at the IFUW, in the opinion of its founders; women who maintained international friendships served the cause of peace.

Virginia's global vision pervaded both her Barnard years and her activism in public life. Inspired by the World War I era, Virginia fastened on internationalism as her special focus and vocation. At Barnard, her global vision led to annual invitations to foreign students, offers to visiting faculty from abroad, and to an international studies program. In public life, it led her first to a fascination with the Middle East and entry into a network of the region's supporters. At the same time, Virginia's concern for world affairs made her a leader in women's organizations in the interwar years and then, as opportunities slightly opened up in the 1940s, brought her to new roles beyond women's groups—to all the committees and commissions that led up to the UN Charter meeting. As Virginia's colleague, rival, and onetime mentor William Allan Neilson observed, the dean was "not an amateur."

Gender played a varied role in Virginia's international ventures. In the all-women public spaces of the interwar era—the AAUW International Relations Committee and the IFUW—settings that Virginia controlled, she was most inventive. The all-woman household that Virginia created with Caroline Spurgeon and Lilian Clapham at Alciston, a community to which they invited visitors from around the world, was another creative endeavor. Virginia's World War II opportunities brought wider involvement though less control. The navy, which needed women's enrollment, provided a surprisingly hospitable situation; the Shotwell Commission of 1941–1945 offered a venue in which to make contacts among foreign policy devotees and to work toward peace, an effort in which the IFUW had by then failed. Diplomacy proved a less-welcoming venue. At the UN Charter meeting, where women delegates were few, Virginia arrived with some of the drawbacks of an "outsider"; she lacked the political experience that her fellow members of the U.S. delegation brought to the task and faced considerable challenge. Unexpectedly, a further challenge arose: She had to deal with a major clash over equal rights, a feud for which she was unprepared, that brought recrimination, and that was much better handled by the *next* woman on the U.S. delegation, Eleanor Roosevelt. Postwar anti-Zionism offered yet another type of experience: Outnumbered and beleaguered, the entrenched US anti-Zionists were grateful to have a woman nominally at the helm, especially an "Insider." But Virginia was then in her seventies, and her anti-Zionist colleagues really preferred Dorothy Thompson, who was far better known and who quickly moved into the leadership spot. For the third time in her later years, Virginia had been in a sense displaced: first by Millicent McIntosh at Barnard and Eleanor Roosevelt at the United Nations, and then by Dorothy Thompson in U.S. anti-Zionism.

Beyond her roles as an administrator and internationalist, Virginia took on a final role as an autobiographer, a highly original addition to her list of achievements. Her prime motive was to deter and preempt biographers, who might be interested in some facet of her experience best left alone. She sought instead to keep control of the narrative: to create her own story.

Virginia was highly conscious of her role in history. In her decades of deanship at Barnard, she depended on the college publicity office, the alumnae magazine, and local journalists to keep a record of her part in public life; she also relied on her favored trustees, those with power in the press, Helen Reid and Agnes Meyer. At the same time, as she generated a presence in print, Virginia preserved all her academic, administrative, and organizational records; every scrap and morsel (save the personal correspondence that she methodically purged) fell into the archival jaw. After Barnard, at midcentury, Virginia began to contemplate shaping the historical record in print, though she had not published a book since her doctoral dissertation. Alone among her cohort of women's college leaders, Virginia turned to autobiography. Enlisting assistance, she prepared methodically for the role of self-analyst. The volume she produced in 1954 was a dramatic public performance, full of risk—an exceptional act commensurate with her long stewardship of Barnard and her decades of involvement in foreign affairs.

As *Many a Good Crusade* made clear, Virginia had been both a witness to history and a participant in it. Unpacking the highlights of her dual career, Virginia offered an advice manual for women in leadership roles. A triumph of revisionism, the book glossed over trouble spots and marginalized rivals. An exercise in self-justification, it was at once self-serving and self-exposing. A major question Virginia never tackles is whether she had ever made any mistakes; admission of error was not in her repertoire. Thus, she omits entirely her vocal indulgence of Nazi policies in the early 1930s, a series of unforced errors that she subsequently ignored but could never erase, and moves on to less damaging topics. Defiant and defensive, engaging and revealing—and surprisingly readable, *Crusade* was an impressive finale, a tour de force performance.

Virginia's autobiography spoke to many responsive readers of the 1950s. A decade later, social movements of the 1960s began to disrupt every framework on which her life and career had rested. The antiwar movement, the civil rights movement, and the women's movement undercut all the assumptions of the 1950s reading audience. Upheavals disrupted campuses, curricula underwent transformations, and coeducation transformed single-sex schools. New causes, from free speech to equal rights, swept whatever interest then existed in Virginia's book off to the margins. But her commitment to the liberal arts and to internationalism remain resilient themes; as Virginia's editors had once hoped, the parts of her memoir that concern running a college and the UN Charter meeting continue to win attention. So do the sections that allude to clashes over the Middle East, the area in which Virginia was most deeply embattled.

Elites seek ways to secure their boundaries, fortify their institutions, and preserve their advantages. Virginia contributed to these processes. Socially entitled, academically mobile, and well connected, she acted to advance the status of women and to secure her own status in professional hierarchies and public life. As an insider, Virginia promoted exclusive institutions and defended restrictive practices, such as biased admissions at selective colleges. She functioned as an outsider, too, most notably as an aspirant in foreign affairs and novice diplomat. Her autobiography, which sought at once to win attention and avoid scrutiny, suggests the tensions among her multiple roles.

Acknowledgments

I am indebted, first, to my friends and colleagues Rosalind Rosenberg, Robert McCaughey, and Herb Sloan for their help throughout this project. I am profoundly grateful for their expertise, indulgence, and invaluable advice. I am similarly indebted to Heather Mayall, who, while plowing an adjacent field, has shared her research and insights. I could not be more appreciative.

At Barnard College: I am grateful to the History Department for years of encouragement, and, most recently, for the privilege of working as a Research Scholar in History. My thanks go to Provost Linda Bell and to Lisa Tiersten and Dorothy Ko, chairs of the History Department. I also appreciate the time I spent in Robert McCaughey's seminar for alumnae, Making Barnard History, in 2014 and 2015 and the generous responses of seminar members.

For (variously) inspiration, encouragement, information, discussion, and comments on chapters, let me thank: Louise Bernikow, Cynthia Gensheimer, Lisa Keller, Helen L. Horowitz, Anya Jabour, Monica Mercado, Monica Miller, Caroline Niemczyk, Deborah Valenze, Susan Ware, and Rona Wilk. Thanks to Frank Smyth for his research on the NRA.

I am grateful to the staff of the Columbia University Rare Book and Manuscript Library and to the Barnard College Archives. My immense thanks go to Shannon O'Neill, now curator of the Tamiment-Wagner Collections at New York University, and to Martha Tenney, Director of the Barnard Archives and Special Collections. Without the extraordinary help that I received from Shannon and Martha, I could never have started or finished this book. Special thanks also to Anna Manthorpe, Archivist, at the East Sussex Brighton and Hove Record Office and to Nicole Westerdahl, Reference Librarian, Special Collections Research Center, Syracuse University Libraries.

I am fortunate to have had the support of the Columbia University Press, whom I thank, and especially lucky to have fallen into the bailiwick of history editor Stephen Wesley, whose suggestions have meant so much to me. What an impressive editor! Thank you, Stephen! Finally, my overwhelming thanks to the members of my family, especially to Isser, for all the help he provided. Thanks also to David, Dana, Alex, Karla, Lewis, and Benjamin, and to Adam and Vali.

March, 2021

A Note on Sources

This study relies on the archival resources of Barnard and Columbia. The Virginia C. Gildersleeve Papers at the Barnard College Archives deal almost entirely with Gildersleeve's career at Barnard. It includes extensive records of correspondence, publications, and speeches. Barnard resources in the archives include college publications, dean's reports, records of the Dean's Office and the Admissions Office, faculty data, and interview collections. The Barnard College Archives also holds the Setzer file, two boxes of material left by a potential biographer, journalist Dorothea Setzer. Labeled "Gildersleeve Biographical Notes and Correspondence, 1951–1954," the Setzer file includes family history items, miscellaneous snippets of research, and records of at least two dozen interviews that Setzer held in the early 1950s with Virginia's friends, colleagues, and associates. Few of the interviews are verbatim; in most cases, Setzer left accounts in her own words, speckled with quotations, of what were once interviews or written statements. Still, the Setzer file remains a lively record of first-hand personal impressions.

The Virginia C. Gildersleeve Papers, 1898–1962, at the Rare Book and Manuscript Library (RBML) of the Columbia University Libraries (81 boxes) include biographical materials and family history, records of Gildersleeve's student years, and extensive institutional records that cover her work with the American Association of University Women, the International Federation of University Women, the Middle East College Association, the UN Charter Conference of 1945, and the committee that visited Japan in 1946. The collection includes material related to the writing of Virginia Gildersleeve's autobiography and other manuscripts. The RBML also contains collections of the papers of Nicholas Murray Butler and Charles R. Crane.

Documents on the Old Postman's Cottage in Alciston, UK are in the East Sussex Record Office. Several document collections used in this study appear online, including the Records of the International Federation of University Women (https://atria.nd/search/collection/arch /show//11AV000005333).

Previous scholarship on Virginia C. Gildersleeve informs this study. Much valuable work appears in institutional histories, most prominently Robert McCaughey, *A College of Her Own: A History of Barnard* (New York: Columbia University Press, 2020) and Rosalind Rosenberg, *Changing the Subject: How the Women of Columbia Shaped the Way We Think About Sex and Politics* (New York; Columbia University Press, 2004). Patrick Dilley insightfully explores Virginia Gildersleeve's contribution to education in *The Transformation of Women's Collegiate Education: The Legacy of Virginia Gildersleeve* (New York: Palgrave/Macmillian, 2017).

A rich periodical literature discusses Virginia Gildersleeve's impact on higher education and international affairs. Some of the many articles on which this study depends are: Lynn D. Gordon, "Annie Nathan Meyer and Barnard College: Mission and Identity in Women's Higher Education, 1889–1950," *History of Education Quarterly* 26, no. 4 (Winter 1986), 503–522; Caroline Niemczyk, "Barnard and Columbia in Historical Perspective: Opening the Doors of Academe," *Barnard Alumnae Magazine* (Summer 1988), 2–7; Rosalind Rosenberg, "Virginia Gildersleeve: Opening the Gates" in *Living Legacies: Great Moments and Leading Figures in the History of Columbia University*, http://www.columbia.edu/alumni /Magazine/Summer2001/Gildersleeve; Christy Jo Snider, "Planning for Peace: Virginia Gildersleeve at the United Nations Conference on International Organization," *Peace and Change* 32, no. 2 (April 2007), 168–185; Stephen Turner, "When Empathy Fails: Some Problematic 'Progressives' and Expertise: Crystal Eastman and Virginia Gildersleeve," http://usf .academia.edu/StephenTurner; and Andrea Walton, "Achieving a Voice and Institutionalizing a Vision for Women: The Barnard Deanship at Columbia University, 1889–1947," *Historical Studies in Education* 13, no. 2 (Fall 2001), 113–146.

ABBREVIATIONS

ANM: Annie Nathan Meyer
BC: Barnard College
CU: Columbia University
DT: Dorothy Thompson
GAP: George A. Plimpton
IFUW: International Federation of University Women
NMB: Nicholas Murray Butler
OPC: Old Postman's Cottage
RBML: Rare Book and Manuscript Library
TC: Teachers College
VCG: Virginia Crocheron Gildersleeve
ZNH: Zora Neale Hurston

Notes

INTRODUCTION

1. VCG, "The Strange Flotsam of Time" (typescript of memories), 6–7, box 66, Virginia C. Gildersleeve Papers, RBML, CU; "New Dean of Barnard College," *New-York Daily Tribune*, December 18, 1910, 56.
2. Dorothea Setzer interview with Meta Glass, n.d. BC2.4, box 2, Setzer File, Barnard Archives.
3. Stephen Turner, "When Empathy Fails: Some Problematic 'Progressives' and Expertise: Crystal Eastman and Virginia Gildersleeve," http://usf.academia.edu/Stephen Turner.

1. ROOTS: 1877–1911

1. VCG, *Many a Good Crusade* (New York: Macmillan 1954), 23.
2. "Clings to Ancestral Estate: Last of the Crocherons Would Retain Her Staten Island Home," *New York Times*, October 11, 1904, 6; for Mary Elizabeth Crocheron, see also "Dead Behind Locked Doors: Woman Recluse Once Repelled Eviction in Staten Island," *New York Times*, September 4, 1909, 3.
3. John Butler, *Huguenots in America: A Refugee People in a New World* (Cambridge, MA: Harvard University Press, 1983), 45; Lori R. Weintrob, "When New York Spoke French: Traces of Huguenot Refugees on Staten Island." Paper given at the New York Area French History Group, CUNY Graduate Center, October 13, 1916. For the progenitor, Jean Crocheron, see *The Crocheron Family of Staten Island*, compiled by Charlotte Louise Megill Hix (Garden City, NY: n.p., 1954), 1–3. VCG discusses Crocheron history in *Many a Good Crusade*, 3–10.

4. For the Jean Crocheron inventories, see Hix, *The Crocheron Family*, 3. The comment on slavery is from J. J. Clute, *Annals of Staten Island, from its Discovery to the Present Times* (New York: Press of C. Vogt, 1877), 76.

5. Hix, *The Crocheron Family*, 23 and passim; J.J. Clute, *Annals of Staten Island*, 140, 141, 147.

6. Hix, *The Crocheron Family*, 77–78; Mary St. J. Mairs to Alger Gildersleeve, September 11, 1945, box 1, VCG Papers, RBML, CU.

7. Hix, *The Crocheron Family*, 77–78, 79, 81–83; VCG, *Crusade*, 4–7.

8. Anna M. Gayle Fry, *Memories of Old Cahaba*, printed for the author (South Nashville, Tenn., and Dallas, Tex.: Publishing House of M.E. Church, 1908), 13, 18; Alger C. Gildersleeve, "Some Notes on the Crocheron Family, 1928, Typewritten by Alger Crocheron Gildersleeve . . . With Remarks Interjected by the Typist," 11, box 1, VCG Papers, RBML, CU. For Cahaba, see also Tom Bailey et al., *The Five Capitals of Alabama: The Story of Alabama's Capital Cities from St. Stephens to Montgomery* (Montgomery, Ala.: New South Books, 2020).

9. Gayle, *Memories of Old Cahaba*, 13, 19

10. Gayle, *Memories of Old Cahaba*, 27; letter from VCG to her mother, May 28, 1917, box 1, VCG Papers, RBML, CU; VCG, "The Strange Flotsam of Time" (typescript memories), box 66, CU; VCG, *Crusade* (New York: Macmillan, 1954), 7; David J. Eicher, *The Longest Night: A Military History of the Civil War* (New York: Simon & Schuster, 2001), 237–238.

11. Willard Harvey Gildersleeve, M.A., *Gildersleeve Pioneers* (Rutland, Vt.: The Tuttle Publishing Co., 1941), chaps. 1–5.

12. Gildersleeve, *Gildersleeve Pioneers*, 276–277.

13. Accounts of Henry A. Gildersleeve's life include John W. Leonard, ed. *Men of America: A Biographical Dictionary of Contemporaries* (New York: L. R. Hamersly & Co., 1908, vol. 1), 981–982; Delancey Nicoll, "Memorial of Henry Alger Gildersleeve," in New York County Lawyers' Association, *Yearbook, 1923* (New York: J.J. Little & Ives Company, 1923), 218–221; ACG [Alger C. Gildersleeve], "Biography of Henry Alger Gildersleeve," privately printed, VCG Papers, Setzer file, BC2.4, box 1, Barnard Archives.

14. Prof. George Chase, "The Dwight Method of Legal Instruction," *The American Lawyer* 15, no. 9 (September 1907), 419–422.

15. Michael A. Gordon, *The Orange Riots: Irish Political Violence in New York City, 1870–1871* (Ithaca, NY: Cornell University Press, 1993); Henry A. Gildersleeve, *Rifles and Marksmanship* (New York: Spirit of the Times, 1878, reprint of 1876 edition); Henry A. Gildersleeve, Obituary, *American Rifleman* (July 1, 1923); Delancey Nicoll, "Memorial of Henry A, Gildersleeve," 218–222.

For the early history of the NRA, rooted in marksmanship and competitive shooting matches, see Frank Smyth, *The NRA: The Unauthorized History*. New York: Flatiron Books, 2020, chaps. 1–2.

16. Leonard, *Men of America*, 980–981.

17. "Henry A. Gildersleeve." *The University Magazine* 10–11 (1894): 280–281.

18. "Edward Corrigan's Suit Against the Coney Island Jockey Club," *Brooklyn Daily Eagle* (June 6, 1892), 6.

19. *Edward Corrigan, Respondent v. The Coney Island Jockey Club, Appellant*, decision of October 24, 1892, *Reports of Cases Argued and Determined in the Superior Court of the City of New York* (New York and Albany, NY: Banks & Brother, Law Publishers, 1893), vol. 61, 393–399.

20. *Homiston v. Long Island Railroad*, 3 Misc. 342 22 N.Y. 78, decision of April 1, 1893.

21. *Jaeger's Sanitary Woolen System Co. v. Le Boutillier* 5 Misc. 78 (N.Y. Misc. 1893) or 5 Misc. 78 (24 N.Y.S. 890), a decision of September 1, 1893.

22. VCG, *Crusade*, 20.

23. Clifton Hood, *In Pursuit of Privilege: A History of New York's Upper Class and the Making of a Metropolis* (New York: Columbia University Press, 2017), 107, 210, 211. In some accounts, Murray Hill's uptown boundary was closer to Thirty-Fourth Street than to Fiftieth Street.

24. Michael Rosenthal, *Nicholas Miraculous: The Amazing Career of the Redoubtable Nicholas Murray Butler* (New York: Farrar, Straus, and Giroux, 2006), 401–403; Robert A. McCaughey, *Stand, Columbia: A History of Columbia University in the City of New York* (New York: Columbia University Press, 2003), 541; Alger C. Gildersleeve, "Notes on the Youth of VCG." Statement to Dorothea Setzer, BC.2.4, box 2, folder 2, Barnard Archives.

25. VCG, *Crusade*, 20, 23.

26. VCG, *Crusade*, 19–20; VCG, "The Strange Flotsam of Times," 1–2, box 66, VCG Papers, RBML, CU.

27. [Dorothea Setzer], "People Who Influenced the Life of Virginia C. Gildersleeve," 1, 7, box 1, VCG Papers, RBML, CU

28. [Setzer] "People Who Influenced the Life of VCG," 7; VCG, *Many a Good Crusade*, 25, 33.

29. VCG, *Crusade*, 22; ACG, statement to Dorothea Setzer, circa 1952, Setzer file, BC2.4, box 2.

30. "Alger Crocheron Gildersleeve," *Biographical Dictionary of the State of New York, 1900*, 158; "The Story of the Columbia University Club," *Columbia Alumni News*, February 15, 1918, vol. 9, no. 20, 500; ACG, "Some Notes on the Crocheron Family, 1928, Typewritten by Alger Crocheron Gildersleeve . . . With Remarks Interjected by the Typist," VCG papers, RBML, CU; ACG, "John Gelb

and His Seven Children" (Far Rockaway, NY, 1945), box 1, VCG Papers, RBML, CU; ACG to Mr. [Edmund Parker] Crocheron, March 12, 1928, box 1, VCG Papers, RBML, CU. For ACG, see also BC2.4, box 29, VCG Papers, Barnard Archives.

31. *Letters and Writings of James Greenleaf Croswell: Late Master of the Brearley School* (Boston: Houghton Mifflin, 1917); Alice Castree to VCG (June 13, 1895), box 1. VCG Papers, RBML, CU; Richard Schwartz, "Brearley School," *Encyclopedia of New York City*, 2nd ed., ed. Kenneth T. Jackson, 312 (New Haven, Conn: Yale University Press, 2010), 132.

32. Annie Nathan Meyer, *Barnard Beginnings* (Boston: Houghton Mifflin Company, 1935), 100–102; Marian Churchill White, *A History of Barnard College* (New York: Columbia University Press, 1954), 13, 16, 118; Rosalind Rosenberg, *Changing the Subject: How the Women of Columbia Changed the Way We Think About Sex and Politics* (New York: Columbia University Press, 2004), 33, 43,50–51, 189; VCG, *Crusade*, 39. The "no nerves" comment made by Virginia the elder would have been clear to VCG's contemporaries. It refers to the recommendation of an eminent physician in the 1870s that young women stay out of college to protect their health and prevent nervous breakdowns. For the argument against higher education for women, see Edward H. Clarke, MD, *Sex in Education, or A Fair Chance for the Girls* (1873); for a counterattack, see Julia Ward Howe, ed., *Sex in Education: A Reply to Dr. E. H. Clarke*, (Cambridge, Mass.: Roberts Brothers,1874).

33. Annie Nathan Meyer describes her role in Barnard's founding in *Barnard Beginnings;* the words quoted are from p. 3. For Barnard's early years, see also Caroline Niemczyk, "Barnard and Columbia in Historical Perspective: Opening the Doors of Academe," *Barnard Alumnae Magazine* (Summer 1988): 2–7; Robert McCaughey, *A College of Her Own: The History of Barnard* (New York: Columbia University Press, 2020), chap. 1; Horowitz, *Alma Mater*, 134–142; and Rosenberg, *Changing the Subject*, chap. 1 and 53–58.

34. Annie Nathan Meyer, "A New Phase of Women's Education in America," *Transactions of the National Council of Women in the United States, Assembled in Washington, DC, February 22 to 25, 1891* (Philadelphia: J. B. Lippincott, 1891), 171, 182–183 (Tuesday, February 24, 1891, evening session); James Axtell, *The Making of Princeton University from Woodrow Wilson to the Present* (Princeton: Princeton University Press, 2006), 156.

35. VCG, "The Charm of the New Site," May 6, 1898, 2, 3, 6 (student essay), box 2, folder: "Undergraduate themes, BA thesis, MA thesis," VCG Papers, RBML, CU; VCG, *Many a Good Crusade*, 42.

36. VCG, *Crusade*, 41; VCG, "The Purpose of College Greek," *Educational Review* (September, 1916), 174–175; Mrs. N.W. Liggett to VCG, July 1, 1896, box 2, VCG

Papers, RBML, CU, folder: "Personal Items in Student Days at Barnard." Mrs. N. W. Liggett, Barnard's bursar/registrar, listed under that name in Barnard/Columbia records, was also, in the records of Vassar College, Anna Coates Wardle [Liggett], Vassar '80. A former teacher, most recently at Packard Collegiate Institute, Mrs. Liggett had been married in 1889 to William Leigh Liggett, a lawyer, widowed since 1890, and hired at Barnard in 1891. See *Catalogue of Officers and Graduates of Columbia University* (New York: Printed for the University, 1912), 60; *General Catalogue of the Officers and Graduates of Vassar College*, vol. 5, 37; and *Woman's Who's Who of America: A Biographical Dictionary, 1914*, ed. John William Leonard, vol. 1, (New York: American Commonwealth Company, 1914), 491. No one who referred to Mrs. Liggett at Barnard ever used a first name, nor did the Columbia University catalogue.

37. VCG, *Crusade*, 40; VCG, "College Friendships," *Barnard Bulletin* (April 8, 1914), quoted in Rona M. Wilk, "'What's a Crush?' A Study of Crushes and Romantic Friendships at Barnard College, 1900–1920," *Magazine of History* 18, no. 4 (July 2004): 21; Agnes Ernst Meyer, interview with Dorothy Setzer on February 2, 1953 in "Notes for a Biography," BC2.4 box 2, folder 1, Barnard Archives.

38. VCG, *Crusade*, 44; McCaughey, *A College of Her Own*, chap. 3; Alice Duer Miller, "Twenty-five Years a Dean," *Barnard College Alumnae* XXV, no. 6 (March 1936), 23–24; VCG, "The Strange Flotsam of Times," typescript, pp. 5–6, box 66, VCG Papers, RBML, CU. Alice Duer Miller's books include a 1939 history of Barnard College

39. McCaughey, *A College of Her Own*, chap. 3; McCaughey, "Profile of the Class of 1899"; Mrs. George McAnemy interview with Dorothea Setzer of January 14, 1952, BC2.4, box 2. Science trumped religious belief in the Putnam/Jacobi family. Dr. Abraham Jacobi, socialist and anticleric, professed no faith, nor did Dr. Mary Putnam Jacobi; their daughter, Marjorie, grew up with no religion. See Carla Jean Bittell, *Mary Putnam Jacobi and the Politics of Medicine in Nineteenth-Century America* (Chapel Hill: University of North Carolina Press, 2009), 169.

40. McCaughey, *A College of Her Own*, chap. 3; Diana B. Turk, *Founded By a Mighty Vow: Sisterhood and Women's Fraternities, 1870–1920* (New York: New York University Press, 2004), 26; Turk discusses fraternities and anti-Semitism in chap. 3; VCG, *Crusade*, 42; Annie Nathan Meyer, interview with Dorothea Setzer, "Notes for a Biography of VCG," BC2.4, box 2, folder 1, Barnard Archives.

41. VCG, *Crusade*, 43, 44, 46–47; VCG, "The Ideals of Social Regeneration of the Terrorists," 69–70; untitled essay for Rhetoric I, October 20, 1897, both in box 2, folder: "Undergraduate themes, BA Thesis, MA thesis," VCG Papers, RBML, CU.

42. VCG, "The Change in the Spirit of Barnard," April 25, 1899, box 2, folder: "Undergraduate themes, BA Thesis, MA Thesis," VCG Papers, RBML, CU; see also, for the changing pattern of women's college attendance, Alice Duer Miller, "Social Life at Barnard," *Columbia University Quarterly* 2 (1900), 219; Lois Kimball Matthews Rosenberry *The Dean of Women* (Boston: Houghton Mifflin, 1915), 4; and Helen Lefkowitz Horowitz, *Alma Mater: Design and Experience in the Women's Colleges from Their Nineteenth-Century Beginnings to the 1930s* (New York: Knopf, 1984), 252.

43. *Mortarboard for 1900, created by the Class of 1899* [the Barnard College Yearbook], 38, 39, 59, 94.

44. VCG, *Crusade*, 39, 49.

45. McCaughey, "Profile of the Barnard Class of 1899"; Mary E. Cookingham, "Bluestockings, Spinsters, and Pedagogues: Women College Graduates, 1865–1910." *Population Studies* 38 (November 1984), 349–364; Patricia A. Graham, "Expansion and Exclusion: A History of Women in Higher Education." *Signs* 3 (Summer 1978), 759–773; Millicent Washburn Shinn, "The Marriage Rate of College Women." *The Century Magazine* 50 (October 1895): 946–948.

46. For the family claim, see Joyce Antler, "After College, What? New Graduates and the Family Claim." *American Quarterly* 32 (Fall 1980), 409–434.

47. Patrick Dilley, *The Transformation of Women's Collegiate Education: The Legacy of Virginia Gildersleeve* (Cham, Switzerland: Palgrave/Macmillan, 2017), 19.

48. Rosenberg, *Changing the Subject*, 74–75. The Faculty of Political Science included several social science departments, plus the History department. Earlier in the 1890s, as historian Rosalind Rosenberg reveals, Dean John W. Burgess of the Faculty of Political Science had hounded younger colleagues who admitted women to their graduate courses to reverse direction and exclude them.

49. MA thesis is in box 2, VCG Papers, RBML, CU.

50. VCG, *Crusade*, 51.

51. VCG, *Crusade*, 51; "A Bow to Mr. Brewster," *Barnard College Alumnae Magazine* 26 no. 2 (November 1936): 9; William T. Brewster to VCG, October 8, 1900, box 2 VCG Papers, RBML, CU, folder: "VCG: Postgraduate."

52. VCG, *Crusade*, 53; White, *History*, 65.

53. Preliminary Examination, October 19, 1907, box 2, VCG Papers, RBML, CU.

54. VCG, *Government Regulation of Elizabethan Drama*. New York: Columbia University Press, 1908, 1–3.

55. VCG, *Crusade*, 57–60; VCG to Prof. [William P.] Trent, November 22, 1909, 2, Dean's Office Correspondence 1910–1911, box 12, VCG Papers, Barnard Archives.

56. VCG, *Crusade*, 59–61; "The Development of English Versification, My Graduate Course, English 255, Given at Columbia, 1910–1911," box 2, folder: "College Course Notes," VCG Papers, RBML, CU.

57. VCG, *Crusade*, 61, 63.

58. Andrea Walton, "Achieving a Voice and Institutionalizing a Vision for Women: The Barnard Deanship at Columbia University, 1889–1947." *Historical Studies in Education* (2001): 113–146; this section also depends on McCaughey, *A College of Her Own*, 31–33, 66–70; and Rosenberg, *Changing the Subject*, 120–122.

59. Nicholas Murray Butler to Annie Nathan Meyer, May 26, 1905, quoted in McCaughey, *A College of Her Own*, 81–82; Butler to George A. Plimpton, January 5, 1908, GAP Papers, 1889–1936, BC1.3, box 2, folder: correspondence, 1907–08; VCG, *Crusade*, 52–53; Laura Drake Gill to Silas Brownell, December 10, 1907, BC1.6, Board of Trustees Correspondence, box 2, folder 34, Barnard Archives.

60. Rosenthal, *Nicholas Miraculous*, 8, 14; McCaughey, *Stand Columbia*, chap. 7; Diane Ravitch, *The Great School Wars*, part 2; Upton Sinclair, *The Goose Step: A Study of American Education*, rev. ed. (Girard, Kans.: Haldeman-Julius Publications, 1923), 30, 31, 40–41, 44.

61. James M. Bruce to George A. Plimpton, January 14, 1909; Caroline Hazard to GAP, October 8, 1909; M. Carey Thomas to GAP, October 12, 1909; GAP to Mrs. A. A. Anderson, October 21, 1909, all in George A. Plimpton Papers. 1889–1936, box 3, folder: "Selecting a Dean, 1894–1910," Barnard Archives. For the distinguished career of Lucy Sprague Mitchell, a prominent progressive educator, see Joyce Antler, *Lucy Sprague Mitchell: The Making of a Modern Woman* (New Haven: Yale University Press, 1987); and Antler, "Feminism and Life Process: The Life and Career of Lucy Sprague Mitchell." *Feminist Studies* 7, no. 1 (Spring 1981): 134–157. Involved in settlement work and labor reform, Mitchell (who married in 1912) founded a Bureau of Educational Experiment in New York City that eventually became the Bank Street College of Education. Additional letters on Mitchell, who impressed Butler and Plimpton, during the Barnard search include NMB to Lucy Sprague, May 28 and July 14, 1909, Lucy Sprague Mitchell Papers, CU, and Benjamin Wheeler to NMB, April 16, 1910, Dean's Office Correspondence, 1909–1910, box 9, folder 23, Barnard Archives.

    For debate over the Barnard deanship in 1908, see Walton, "Achieving a Voice," 134–137.

62. GAP to M. Carey Thomas, November 11, 1909, GAP Papers, box 3, folder: "Seeking a Dean, 1894–1910," Barnard Archives. For Breckinridge, see Helen L. Horowitz, "With More Love Than I Can Say: A Nineteenth-Century Father to His Daughter," *Wellesley* 65 (1980): 16–20; Becky Beaupre Gillespie, "Sophonisba in Love: A Law School Pioneer and the Women Who Vied for Her Affection," February 19, 2015, University of Chicago Law School (online) www.law.uchicago .edu/news/sophonisba-in-love; and Anya Jabour, *Sophonisba Breckinridge: Championing Women's Activism in Modern America* (Chicago: University of

Illinois Press, 2019). Jabour discusses the feud over social work on pp. 114–115 and 136.

63. Nicholas Murray Butler to GAP, October 23, 1909, BC5.1 Dean's Office Correspondence, 1909–1910, box 9, folder 8, Barnard Archives; Walton, "Finding a Voice," 135.

64. Nicholas Murray Butler to Silas Brownell, December 27, 1909, BC5.1 Dean's Office Correspondence 1909–1910, box 9, folder 8, Barnard Archives.

65. Butler to Trustees of Barnard College, n.d. [April 1910], GAP Papers, box 3, folder: "Seeking a Dean, 1894–1910"; Meeting, Board of Trustees, April 18, 1910, 1–3, BC1.6, Board of Trustees Correspondence, 1896–1915; Butler to Plimpton, June 7, 1910, Dean's Office Correspondence, 1909–1910, BC5.1, box 9, folder 2, Barnard Archives; VCG, *Crusade*, 63.

66. Plimpton to Butler, June 18, 1910, Dean's Office Correspondence, 1909–1910, box 9, folder 8, BC5.1, Barnard Archives. Sociologist Elsie Clews Parsons, Barnard '96, who would serve as a Barnard trustee 1911–1915, proposed mothers as best suited for the Barnard deanship; her nominees included her friends Alice Duer Miller, social scientist Mary Simkhovitch, and former dean Emily James Smith Putnam; see Rosenberg, *Changing the Subject*, 122.

67. Plimpton to Mrs. A. A. Anderson, June 16, 1910. BC5.1 Dean's Office Correspondence, 1909–1910, box 9, folder 23, Barnard Archives.

68. Lida Shaw King to Plimpton, October 18, 1910, GAP Papers, 1889–1936, BC1.3, box 3, folder: "Selecting a Dean, 1894–1910," Barnard Archives. Butler's revised rules for the deanship were discussed in the *Columbia University Quarterly*, 12 (June 1910): 318, where Lida Shaw King read about them.

69. Butler to Plimpton, November 14 and November 18, 1910, George A. Plimpton Papers, 1889–1936, BC1.3 box 2, folder: "GAP Correspondence, 1909–1910." For the "first merger crisis," see McCaughey, *A College of Her Own*, chap. 3.

70. Meeting, Board of Trustees, December 9, 1910, p. 7, BC1.6 Board of Trustees Correspondence, 1896–1915, Barnard Archives; Gano Dunn, First Interview, n.d. Setzer File, box 2, BC2.4, Barnard Archives.

71. Plimpton to Mrs. A. A. Anderson, December 16, 1910 and Plimpton to Albert G. Milbank, December 21, 1910, GAP Papers, BC1.3, GAP Correspondence, 1909–1910 box 2, GAP Papers, Barnard Archives; VCG, *Crusade*, 63.

72. VCG to Edward W. Sheldon, March 27, 2011, BC5.1, Dean's Office Correspondence, 1910–1911, box 11, Barnard Archives (lawyer Sheldon, Princeton '79, donated time to Columbia, where he had attended law school. VCG asked for his help in restoring power to the dean's role at Barnard); VCG, *Crusade*, 64.

73. Silas Brownell to Friends of Barnard College, February 16, 1911, BC1.6 Board of Trustees Correspondence, 1896–1915, Barnard Archives.

2. THE INSIDER: 1911 THROUGH WORLD WAR I

1. "Building the Barnard Tradition: The text of the address given at the dinner by Nicholas Murray Butler, President of Columbia University," *Barnard College Alumnae Monthly* XXV, no. 6 (March 1936), 15. For another version of the statement, see "First Interview with Mr. Gano Dunn (n.d.) Verbatim Report," BC2.4, Setzer file, box 2, Barnard Archives.

2. "Miss Gildersleeve Now Heads Barnard," *New York Times*, February 17, 1911, 6.

3. "New Dean of Barnard College," *New-York Daily Tribune*, December 18, 1910, 56; VCG, *Many a Good Crusade: Memoirs of Virginia Crocheron Gildersleeve* (New York: Macmillan, 1954), 66–67; Comment from the Provost, William T. Brewster; Greetings of Miss Alice G. Chace, President of the Associate Alumnae of Barnard College on the Installation of Dean Gildersleeve, February 16, 1911; Greetings of Mary B. Polhemus, class of '11, from Dean's Office Correspondence, BC5.1, box 11, folder 5, Barnard Archives.

4. VCG, *Crusade*, 65. Nicholas Murray Butler to Henry A. Gildersleeve, April 14, 1915, February 12, 1917, December 2, 1920, and December 23, 1921; VCG to Sarah S. Butler, March 26, 1913; VCG to Nicholas Murray Butler, February 8, 1935, October 10, 1938, and August 13, 1943; Nicholas Murray Butler to VCG, February 13, 1936 and October 6, 1938, in Nicholas Murray Butler Papers, series II, box 157, RBML, CU.

5. Nicholas Murray Butler to George L. Rives, president of Columbia University Board of Trustees, November 20, 1914, Rives Papers, CU, quoted by Robert A. McCaughey in *Stand Columbia: A History of Columbia University in the City of New York, 1754–2004* (New York: Columbia University Press, 2003), 226; Andrea Walton, "Achieving a Voice and Institutionalizing a Vision for Women: The Barnard Deanship at Columbia University, 1889–1947," *Historical Studies in Education* 13 no. 2 (Fall 2001), 140.

6. Statement of Francis Plimpton is in the Setzer file, BC5.1, box 2, Barnard Archives.

7. George A. Plimpton to George F. Baker, March 22, 1923, GAP Papers, box 2, folder: correspondence, 1921–1934, RBML, CU; fundraising letter to Henry L. Harrison (n.d., c. 1930), folder 19, GAP correspondence, 1921–1934, GAP Papers, RBML, CU; GAP to Mrs. Russell Sage, June 17, 1909, GAP Papers, folder: Correspondence, 1909–1910, BC1.3, box 2, Barnard Archives.

8. For Plimpton's success as treasurer, see Robert A. McCaughey, *A College of Her Own: The History of Barnard* (New York: Columbia University Press, 2020), chap. 3; for VCG's reports to Plimpton on Barnard's needs, to be used in fundraising efforts, see VCG to GAP, March 29, 1911 and March 30, 1911 (letters of different lengths), GAP Papers, box 2, folder: 1911, BC1.3, Barnard Archives,

and VCG to GAP, "An Appeal for Barnard College," November 11, 1912, box 2, GAP Papers, folder: 1912. For the opening of Students' Hall in 1917, see VCG, "Dean's Report for 1918," 5; the last comment is from VCG, "Dean's Report for 1913," 10.

9. VCG to Annie Nathan Meyer, May 15, 1912 and January 2, 1912, BC5.1, Dean's Office Departmental Correspondence, 1911–1912, box 13; Lynn D. Gordon, "Annie Nathan Meyer and Barnard College," *History of Education Quarterly* 26 (Winter 1986), 515ff. See also Joyce Antler, *The Journey Home: How Jewish Women Shaped Modern America* (New York: Schocken Books, 1997), 67.

10. VCG to Silas B. Brownell, June 7, 1912; J. B. Jennings to VCG, January 13, 1912; VCG to Captain of the 36th Precinct, June 13, 1912; VCG to Hon. Rhinelander Walso, Police Commissioner, September 14, 1911, December 20, 1911, and January 6, 1912, in BC5.1, Dean's Office and Departmental Correspondence, 1911–1912, box 13, folders 1–14, Barnard Archives; VCG, *Crusade*, 199–201.

11. "Regulations for the Election of the Alumnae Trustee, May 16, 1912; VCG to Mrs. Charles Cary Rumsey, February 19, 1912; VCG to George A. Plimpton, November 23, 1911, all from BC5.1, Dean's Office and Departmental Correspondence, 1911–12, box 13, folders 1–14; "Dean's Report for 1911," 5.

12. VCG, "Statement of Educational Changes, May 2, 1912," BC5.1, Dean's Office and Departmental Correspondence, 1911–1912, box 13, folder 7, Barnard Archives; Talcott Parsons to VCG, May 11, 2014, Dean's Office Correspondence, 1913–1914, box 21, folder 5; and VCG to Dean James E. Russell, April 22, 1914, folder 6; "Dean's Report for 1913," 3; "Recruitment Materials, Barnard College, 1918," 3, in BC11.2, Barnard Archives; VCG, *Crusade*, 99; Walton, "Achieving a Voice," 140; and Rosalind Rosenberg, *Changing the Subject: How the Women of Columbia Shaped The Way We Think About Sex and Politics* (New York: Columbia University Press, 2007), 124–125. The New York School of Social Work became affiliated with Columbia in 1940.

For the contested relations between Barnard and Teachers College, see Bette Weneck, "Social and Cultural Stratification in Women's Higher Education: Barnard College and Teachers College, 1898–1912," *History of Education Quarterly* 31, no. 1 (Spring 1991), 1–25. Under an agreement that VCG imposed in 1912, Barnard retained access to TC resources while keeping TC students (a "heterogeneous" group, according to Laura D. Gill) out of Barnard courses.

13. VCG, *Crusade*, 99; BC5.1, Dean's Office Correspondence, 1913–1914, box 21, folder 3; "Dean's Report for 1913," 1; Walton, "Achieving a Voice," 138–139.

14. VCG, *Crusade*, 68–69 (on "working from within"); Statement of George Pegram (physicist and dean of the Engineering School, 1918–1930), early 1950s, Setzer file, BC24.1, box 2, folder 1, Barnard Archives; Rosenberg, *Changing the Subject*, 124–125.

15. VCG, *Crusade*, 98. Facebook executive Sheryl Sandburg urged more direct ways of demanding equity in *Lean In: Women, Work, and the Will to Lead* (New York: Knopf, 2013).

16. Ibid.

17. For the early twentieth-century women's movement, see Nancy F. Cott, *The Grounding of Modern Feminism* (New Haven: Yale University Press, 1987). Historian William L. O'Neill defines "social feminism," the antimilitant stance of many activists in the women's movement, in *Feminism in America*, 2nd ed. (New Brunswick, NJ: Transaction Publishers, 1989), xxiv; see also chap. 3, and *passim*. Those who promoted advances for women in higher education, like VCG, generally fall into the social feminist category; it was not a term used at the time.

18. VCG, "Constructive Elements in the Curriculum," *Educational Review* 53 (February 1917), 137–145. For VCG's defense of the liberal arts tradition, see also "Growth of Barnard: Dean Gildersleeve Tells of a Successful Experiment," *New York Times*, January 25, 1913, 14 (a letter to the editor).

19. VCG, "Constructive Elements," 143, 145.

20. "Dean's Report for 1918," 7.

21. Freda Kirchwey, "Fraternities Versus Democracy," *Barnard Bear* 8 (October 1912), 3–6; "Barnard Puts Ban on Secret Societies," *New York Times*, June 8, 1913, 10; "Dean's Report for 1913," 5; Sara Alpern, *Freda Kirchwey: A Woman of the Nation* (Cambridge: Harvard University Press, 1987), 12; McCaughey, *A College of Her Own*, chap. 3.

22. "Dean's Report for 1913," 5–6 and 8–9.

23. "Dean's Report for 1913," 7; "Dean's Report for 1916," 7–8.

24. " 'Frats' at Barnard Missed by the Dean," *New York Times*, October 31, 1915, 13; VCG's letter to a dean at Swarthmore is quoted in McCaughey, *A College of Her Own*, 91.

25. John Milton Cooper, *Woodrow Wilson: A Biography* (New York: Knopf, 2009), 88–95; *Princeton Alumni Weekly*, June 12, 1907.

26. VCG to Naomi Harris, April 11, 1911 and April 26, 1912; Katrina Ely Tiffany to VCG, April 15, 1912; VCG to Mrs. Charles Ely Tiffany, April 18, 1912, all in BC5.1, Dean's Office Correspondence, 1911–1912, box 14, BC. Thanks to Rona Wilk for the documents.

27. Annie Nathan Meyer to VCG (n.d., 1912); VCG to Annie Nathan Meyer, April 16, 1916; VCG to Miss Elizabeth Hall, October 19, 1915; all in BC5.1, Dean's Office Correspondence, 1915–1916, box 28, Barnard Archives; for the Nathan sisters, see Louise Bernikow, "Sisters in a House Divided: Annie Nathan Meyer and her Sister, Maud Nathan, Debate the Question of Women's Suffrage" *Barnard Magazine* CIV, no. 1 (Winter 2016), 32–33. The comment by Iphigene

Ochs is mentioned in Lynn D. Gordon, "Annie Nathan Meyer and Barnard College," 513. For the Barnard Suffrage Club, see Juliet Stuart Poyntz, "Suffragism and Feminism at Barnard," *Barnard Bear* (April 1914) IX, no. 7, 3–4.

28. Christy Jo Snider, "Planning for Peace: Virginia Gildersleeve at the United Nations Conference on International Organization," *Peace and Change* 32, no. 2 (April 2007), 170; VCG, *Crusade*, 65–68, 116–117, 122–123, 126; "Dean's Report for 1919," 4–5. For admission of women to Columbia's medical school, see also McCaughey, *A College of Her Own*, 103, and Rosenberg, *Changing the Subject*, 127.

29. VCG, "Women Farmer Workers," *New Republic* 12, no. 6 (September 1, 1917), 132–134; Lynn Dumenil, *Second Line of Defense: Women and World War I* (Chapel Hill: University of North Carolina Press, 2020), 190–191.

30. Snider, "Planning for Peace," 170–171; Marion Talbot and Lois Mathews Rosenberry, *The History of the American Association of University Women, 1881–1913* (Boston and New York: Houghton Mifflin, 1931), 73, 242–247, 267–271; Gertrude S. Martin to VCG, May 13, 1918, VCG Papers, box 44, RBML, CU.

31. Edith C. Batho, *A Lamp of Friendship, 1918–1968: A Short History of the International Federation of University Women* (Eastbourne, UK: Sumfield & Day, 1968), 3; and Christine von Oertzen, *Science, Gender, and Internationalism: Women's Academic Networks, 1917–1955* (New York and London: Palgrave Macmillan, 2014), 18, 24–25. For the reception committee, see "Visit of the British Educational Mission to the United States, October-December, 1918," 5 (pamphlet) box 44, VCG Papers, folder: 1918, RBML, CU.

32. Spurgeon quote from "The British Educational Mission to the United States, October-December, 1918), 12, BC.05 Dean's Office Papers, 1918–1919, box 4, Barnard Archives.

33. Batho, *Lamp of Friendship*, 4; Katherine Lee Bates to Caroline Spurgeon, February 11, 1919, box 47, VCG Papers, RBML, CU.

34. VCG, handwritten manuscript of "How It Started," for the IFUW Newsletter, n.d., c. December 1950, 1–2, VCG Papers, box 46, folder: 1948–54, RBML, CU.

35. "Report of the Conference on After-War Problems, December 6, 1918, pt. II, International Relations," VCG Presiding, 14 pp., VCG Papers, box 44, folder: 1918, RBML, CU. See also VCG, "Committee on International Relations," *Journal of the Association of Collegiate Alumnae*, 12, no. 3 (April 1919), 150–153.

36. Report of the First Conference, July, 1920; Batho, *Lamp of Friendship*, 4–5; von Oertzen, *Science, Gender, and Internationalism*, 27–31; von Oertzen, "Whose World? Internationalism, Nationalism, and the Struggle Over the Language Question in the International Federation of University Women, 1919–1932," *Contemporary European History* 25, special issue 2 (May 2016), 275–276. For

British academic women's activism, see Carol Dyhouse, "The British Federation of University Women and the Status of Women in Universities, 1907–1959," *Women's History Review*, 4, no. 4 (1995), 465–485; and also, on the careers of pioneer women academics, Dyhouse, *No Distinction of Sex? Women in British Universities, 1870–1939* (London and New York: Routledge, 1995).

37. For groups formed after World War I, see Mona L. Siegel, *Peace On Our Terms: The Global Battle for Women's Rights After the First World War* (New York: Columbia University Press, 2019).

38. For Spurgeon's remarks, see IFUW, Report of the First Conference, London, 1920, 15; Von Oertzen, *Science, Gender, and Internationalism*, 28.

39. VCG, "How It Started," pp. 4–5.

40. Ada Comstock, "Report of the First Conference of the IFUW," *Journal of the Association of Collegiate Alumnae* 14, no. 1 (October 1920), 4–6; IFUW, Report of the Meeting of 1922; Von Oertzen, *Science, Gender, and Internationalism*, 24–26.

41. Juliette Dor, "Caroline Spurgeon (1869–1942) and the Institutionalization of English Studies as a Scholarly Discipline," *PhiN-Bieheft Supplement* 4/2009, 57. Spurgeon's letters to her aunt of March 2, 1913 and March 21, 1913, are in the Caroline Spurgeon Papers, Royal Holloway, London. See also, for Spurgeon, Renate Haas, "Caroline Spurgeon—English Studies, the United States, and Internationalism," *International Review of English Studies* 38 (2002), 215–228, and, for bibliography, Renate Haas, "Caroline Spurgeon," chap. 8 in Jane Chance, ed., *Women Medievalists and the Academy* (Madison: University of Wisconsin Press, 2005), 99–110. I am indebted to Heather Mayall for sharing her research and for her extensive advice on Caroline Spurgeon.

   The college in London attended in the 1890s by Caroline Spurgeon and Edith Morley began in 1885 as Kings College London Ladies Department, and, after various name changes, became in 1908 Kings College for Women.

42. For British women's difficulties with academic careers, see Edith Morley's essay on university teaching in Morley, ed., *Women Workers in Seven Professions: A Survey of Their Economic Conditions and Prospects* (New York and London: G. Routledge, 1914), 15. For the first generation of women students at Oxford, who entered Somerville College in 1912 and earned degrees in 1920, see Mo Moulton, *The Mutual Admiration Society: How Dorothy Sayers and Her Oxford Circle Remade the World for Women* (New York: Basic Books, 2019). Caroline Spurgeon's work on Chaucer, *Five Hundred Years of Chaucer Criticism and Allusion, 1357–1900*, appeared in English first, from 1908 to 1917, in seven parts, under the auspices of the Chaucer Society (1868–1912) and the Oxford University Press, and then as a 3-volume book (Cambridge: Cambridge University, 1925).

43. For Caroline Spurgeon as a teacher of English, see "Focus on Research: Rachel Buurma F'12 and Laura Heffernan F'12: Exploring the History of a Discipline Through Classroom Records," *ACLS News* (10/3/2014); Buurma and Heffernan, *The Teaching Archive: A New History for Literary Study* (Chicago: University of Chicago Press, 2020), chap. 1 on "Caroline Spurgeon: The Art of Reading (1913)"; and Spurgeon, "The Refashioning of English Education: A Lesson of the Great War," *The Atlantic Monthly* (January 1922), 55–67. For Spurgeon's course on "How to Teach English," see VCG Papers, box 44, RBML, CU. For her comments on Virginia's achievements, see Gena Tenney Phenix '33 (Mrs. Philip Phenix), "Sketch of Interview with Miss Caroline Spurgeon Regarding the Life Abroad and Activity in International Affairs of Virginia C. Gildersleeve," February, 1936, in the Setzer file, BC2.4, box 2, Barnard Archives.

44. Edith Morley, *Before and After: Reminiscences of a Working Life* (Morris, Reading, UK: Two Rivers Press, 2016), 53–54. The University of Reading began in 1892 as a branch of Oxford called "University College, Reading." Morley, who arrived to teach in 1901, refers to the institution as "the College" (*Before and After*, 97ff).

45. n.a. "Personalities and Power: Professor Caroline Spurgeon," *Time and Tide* (July 9, 1920); VCG, *Crusade*, 139–140, 204–206. In this instance, as in others, VCG uses the word "intimate" to mean "close."

46. Morley, *Before and After*, 62–64, 186.

47. Morley, *Before and After*, 186; E.W. Pawell, "The Women's University Settlement in Southwark," *Charity Organization Review*, New Series, 35, no. 208 (April 1914), 178–186; Chris Northcott, *MI5 At War: How MI5 Foiled the Spies of the Kaiser in the First World War* (Ticehurst, East Sussex: Tattered Flag Press, 2015), 117

48. Mo Moulton, *The Mutual Admiration Society*, 177–185.

49. VCG, *Crusade*, 192–193, 290, 397.

50. For Virginia's letters of 1919, see VCG to Caroline Spurgeon, January 5 and February 28, 1919, Personal Papers of Caroline Spurgeon, Folger Shakespeare Library, cited in Natalie Francesca Wright, "Pragmatic Criticism: Women and Femininity in the Inauguration of Academic English Studies in the UK, 1900–1950," Ph.D. dissertation, University of Sussex, August, 2020, 150. VCG served as Caroline Spurgeon's executor and donated at least two boxes of Cara's papers to the Folger Library. Although Virginia and Cara had agreed to destroy their correspondence, a portion of that correspondence, perhaps unnoticed by VCG, is in the Folger collection. For the agreement to destroy correspondence, see "Idris" (unknown correspondent) to "Markie" (Mrs. Clifford Markham), October 16, 1960, box 4, VCG Papers, RBML, CU. For VCG's

contributions to the Folger Library, see Louis B. Wright, "More of Miss Spurgeon's Notes," January 4, 1950, vol. 2, no. 2 in Wright, ed. *The Folger Library, Two Decades of Growth: An Informal Account* (Charlottesville: University of Virginia Press, 1968), 25.

Another small cache of correspondence between VCG and Caroline Spurgeon survives as well: About a dozen letters, all from the summer of 1939, are in the VCG Papers, box 4, RBML, CU. The quotes at the end of this paragraph are from Virginia's letters to Cara of July 29 and August 1, 1939.

51. M. Carey Thomas to Helen Taft, January 23, 1920, M. Carey Thomas Papers, reel 51, Bryn Mawr Archives, quoted in Von Oertzen, *Science, Gender, and Internationalism*, 26; Spurgeon quote from IFUW, Report of the First Conference, 1920, 11–12, in Von Oertzen, 35. Leila J. Rapp suggests the roles of single-sex couples in the international women's movement in *Worlds of Women: The Making of an International Women's Movement* (Princeton: Princeton University Press, 1997), 96–101.

52. Helen L. Horowitz, *The Power and Passion of M. Carey Thomas* (New York: Knopf, 1994), 287–291, 450; Anna Mary Wells, *Miss Marks and Miss Woolley* (Boston: Houghton Mifflin, 1978), 111; Patricia M. Palmieri, *An Adamless Eden: The Community of Women Faculty at Wellesley* (New Haven: Yale University Press, 1995), 137–138; Anya Jabour, *Sophonisba Breckinridge: Championing Women's Activism in Modern America* (Urbana, Chicago, and Springfield: University of Illinois Press, 2019), 261–268. For the British women academics, see Carol Dyhouse, *No Distinction of Sex? Women in British Universities, 1870–1939* and, on Sidgwick and Fry, Emily Rutherford, "Friendship, Idealism, and Federating University Women in the Early Twentieth Century," February 15, 2016 at http://jhiblog.org/2016/02/15/friendship-idealism-and-federating-university-women-in-the-early-twentieth-century/.

53. Elizabeth Clement and Beans Velocci, "Modern Sexuality in Modern Times (1880s-1920s)," in Don Romesburg, ed., *Routledge History of Queer America* (New York and London: Routledge, 2018, chaps. 4, 54, and 63.

54. VCG, *Crusade*, 105, 108; Rosenberg, *Changing the Subject*, 169–170.

55. Francesca Wade, *Square Haunting: Five Writers in London Between the Wars* (New York: Random House/Tim Duggan Books, 2020), 168.

56. Wright, "Pragmatic Criticism," 116, 143–153. Academic women's writings of Spurgeon's era "rarely mention homosexuality explicitly," Wright observes, "instead encoding queerness into character tropes, symbolism, ellipses, and literary references" (116).

57. VCG, "The Strange Flotsam of Time," 9 (typescript about fragments of memory), VCG Papers, box 66. RBML, CU.

58. VCG, *Crusade*, 171, 172–174.

59. For Crane, see Norman E. Saul, *Life and Times of Charles R. Crane, 1858–1939* (Lantham, Md.: Lexington Press, 2013); F. W. Brecher, "Charles R. Crane's Crusade for the Arabs, 1919–39," *Middle Eastern Studies* 24, no. 1 (January 1988), 42–55; and David A. Hollinger, *Protestants Abroad: How Missionaries Tried to Change the World But Changed America* (Princeton: Princeton University Press, 2017), chap. 5. For the King-Crane Commission, see Saul, *Life and Times*, 187–191 and Hollinger, *Protestants Abroad*, 120–123.

60. Brecher, "Charles R. Crane's Crusade," 42–43.

61. Brecher, "Charles R. Crane's Crusade," 42, 50.

62. VCG, *Crusade*, 171, 176.

63. VCG, *Crusade*, 171–172, 176–177, 178; for John Crane's statement, see "VCG: John Crane," n.d., VCG Papers, box 47, folder: IFUW, RBML, CU. Another copy of John Crane's statement, dated June 25, 1952, is stored with other interviews in the Setzer file, BC 2.4, box 2.

64. VCG, *Crusade*, 178; Hollinger, *Protestants Abroad*, 118–120. Relevant documents on "Near East Relief, 1915–1930," are in VCG Papers, box 38, RBML, CU.

65. "Report to the Trustees of the American College for Girls for the Academic Year 1950–51," 1–2, sums up the school's philosophy and "delicate balance" between American and Turkish cultures, VCG Papers, box 48, "American College for Girls, 1917–53," RBML, CU.

66. VCG, *Crusade*, 177, 178, 406. VCG's papers on "Near East Colleges," are in VCG Papers, box 52, RBML, CU.

67. Hollinger, *Protestants Abroad*, 118; VCG, *Crusade*, 182–183.

68. VCG, *Crusade*, 176.

69. John B. Pine to Nicholas Murray Butler, November 8, 1902, Pine Papers, Columbia Archives, quoted in Rosenthal, *Nicholas Miraculous: The Amazing Career of the Redoubtable Dr. Nicholas Murray Butler* (New York: Farrar, Straus, Giroux, 2006), 333–334; Mrs. N. W. Liggett to George A. Plimpton, June 20, 1906, GAP Papers, BC1.3, box 1, folder: "Correspondence, 1906."

70. McCaughey, *A College of Her Own*, chap. 3; Rosenthal, *Nicholas Miraculous*, 338; "Candidates Entering in 1906," list attached to letter of Mrs. N. W. Liggett to George A. Plimpton of June 20, 1906. Of 102 entrants, 40 were Jewish, according to Mrs. Liggett's calculation.

71. Rosenthal, *Nicholas Miraculous*, 333, 336; M. Carey Thomas, "Address to 1916 College Opening," *The College News*, Bryn Mawr (October 11, 1916), 1; Helen Lefkowitz Horowitz, *The Power and Passion of M. Carey Thomas* (New York: Alfred A. Knopf, 1994), 231, 341.

72. George A. Plimpton to Adolph Ochs, January 15, 1912, GAP Papers, BC1.3, box 2, folder: Correspondence, 1912, Barnard Archives.

73. "Re Mrs. N. W. Liggett," BC3.4, Faculty/Staff/Visitor Bio Files, box 28; N.W. Liggett to Laura Drake Gill, July 20, 1901, BC5.1 Laura Drake Gill Correspondence, box 225, folder 9 (July-August 1901); Marian Churchill White, *A History of Barnard College* (New York: Columbia University Press, 1954), 22–23; Annie Nathan Meyer, *Barnard Beginnings*, 93–94. For Mrs. Liggett, see chap. 1, footnote 36.

74. Laura Drake Gill, "Dean's Report for 1901–1902," 143; William T. Brewster to Nicholas Murray Butler, September 22, 1909, 8 in BC5.1 Dean's Office Correspondence, 1909–1910, box 9, folder 8. Brewster, when dean of Barnard, 1907 to 1911, wrote ten-page letters regularly to the university president to tell him in great detail about all the college affairs.

75. "Minutes of Staff Conference, January 10, 1921," cited in Rosenberg, *Changing the Subject*, 139–140.

76. McCaughey, *A College of Her Own*, chap. 3; VCG, "Dean's Report for 1915," 8–11.

77. VCG to Adam Leroy Jones, October 23, 1913, Dean's Office Correspondence, 1913–1914, box 21, folder 4, Barnard Archives.

78. For Columbia's admissions restrictions, see Harold S. Wechsler, *The Qualified Student: A History of Selective College Admissions in America* (New Brunswick: Transaction, 2014), especially chap. 7. Dean Keppel's quote is from his book, *Columbia* (New York: Oxford University Press, 1914), 180. For Dean Hawkes, see Wechsler, 154.

79. VCG, "Dean's Report for 1914," 2; "Dean's Report for 1918," 11, and "Dean's Report for 1920," 4.

3. GATEKEEPING: THE 1920s

1. VCG, *Many a Good Crusade* (New York: Macmillan, 1954), 213.

2. VCG, *Crusade*, 201, 213; "People Who Influenced the Life of VCG" (typescript), 4, VCG Papers, box 1, RBML, CU, also in BC2.4, Setzer file, Barnard Archives.

3. VCG, *Crusade*, 132–133, 213; Marian Churchill White, *History of Barnard College* (New York: Columbia University Press, 1954), 104, 119–20; Robert McCaughey, *A College of Her Own: A History of Barnard* (New York: Columbia University Press, 2020), chap. 5.

4. VCG, *Crusade*, 201–204.

5. VCG, *Crusade*, 205–206; "Caroline Spurgeon," *Time and Tide* (June 9, 1920).

6. Caroline F. E. Spurgeon. "The Refashioning of English Education," *Atlantic Monthly* (January 1922), 55–67, quote from 59; Renate Haas, "Caroline Spurgeon" in *Women Medievalists and the Academy*, ed. Jane Chance (Madison: University of Wisconsin Press, 2005), 99–110.

7. Haas, "Caroline Spurgeon," 106; VCG, *Crusade*, 231–232 For Henry Fairfield Osborn, his impact on racist ideology, and his intersection with Barnard, see Daniel Okrent, *The Guarded Gate: Bigotry, Eugenics, and the Law That Kept Two Generations of Jews, Italians, and Other European Immigrants Out of America* (New York: Simon & Shuster, 2019).

8. Margaret Mead, *Blackberry Winter: My Earlier Years* (New York: Morrow, 1972), 108; Julie V. Marsteller, "Interview with Eleanor Rosenberg, May 1, 1973," Marsteller Collection, B1.6, box 1, folder 5, Barnard Archives; VCG, *Crusade*, 216–217; "Bids Barnard Girls Justify College," *New York Times*, October 8, 1930, 40. For college life in the women's colleges, see Helen Lefkowitz Horowitz, *Campus Life: Undergraduate Cultures from the Eighteenth Century to the Present* (New York: Knopf, 1987), chap. 9. A classic study of college life in the 1920s is Paula Fass, *The Damned and the Beautiful: American Youth in the 1920s* (New York: Oxford University Press, 1977).

9. Marsteller, "Interview with Eleanor Rosenberg, May 1, 1973."

10. This discussion of VCG as dean rests on Andrea Walton, "Achieving a Voice and Institutionalizing a Vision for Women: The Barnard Deanship at Columbia University, 1889–1947," *Historical Studies in Education* 13, no. 2 (Fall 1991), 137–138 and Robert McCaughey, *A College of Her Own* (New York: Columbia University Press, 2020), chap. 5. For quotes, see *Barnard Alumnae Magazine* XV, no. 2 (May 1926), 2,4, 5, and VCG, *Crusade*, 89.

11. VCG, *Crusade*, 218–219.

12. "Dean of Barnard Favors Expansion," *New York Times*, August 31, 1924, E3; Walton, "Achieving a Voice," 141; VCG, *Crusade*, 82; VCG, "Dean's Report for 1927," 13–14. For the conflicted role of the School of Euthenics at Vassar, see Elizabeth A. Daniels, *Bridges to the World: Henry Noble MacCracken and Vassar College* (Clinton Corners, NY: College Avenue Press, 1994), chap. 10.

13. "Interview with Mrs. Eugene Meyer, February 18, 1953" (as recorded by Dorothea Setzer), Setzer file, BC2.4, box 1, Barnard Archives. For Boas, see Charles King, *Gods of the Upper Air: How a Circle of Renegade Anthropologists Reinvented Race, Sex, and Gender in the Twentieth Century* (New York: Doubleday, 2019), 116. For Power, see Francesca Wade, *Square-Haunting: Five Writers Between the Wars* (New York: Random House, 2020), 234.

14. McCaughey, *A College of Her Own*, chap. 5 and VCG, *Crusade*, 78–79, 81.

15. William Allan Neilson, letter to the Boston Smith Club, February 1, 1921, quoted in Margaret Farrand Thorp, *Neilson of Smith* (New York: Oxford University Press, 1956), 166–167; McCaughey, *A College of Her Own*, chap. 5; Rosalind Rosenberg, *Changing the Subject*, 169; VCG, *Crusade*, 106–107.

16. VCG, "Dean's Report for 1927," 8–9. For the Bryn Mawr model, see Rita Heller, "Blue Collars and Blue Stockings: The Bryn Mawr Summer School for Women

Workers, 1921–1938," in *Sisterhood and Solidarity: Workers' Education for Women, 1914–1984*, ed. Joyce L. Kornbluh and Mary Frederickson (Philadelphia: Temple University Press, 1984), 107–145; for Barnard, see 193. See also Hilda Worthington Smith, *Opening Vistas in Women's Education: The Autobiography of Hilda A. Worthington Smith*, ed. Lyn Goldfarb and Stephen MacFarlane (Washington DC: By the Author, 1978), 171–173.

17. VCG, "Dean's Report for 1928," 7–8; Emilie J. Hutchinson, "The Barnard Summer School for Women Workers in Industry," *Barnard Alumnae Bulletin* XVII, no. 1 (January 1928), 7–8; Ernestine J. Friedman, "Barnard's Contribution to a New Educational Movement," *Barnard Alumnae Bulletin* XVIII, no. 2 (May 1929), 7–8; Summer School records in the Barnard Archives are in BC13.6 Record Group: Summer School for Women Workers, 1927–1933. Box 1 includes course materials; for workers' publications see folder: Spring Magazine of the Affiliated Schools for Women Workers in Industry, 1930. Box 2 contains "List of Students."

18. VCG, *Crusade*, 101–103; Rosenberg, *Changing the Subject*, 128–129; Barbara Aronstein Black, "Something to Remember, Something to Celebrate: Women at Columbia Law School," *Columbia Law Review* 102, no. 6 (October 2002), 1451–1468. Black cites the correspondence of November 1915 between VCG and Harlan Stone on 1452.

19. VCG to Dean Emily H. Dutton (Sweet Briar), February 4, 1929, BC2.4, Setzer file, box 1, VCG Papers, Barnard Archives.

20. Thorp, *Neilson of Smith*, 334; Elizabeth Daniels, *Bridges to the World*, 167.

21. VCG, *Crusade*, 89–90; Thorp, *Neilson of Smith*, 334; Elizabeth Daniels, *Bridges to the World*, 168.

22. VCG et al, "The Question of the Women's Colleges," *Atlantic Monthly* 140, no. 5 (November 1927), 577–584. The authors, as listed, alphabetically, by college, are VCG (Barnard), Marion Edwards Park (Bryn Mawr), Mary E. Woolley (Mount Holyoke), Ada L. Comstock (Radcliffe), William Allan Neilson (Smith), Henry Noble MacCracken (Vassar), and Ellen F. Pendleton (Wellesley). For an abridged version of the article, see *Bulletin of the American Association of University Professors* 14, no. 2 (February 1928), 144–146.

23. "Dean's Report for 1928," 11–12; see also "Lack of Funds Balks Barnard, Declares Dean," *New York Herald Tribune*, January 22, 1928, 13 and "Gifts to Girls' Colleges Asked by Barnard Dean," *New York Herald Tribune*, October 21, 1928, A14.

24. VCG, *Crusade*, 89–91; Thorp, *Neilson of Smith*, 334–335; Daniels, *Bridges to the World*, 168–69; Walton, "Achieving a Voice," 144.

25. Daniels, *Bridges to the World*, 169; "The Seven Colleges at St. Louis," *Vassar Quarterly* XIX, no. 1 (February 1934), 43–44.

26. "Report of the Alumnae Committee of the Seven Colleges, May 11, 1934," *Vassar Quarterly* XIX, no. 3 (July 1934), 250–253.

27. Daniels, *Bridges to the World*, 171; Walton, "Achieving a Voice," 144; "National Scholarships for Girls Offered by Leading Colleges," *New York Times*, November 14, 1943, 50; "Conference of the Seven Colleges, New York City, October 25, 1944," BC2.4, VCG Correspondence, box 1, folder 86, VCG Papers, Barnard Archives. For "sparse country," see Anemona Hartocollis, "Affirmative Action Trial Begins with Details on How Harvard Treats Rural Areas," *New York Times*, October 16, 2018.

28. Horowitz, *Alma Mater*, 260–262; Mary J. Oates and Susan Williamson, "Women's Colleges and Women Achievers," *Signs: Journal of Women in Culture and Society* 3, no. 4 (Summer 1978), 799; Elaine Kendall, *Peculiar Institutions: An Informal History of the Seven Sister Colleges* (New York: Putnam, 1975), 30. For the Seven Sisters' imprint on fashion, see Rebecca C. Tuite, *Seven Sisters Style: The All-American Preppy Look* (New York: Rizzoli Universe Promotional Books, 2017).

29. "Anti Semitism at Barnard" (letter from Rebecca Grecht to the Editor), *Nation* 115, no. 2987 (October 4, 1922), 337. See also "May Jews Go to College?" *Nation* 114, no. 2971 (June 14, 1922), 708, an unsigned editorial, probably by Freda Kirchwey, and "Anti-Semitism and the Colleges," *Nation* 115, no. 2975 (July 12, 1922), 45–46, a series of letters to the editor.

30. "Class and Creed at Barnard" (letter from VCG to the Editor) *Nation* 115, no. 2996 (December 6, 1922), 607.

31. NMB to VCG, November 19, 1912 and October 4, 1911, Nicholas Murray Butler Papers, Series II, Box 157, RBML, CU.

32. Two leading studies of anti-Semitism in college admissions are Jerome Karabel, *The Chosen: The Hidden History of Admission and Exclusion at Harvard, Yale, and Princeton* (Boston and New York: Houghton Mifflin, 2005) and Harold S. Wechsler, *The Qualified Student: A History of Selective College Admissions in America* (New Brunswick: Transaction, 2014).

33. The two quotes are from "May Jews Go to College?" *Nation* 114, no. 2971 (June 14, 1922), 708 (editorial) and Harold A. Woodruff (pseud.), "Jews Go to College," *Harper's Monthly Magazine* (September 1, 1931), 419. For restricted admissions, in general and at Columbia and Barnard, see Harold S. Wechsler, "The Rationale for Restriction: Ethnicity and College Admissions in America, 1910–1980" *American Quarterly* 36 (Winter 1984): 643–667; Robert A. McCaughey, *Stand Columbia: A History of Columbia University in the City of New York, 1754–2004* (New York: Columbia University Press, 2003), chap. 9; McCaughey, *A College of Her Own*, chap. 4; Lynn D. Gordon, "Annie Nathan Meyer," 519; Helen Lefkowitz Horowitz, *Alma Mater: Design and Experience in the Women's Colleges*

from Their Nineteenth-Century Beginnings to the 1930s (Boston: Beacon Press, 1984), 258–259; and Rosalind Rosenberg, *Changing the Subject: How the Women of Columbia Changed the Way We Think About Sex and Politics* (New York: Columbia University Press, 2004), 135–141.

34. McCaughey, *A College of Her Own*, chap. 4

35. Herbert Hawkes to Edwin B. Wilson, June 16, 1922, Hawkes Papers, CU Archives, quoted in Wechsler, *The Qualified Student*, 153–154, and Michael Rosenthal, *Nicholas Miraculous: The Amazing Career of Redoubtable Nicholas Murray Butler* (New York: Farrar, Straus Giroux, 2006), 343.

36. Rosenthal, *Nicholas Miraculous*, 345–347 and McCaughey, *Stand, Columbia*, 270–271.

37. Jerold S. Auerbach to the Editor, *Commentary* 76, no. 2 (August 1983), 9; Barbara Miller Solomon, *In the Company of Educated Women: A History of Women in Higher Education* (New Haven: Yale, 1985), 144.

38. VCG, "Dean's Report for 1918," 11 and "Dean's Report for 1920," 4; VCG, "Trends in College Admissions," *Barnard Alumnae Bulletin* XVI, no. 1 (January 1927); and Rosenberg, *Changing the Subject*, 137–138.

39. "Adams Leroy Jones, Director of Admissions at CU for 25 Years," *Columbia University Spectator* LVII, no. 91 (March 7, 1934), 2; Jones, "Some New Methods of Admissions to College," *Educational Review* 46 (November 1913), 355.

40. McCaughey, *A College of Her Own*, chap. 4.

41. Committee on Admissions, September 25, 1922 and September 19, 1925, in BC19.3, Admissions Office Files, Barnard Archives; Arlene M. Winer, interview with Mary Dublin Keyserling, Washington, D.C., March 13, 1989, Barnard Archives.

42. For Komarovsky, see Shulamit Reinharz, "Finding a Sociological Voice: The Work of Mirra Komkarovsky," *Sociological Inquiry* 59, no. 4 (October 1989), 374–395; for Max, see Elisabeth Israels Perry, *After the Vote: Feminist Politics in LaGuardia's New York* (New York: Oxford, 2019), 11–13. On admissions, see Heywood Broun and George Britt, *Christians Only: A Study in Prejudice* (New York: Vanguard Press, 1931), 74, cited in McCaughey, *A College of Her Own*, 323, n. 35.

43. "Admissions," *Barnard Alumnae Bulletin* XIII, no. 1 (December 1923), 5; "A Glimpse Into the Future," *Barnard Alumnae Bulletin* XIII, no. 2 (May 1924), 10–11.

44. McCaughey, *A College of Her Own*, chap. 5; VCG to Wilfrid M. Aiken, founder of the Scarborough School, December 18, 1935, Dean's Office Correspondence, cited in Gordon, "Annie Nathan Meyer," 516; "Report of the Dean for 1938," 7.

45. VCG to Mrs. Alfred Meyer, January 12, 1932 and March 30, 1933, Annie Nathan Meyer Papers, American Jewish Archives, quoted in Helen Lefkowitz Horowtz, *Alma Mater: Design and Experience in the Women's Colleges from Their Nineteenth-Century Beginnings to the 1930s* (Boston: Beacon Press, 1984), 259.

46. ANM to Emily James Smith, May 23 and October 17, 1898, BC5.1, box 219, Emily James Smith Correspondence (1898–1900), Barnard Archives (thanks to Rona Wilk for these letters); Gordon, "Annie Nathan Meyer," 516–517; Joyce Antler, *The Journey Home: How Jewish Women Shaped Modern America* (New York: Schocken Books, 1997), 64–70; Linda K. Kerber, "Annie Nathan Meyer," in *Notable American Women: The Modern Period*, ed. Barbara Sicherman and Carol Hurd Green (Cambridge: Harvard University Press, 1980), 473–474.

47. William Allan Neilson, "Report to the Trustees of Barnard College," December 4, 1941, Annie Nathan Meyer Papers, box 5, folder 3, Barnard Archives, quoted in Gordon, "Annie Nathan Meyer," 520.

48. Gordon, "Annie Nathan Meyer," 520.

49. VCG, "The Barnard Admissions Policy," *Barnard College Alumnae Monthly* 28, no. 8 (May 1939), 4–5.

50. Gordon, "Annie Nathan Meyer," 517; ANM to W. E. B. DuBois, March 16, 1932, W.E.B. DuBois Papers, Series 1A, Correspondence, University of Massachusetts, Amherst, https://credo.library.umass.edu/view/full/mums312-b063-i044.

51. Zora Neale Hurston to Constance Sheen (friend and future sister-in-law), January 5, 1926 and ZNH to Annie Nathan Meyer, May 12, 1925, in *Zora Neale Hurston: A Life in Letters*, ed. Carla Kaplan (New York: Anchor Books, 2002), 55, 75. This section relies on Kaplan's book and on Valerie Boyd, *Wrapped in Rainbows: The Life of Zora Neale Hurston* (New York: Scribners, 2003), especially chap. 12. Another version of that chapter is Boyd, "Enter the Negrotarians," in "Jumpin' At the Sun: Reassessing the Work of Zora Neale Nurston," ed. Monica L. Miller, *Scholar and the Feminist Online* 3, no. 2 (special issue, Winter 2005). For Hurston see also Alice Walker, ed. *I Love Myself . . . A Zora Neale Hurston Reader* (New York: The Feminist Press, 1979); Robert E. Hemenway, *Zora Neale Hurston: A Literary Biography* (Urbana and Chicago: University of Illinois Press, 1980); and Monica L. Miller and Tami Navarro, eds., "Undiminished Blackness: Zora Neale Hurston on Theory and Practice," *Scholar and the Feminist Online* 16, no. 2 (Fall, 2020).

52. VCG to Annie Nathan Meyer, June 9, 1925 and October 2, 1925, ANM Papers, folder 7, American Jewish Archives, quoted in Rosalind Rosenberg, *Changing the Subject*, 145; Boyd, *Wrapped in Rainbows*, 104; "Committee on Transfers, September and October, 1925" and "Record of Freshman Interest," dated December 16, 1925, in Miller, "Jumpin' At the Sun," Part VI: "From the Archives: Documents on Zora Neale Hurston from the Barnard College Archives."

53. VCG to ANM, October 2, 1925, ANM Papers; Boyd, *Wrapped in Rainbows*, 101, 104.

54. ZNH to Fannie Hurst, March 15, 1926, in Kaplan, 85; ZNH, *Dust Tracks on a Road: An Autobiography* (New York: HarperCollins, 2010) (first published in

1942), 139; VCG to ANM, November 5, 1925, ANM Papers; Boyd, *Wrapped in Rainbows*, 104–106, 107, 109.

55. ZNH to ANM, n.d. 1925, in Kaplan, 79; VCG to ANM, February 9, 1926, ANM Papers, cited in Boyd, *Wrapped in Rainbows*, 110

56. ZNH to ANM, February 22, 1926, in Kaplan, 81–82; ZNH to Constance Sheen, February 2, 1926, in Kaplan, 80–81; Boyd, *Wrapped in Rainbows*, 99, 110, 118. For disputes, see Kaplan, 17, 144, 175–178, 251. Alain Locke's classic collection is *The New Negro: An Interpretation* (New York: Albert & Charles Boni, 1925).

57. King, *Gods of the Upper Air*, 96, 116, 117; Rosemary Levy Zumwalt, *Franz Boas: The Emergence of Anthropology* (Lincoln, Neb.: University of Nebraska Press, 2019), 65, 135, 256–257, 261; Rosenberg, *Changing the Subject*, 133–135, 157; VCG, *Crusade*, 417.

58. King, *Gods of the Upper Air*, 117; Margaret Mead, *Blackberry Winter: My Earlier Years* (New York: William Morrow & Company, 1972), 112.

59. ZNH, *Dust Tracks*, 140, 171; ZNH to ANM (n.d., c. Spring 1926) in Kaplan, 82; King, *Gods of the Upper Air*, 116, 185–186.

60. King, *Gods of the Upper Air*, 194, 210; ZNH to Charlotte Osgood Mason, May 8, 1932, in Kaplan, 254; Boyd, *Wrapped in Rainbows*, 100.

61. VCG to James Weldon Johnson, January 22, 1934, in Kaplan, 287; VCG to B. (Bertram) Lippincott, May 28, 1934, "Documents on Zora Neale Hurston from the Barnard Archives," in Miller, ed., "Jumpin' At The Sun."

62. ZNH, *Mules and Men* (New York: Lippincott, 1935), 1, spyglass quote; Sterling Brown, review of February 1936, clipping, quoted in Hemenway, *Zora Neale Hurston*, 219; ZNH to Dorothy A. Elvidge, February 4, 1935 and to George Arthur, February 5, 1935, in Kaplan, 344–345, 346.

63. ZNH to Miss Dorothy A. Elvidge, February 4, 1935 and to George Arthur, February 5, 1935, in Kaplan, 344–345. 346; Boyd, *Wrapped in Rainbows*, 102; ZNH to ANM, October 12, 1925, in Kaplan, 66.

64. W. E. B. DuBois, "Negroes in College," *The Nation* 122 (March 3, 1926), 229.

65. Linda M. Perkins, "The Racial Integration of the Seven Sisters Colleges," *Journal of Blacks in Higher Education* 19 (Spring 1998), 107; Perkins, "The African American Female Elite: The Early History of African American Women in the Seven Sisters Colleges, 1880–1960," *Harvard Educational Review* 67, no. 4 (Winter 1997), 741–742, 744. For Eleanor Roosevelt on Channing Tobias, see ER, "Some of My Best Friends Are Negro," *Ebony* 9 (February 1953), 17–20, 24–26.

66. Perkins, "African American Female Elite," 742, 744, 745; VCG to Rev. James H. Robinson, n.d. in *Barnard Bulletin*, March 1, 1943, cited in Perkins, "African American Female Elite," 742. See also McCaughey, *A College of Her Own*, 150.

67. Rosalind Rosenberg. *Jane Crow: The Life of Pauli Murray* (New York: Oxford University Press, 2017), 29, 31.

68. *Columbia Daily Spectator* XCVIII, no. 90, March 30, 1954; Marian White Churchill, *A History of Barnard College* (New York: Columbia University Press, 1954); Alice Walker, ed., *And Then Again When I Am Angry and Impressive: A Zora Neale Hurston Reader* (Westbury, NY: The Feminist Press, 1979).

69. "Near East Colleges," VCG Papers, box 52, CU; "VCG: John Crane," statement of June 25, 1952, box 47, VCG Papers, folder: "IFUW: Speeches."

70. Meeting of the Committee on International Relations of the AAUW, October 31, 1924, February 18, 1925, April 7, 1925, and May 15, 1925, box 44, VCG Papers, CU, folder: "AAUW/Committee on International Relations, 1924–1927."

71. Meeting of the Committee on International Relations, October 31, 1924.

72. VCG, *Crusade*, 135; *New York Times*, June 18, 1924; *Barnard Alumnae Bulletin* XIV, no. 1 (December 1924), 15; Christine von Oertzen, "Whose World? Internationalism, Nationalism, and the Struggle Over the Language Question in the International Federation of University Women, 1919–1932," *Contemporary European History* 25, special issue no. 2 (on "The Age of Internationalism"), 276–277; and IFUW, "Report of the Third Conference, Oslo, 1924," quoted in von Oertzen, *Science, Gender, and Internationalism: Women's Academic Networks, 1917–1955* (New York and London: Palgrave, Macmillan, 2014), 31.

73. VCG, "Speech at the Paris Conference of the IFUW, September, 1922," box 47, VCG Papers, RBML, CU, folder: "IFUW: Speeches"; von Oertzen, "Whose World?" 279, 281–282.

74. Meeting of the Committee on International Relations, May 15, 1925, 2–3, box 44, VCG Papers, RBML, CU, folder: AAUW/Committee on International Relations, 1924–1927; von Oertzen, "Whose World?" 181–182.

75. Von Oertzen, "Whose World?" 279.

76. Marion Talbot and Lois Kimball Matthews Rosenberry, *History of the American Association of University Women, 1681–1931* (Boston: Houghton Mifflin, 1931), 285; von Oertzen, "Whose World?" 277, 283; VCG, *Crusade*, 145.

77. Von Oertzen, "Whose World?" 283–287; von Oertzen, *Science, Gender, and Internationalism*, chap. 2; VCG, *Crusade*, 148.

78. Caroline Niemczyk, "Elisabeth Mills Reid and Helen Rogers Reid: The Founder and Perpetuator of Reid Hall, 1893–1964" (paper given at Columbia, June, 1993); Talbot and Rosenberry, *History of the American Association of University Women*, 274–275; von Oertzen, *Science, Gender, and Internationalism*, 37 and chap. 3.

79. "American University Women's Paris Club," *Barnard Alumnae Bulletin* XIII, no. 1 (December 1923), 9; VCG, *Crusade*, 127, 140. Barnard graduate Dorothy Leet, class of '17, Reid Hall's first director, served until World War II, returned

after the war to run a study abroad center, and remained until 1964, when Helen Rogers Reid bequeathed the property to Columbia. Reid died in 1970; Columbia now runs Reid Hall as one of ten global centers.

80. "Report of the Fifth Conference, Geneva, August 7 to August 14, 1929," (London: International Federation of University Women, 1929).

81. VCG Speech. "Report of the Fifth Conference, Geneva, August 14, 1929," IFUW, Bulletin no. 11 (London, 1929), 61–62, 64–65, box 43, VCG Papers, RBML, CU.

82. "Administrative/Biographical Background" and "Copies of Documents Relating to the Old Postman's Cottage, Alciston, and Professor Caroline Spurgeon," AMS6516, East Sussex Record Office, UK.

83. M. Dane, "The Old Postman's Cottage, Alciston: The Sussex Home of Professor Caroline Spurgeon," *Homes and Gardens* (July 1931); "Administrative/ Biographical Background," AMS6516, East Sussex Record Office, UK; VCG, *Crusade*, 290.

84. "The Dean Comes Home, as told to Emma Bugbee," *Barnard Alumnae Magazine* XXV, no. 1 (October 1935), 10–12.

85. "Old Postman's Cottage, Alciston, Visitors Book," East Sussex Record Office AM6516/7, *passim*. For the remark on Edith Thompson, see Theodora Bosanquet, Diary, Entry for August 3, 1924, Harvard University. Many thanks to Heather Mayall for sharing her research on Theodora Bosanquet and her work-in-progress on Caroline Spurgeon.

86. VCG, *Crusade*, 194; for Lydia Lopokova and the intrigue of her mental choreography, see also 210. Keynes and VCG shared the speakers' platform at the opening of the new village hall at Selmeston, just north of Alciston, in July 1935.

87. Caroline Spurgeon to Virginia Woolf, November 7, 1929 (a handwritten note with the letterhead of "The Deanery"), in Beth Rigel Daugherty, ed. "'You See You Kind of Belong to Us and What You Do Matters Enormously': Letters from Readers to Virginia Woolf," *Woolf Studies Annual* 12 (2006), 65–66. The letter is mentioned in Natalie Francesca Wright, "Pragmatic Criticism: Women and Femininity in the Inauguration of Academic English Studies in the UK, 1900–1950," Ph.D. dissertation, University of Sussex, August, 2020, 147. This study discusses the work of three literary critics: Edith Morley, Spurgeon, and Q. D. Leavis.

88. "Old Postman's Cottage, Alciston, Visitors Book," *passim*. For Mead on Latham, see *Blackberrry Winter*, 103.

89. For Crane and Antonius, see OPC, Visitors Book, entry for July 13, 1934, 12 and also "People Who Influenced the Life of VCG," 5, Setzer File, box 1, BC2.4, Barnard Archives. The latter, a typed document, has unclear roots; it probably represents Virginia's memories of the many persons listed, as conveyed to and recorded by potential biographer Dorothea Setzer in the early 1950s.

The visit of Crane and Antonius to the Old Postman's Cottage, as recorded in the Visitors Book in 1934, and recounted again in VCG, *Crusade*, 175, does not appear in the literature on either Crane or Antonius. See, for instance, Norman Saul, *Life and Times of Charles R. Crane*; Martin Kramer, "Ambition, Arabism, and George Antonius" in *Arab Awakening and Islamic Revival: Politics of Ideas in the Middle East*, ed. Martin Kramer (New Brunswick: Transaction, 1996), 111–123; and Susan Sisby Boyle, *Betrayal of Palestine: The Story of George Antonius* (Boulder: Westview Press, 2001). For a relevant interchange between Charles R. Crane and FDR's ambassador to Germany, William P. Dodd, see Erik Larson, *In the Garden of Beasts: Love, Terror, and an American Family in Hitler's Germany* (New York: Crown, 2011), 38–39. Crane's letter to Dodd of June 14, 1938, which conveys his support for Hitler and anti-Semitic views ("Let Hitler have his way") is in box 40, William E. Dodd Papers, Library of Congress and cited by Larsen.

90. "Old Postman's Cottage, Alciston, Visitors Book," "General Remarks" at end of entry for September 18, 1928, 4 and entry titled "Some Remarks," under September, 1933, 11.

91. VCG drove Lilian home from a local nursing home where she had recuperated from an operation for tonsils; see Visitors Book, June 21, 1930.

92. Caroline Spurgeon to Lilian Clapham, January 18, 1931, Papers of Caroline Spurgeon, Folger Shakespeare Library, quoted in Wright, "Pragmatic Criticism," 153.

93. Cara's extensive photograph collection, starting with her youth though featuring the Old Postman's Cottage, is with the OPC Visitors Book at the East Sussex Record Office. Included in the photos, in addition to Cara, Virginia, and Lilian, are Meta Tuke, Mary Aeldrin Cullis, and the scene-stealing terriers, Jock and Jeannie.

94. VCG, *Crusade*, 191–192.

95. VCG, *Crusade*, 192–193.

96. VCG, *Crusade*, 193–194. It is regrettable, observes an archivist at the East Sussex Record Office, that Virginia's account of the days at the Old Postman's Cottage, the "rather self-conscious" memoirs of "a self-confessed outsider," is the only written record available. This remark is too generous. "Self-congratulatory," "simpering," "cloying," and "smug" would be accurate terms for Virginia's account of the village fête and the annual garden party. Virginia, in her snobbish mode, could be insufferable. See "Administrative/Biographical Background," AM6516/7, East Sussex Record Office, UK.

97. Visitor's Book, last page, and "Administrative/Biographical Background"; VCG, *Crusade*, 196, 397–398.

4. EMERGENCIES: 1930–1947

1. Eunice Barnard Fuller, "Barnard Hails Her Dean," *New York Times Sunday Magazine* (February 16, 1936), 10–11.

2. "Barnard Alumnae Honor Their Dean," *New York Times*, February 19, 1936, 15; VCG, *Many a Good Crusade: Memoirs of Virginia Crocheron Gildersleeve* (New York: Macmillan, 1954), 320.

3. Robert McCaughey, *A College of Her Own: The History of Barnard* (New York: Columbia University Press, 2020), 130–131, 133–138; Marion Churchill White, *A History of Barnard College* (New York: Columbia University Press, 1954), 125–132; "Barnard 'Deficit' is $7,077 Surplus," *New York Times*, October 11, 1933, 25; VCG, *Crusade*, 88 (on Plimpton); VCG, "Why Cannot Barnard Merge With Columbia to Solve Its Financial Problems?" typed paper of October 12, 1937, carbon copy, Setzer file, box 1 BC2.4 Barnard Archives; "Report of the Dean for the Year Ending June 30, 1939," 5, Barnard Archives.

4. "Comes Out For President," *New York Times*, October 11, 1936, 41; "Backs Roosevelt's Policy," *New York Times*, October 16, 1936, 6; "Barnard Dean Defends Wives Holding Jobs," *New York Herald Tribune*, June 7, 1939, 25; " 'Diluted' Education for Women Is Decried By Miss Gildersleeve," *New York Herald Tribune*, February 19, 1936, 1; "Teacher-Training Termed a Racket" *New York Times*, April 25, 1935, 23; "Puts College Girls on a Par With Men," *New York Times*, June 2, 1932, 14; "Girls At College No Longer Blasé," *New York Times*, February 14, 1933, 13.

5. McCaughey, *A College of Her Own*, 138–141; "First Interview with Mr. Gano Dunn, verbatim report," Setzer file, box 2, BC2.4, Barnard Archives. For Komarovsky's career at Barnard, see "Interview with Mirra Komarovsky, March 13, 1984," William E. Wiener Oral History Library, The American Jewish Committee, New York Public Library Dorot Collection, and Komarovsky, "Women Then and Now: A Journey of Detachment and Engagement," *Barnard Alumnae Magazine* LXXI, no. 2 (Winter 1982), 7–11.

6. "Report of the Dean for Year Ending June 30, 1938," 7 (on admisssions); VCG, "The Barnard Admissions Policy," *Barnard College Alumnae Magazine* 27, no. 8 (May 1939), 4–5; VCG, *Crusade*, 86.

7. "Dr. Gildersleeve to Rest," *New York Times*, August 13, 1931, 14. Caroline Spurgeon's book was published in England by Cambridge University Press in 1935 and in 1936 by Macmillan in the United States. The quote from Bosanquet's review is from *English: Journal of the English Association* 1, no. 1 (April 1936), 64–66. The Eisenstein comments are in Michael Glenny, ed. & trans., *Toward a Theory of Montage: Sergei Eisenstein's Selected Works*, 2nd ed. (London and New York: I.B. Taurus, 2010) vol. 1, 189.

8. Account of interview with Catherine Weiser, Setzer file, BC2.4, box 2, Barnard Archives; Gildersleeve, *Crusade*, 223; "Class of 1917," *Annual Register of the Alumnae Association of Smith College*, 239. For Dorothy Sayers, see Mo Moulton, *The Mutual Admiration Society: How Dorothy L. Sayers and Her Oxford Circle Remade the World for Women* (New York: Basic Books, 2019).

9. Frank Fackenthal interview with Dorothea Setzer, undated (c. early 1950s), notes for a biography of VCG, Setzer file, BC2.4, box2.

10. Frank Fackenthal interview (n.d.), Setzer file, box 2, Barnard Archives. Setzer's account of her interview with Catharine Weiser is also in the Setzer file, box 2, Barnard Archives, as is Setzer's typed account of VCG's letters to Catharine Weiser, 1938–1942. The letter quoted is VCG to "Bunter," September 15, 1942.

11. VCG to Caroline Spurgeon, letters of August 1, 4, 7, 18, 24, and 31, 1939, box 4, VCG Papers, RBML, CU.

12. Winifred C. Cullis to VCG, July 15, 1942, box 45 (IFUW Correspondence 1939–1942), VCG Papers, RBML, CU; Nicholas Murray Butler to VCG, October 27, 1942, Nicholas Murray Butler Papers, Series II, box 157, RBML, CU.

13. Christine von Oertzen, "Whose World? Internationalism, Nationalism, and the Struggle Over the 'Language Question' in the International Federation of University Women, 1919–1932," *Contemporary European History* 25, no. 2 (2016), 283–287; von Oertzen, *Science, Gender, and Internationalism: Academic Women's Networks, 1917–1955* (New York & London: Palgrave Macmillan, 2014), 59–109.

14. Von Oertzen, "Whose World?" 277, 290; von Oertzen, *Science, Gender, and Internationalism*, 107, chap. 4 on Nazification; VCG, *Crusade*, 149–152; VCG, "Some Highlights on the Council Meeting," *AAUW Journal* 28, no. 2 (Winter 1934/5), 121–122; Meta Glass comments, 2, Setzer file, box 2, BC2.4, VCG Papers, Barnard Archives. President of Sweet Briar from 1926–1945, President of the AAUW, and frequent VCG ally in the 1930s and 1940s, Meta Glass was the younger half-sister of Virginia Senator Carter Glass (1941–1945).

15. "Report of the Seventh Conference, Cracow, August 22–September 1, 1936" *IFUW Bulletin* no. 18 (1936), 67–70.

16. Von Oertzen, *Science, Gender, and Internationalism*, chap. 5 on IFUW aid to refugees; Edith C. Batho, *A Lamp of Friendship* (London: International Federation of University Women, 1969), 17; VCG, "The International Federation Greeting to the AAUW from the University Women of Other Countries," *Journal of the AAUW* 30, no. 4 (June 1937), 204–206, quoted in Christy Jo Snider, "Planning for Peace: Virginia Gildersleeve at the United Nations Conference on International Organization," *Peace and Change: A Journal of Peace Research* 32, no. 2 (March 2007), 174.

17. Michael Rosenthal, *Nicholas Miraculous: The Amazing Career of the Redoubtable Dr. Nicholas Murray Butler* (New York: Farrar, Straus, and Giroux, 2006), chap. 16; "VCG: John Crane," n.d., statement of John Crane about VCG and Charles R. Crane, box 47, VCG Papers, CU, folder: IFUW/ Speeches; Stephen H. Norwood, *The Third Reich in the Ivory Tower: Complicity and Conflict on American Campuses* (Cambridge: Cambridge University Press, 2009), chap. 4; Bradley W. Hart, *Hitler's American Friends: The Third Reich's Supporters in the United States* (New York: St. Martin's Press, 2018), 19.

18. "Urge World Unit to Avert Disaster," *New York Times*, April 30, 1933, 15.

19. VCG to Mrs. Alfred Meyer, December 15, 1933, box 7, folder 1, Annie Nathan Meyer Papers, quoted in Lynn D. Gordon, "Annie Nathan Meyer and Barnard College: Mission and Identity in Women's Higher Education, 1889–1950," *History of Education Quarterly* 26, no. 4 (Winter 1986), 518.

20. AAUW *Journal* 28, no. 2 (Winter 1934/35), 121–122. For Matthias's duplicity, see von Oertzen, *Science, Gender, and Internationalism*, 109–110.

21. Cornelia Geer le Boutillier, "Dean Gildersleeve, Interviewed by Cornelia Geer le Boutillier," *Barnard Alumnae Magazine* XXIV, no. 1 (October 1934), 9.

22. "Group Protests Italian Award," *Columbia Daily Spectator* LVIII, no. 20 (October 24, 1934), 1; Stephen H. Norwood, "Complicity and Conflict: Columbia University Responds to Fascism, 1933–1937," *Modern Judaism* 27, no. 3 (October 2007), 266, 274.

23. VCG, "To the Editor of the *Barnard Bulletin*," April 4, 1935, carbon copy in box 3, VCG Papers, Columbia University, folder: "VCG: Personal and Confidential Correspondence."

24. "Dean Gildersleeve Back from Europe," *New York Times*, September 11, 1935, 25. For Butler's remarks to the press in support of German and Italian expansionism, see Rosenthal, *Nicholas Miraculous*, 390.

25. For German enrollment see Frieda Wunderlich (a sociologist at the New School), "Education in Nazi Germany," *Social Research* 4, no. 3 (September 1937), 355. Between 1931 and 1935/36, the numbers of German university students dropped by 38 percent (men) and 50 percent (women), from 126,537 to 76,808. VCG's onetime mentor Charles R. Crane, by 1933 a Nazi sympathizer, voiced a counterpart of the "overcrowding" myth that year when he asserted that Jews held "a great many more key positions in Germany than their numbers or their talents entitled them to"; see F. W. Blecher, "Charles R. Crane's Crusades for the Arabs, 1919–1939," *Middle Eastern Studies* 24, no. 1 (January 1988), 47.

26. "The Dean Comes Home, as Told to Emma Bugbee," *Barnard Alumnae Magazine* XXV, no. 1 (October 1935), 10–12.

27. Rosenthal, *Nicholas Miraculous*, 394; Norwood, "Complicity and Conflict," 276; "FDR: Day by Day," March 3, 1936 and ER, Engagement Book, March 3, 1936, Series 45, Box 1386, FDR Library.

28. *Barnard Bulletin*, January 15 and December 10, 1937, cited in Norwood, "Complicity and Conflict," 258. In a report to alumnae on the history of the student aid program (retroactive), VCG struck a characteristic pose. Conceding the presence of a Nazi propagandist, the dean defended the wartime presence of students from Axis powers as well as the overall benefit of the program; it offered an "opportunity to test the open-mindedness and generosity of spirit of Barnard undergraduates." See "Dean Emeritus Virginia C. Gildersleeve Recalls the Development of the Student Exchange Program," *Barnard Alumnae Magazine* 46, no. 1 (November 1956), 2.

29. VCG to Nicholas Murray Butler, September 27, 1938, NMB Papers, Series II, box 157, RBML, CU; Rosenthal, *Nicholas Miraculous*, 435; Batho, *A Lamp of Friendship*, 18.

30. VCG, *Crusade*, 82; Laurel Leff, *Well Worth Saving: American Universities' Life and Death Decisions on Refugees from Nazi Europe* (New Haven: Yale University Press, 2019), 105, 109; VCG quote from "Miss Gildersleeve Returns from Europe," *New York Times*, September 14, 1938, 23, cited in Leff, 96.

31. Larissa Bonfante, "Margaret Bieber (1879–1978)," in Claire Richter Sherman, *Women as Interpreters of the Visual Arts, 1929–1981* (Westport, CT: Greenwood, 1981), 265 ff.; Interview with Julius Held, 1.7 Tape Number: IV, Side Two, June 25, 1991, TET Project, Oral History, UCLA, https://oralhistory.library .ucla.edu/catalog/21198-zz0008znn6.

32. For instance, Stephen Norwood tracks VCG's anti-Semitism, as in his book and article, cited above; Anthony Grafton suggests that VCG was a "complex character" in "A Nazi at Harvard," *NYRblog*, November 2, 2009.

33. VCG, *Crusade*, 183; VCG, "Scattered Reminiscences of the IFUW," May 19, 1950, 3–5, VCG Papers, box 47, CU, unidentified folder on the 1950s; "Barnard's Dean Says U.S. People Favor the Allies," *New York Herald Tribune*, October 11, 1939, 14.

34. Joseph Gerard Brennan, *The Education of a Prejudiced Man* (New York: Scribner, 1977), 117; Elizabeth Reynard, *Ports of Youth: Fragments of an Autobiography* (Printed for Virginia Gildersleeve, 1962), intro by VCG, 9–10.

35. Reynard, *Ports of Youth*, 27–28, 40, 43, 47, 49. For biographical information, see also "Tributes to Elizabeth Reynard, Read at the Memorial Meeting Held at Barnard College, February 1, 1962," BC34, Faculty/Staff/Visitor Bio Files, box no. 40, Barnard Archives.

36. VCG quote from Reynard, *Ports of Youth*, introduction, 9; "Elizabeth Reynard Dead at 64; Ex-Barnard English Professor," *New York Times*, January 10, 1962, 47. A reference to "B. Litt. Oxford Univ. (Eng.) 1927" appears in the entry for

Elizabeth Reynard in *American Publications, 1939* (Los Angeles, 1939), vol. 3, found in the Barnard Archives, BC3.4 Faculty/Staff/Visitor Bio Files, folder on Reynard. For the connection of Ida Ogilvie and VCG, who served together on the Committee on Women Graduate Students, see Rosalind Rosenberg, "Virginia Gildersleeve: Opening the Gates," *Living Legacies: Great Moments and Leading Figures in the History of Columbia University*, http://www.columbia.edu/cu/alumni/Magazine/summer2001/Gildersleeve.html. Eleanor Rosenberg, Barnard '29, discusses Reynard's success as an instructor in her contribution to "Tributes to Elizabeth Reynard," February 1, 1962, 1–2.

37. Reynard, *Ports of Youth*, 9 (VCG quote), 56 (on Boas), 69; Elizabeth Reynard, *The Narrow Land: Folk Chronicles of Old Cape Cod* (Boston: Houghton Mifflin, 1934); "Cape Cod Chronicles: The Narrow Land," *New York Times Book Review*, December 9, 1934, 12.

38. Reynard, *Ports of Youth*, 30; VCG quote from intro to *Ports of Youth*, 9–10; VCG, *Crusade*, 250–251; "Barnard to Offer Course on America: Dean Gildersleeve Plan to Give Better Understanding of Tradition," *New York Times*, April 2, 1939, 59; Elizabeth Reynard, draft of an article of February 4, 1946, sent to the *Barnard Alumnae Magazine*, Barnard College Archives, BC13.1, American Studies, box no. 1, folder: American Studies, 1946–1948. For Reynard's shaping of the American Studies program, see the contribution of Eleanor Rosenberg to "Tributes to Elizabeth Reynard," February 1, 1962, 3. Barnard student Elspeth Davies Rostow, '38, future political scientist and presidential advisor to Lyndon Baines Johnson, claimed to have proposed the plan for American studies to Reynard, who then suggested it to VCG, and to have shaped the curriculum for the program. See "Barnard Establishes American Studies, 1937," *Columbia Spectator* CXXIII, no. 136 (December 13, 1999), 13.

39. Elizabeth Reynard, "Merrily We Roll Along: The Book of the Recruit" (scrapbook), introduction, 2, Elizabeth Reynard Papers, Schlesinger Library, Radcliffe College. The Schlesinger Library collection includes, besides the scrapbook, Reynard's lectures at the *U.S.S. Hunter*, the United States Naval Training School, and notes and materials for *The Narrow Land*. For Reynard's navy career, see Jean T. Palmer's contribution to "Tributes to Elizabeth Reynard," February 1, 1962, 1–3 and Dorothea Setzer, "Former WAVE Commandant Views Military Training," *Christian Science Monitor*, February 14, 1952, 12. For a perceptive interpretation of women's experience in the World War II Navy, see Mildred McAfee Horton, "Women in the United States Navy," *American Journal of Sociology* 51, no. 5, 448–450.

40. "Women—Miss Mac," *Time* 45, no. 1 (March 12, 1945), 20–23; Horton, "Women in the United States Navy," 448; Emily Yellin, *Our Mothers' War: American Women at Home and on the Front During World War II* (New York: The Free

Press, 2004), 137–142; Allan Berube, *Coming Out Under Fire: The History of Gay Men and Women in World War Two* (New York: The Free Press, 1990), 28, 35, 56–7. Congress started the Women's Army Auxiliary Corps (WAAC) on May 15, 1942; the unit became the Women's Army Corps (WACS) and assumed active-duty status on July 1, 1943. FDR signed the law that started the WAVES on July 30, 1942.

41. Christy Jo Snider, "Planning for Peace," 176–77; "Dean at Barnard Scores Lindbergh," *New York Times*, June 4, 1941, 11; VCG, *Crusade*, 258–259.

42. Snider, "Planning for Peace," 177; "Women—Miss Mac," 20–23; VCG to Catharine Weiser (Bunter), July 6, 1942, typescript in Setzer file, box 2, Barnard College Archives; "Aims of Britain Seen as Similar to Ours; Dean Gildersleeve Urges More Cooperation Between Allies," *New York Times*, October 13, 1943, 33; "Speech delivered by Dean Virginia C. Gildersleeve of Barnard College over Station WABC, September 13, 1943, 5:15–5:30 p.m.," VCG Papers, 2.4, box 1, Speeches and Addresses, file for 1943; "Dean Gives Warning on Teaching Germans," *New York Times*, November 7, 1943, 58; and Laura Micheletti Puaca, *Searching for Scientific Womanpower: Technocratic Feminism and the Politics of National Security, 1940–1980* (Chapel Hill: University of North Carolina Press, 2014), 17. For Eleanor Roosevelt's trip to England in 1942, see Doris Kearns Goodwin, *No Ordinary Time: Franklin and Eleanor Roosevelt: The Home Front in World War II* (New York: Simon and Schuster, 1994), 379–383.

43. VCG, *Crusade*, 299–301; Isser Woloch, *The Postwar Moment: Progressive Forces in Britain, France, and the United States After World War II* (New Haven: Yale University Press, 2019), 263–267. For the introduction of a modern educational system, see Peter Mandler, *The Crisis of the Meritocracy: Britain's Transition to Mass Education Since the Second World War* (New York: Oxford University Press, 2020).

44. "How Barnard Can Help Win the War," Address by Dean Gildersleeve at the College Assembly, January 13, 1942, BC2.4, box 1 (Addresses); "Women's Colleges and National Defense," CBS Broadcast of September 26, 1944, BC2.4, box 1 (Folder for 1944); "Educating Girls for the War and Postwar World, Postscript," Speech of October 20, 1943, BC2.4, box 1, Barnard Archives. For VCG in the World War II era, see Rosalind Rosenberg, *Changing the Subject: How the Women of Columbia Changed the Way We Think About Sex and Politics* (New York: Columbia University Press, 2004), 179–180; Rosenberg, "The Legacy of Dean Gildersleeve," 4; and Puaca, *Searching for Scientific Womanpower*, chap. 1. For the entry of women to Columbia's engineering school, see VCG, *Crusade*, 103–104 and Robert McCaughey, *A Lever Long Enough: A History of Columbia's School of Engineering and Applied Science Since 1864* (New York: Columbia University Press, 2014), 112. "It is easy to grant this so-called right to women,"

observed the engineering dean, "but it will probably be impossible to withdraw it should we decide to do so at a later date."

45. "The Shortage of Trained Brains," address of February 1942, Barnard Archives, BC 2.4, box 1 (speeches), folder 1942. For the draft, see "Dean at Barnard Scores Lindbergh," *New York Times*, June 4, 1941, 17; "Gildersleeve Against Draft of Girls in College for War Jobs," *New York Herald Tribune*, February 10, 1943, 15; "Conscript Women, Too, Dean Gildersleeve Urges," *Wall Street Journal*, August 17, 1943, 1; "Dean Gildersleeve Expects U.S. to Draft Women for War or Jobs," *New York Herald Tribune*, August 17, 1943, 13; Adelaide Kerr, "Should the United States Draft Its Womanpower?" *Washington Post*, September 3, 1943, B4; Minutes, Conference of the Seven Colleges, New York City, October 28, 1944, BC2.4, box 29 (Correspondence), folder 86, Barnard Archives.

46. VCG, *Crusade*, 253–255; Rosalind Rosenberg, "Virginia Gildersleeve: Opening the Gates" in *Living Legacies of Columbia*, ed. Theodore de Bary, 474; Margaret Farrand Thorp, *Neilson of Smith* (New York: Oxford University Press, 1956), 347–348.

47. Smith Simpson, "The Commission to Study the Organization of Peace," *American Political Science Review* 35, no. 2 (April 1941), 317–324; Commission to Study the Organization of Peace, *Fourth Report: Fundamentals of International Organization*, New York, November 1943, 27 pp.; Clark M. Eichelberger to Governor Herbert Lehman, letter of December 30, 1942, New York Public Library; Harold Josephson, *James T. Shotwell and the Rise of Internationalism in America* (Rutherford, NJ: Fairleigh Dickinson University Press, 1974), 238–239, 242.

48. "Dean Gildersleeve Would Exile Hitler and Impose Hard Peace," *New York Herald Tribune*, February 16, 1945, 1, 18.

49. "Dean Gildersleeve Would Exile Hitler," 1; Mary Hornaday, "Choice of Dean Gildersleeve Lauded," *Christian Science Monitor*, February 15, 1945, 3; Bess Furman, "Hails Honor Given Dean Gildersleeve," *New York Times*, February 15, 1945, 22; Robert C. Hildebrand, *Dunbarton Oaks: The Origins of the United Nations and the Search for Postwar Security* (Chapel Hill: University of North Carolina Press, 1990), 81. For the White House Conference of June 14, 1944, see Judy Barrett Litoff and David C. Smith, eds., *What Kind of World Do We Want? American Women For Peace* (Wilmington, Del.: Scholarly Resources, 2000), chaps. VI and VII. In her speech at the conference, Eleanor Roosevelt called for women's presence at "every meeting that deals with postwar problems," 104.

50. VCG, *Crusade*, 320; Christy Jo Snider, "Planning for Peace: Virginia Gildersleeve at the United Nations Conference on International Organization," *Peace & Change* 32, no. 2 (April 2007), 168. The transnational women's organization, Snider suggests, was VCG's springboard into professional diplomacy.

51. William Allan Neilson, Press Release, Friday, March 23, 1945, Commission to Study the Organization of Peace, BC2.4, box 3: "Addresses, Publications Events," Barnard Archives.

52. "Letter Inviting Delegates to the United Nations Conference at San Francisco," February 28, 1945 from *The American Presidency Project*, https://www.presidency.ucsb.edu/documents/letter-inviting-delegates-the-united-nations-conference-san-francisco; a major article for the following section is Torild Skard, "Getting Our History Right: How Were the Equal Rights of Women and Men Included in the Charter of the United Nations?" *Forum for Development Studies* 35, no. 1 (2008), 37–60. The Stettinius remark is from Dorothea Selzer's account of an interview with Mrs. George McAnemy (Marjorie Jacobi, VCG's college classmate) on January 14, 1952 in Setzer File, box 2.

53. VCG, "Inside Story" of the United Nations, August 17, 1945, box 65, VCG Papers, RBML, CU; VCG, *Crusade*, 326–327.

54. "Interview with Durward V. Sandifer by Richard D, McKinzie, Chevy Chase, Md., March 15, 1973," 31, Harry S. Truman Library; Skard, "Getting Our History Right," 38–46. The five invited women's organization, which represented a range of views on equal rights for women, were the AAUW, the General Federation of Women's Clubs, The National Federation of Business and Professional Women's Clubs, the National League of Women Voters, and the Women's Action Alliance on Victory and Lasting Peace.

55. Agnes Meyer, "Dean Gildersleeve Popular Choice," *Washington Post*, March 11, 1945, B1; Skard, "Getting Our History Right," 40. For the international dimensions of the clash over women's rights at the United Nations 1945 conference, see Katherine M. Marino, *Feminism for the Americas: The Making of an International Human Rights Movement* (Chapel Hill: University of North Carolina Press, 2019) and Rebecca Adami, *Women and the Universal Declaration of Human Rights* (New York & London: Routledge, 2020, chaps. 1 and 2. Conflict between equal rights feminism and social feminism at the United Nations is also discussed in Helen Laville, "A New Era in International Women's Rights? American Women's Associations and the Establishment of the United Nations Commission on the Status of Women," *Journal of Women's History* 20, no. 1 (2008), 34–56.

56. Skard, "Getting Our History Right," 38–42; VCG, *Crusade*, 349–50; Meyer, "Dean Gildersleeve Popular Choice."

57. VCG, *Crusade*, 349–350, 352–353.

58. Katherine M. Marino, *Feminism for the Americas*, 202–205; Jessie Street, "Letter from San Francisco to the United Associations," May 6, 1945, in *Jessie Street: Documents and Essays*, ed. Heather Radi (Marickville, New South Wales: Southwood Press, 1990), 197.

59. Skard, "Getting Our History Right," 38, 50–51.

60. Skard, "Getting Our History Right," 53–56; Helen Laville, "A New Era in International Women's Rights?" 45; Arvonne S. Fraser, "Equality and Non-Discrimination Under International Law," *Human Rights Quarterly* 21 (1999), 886–888.

61. VCG, *Crusade*, 353; Skard, "Getting Our History Right," 55–56; Fraser, "Equality and Non-Discrimination," 88; Paula F. Pfeffer, "Eleanor Roosevelt and the National and World's Woman's Parties," *The Historian* 59, no. 1 (Fall 1996), 53–54; "Report from the San Francisco Conference, June 16, 1945," with Archibald MacLeish and Virginia Gildersleeve, NBC, recording by Gordon Skene.

62. Jessie Street to Muriel Tribe, February 5, 1952, in *Jessie Street*, ed. Heather Radi, 219; Marino, *Feminism for the Americas*, 218, 223, 233–234.

63. When appointed to her UN post, VCG had used her allies Agnes E. Meyer and Helen Reid to secure good press coverage. Reid praised the appointment to reporter Bess Furman in "Hails Honor Given Dean Gildersleeve," *New York Times*, February 15, 1945, 22 and Meyer published articles elsewhere, such as "Dean Gildersleeve Popular Choice," *Washington Post*, March 11, 1945, 11 and "Dean Gildersleeve Explains Her Outlook on World Issues," *New York Herald Tribune*, March 11, 1945, 5. The articles quoted here are Margaret Parton, "Barnard Dean Works Hard at Being Delegate," *New York Herald Tribune*, June 3, 1945, 8; Edith Efron, "Portrait of a Dean and a Delegate," *New York Times Magazine*, April 1, 1945, 7; and, after VCG returned from San Francisco to New York, n.a., "'America First' As Defined By Barnard Dean," *New York Herald Tribune*, June 29, 1945, 7.

64. VCG left an "inside history" of the UN conference, written on August 17, 1945, a few months after the meeting ended, while memories were "still fresh in my mind"; see untitled folder, box 65, VCG Papers, RBML, CU. Though she labeled the document "not to be published, at least for a long time," it formed the start of the chapter on the UN conference included in her autobiography, *Many a Good Crusade*, 315–357.

65. Leroy Stinebower Oral History, Columbus, N. C. by Richard D. McKinzie, June 9, 1974, 43, Harry S. Truman Library; Dorothea Setzer's account of interview with Leroy Stinebower, n.d., Setzer File, box 2, file 2, Barnard Archives.

66. "Interview with Durward V. Sandifer," 42; Margaret Parton, "Barnard Dean Works Hard at Being Delegate," 8; James Loeffler, "'The Conscience of America': Human Rights, Jewish Politics, and American Foreign Policy at the 1945 United Nations San Francisco Conference," *Journal of American History* (September 2013), 415.

67. VCG, *Crusade*, 344; for Stassen's memory of VCG's proposal, see William Branigin, "UN: 50 Years Fending Off World War III," *Washington Post*, June 25, 1995.

68. VCG, *Many a Good Crusade*, 315, 323–324, 326–327, 331–332, 333–334, 335, 343. "WAVES Chief at Hunter Will Aid Miss Gildersleeve at Conference," *New York Herald Tribune*, April 2, 1945, 36.

69. VCG, *Crusade*, 339, 357; Bertha Lutz to Carrie Chapman Catt, May 21, 1945, reel 12, National American Woman Suffrage Association Papers, quoted in Marino, *Feminism for the Americas*, 214.

70. VCG, "The World is a Community," Broadcast over NBC, Station WEAF, July 14, 1945; VCG, "Report on San Francisco," September, 1945, sent to the General Federation of Women's Clubs, both in BC2.4, box 3 ("Addresses, Publications, Events"), Barnard Archives.

71. Mary Ann Glendon, *A World Made Anew: Eleanor Roosevelt and the Universal Declaration of Human Rights* (New York: Random House, 2001); E. J. Kahn, "Profiles: The Years Alone—1," *The New Yorker* 24 (June 12, 1948), 30–4; Eleanor Roosevelt, "My Day," May 25, 1951; Bertha Lutz to Carrie Chapman Catt, June 3, 1945, reel 12, NAWSA Papers, quoted in Marino, *Feminism for the Americas*, 222

72. "On and Off Campus," *Barnard Alumnae Magazine* XXV, no. 2 (November 1935), 3; Eleanor Roosevelt, "Press Conference of April 12, 1945," in *The White House Press Conferences of Eleanor Roosevelt*, ed. Maureen Beasley (New York: Garland, 1983), 334. Correspondence between VCG and Eleanor Roosevelt regarding ER's visit to Barnard in 1935 is in Anna Eleanor Roosevelt Papers, 1884–1964, Part 1, box 612, folder: Gildersleeve, FDR Library.

73. Eleanor Roosevelt refers to VCG in "My Day" on April 16, 1942, March 4, 1943, and September 15, 1947.

74. VCG, *Crusade*, 358–391; *Report of the United States Education Mission to Japan, Tokyo, March 30, 1946* (Washington, DC: Government Printing Office, 1946), 57–58; "Barnard Dean Sees a Revivified Japan," *New York Times* (April 6, 1946), 6. For implementation of the committee's recommendations, see Brian W. Lagotte, "Because We Said So: Educational Reform in Occupied Japan," *Sungkyun Journal of East Asian Studies* 6, no. 2 (October 2006), 239–256.

75. VCG, *Crusade*, 358, 382, 289; Wlllard E. Givens, "Tokyo and Return," 4 and 6 (entries for March 11 and March 14, 1946), in box 76, VCG Papers, RBML, CU, folder: Trip to Japan—Educational Mission. See also Jennifer M. Miller, *Cold War Diplomacy: The United States and Japan* (Cambridge: Harvard University Press, 2019).

76. "Letters to the Editor," *New York Times*, October 9, 1945, 20; VCG to the Chairman, The Anglo-American Committee of Inquiry on Palestine, January 10, 1946, Barnard Archives.

77. George C. Marshall to VCG, July 29, 1947, Series I, box of catalogued correspondence, Folder: Marshall, George C., VCG Papers, RBML, CU; Glendon, *The World Made Anew*, 32; VCG, *Crusade*, 404.

78. VCG, *Crusade*, 398–400.

79. Michael Rosenthal, *Nicholas Miraculous*, 448–451, 454; VCG, *Crusade*, 399–403.

80. McCaughey, *A College of Her Own*, 149–153.

81. "Dean Gildersleeve of Barnard Asks to Retire by June 30, 1947," *New York Times*, November 27, 1945; Brennan, *The Education of a Prejudiced Man*, 117; McCaughey, chap. 5.

82. "Dr. M. C. M'Intosh Dean of Barnard," *New York Times*, November 26, 1946, 30; Millicent McIntosh to VCG, December 5, 1947, box 35, VCG Papers, CU (this letter is mixed in with VCG's Papers on the Middle East).

83. VCG, *Crusade*, 399, 401; McCaughey, *A College of Her Own*, 152–153.

84. "Women College Presidents," *Life*, October 27, 1947, 96.

85. McCaughey, *A College of Her Own*, 153–154; Frank Fackenthal, interview with Dorothea Setzer, undated (c. early 1950s), 3, Setzer file, box 2, Barnard Archives.

86. "Dean Gildersleeve Decorated by France for Aid During War," *New York Herald Tribune*, April 27, 1947, 44; "Speech at a Luncheon, April 26, 1947," 3, box of Addresses and Publications, folder for 1947, Barnard Archives; McCaughey, *College of Her Own*, chap. 5.

87. Reynard, *Ports of Youth*, 10.

88. Harold S. Wechsler, "The Rise and Fall of Discrimination at Columbia" (talk at Columbia, November 10, 1998), 4; Wechsler, "The Rationale for Restriction: Ethnicity and College Admissions in America, 1910–1980," *American Quarterly* 36 (Winter 1984), 662–663; Wechsler, *The Qualified Student: A History of Selective College Admissions in America* (New Brunswick, NJ: Transaction, 2014), 188–198.

89. Wechsler, "The Rationale for Restriction," 663; Wechsler, *The Qualified Student*, 190. For immediate consequences of the postwar laws, see "Fair Educational Practices Acts: A Solution to Discrimination?" (Editorial Board/Notes) *Harvard Law Review* 64 no. 2 (December 1950), 307–317, and Edward N. Saveth, "Fair Educational Practices Legislation," *Annals of the American Academy of Political and Social Science* 275 (May 1951), 41–46.

90. Brennan, *The Education of a Prejudiced Man*, 115.

5. EMBATTLED: AFTER BARNARD, 1947–1965

1. VCG, *Many a Good Crusade* (New York: Macmillan, 1954), 403–44, 416; "Retires from Faculty of Barnard College," *New York Times*, May 10, 1950.

2. VCG, *Crusade*, 404.

3. VCG, *Crusade*, 418–419.

4. VCG to Catharine Weiser ("Bunter"), September 7, 1942, in Dorothea Setzer's transcript of VCG-"Bunter" correspondence, BC2.4, Setzer file, box 2, Barnard Archives; Marion Churchill White, *A History of Barnard College* (New York: Columbia University Press, 1953), 147.

5. Julie V. Marsteller, interview with John Kouwenhoven, retiring professor of English, April 22, 1975, BC16, Record Group: Oral History, box 2, Barnard Archives.

6. Elizabeth Reynard, draft of article on her plan for American Studies, sent to the *Barnard Alumnae Magazine*, February 4, 1946, 1, 3, BC13.1, box 1, Record Group: American Studies; Elizabeth Reynard to Helen Rogers Reid, July 17, 1947, BC 2.4 box 1, VCG Correspondence, Barnard Archives. Reynard's proposed focus would have made Barnard's program singular among pioneer American Studies programs of the 1ate 1940s. But a similar internationalist impulse—an interest in "how others see us"—arose later in the century in the field of American studies. See Lucy Maddox, ed., *Locating American Studies: The Evolution of a Discipline* (Baltimore: Johns Hopkins University Press, 1999).

7. VCG to Millicent McIntosh, May 21, 1948, BC13.1, box 1, Record Group: American Studies, Barnard Archives.

8. Elizabeth Reynard to the Barnard Board of Trustees, December 5, 1949, VCG Papers, box 71, RBML, CU; Elizabeth Reynard to Mrs. Ogden Reid, December 26, 1949, Elizabeth Reynard file in BC3.4, box 40, Faculty/Staff/Visitor Bio Files; "Retires from Faculty of Barnard College," *New York Times*, May 10, 1950, 18; "Miss Reynard Resigns," *Barnard College Alumnae Monthly* XXXIX, no. 9 (June, 1950), 2; White, *History of Barnard College*, 163; Linda Kaufman Kerber, '60, "Angles of Vision: What American Studies Has Been, What American Studies Must Be," typescript, p. 4, on the sixtieth anniversary of American Studies, 1999, BC13.1, box 2, Barnard Archives.

9. VCG, introduction to Elizabeth Reynard, *Ports of Youth: Fragment of an Autobiography* (Printed for Virginia C. Gildersleeve, Columbia University Press, 1962), 9–10; Kerber, "Angles of Vision," 4; "Civ. Lectures Emphasize Business," *Barnard Bulletin* (March 12, 1956), 1; VCG, memorandum on establishment of the "Navarre" professorship, February 120, 1953, Setzer file, box 2, Barnard Archives.

10. Jean T. Palmer to VCG, January 21, 1963, BC2.4, box 29, folder of correspondence for 1953–1964, Barnard Archives. At this date, Palmer headed Barnard's Public Relations Office.

11. Dorothea Setzer, Notes of February 25, 1953, in the Setzer file, BC2.4, box 2, Folder 2, Barnard Archives

12. Millicent McIntosh to VCG, March 23, 1953; Reception list for VCG's visit to Barnard on November 9, 1954; Announcement of June 17, 1955, Barnard Public

Relations Office; Millicent Mcintosh to VCG, September 26, 1957, all in BC2.4, box 1, Correspondence, folder for 1953–1964, Barnard Archives.

13. VCG, *Crusade*, 406; "Meeting of the Board of Trustees, American College for Girls at Istanbul, May 13, 1952," box 48, VCG Papers, RBML, CU; for Near East College Association in the 1940s, see box 50, VCG Papers, RBML, CU; for VCG's early interest in the Middle East, see *Crusade*, 182–187.

14. VCG, *Crusade*, 405; VCG, Letter to the Editor, *New York Times*, October 9, 1945, 20; VCG to the Chairman, The Anglo-American Committee of Inquiry on Palestine, January 10, 1946, BC2.4, box 29, "Correspondence," Barnard Archives; VCG et al., "Letters to the Times: Against Palestine Partition," *New York Times*, November 21, 1947.

15. VCG, *Crusade*, 409.

16. For the background and stance of Arabists (aficionados of the Arab world who spend much of their lives in it), see David A. Hollinger, *Protestants Abroad: How Missionaries Tried to Change the World but Changed America* (Princeton: Princeton University Press, 2017), chap. 5; Robert D. Kaplan, *The Arabists: The Romance of an American Elite* (New York: The Free Press, 1993); and, for the postwar era, G. David Cohen, "Elusive Neutrality: Christian Humanitarianism and the Problem of Palestine, 1947–1967," *Humanity* 5, no. 2 (Spring 2014), 183–210.

17. VCG, *Crusade*, 409; "Leaders Propose Truce in Palestine," *New York Times*, February 20, 1948, 15; "New Committee Opposes UN's Palestine Plan," *New York Herald Tribune*, March 3, 1948, 10; VCG to Prof. William Ernest Hocking, February 7, 1947, VCG Papers, box 35, folder: "Arabs—Current, 1949," RBML, CU.

18. VCG, *Crusade*, 410; VCG to Clark M. Eichelberger, March 11, 1948 and VCG to Dr. William Emerson, March 17, 1948, both in folder 6, box 35, VCG Papers, RBML, CU.

19. Martin E. Marty, *Under God, Indivisible, 1941–1960* (Chicago: University of Chicago Press, 1999), vol. 3 of *Modern American Religion*, 185, 188–189; Thomas A. Kolsky, *Jews Against Zionism: The American Council for Judaism, 1944–1948* (Philadelphia: Temple University Press, 1990), 25, 35. For Brandeis and Zionism, see Melvin I Urofsky, *Louis D. Brandeis: A Life* (New York: Pantheon, 2009), 399–418 and chap. 21.

   The ACJ declined after Israel's founding in 1948 and even more so after the Six-Day War of 1967.

20. Kolsky, *Jews Against Zionism*, 181; Henry Sloane Coffin to VCG, March 25, 1948, in VCG Papers, box 35, untitled folder, RBML, CU; Elmer Berger to VCG, August 25, 1949, box 38, folder: Middle East Relief, RBML, CU; Hugh Wilford, *America's Great Game: The CIA's Secret Arabists and the Shaping of the Modern Middle East* (New York: Basic Books, 2013), 90.

21. VCG, *Crusade*, 410–412; Wilford, *America's Great Game*, 93.

22. Wilford, *America's Great Game*, 116; Garland Evans Hopkins to Members of the Organizing Committee, March 7, 1949; Kim Roosevelt to VCG, September 13, 1948; Kim Roosevelt to VCG, February 21, 1949, all in box 35, VCG Papers, RBML, CU.

23. VCG, "Letter to the Editor," *New York Times*, January 22, 1948; Maud Tarleton Winchester to VCG, January 23, 1948, untitled folder, box 35, VCG Papers, RBML, CU; VCG, "Letter to the Editor," *New York Times*, April 17, 1949; Blanche Watson to VCG, April 26, 1949, untitled folder, box 35, VCG Papers, RBML, CU.

24. Nancy Cott, *Fighting Words: The Bold American Journalists Who Brought the World Home Between the Wars* (New York: Basic Books, 2021), 299; see also Peter Kurth, *American Cassandra: The Life of Dorothy Thompson* (Boston: Little, Brown, 1990) chap. 17.

25. Dorothy Thompson to VCG, March 15, 1951, box 38, VCG Papers, RBML, CU.

26. Dorothy Thompson, press release of June 23, 1951, in AFME newsletter, "News: American Friends of the Middle East," box 38, RBML, CU; Hugh Wilford, "American Friends of the Middle East: The CIA, US Citizens, and the Secret Battle for American Public Opinion in the Arab-Israeli Conflict, 1947–1967," *Journal of American Studies* 51, no. 1 (February 2017), 93–116; see 100–101 for the founding of AFME.

27. Wilford, "American Friends of the Middle East," 101, 105, 107; VCG, *Crusade*, 412.

28. "Project for Developing Crafts and Tradework, March 23, 1953," box 38, folder: "April 1953," VCG Papers, RBML, CU; Janet Salisbury, "'Rehabilitator' Extraordinary is Called to Chicago From Her Minnesota Labors," *Minneapolis Star-Tribune*, August 23, 1936, 13.

29. VCG to Nicholas Murray Butler, September 27, 1938, NMB Papers, Series II, box 157, CU; VCG to Dorothy Thompson, November 25, 1949, with DT's handwritten draft of a response, Special Collections Research Center, Syracuse University, box 12; Dorothy Thompson to VCG, June 13, 1951, box 38, VCG Papers, RBML, CU, folder: American Friends of the Middle East.

30. Dorothy Thompson, "America Demands a Single Loyalty: The Perils of a 'Favorite' Foreign Nation," *Commentary* 9, no. 3 (March 1950), 210–21; Dorothy Thompson to VCG, August 2, 1951, Dorothy Thompson Papers, box 38, Syracuse University, quoted in Susan Hertog, *Dangerous Ambition: Rebecca West and Dorothy Thompson, New Women in Search of Love and Power* (New York: Ballantine, 2011), 359, 369; Wilford, *America's Great Game*, 117, 126, 309.

31. VCG, "The Self-Segregation of American Jews," Address given before the New York Chapter of the American Council for Judaism, May 25, 1950, 6 pages, box 29, folder for 1950, BC2.4 Barnard Archives.

32. VCG, "Self-Segregation of American Jews," 1–6.

33. "Zionist Move is Attacked: Dean Gildersleeve Says Self-Segregation is Urged," *Baltimore Sun*, June 8, 1950, 28; "Anti-Zionists Are Attacked: Rabbi Goldman Calls Them 'Fanatical and Reckless,'" *Baltimore Sun*, June 8, 1950, 28; Letter to the Editor from Robert S. Nyburg, *Baltimore Sun*, June 16 1950, 18; Alger C. Gildersleeve to Dr. Norman Salit, October 8, 1950, BC2.4, Setzer file, box 1, Barnard Archives. For the cultural scene of the 1940s, see George Hutchinson, *Facing the Abyss: American Literature and Culture in the 1940s* (New York: Columbia University Press, 2019). John Haynes Holmes (1879–1964), prolific and prominent liberal, was a friend of Rabbi Stephen Wise. See Walter Robins, "Cultural Zionism and Bi-nationalism among American Liberal Protestants," *Israel Studies* 23, number 2 (Summer 2018), 142–167; and Carl Herman Voss, *Rabbi and Minister: The Friendship of Stephen S. Wise and John Haynes Holmes* (Cleveland: World Publishing Company, 1964). The article by Holmes that mentioned VCG was "Zion and American Jewry."

34. VCG, *Many a Good Crusade*, 171–187; Dr. Ralf Bellanna, Assistant Secretary General, League of Arab States, to VCG, August 14, 1956, VCG Papers, BC2.4, box 29, "Correspondence"; VCG to Lessing J. Rosenwald, March 9, 1957, VCG Papers, box 4, RBML, CU.

35. VCG, "Scattered Reminiscences of the IFUW," May 19, 1950, 3–5, VCG Papers, box 47, VCG Papers, CU, untitled folder on the 1950s.; Edith C. Batho, *A Lamp of Friendship, 1918–1968: A Short History of the International Federation of University Women* (Eastbourne, UK: Sumfield & Day, 1968), 44. For changing attitudes, see James Loeffler, *Rooted Cosmopolitans: Jews and Human Rights in the Twentieth Century* (New Haven: Yale University Press, 2018).

36. Storer B. Lunt (editor at W. W. Norton) to VCG, May 3, 1949; Wallace Meyer (editor at Charles Scribner's) to VCG, July 10, 1950; VCG to Mr. Ralph J. Cordiner (President of General Electric), December 23, 1950; VCG, "Merchants of Light: Problems in the Practice of Public Speaking," with commentary by Elizabeth Reynard, 8–9 (typed manuscript); VCG to Mrs. C. Raymond Everett (Helen Everett, editor at Houghton Mifflin), November 9, 1951; all in box 71, VCG Papers, RBML, CU.

37. Dorothea Setzer's correspondence with VCG is in the Setzer file, box 2, Barnard Archives; Alger Gildersleeve, "Forebears of Virginia C. Gildersleeve," VCG Papers, box 65, RBML, CU; John Randall Williams to Elizabeth Reynard, December 2, 1953, box 69, VCG Papers, folder: "Macmillan, 1952–1954."

38. Manuscript materials for *Many a Good Crusade* are in box 65, VCG Papers, folder: "VCG: Memories and Notes," CU; VCG, "The Strange Flotsam of Time," 24 pp., is in box 66, VCG Papers; VCG, handwritten document on the UN, untitled, August 17, 1945, is in an unlabeled folder, box 65; verbatim minutes of Committee I/1, for June 7, 1945, are also in box 65, VCG Papers, RBML, CU.

39. J. R. Williams to VCG, November 24, 1952; December 12, 1952; and January 23, 1953, box 69, VCG Papers, folder: "Macmillan, 1952–1954," RBML, CU.

40. Reader One report, included in letter of R. L. De Wilton to VCG, August 10, 1953, box 69, folder: "Macmillan, 1952–1954," VCG Papers, RBML, CU.

41. Reader Two report, included with letter of R. L. De Wilton to VCG, August 10, 1053, box 69, folder: "Macmillan, 1952–1954," VCG Papers, RBML, CU.

42. J. R. Williams to VCG, October 3, 1953, November 19, 1953, and December 2, 1953, and J. R. Williams to Elizabeth Reynard, December 2, 1953, box 69, folder: "Macmillan, 1952–1954," RBML, CU. *Crusade* enjoyed at least three printings.

43. VCG to Dorothea Setzer, April 23, 1954, Setzer file, box 2, BC; VCG to J. R. Williams, August 30, 1954, box 69, folder: "Macmillan Correspondence, 1954–1959," VCG Papers, RBML, CU; VCG, undated list, folder: "publicity for book," box 69, VCG Papers, RBML, CU.

44. J. R. Williams to VCG, December 6, 1954 and November 19, 1954; Virginia H. Patterson to VCG, October 7 and November 10, 1954, and March 11 and 12, 1955; Jean Flinner to Elizabeth Reynard, December 8, 1954; all in box 69, folder: "Macmillan, 1954–1956," CU; VCG to Dorothea Setzer, October 12, 1954 and undated note, Setzer file, box 2, Barnard Archives.

45. Margaret Irwin, review, *Worcester Telegram*, December 12, 1954, folder: "Reviews from the Northeast," box 69, VCG Papers, CU; Lewis Gannett, *New York Herald Tribune Book Review*, October 22, 1954; Elizabeth Janeway, "A Lifelong Journey," *New York Times Book Review*, October 24, 1954, in folder: "Reviews in Leading Newspapers and Magazines," box 69, VCG Papers, RBML, CU.

46. Harry Emerson Fosdick, "Barnard's Virginia Gildersleeve Pens a Most Valuable Memory Book," *New York Herald Tribune*, November 7, 1954, E3; Robert W. Wells, "Woman Educator Helped Organize the UN," *Milwaukee Journal* November 7, 1954; Mildred McAfee Horton, "Woman in Command," *Saturday Review* (October 10, 1954); Millicent Taylor, review in *Christian Science Monitor*, October 30, 1954; Glendy Dawedest, "A Lady Who Fell in Love With a College," *Washington Post*, October 24, 1954; Emily Taft Douglas, "Dean Gildersleeve's Story," *The New Leader* (January 17, 1955), all from folder: "Reviews in Leading Newspapers and Magazines," box 69, VCG Papers, CU; "Cahaba's Dead Glory Relives Through Author," *Selma Times Journal*, December 4, 1954, in folder: "Reviews from Washington DC, the South, and the Southwest," box 69, VCG Papers, RBML, CU.

47. Margaret Pickel to VCG, October 19, 1954; Mrs. George McAnemy to VCG, November 9, 1954; Meta Glass to VCG, November 2, 1954; Susan Brandeis to VCG, October 5, 1954; Iphigene Sulzberger to VCG, October 2, 1954; Margaret Bieber to VCG, October 27, 1954, all in folder: Letters of a More Personal Nature, box 68, VCG Papers, CU; Frank de Heyman to VCG, November 8,

1954, folder: "The Chess Portrait of Shakespeare," or "Some Factual Notes Used for *Many a Good Crusade.*" box 66, VCG Papers, RBML, CU.

48. Jessie Oakley Thornton (Charlottesville, Va.) to VCG, c. 1954, box 68, VCG Papers, RBML, CU; Elsa Becker to VCG, March 5, 1959, Setzer file, box 2; Mabel Alden Hunter to VCG, November 29, 1954 and Nettie Zook Cronemeyer to VCG, November 22, 1955, folder: "Letters from AAUW Women and Other Women's Organizations," box 68, VCG Papers, RBML, CU; Luella A. Huggins, attorney, to VCG, June 6, 1955, folder: "Spontaneous Letters of Appreciation," box 68, VCG Papers, RBML, CU.

49. Leroy Arnold to VCG, January 30, 1955, box 68; Mohammed Fadjil Jamali, Permanent Iraqi Delegate to the UN, to VCG, October 22, 1954, folder: "Letters from Notable People," box 68; William T. Brewster to VCG, November 2, 1954, and Esther Rosker to VCG, November 11, 1955, both in folder: "Letters of a More Personal Nature," box 68, VCG Papers, RBML, CU.

50. VCG to Dorothy Thompson, October 30, 1954, Dorothy Thompson Papers, box 12, Special Collections Research Center, Syracuse University; Dorothy Thompson to VCG, November 4, 1954, unlabeled folder, box 35, VCG Papers, RBML, CU; VCG to Dorothy Thompson, August 21, 1958, box 12, Dorothy Thompson Papers, Special Collections Research Center, Syracuse University.

51. VCG, *Crusade*, vii, 73, 182–183.

52. Terry Castle, *The Apparitional Lesbian: Female Homosexuality and Modern Culture* (New York: Columbia University Press, 1993), 2.

53. Thanks to Rona Wilk for her research.

54. "Educators Honored," *New York Times* (October 5, 1957); Dorothea Setzer, "Former WAVE Commander Views Military Training," *Christian Science Monitor*, February 14, 1952, 12.

55. VCG, preface to Elizabeth Reynard, *Ports of Youth: Fragments of an Autobiography* (New York: Columbia University Press, 1962); The Chatham Historical Society Spring Newsletter, 1997 and *Cape Cod Chronicle* (January 2, 1997), letter to the editor from Primrose Craven in BC3.4 Record Group: Faculty/Staff/Visitor Bio File, box 40, folder: Elizabeth Reynard, Barnard Archives; Nicole Miller, "Tea and Talk" at Jericho in West Dennis, posted February 6, 2014. For the reference to "cousins," see Francesca Wade, *Square Haunting: Five Writers in London Between the Wars* (New York: Random House/Tim Duggin Books, 2020), 168–169.

56. VCG, letter to the editor, *New York Times*, Washington's Birthday [February 22], 1953, in VCG Papers, BC2.4, box 29, folder: VCG correspondence, 1953–1964, Barnard Archives; VCG to Alan Nevins, February 6, 1956, VCG Papers, box 4, RBML, CU; Unknown correspondent to "Markie" (Mrs. Clifford Markle, at Navarre), October 16, 1960, VG Papers, box 4, RBML, CU. In the words of

the letter writer, "The Dean once told me that she and Miss Spurgeon agreed to destroy their correspondence so that nothing would be left of it."

57. "Elizabeth Reynard Dead at 64; Ex-Barnard English Professor," *New York Times*, January 10, 1962, 47; "Tributes to Elizabeth Reynard," Memorial Meeting at Barnard College, February 1, 1962, by Eleanor Rosenberg, Jean Palmer, and VCG, BC34 Record Group: Faculty/Staff/Visitor Bio Files, box no. 40, folder: Elizabeth Reynard, Barnard Archives.

58. *Cape Cod Chronicle*, December 2, 1996, Elizabeth Reynard folder in BC34, Record Group: Faculty/Staff/Visitor Bio Files, box 40, Barnard Archives; Elizabeth Reynard, *The Narrow Land: Folk Chronicles of Cape Cod*, 2nd ed. ed Andrew Oliver, preface, vii–viii; Reynard, *Ports of Youth*, preface by VCG.

59. Reynard, *Ports of Youth*, 56–57, 67, and preface by VCG.

60. VCG, preface, *A Hoard for Winter* (New York: Columbia University Press, 1962).

61. VCG, *A Hoard for Winter*, 6; the essays mentioned are, in order of mention, "The Lost Half Century," "Calling All Women," and "The Abuse of Democracy."

62. "Alger C. Gildersleeve: Brother of Ex-Dean," *New York Times* (May 5, 1952), 25; entry for VCG by Annette Baxter, *Notable American Women: The Modern Period* (Cambridge: Radcliffe College, 1980), 275.

63. "Virginia C. Gildersleeve, Women Educators' Dean," *New York Times*, July 9, 1965, 27.

64. Barnard College biography of VCG in BC2.4, box 1, Barnard Archives.

65. Margaret Pickel statement, February 26, 1953, Setzer file, box 2, Barnard Archives.

ENDNOTE: "WORKING FROM WITHIN"

1. "On and Off the Avenue," *Barnard College Alumnae Magazine* 25, no. 2 (November 1935), 3.

2. Account by Dorothea Setzer of interview with Meta Glass, n.d. BC2.4, VCG Papers, Barnard Archives.

Index

Photos are indicated by *p1, p2, p3*, etc.

Columbia College, 26, 29, 72; admission
to, 80, 84–85; anti-Semitism and,
105–106; attendance at, 19, 20;
Barnard College and, 48, 136,
188; "Collegiate Course," 22, 50;
professors at, 30; tax-exempt status,
180–181; teaching at, 33–34, 41;
women refused admission, 22. *See
also* Barnard College
Columbia College School of Mines, 20
Columbia Dames, 52
Columbia Law School, 96
Columbia School of Journalism, 52, 53
Columbia University, 17, 53–54; N. M.
Butler at, 35, 36, 48; Committee on
Educational Policy, 53; Committee on
Women's War Work, 61; engineering
school, 157, 264n44; graduate course
by VCG at, 42; Graduate Faculties,
52; Jewish students at, 81–83;
Johnson Hall, 53; journalism school,
52, 53; law school and admission
of women, 53, 96; medical school,
61–62; Teachers College, 35, 52
Coman, Katherine, 73
Commentary (journal), 197, 198–199
Commission on Human Rights, 166
Commission on the Status of Women,
166–167, 172
Commission to Study the Organization
of Peace, 158–159
Committee for Justice and Peace in the
Holy Land (CJP), 191–192, 195
"Committee of Public Safety in the French
Revolution" (thesis) (Gildersleeve,
Virginia Crocheron), 26
Committee of Women on National
Defense, New York, 61, 62
Committee on Educational Policy,
Columbia University, 53

Committee on Women Graduate
Students, 53
Committee on Women's War Work,
Columbia University, 61
Committee to Defend America by
Aiding the Allies, 155
communication, process of, 221
communism, 146
community, campus and, 80–86
companions, intimate, 29, 89
competitiveness, 171
Comstock, Ada L., *p8*
Coney Island Jockey Club, 14–15
Confederacy, 38
conferences: five-power, 170–171;
IFUW, 122–124, 142, *p9, p15*; UN
Charter, 163–168, 186, 204, 222, *p16,
p18, p19*; Yalta, 160. *See also* Seven
College Conference
Converse, Florence, 73
Corrigan, Edward, 14–15
Cottage Hill Academy, 10, 11
country life, 128–130
Cracow, IFUW conference in, *p15*
Cracow, Poland, IFUW conference in,
142, *p15*
Crane, Charles R., 76--79, 121, 143,
150, 190, 212, 256n89; Institute
of Current World Affairs, 77–78,
121, 220; Middle East interests of,
76–78; Nazi sympathies of, 143,
212, 259n25; visit to Old Postman's
Cottage, 131
Crane, John, 78
Creative Writing course (Reynard), 153
criticism, 170; of N. M. Butler, 36–37,
48; of Judge Gildersleeve, 14; of
Jonah's Gourd Vine, 117–118; of
Many a Good Crusade, 207–208; of
VCG, 2, 3, 20, 56, 92, 104–105, 111

eating clubs, at Princeton, 59
Eatonville, Florida, 113, 117, 118
Economic and Social Council, 166,
    169–170
education: at Columbia College, 30; in
    England, 157; funding for women
    for, 97–99; in Middle East, 78–80;
    transatlantic exchange, 63–64, 68;
    VCG in early life, 18, 20–24; war
    impact on women in higher, 62–63
Educational Review, 55
educational system, 69
*Edward Corrigan v. The Coney Island
    Jockey Club* (1892), 14–15
Edwards, Katherine M., 37
Efron, Edith, 168
Egypt, 79, 171, 200
Eisenhower, Dwight D., 177, 195, 200
Eisenstein, Sergei, 138
Eliot, Clara, 95
Elizabethan theater, 32–33
empathy, 3
employment, for women, 28
endowments, of women's colleges,
    97–102
England: education in, 157; travels to,
    72, 156–157
English department, at Barnard
    College, 33–34, 180
English language, 32
English literature, 32–33, 90–91
English Women's Hockey Association,
    70
entitlement, 5, 173, 219
entrance requirements, Barnard
    College, 119–120
epidemic, Spanish flu, 64
Episcopal Church, 10
equal rights, 55, 165–167, 168, 222, 224,
    264nn54–55

Equal Rights Amendment, US, 55
errors, admission of, 223–224
Europe, 6, 20–21
Evelyn College at Princeton, 22
exclusion: admission and, 102–112;
    Jewish, 81, 86, 102–104, 106, 108–
    110; of women, 236n48

Fackenthal, Frank, 139, 177, 179
faculty: at Barnard College, 93–95;
    Political Science, 30, 236n48; women
    on, 94–95
Faculty Committee on Student
    Organizations, 57–58
"failure of empathy," 3, 150
Fair Educational Practices Act (1948),
    New York, 181
"family claim," 28–29
family history, of VCG: Crocherons
    of State Island, 6–10; genealogy
    and, 20, 202–203; of Henry Alger
    Gildersleeve, 11–17
"farmerettes," 62
fascism, 143–144, 148, 149, 211;
    antifascist students and, 145–146;
    denial of, 150
favoritism, 151; toward male faculty, 94
FDR. *See* Roosevelt, Franklin Delano
Federal Emergency Relief
    Administration (FERA), 136
female partnership, 74
feminism, 164, 264nn54–55; anti-, 165;
    discrimination and, 81; militant,
    54–55, 164; social, 55, 172; suffrage
    and, 60–61; of VCG, 157–158, 163–
    166, 168, 221, *p18*
FERA. *See* Federal Emergency Relief
    Administration
Fiftieth Anniversary Committee, *p14*
finance, of women's education, 96, 97

Jews, 192, 210–211; anti-Zionism and, 191–192: Crane views on, 77; culture and, 198; discrimination against, 2, 81; IFUW concern for, 142; as immigrants to Palestine, 190, 193; and nationalism, 197–198; in New York, 80, 81; in Palestine, 76, 79, 175; as refugees, 176, 190; VCG stance toward, 79–80, 109–110, 210–211

Johnson, Henry W., 12

Johnson, James Weldon, 117

Johnson Hall, 53

Jonah's Gourd Vine (Hurston), 117–118

Jones, Adam Leroy, 84, 86, 105, 107–108

Joseph, Vera, 119

Judaism, 199

Julius Rosenwald Fund, 117, 118

Kappa Kappa Gamma (KKG), 25–26, 58, 180, *p2*

Kenyon, Dorothy, 167

Keppel, Frederick P. 26, 53, 81, 85

Kerr, Alma B., 196

Keynes, John Maynard, 129–130, 255n86

Keyserling, Mary Dublin, 108

King, Lida Shaw, 37, 39, 40, 41

King-Crane Commission of Inquiry, 76

King's College for Women, 68, 69, 70, 243n41

Kirchwey, George, 56

Kirchwey, Freda, 56

KKG. *See* Kappa Kappa Gamma

knockoffs, garment trade, 16

Komarovsky, Mirra, 108, 137, *p14*

Kouwenhoven, John, 185

Krapp, George P., 32

La Follette, Robert, 76–77

Lamont, Charles Evans, 100

land ownership, 7–8

"language question," 124–125, 140–141

languages: IFUW and German, 124–125, 140; Japanese, 174

Latham, Minor, 131

Latin American women, 164

Latin requirement, at Barnard College, 135

"Law Against the Overcrowding of German Schools and Universities," Germany, 144

Lawrence, Martha, 162

Lawrence, William W., 32

law school admission of women, at Columbia, 96

leadership, 222

League of Nations, 66–67, 76, 122, 162–163

Leet, Dorothy, 130, 189, 255n79

Leff, Laurel, 149

legacy, of VCG, 180–181, 217, 224

Legend of America, The (course), 185–187

lesbians, 73, 74

letters, with Spurgeon, 139–140

liberal arts education, 1, 22, 43, 55–56, 93, 224

liberal education, 26, 147

Liggett, N. W., 35, 80–81, 235n36, 246n70; anti-Semitism of, 82–83

Lippincott publishers, 117, 118

Lippmann, Walter, 100

Locke, Alain, 113, 115

Long, Robert, 196

Lopokova, Lydia, 129–130

Low, Seth, 29–30, 116

Lutz, Bertha, 164–168, 171, 172, 211, *p18*

MacArthur, Douglas, 174, 175

MacCracken, Henry Noble, 97, 101, *p8*

VCG. *See* Gildersleeve, Virginia Crocheron

Velocci, Beans, 74

Virginia C. Gildersleeve Professorship, Barnard, 189

Visitors Book, Old Postman's Cottage, 129

visitors to, Old Postman's Cottage, 130–131

vocational ambition, 56

vocational training, 54, 56

WACS. *See* Women's Army Corps

Wade, Francesca, 74–75

Waldensians, 6–7

Walker, Jimmy, 93

Walton, Andrea, 35, 53, 92

WAVES. *See* Women Accepted for Volunteer Emergency Service

Wechsler, Harold, 181

Weed, Ella, 35, 59, 82

Weiser, Catharine, 156

Weiser, Catharine ("Bunter"), 139, 156, 185

Wellesley College, 37, 73, 97, 106, 118, 119, 154, 208

Wells, Robert W., 207–208

White, Marion Churchill, 89

white supremacy, 116

Wilford, Hugh, 192

will, of VCG, 152–153

Williams, J. Randall III, 203–204, 205

Wilson, James H., 10

Wilson, Woodrow, 59, 76, 77

De Wilton, R. L., 204, 205

winter, hoarding for, 212–217

women, 1, 68, 155–156; admission to Barnard College refused to, 22; admission to Columbia Law School, 96; British, 63–65; on campus, 52–53; college graduates, 28–29; Columbia College engineering school, 262n44; at Columbia's medical school, 61–62; as deans, 39–41; employment options for, 28; exclusion of, 236n48; on faculty, 94–95; "farmerettes," 62; funding for education of, 97–99; German, 123–124, 141–142; Jewish, 142; Latin American, 164; mental health of, 234n32; in military, 154–155, 157–158, 262n40; politics of, 66; professional training for, 52; representation of, 163; rights for, 4, 55, 163–165, 221, 264nn54–55, *p18*; self-consciousness and, 26–27; suffrage of, 55, 56–63; of Turkey, 79; unmarried, 73–74; war impact on higher education for, 62–63

Women Accepted for Volunteer Emergency Service (WAVES), 154–155, 156, 208, 211, 262n40; Reynard participation in, *p15*

women delegates, UN, 163, 164–167

women graduates, 28–29

women professors, 94–95

Women's Advisory Council, Navy, 156

Women's Army Corps (WACS), 262n40

women's groups, international, 66

women's movement, 3–4, 54–55, 95, 127. *See also* International Federation of University Women

women's movement, 55, 66; international, 72

Women's Paris Club, AAUW, 125

women's press corps, 168

Women's University Settlement in Southwark, 70

Woolley, Mary, 101

Woolf, Leonard, 130

Woolf, Virginia, 130
Woolley, Mary E., 73, *p8*
"working from within" strategy, 3,
    53–54, 163, 221
working women, 62
works, of Gildersleeve, Virginia
    Crocheron, 2–3; "Committee
    of Public Safety in the French
    Revolution" (thesis), 26;
    "Government Regulation of
    Elizabethan Drama" (dissertation),
    32; *A Hoard for Winter*, 215; *Many
    a Good Crusade*, 5, 30–31, 74, 132,
    202–212, 223–224; "The Roots of
    our Crisis in the Middle East," 200;
    "Scattered Reminiscences of the
    IFUW," 200–201; "Some Materials
    for Judging the Actual Effects of
    Feudalism in France" (thesis), 30

World War I, 46, 56–63; Clapham
    assignment during, 71; Middle East
    during, 76
World War II, 154–155, 156–161,
    176–177, *p15*; allies, 155; WAVES and,
    154–155
Wright, Natalie Francesca, 75
writing: of essays, 215; with Reynard,
    201–202
Wu Yi-Fong 166

Yalta Conference, 160
Young, Josephine Sheldon Edmonds, *p8*

Zahn-Harnack, Agnes von, 123, 126
Zionism, 2, 79–80, 150, 176, 177–178,
    190–193, 197–199, 200, *p20*; D.
    Thompson and, 194–195. *See also*
    anti-Zionism